PRAISE FOR *TAROT MYS...*

"This book plumbs the depths of tarot mysticism and takes you on an unparalleled journey into the heart of Western esotericism. Joe Monteleone's expertise and wisdom shines in this tome that both demystifies the Thoth system and illuminates its Mysteries. If you are ready to transcend the ordinary, then *Tarot Mysticism* is the handbook on the tarot meant for you. A truly noteworthy and remarkable achievement."
—**BENEBELL WEN**, author of *Holistic Tarot* and creator of the *Spirit Keeper's Tarot*

"*Tarot Mysticism* is an enlightening journey into the psycho-spiritual side of the Thoth Tarot, delivered in a way only Joe can. This book artfully blends the wisdom of the Thoth Tarot and its multifaceted applications for the modern tarot reader with rich insight, making it a must-read for both beginners and seasoned practitioners. I can't recommend this book enough. There is no one like Joe Monteleone, and his passion for the tarot, life, and the beauty and mystery of the universe can't be replicated."
—**ETHONY DAWN**, author of *Tarot Grimoire*

"Joe Monteleone is the ultimate guide for anyone venturing into the landscape of the Thoth Tarot. His profound esoteric knowledge and extensive experience make him an unparalleled teacher, and *Tarot Mysticism* an essential one-stop resource for your journey into this iconic tarot deck."
—**STEVEN BRIGHT**, author of *In Focus Tarot* and *Rainbow Kipper*

"*Tarot Mysticism* isn't a book; it is a portal. Within these pages you will decode into the most enigmatic tarot ever created. A dazzling debut!"
—**SASHA GRAHAM**, author of *The Magic of Tarot* and *Dark Wood Tarot*

"Tarot is more than a divinatory device—it is a sacred apparatus. This book profoundly illustrates why, as it explains the Thoth Tarot as a map for exploring the ineffable truths of the inner reality. With deep wisdom, it delves into tarot as a contemplative experience and a tool for presence. It is a holographic expression of Hermetic philosophy, wherein all things are an emanation of the divine."
—**M. M. MELEEN**, Thoth-based tarot deck creator and author of *Tabula Mundi Tarot* and *Book M: Liber Mundi*; coauthor of *Tarot Deciphered* and cocreator of *Fortune's Wheelhouse* podcast

TAROT
MYSTICISM

ABOUT THE AUTHOR

Joe Monteleone, a "one-man band of magical thinking made reality" (*Huffington Post*), is a master tarot teacher, author, YouTuber, healer, and modern mystic. He has spent more than twenty years researching, reading, teaching, and performing tarot and mystical philosophy all around the physical and virtual world. After a life-changing mystical experience, he created the Tarot Mysticism Academy, where he teaches the esoteric tarot and various mystical disciplines for personal development and accelerated spiritual growth. He also coaches professional readers and spiritual business owners in growing their practice. You can find more information at www.tarotmysticismacademy.com and his YouTube channel, youtube.com/joemonteleone.

TAROT MYSTICISM

JOE MONTELEONE

THE PSYCHO-SPIRITUAL TECHNOLOGY OF THE THOTH TAROT

LLEWELLYN
WOODBURY, MINNESOTA

Tarot Mysticism: The Psycho-Spiritual Technology of the Thoth Tarot Copyright © 2025 by Joe Monteleone. All rights reserved. No part of this book may be used or reproduced in any manner whatsoever, including internet usage, without written permission from Llewellyn Worldwide Ltd., except in the case of brief quotations embodied in critical articles and reviews.

First Edition
First Printing, 2025

Book design by Rordan Brasington
Cover art and chapter opener art by Daniel Martin Diaz
Cover design by Shannon McKuhen
Editing by Laura Kurtz
Interior illustrations
   Llewellyn Art Department: 38, 52, 53, 185, 339
Thoth Tarot Deck
   Copyright © Ordo Templi Orientis and University of London.
   All rights reserved. Thoth Tarot is a trademark of Ordo Templi Orientis.

Llewellyn Publications is a registered trademark of Llewellyn Worldwide Ltd.

Library of Congress Cataloging-in-Publication Data (Pending)
ISBN: 978-0-7387-7834-1

Llewellyn Worldwide Ltd. does not participate in, endorse, or have any authority or responsibility concerning private business transactions between our authors and the public.

   All mail addressed to the author is forwarded, but the publisher cannot, unless specifically instructed by the author, give out an address or phone number.

   Any internet references contained in this work are current at publication time, but the publisher cannot guarantee that a specific location will continue to be maintained. Please refer to the publisher's website for links to authors' websites and other sources.

Llewellyn Publications
A Division of Llewellyn Worldwide Ltd.
2143 Wooddale Drive
Woodbury, MN 55125-2989
www.llewellyn.com

Printed in the United States of America

To my mother, father, and sister

CONTENTS

Exercise List x

Acknowledgments xi

Introduction 1

Chapter 1: The Esoteric Tarot 3

Chapter 2: The Major Arcana 73

Chapter 3: The Court Cards 167

Chapter 4: The Small Cards 245

Chapter 5: Practical Application 331

Chapter 6: What's the Point? 341

Conclusion 345

Recommended Resources 347

Bibliography 351

Index 357

EXERCISES

Measuring Me 24
Being the Observer 26
The Loops 27
The Tetractys Meditation 45
Your Creative Act 170
The Tetragrammatic Method 336

ACKNOWLEDGMENTS

I must first thank Ethony Dawn. Without your guidance and motivation, this book would not have manifested. I must also thank Llewellyn and Barbara for drawing this book down into Malkuth. I couldn't have done it without you.

A special thanks to all my guides, whether on this plane or another. Thank you to the great mystics, philosophers, and sages of the past.

Thank you to my father for the discipline, work ethic, intelligence, and inherited passion. Thank you to Angela, my sister, for your continued support and inspiration. Thank you to Purim, my mentor, for all you've taught me. Thank you, Grandma Betty, for being my first spiritual teacher. Thank you, Joey, for all the love, care, and laughs throughout this process.

Most importantly, an infinite thank you to my mom, Sue. This book and all my successes were only possible because of your love, support, and wisdom. Thank you for fostering my creativity, believing in me, guiding me, and cheering me on in every endeavor.

INTRODUCTION

You're about to learn the tarot as a psycho-spiritual technology of perennial wisdom. Underlying all mystical traditions, philosophies, and religions is one so-called perennial philosophy, one undying current of revelation in continual transmission. It is less of a philosophy and more of an unspeakable truth, a secret so obvious it is often missed. This truth, though ineffable, oftentimes manifests for many seekers as a sense of peace, ease, or radical connection. It is what points to our connection with everything that is.

The search for connection is nothing new, and I would argue it is one of the most common driving forces behind most of our endeavors. When we feel connected, we are at peace and there is a certain kind of flow. When an organ is properly functioning and serving the body, we do not notice it. In the same way, when we are connected to something bigger than ourselves, we don't notice ourselves, and get out of our own way. We become part of something bigger and the energy flows through us.

INTRODUCTION

There are many ways to find this connection. Some find it in the camaraderie of a packed sports stadium. Some find it when they lock eyes with their beloved. Some find it through their busy jobs. Some find it through drugs or alcohol. Some find it in the beauty of art. Some find it with their families. Some find it through suffering. And of course, some find it through tarot.

The tarot connects us in many ways. It connects us to ourselves when reading for ourselves. It connects us to others when reading for others, this much is obvious. But the tarot is not just a *tool* for connecting. It is also a *map* of our connection, our connection to the Divine. And in the journey ahead, we will be exploring that connection.

The truth is, connection is not something you need to find. It does not require a medium. It is something you can realize *directly* as your own nature. Beyond a tool for divination, the tarot symbolically expresses this direct connection between you and the absolute, and you're about to learn how.

The tarot is only the latest mystical technology to do this. Shamans have done so through nature and journeying. Like Empedocles, earlier Greek philosophers had done so by meditating in caves. The Pythagoreans did so through numbers. The rishis did so through direct glimpses recorded in the *Upanishads*. The yogis did so by shutting off their minds. The Zen masters did so by annihilating their minds. The genius Kabbalists did so by overflowing their minds. These are just some examples of entry points into the perennial philosophy. In this book, you will learn the connections between some of these spiritual systems and their synthesis in the Thoth tarot.

The tarot is so much more than a tool for divination or personal insight. It is a symbolic expression of how we create our lives and, more widely, how the universe happens to itself. Luckily for us, tarot has had several hundred years to compact several thousand years of mystical philosophy from so many cultures. You're about to learn the tarot in this context, as a tool of personal, transpersonal, and ontological connection.

CHAPTER 1
THE ESOTERIC TAROT

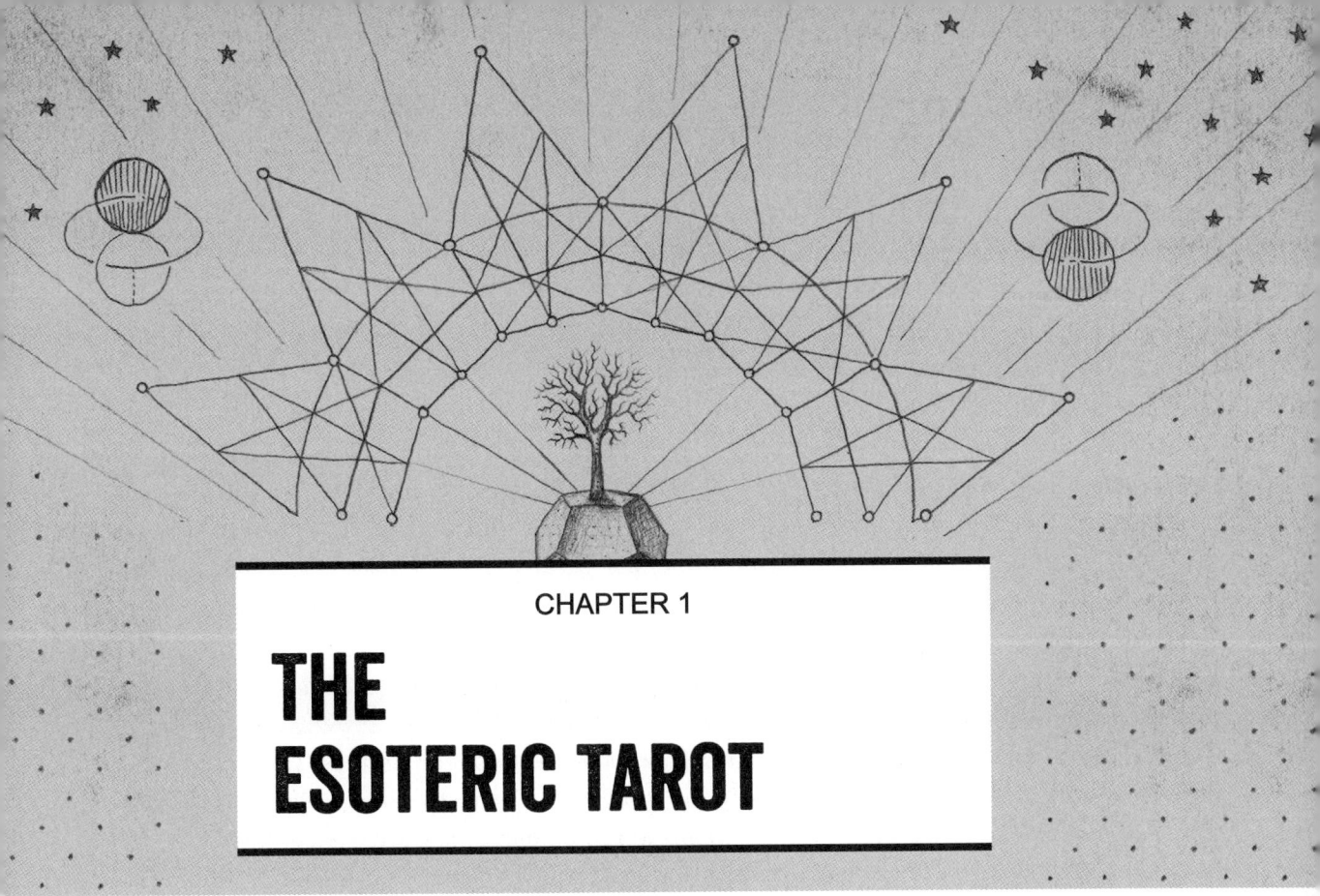

Every detail in the tarot is an expression of one fundamental teaching. Every card, symbol, correspondence, association, number, letter, every pixel of the card itself and every subatomic particle under *that* and quantum mystery under *that* is all, without fail, an expression of one teaching. This teaching is a singularity. One glimpse and you're done; there's no return. This is the teaching of so many mystical traditions: The unity of all things.

What does it mean for something to be esoteric? Esoteric qualifies any subject matter that is meant to be understood by a select few. Most religions have an esoteric and exoteric layer. The esoteric material deals with a more direct understanding of deeper teachings and truth while the exoteric material is offered to a wider audience with less specialization, training, and preparation. This is not to say that what is esoteric is exclusionary, far from it. Esoteric mysteries are now more accessible than ever before. Rather, that which is esoteric will only be sought after, learned, and integrated by those who have an intense desire for truth. Furthermore, it's not something that can be understood by the mind or really taught in books. It is transmitted through initiation. Initiation can happen in many ways: Some use ritual, as in ceremonial magic and the western esoteric traditions. Some follow a more contemplative path, such as the many eastern mystical traditions. Sometimes initiations come spontaneously without any effort. Whereas exoteric disciplines teach how to live a more pleasant life, esoteric teachings cultivate initiatic experiences where the seeker realizes their true nature. This initiation, this realization of truth, is singular. When you experience it, you will see how all the great writings of past mystics, sages, and philosophers echo one truly timeless perennial wisdom. Christ, Buddha, the rishis, the philosophers—all partook of this one indescribable experience. In its ambitious reach toward various esoteric disciplines of different cultures, the tarot took it upon itself to visually express this singular mystical experience. When most people think of tarot, they think of its exoteric discipline, called divination. In this book, you will learn of its esoteric discipline, mysticism.

This book is going to teach you tarot mysticism through the Thoth deck from an esoteric lens. Tarot mysticism is the use of tarot to realize the unity of all things, to understand the lack of separation and arrive at peace. This book will help you do what the tarot does: Analyze reality into a set of ideas, and then merge it back together into one unspeakable united truth. First, let's discuss the topics of tarot, mysticism, and the Thoth deck.

TAROT

What is tarot? Here are some definitions I've used in the past:

- Seventy-eight memes of consciousness
- A psycho-spiritual-historical trainwreck of symbols
- Probably not a spellbook from ancient Egypt (but maybe)
- Definitely a spiritual technology with alchemical, Hermetic, Qabalistic, astrological, soteriological, and magical/esoteric influences
- A method of divination and spiritual unfoldment
- The gateway drug into mysticism and the occult

My favorite definition is this: *A permission slip for presence*. Tarot, like any form of mysticism, facilitates our presence with ourselves and the world. This is both the loftiest and the most terrifying goal. To really know who you are is impressive and no easy feat. To know *what* you are is saintly. Most people distract themselves from themselves by persuading themselves they exist through one identification, addiction, role, or another. When used with desperation and delusion, tarot can be another one of these distractions. When used with integrity, it can illustrate the truth of who we are, pointing to the many layers of our life, choices, and patterns. When used mystically, it can show us what we are (more on that later). I find that tarot has three major uses.

Use 1: Divination

Divination is an excuse for, and allowance of, awareness. That can include insight, guidance, channeling, psychic work, intuition, connection to the higher self, and so many more things. What I don't like to include in my definition of divination is superstition. I do not like superstition. I find most of it boring, unsophisticated, and fear-based, and it usually blocks awareness. What's more, I find superstition distracts from reality, which is so much more mind-blowing than any superstition. I'm not superstitious; I'm quite a skeptic, actually. I had read tarot for about ten years before I ever admitted it "worked." Now with more than two decades of experience reading and teaching, I know it can tell the future, so to speak. But how?

Tarot can tell the future because it can tell the present, and the future is in the present. Remember, tarot is a permission slip for presence. It has been argued that time as we understand it is merely a human invention, another meter of the insatiably measuring mind. The past and future probably don't exist. No one has been there. Ever. When consulting the cards for telling the past or the future, we are really just reflecting on the present.

The tarot is a physical object that acts as a bridge between the perceived "physical" world and other planes that you will learn soon. For now, we can understand tarot as a set of images that trigger reflection. It's like walking through a museum of consciousness, "seventy-eight memes of consciousness." By reflecting on these carefully curated symbols, we reflect on the human experience, and ourselves, a process which is invaluable and one that can make the future.

Use 2: Mystical Philosophy

Mystical philosophy develops from the testimonies of mystics. It often happens like this: A human will intentionally have, or stumble across, a mystical experience. It will turn their understanding of reality inside out. They will go tell everyone they can. Sometimes their words survive. Sometimes those words are copied, adapted, modified, and systematized over a period of time, congealing into mystical philosophy.

Chapter 1

However, the initial mystical experience and the mystical philosophy are never the same. The philosophy is only an attempt at transmitting the mystical experience or direct understanding. The mystical experience always transcends the mind. But mystical philosophy exists in the mind. It's quite man-made. All religions, philosophies, and methods are made up by one person or another, transmitted from mind to mind, whether prophet or madman (the two are usually not too far apart). Language, being an indulgence of mind, always has its flaws. Hermes loves to play tricks. But language and human composition do not invalidate content, especially if that content transcends its container. The western esoteric tradition from which modern tarot descends is a great example of this. It's full of fancy ideas. But the fancy ideas are only fancy ideas until you find out what's really going on.

The more I've studied mysticism, the more I've realized it's all very similar. So much material overlaps. It's almost as if throughout history, there was a "mystical misfit lunch table" at the high school of humanity. So many mystical traditions have influenced each other because everyone asking those deep questions eventually found friends asking the same questions. There sat all the weirdos who had all the odd interests and obscure questions. Perhaps we are both at the mystical misfit lunch table now.

However, it's not just history that connects the many traditions of mysticism. What's more impressive is the lack of historical connection! Hermes Trismegistus and Plotinus used some of the same words as the *Upanishads*, four thousand miles and about five centuries apart.

Some argue that the tarot descends from Egyptian magi or even Atlantis. I love a great magical origin story as much as the next person. But what's more magical is the greater plausibility that Tarot arose out of a complex confluence of various sources that all had something in common. Kabbalah, Hermeticism, Neoplatonism, astrology, Christian mysticism, Gnosticism, Tantra, and more all make their way into tarot because they all share something. They all ask "What are we?" The tarot illustrates these great wisdom traditions; in studying them, we radically update our understanding of reality.

Use 3: The Mystical Experience

We arrive now at the mystical level. This is where the mystical philosophy becomes a direct realization. It is possible to reach profound states of consciousness by pushing the mind into a hyperconnected state where it understands every single thing connected to every other thing. Aleister Crowley explains this in *Wheel And–Whoa!*[1] The idea is that you can

---

1. Aleister Crowley, *The Book of Lies: The Secret to a Bigger Life* (Red Wheel/Weister, 1913), 166.

experience an illuminated state when the mind runs fast enough. A wheel spinning fast enough will appear still. Through an overload of information, association, and symbol, the mind can connect everything with everything and be in communion with all. If you know you are everything, there is nothing that is *not* you and therefore nothing to fear.

These three uses of tarot have a soft parallel to the three planes of tarot practice. After reading tarot professionally for many years and studying various mystical traditions, I have come to discover that most work with tarot will occupy one of the three following levels. I have delineated these three levels for convenience, but you will find similar schemas in Kabbalah, Neoplatonism, and the *Upanishads*.[2] Here I share how the three levels of tarot are mirrored in these older mystical traditions.

The first two levels of tarot concern divination, what most people understand tarot to be. The third level concerns tarot mysticism, which is much less understood and, in my opinion, much more interesting.

Level 1: Mechanical

The mechanical plane of tarot practice focuses on what a person's body will be doing, where, with whom, and when. It answers questions like, "Will I get married? What is my next job? What does my health look like next year?" and famously "When will [my crush] text me back?" The general mode of questioning is "what will happen to me?" These types of readings focus on detail and can be very impressive. Most clients expect something like this from tarot at first.

In the *Mandukya Upanishad*, this would correspond to the *visva*, (the waker and the waker's world). The visva is consciousness associated with the physical body and physical world. In the *Taittiriya Upanishad*, this would correspond to the *annamaya kosha* (food sheath). In Plotinus's chain of being, this would correspond to nature. Elementally, this would correspond to earth. Qabalistically, this corresponds to the world *Assiah*, "action," and the part of the soul called the *nephesh*, the "animal soul."

So how do you experience this? You're experiencing it right now by reading these words. This level is all about sensation, ambulation, action, proprioception, and anything to do with the body. This is the gross (that is, mundane) world most people agree on.

However, there's a big problem with this level. We know that reality isn't just our body. We have a whole mind. Many mystical traditions would say that the body only exists in the

---

2. I use the spelling "Kabbalah" when referring to Jewish Kabbalah or its historical roots. I use the spelling "Qabalah" when referring to its connection with tarot and western esotericism.

mind. After any serious effort in spiritual study or personal development, a seeker will realize that reality is much more interesting (and confusing) than a simple Newtonian universe of physical things knocking into each other. One realizes they are not merely a billiard ball being knocked around, but rather, a full participant in their reality and experience. The inner world and outer world start to blur as we explore the backstage of this phantom material show in level 2.

The glue that connects level 1 to level 2 is the "feeling" sense. By that I refer to the somatic, emotional, and/or energetic responses that occur in the body in response to certain stimuli. Some people label them as simply emotions. But if you look deeply enough, every emotion can be reduced to a feeling in the body. Those feelings give us insight into our energy body and level 2. There are so many therapeutic and personal development modalities focused on the relationship between level 1 and level 2, often centered on the nervous system and feelings. I've learned a lot of this from my own mentor, Purim King. It has allowed extreme transformations for myself and so many of my students.

Level 2: Subtle/Causal

At the subtle/causal level, a reading gives information on what is causing the results that materialize around us. Here, the cards show us patterns in our life, whether energetic, karmic, psychological, or otherwise. The subtle/causal plane is the higher reality above the mechanical. It shows how we are full participants in reality and not its effects. It reveals a tricky cybernetic feedback loop between the internal world (you could say "mind") and outer world ("matter"). It's tricky because there is no real separation, but Hermes has us fooled.

This level answers questions like, "who am I?" This is the place of ideas, archetypes, symbols, and mythologies. Many tarot readers are familiar with this level of work to an extent, and it has become more popular over recent decades.

This level is all about looking within. Instead of identifying with our body, like in level 1, we identify with the inner world. This may appear as thoughts or feelings to some seekers, but it goes deeper.

There are complexes of patterns and subconscious behavior strategies that have been developing in our species for hundreds of thousands of years. On the other hand, some of these behavior strategies have been invented just in the recent weeks of a person's life. You can understand this level like a complex array of fluid dynamics, multiple forces affecting the whole system of our psyche. The history of these fluid dynamic influences starts now, and goes back beyond childhood, all the way to the first single-celled organisms in our unconscious evolutionary record.

This is also the world of dreams and imagination. The tarot can help us explore these conscious and unconscious mechanisms within us that help manifest our life in level 1.

In the *Mandukya Upanishad*, this might correspond to the *taijasa* ("endowed with light," consciousness associated with the dreamer and the dream). In the *Taitiriya Upanishad*, this links with the *pranamaya kosha* and *manomaya kosha* (energy body and mental apparatus). In Plotinus's chain of being, this could correspond to the soul. Elementally, this is air and water. Qabalistically, this is the *ruach* (the intellect) and the world of *Yetzirah* (formation).

However, there is a problem with this level. In the same way that level 1 does not give us the full picture, level 2 falls short as well. The subtle/causal plane has to do with symbolism, the mind, language, and meaning. Each of these shares one huge limitation: They are linear. Language is clearly linear. You are reading the lines right now! Each word leads to another word. However, there is a deeper semiotic linearity with language, symbolism, and meaning. Every word and every symbol draws an invisible line of reference to that which it is signifying or meaning. Words and symbols don't give direct experience of what they refer to. They can only point you in the direction. Now, this is great for the subtle/causal plane as a primarily mental level. The mind loves linearity and association. It is the capacity of this newly updated prefrontal cortex of our species to create endless worlds of abstraction built with countless linear ideas. Civilization exists because of all of these words and symbols that point to something other than themselves. When we can all share in that, we can do amazing things, like build skyscrapers or land on the moon. But let's be honest. The human race is one orgy of semiotics. Everything means something else. And therein lies the problem. If everything means something else, when do we finally arrive? When does a thing just mean itself? When does a line collapse into a point? The answer is mysticism.

I'm going to give a very specific example of this to fully illustrate this point. This won't "break" tarot divination, but it will show you its limitations, and where tarot mysticism picks up. If you pull out the Priestess card of the Thoth deck, you will notice a camel. That could represent a camel showing up to your door, but it isn't likely. The camel is a symbol. That symbol refers to the Hebrew letter gimel. Why gimel? In addition to being near-homophones, that letter is attributed to the Priestess. It is also attributed in the Hermetic Qabalah to the thirteenth path on the Tree of Life. This path leads from Tiphareth to Kether, connecting the hexad and microcosm to the monad and macrocosm. In this way, we could interpret this to mean spiritual connection. But even then, what is spiritual connection? In a reading, this might signify someone following their intuition. But what does intuition mean? It could refer to an immediate understanding without the need for reasoning. But what is that? Every symbol and word leads to some other thing. In the subtle/causal level, this is a good thing. It's the jazz of the collective unconscious/mind stuff to constantly transmute itself. Tarot readers and spiritual seekers love this. It's interesting, creative, imaginative, and engenders a sort of freedom in self-investigation. What we learn from the subtle/causal plane is that everything can be further analyzed or synthesized except one thing: That which transcends all symbol and language. That can only be dealt with in mysticism.

Level 3: Mystical

Mysticism begins where symbolism, language, and meaning end. That is because mysticism often leads to some form of nonduality or monism. Symbolism, language, and meaning are, by definition, dual. They always require some sort of linearity or association. The mind loves them. In this level, we are transcending the mind.

That is why, at the highest level, tarot is not so much about reading (dualism) as it is about direct knowledge (monism/nondualism). Here, tarot is less concerned with our inner identity and more concerned with our even deeper reality. At this level, we stop asking "who am I?" (mind) and start asking "what am I?" (consciousness).

Here, the tarot becomes a holographic system of mystical insight that leads to the highest revelations and the deepest peace. At this level, every symbol starts expressing the whole system directly instead of another symbol, meaning, or semiotic web. In the same way and at this level, you, the seeker, start to express the whole universe, instead of just an aspect of yourself as a tarot reading would reveal. At this level, the tarot starts to point to an apprehension of absolute unity. This is much less commonly understood than the first two levels.

In the *Mandukya Upanishad*, this might correspond to the *prajna*, the experience of deep sleep, where there is no symbol, image, meaning, or duality. There is no dream in deep sleep. In the *Taitiriya Upanishad*, this might correspond to the *vijnanamaya kosha* and *anandamaya kosha* (the part of us that knows and the self that is pure bliss). In Plotinus's chain of being, this might correspond with the *nous* (the intellect) and *to hen* (the one). Nous is not so much the thinking intellect, but the ability of consciousness to be self-aware. Elementally, this is fire and spirit. Kabbalistically, this is the part of the soul known as the *neshamah* (intuition) but mostly *chiah* (creative force) and *yechidah* (our connection to God).

The focus of this book will be mostly on level 3, using a great deal of level 2 to support it. It is important to note that the realization in level 3 can come through an exploration of level 2. However, because I am emphasizing level 3, I won't be teaching much symbolism. I will teach what is beyond that. The way this is done is through recognizing yourself as an unbroken whole in all the parts or symbols of your experience instead of separating yourself into symbols. Level 2 may consist of the tarot cards' many attributions and associations through symbol, name, and meaning. The whole, which level 3 implies, is the consciousness experiencing all of those parts, symbols, names, meanings.

Let's use the Tower card as an example. It's a part of us. It is attributed to Mars, which is our adrenaline, anger, and will to live. Those aspects of us always exist in our consciousness, which is the whole. The conscious whole, as you will learn soon, is the Fool. Connecting the parts of ourselves to the whole of our Self is the aim of mysticism and ceremonial high magick.

The approach of the work ahead is to see each tarot card as a part of you, the whole, not you in each tarot card. On a larger scale, tarot mysticism shows how any moment or place or event in the universe expresses the entire universe by the definition of it "being." This pure being is the unity of all things. It is that which *is*. If it is, it is, and that "is"-ness is the same infinitely anywhere. It's the infinite "I am." In the mechanical plane of level 1, the tarot reads as "I am a body experiencing events." In level 2, the subtle/causal plane, the tarot expresses "I am this person." In level 3, the mystical plane, the tarot reveals simply "…I am." At this level, tarot is no longer a permission slip for awareness. It reveals pure awareness.

Tarot reading is, amongst many things, an opportunity to be present with the contents of the individual self. Tarot mysticism is different. Tarot mysticism is the art of bridging that individual self with the absolute Self, pure being. Where tarot reading explores who you are, tarot mysticism explores what you are. This makes every idea, symbol, and correspondence in the tarot to threshold into unity. Everything in the tarot begins to point to that ineffable "non-thing" through which all "things" exist. And then, everything in life points to it too. Contemplating this material can bring about a "mystical experience," which I can only describe as a radical exhalation of all fear. It is the realization of the connection between everything and everything.

You're about to learn how each card, each symbol, and each idea express a realization that has been documented by every mystical tradition. The result of contemplating the ideas ahead is a paradox, where you, the knower, become no different from the known content of your experience. In the absence of this difference, there is radical peace. To put it simply, tarot mysticism helps us realize there is no difference between any one thing and any other thing. In that knowledge, there is no fear. The information ahead provides the foundation to jailbreak reality.

This book needs to be read actively, slowly, and with participation. Always have a pen with you to scribble notes and underline. Dog-ear the pages. Add sticky notes with journal entries and references. If you look at my library, most books have become notebooks. This material requires integration and patience.

THE THOTH DECK

What does the Thoth deck have to do with everything mentioned so far? The Thoth deck is probably one of the most explicitly esoteric decks, known for its hauntingly beautiful imagery, thick erudition, and intimidating background. Its function, art style, history, and content differ wildly from other decks. But what makes it especially applicable for mystical inquiry is its reach: The Thoth deck brings tarot to the universal and ontological scale. To use the three-level model presented previously, the Thoth deck easily works on the subtle/causal level and the mystical level. Most tarot decks are focused on the mechanical level, peeking occasionally into the subtle/causal. (It's important to note that all levels exist simultaneously, but different tarot decks are made for different levels.)

The Thoth deck is the second most popular tarot deck in the world. It was painted by Lady Frieda Harris under the direction of in/famous occultist Aleister Crowley. The project was proposed by Harris, who paid for Crowley's mentorship. Work on the deck started in 1938 and ended in 1943, to eventually be published in 1969.

The most popular deck is the Rider-Waite-Smith (RWS). It is probably best to understand the Thoth deck in comparison to RWS. This will also help readers that are advancing their studies who have familiarity with the RWS tradition.

Many consider the RWS to be one for beginners, but this is not necessarily so: It is filled with powerful iconography, veiled secrets, and many layers of meaning. It was painted by Pamela Colman Smith under the direction of Arthur Edward Waite, a Christian mystic. What makes this deck appropriate for beginners is the clear scenic imagery. This was one of the earlier decks to illustrate the pip cards (numbered suited cards, ace through ten). Instead of figuring out what the image of ten cups might mean in a reading, the deck illustrates for you a happy family under a rainbow. I wouldn't say it spoon-feeds card meanings, but they are much more apparent. If the RWS was a car, it would be an automatic. If the Thoth was a car, it would be a stick shift.

Yes, the Thoth deck is a "manual" deck. You have more control and participation but also more responsibility. Why is this so? Instead of giving you clear illustrations as in the RWS, the Thoth offers abstraction. Instead of linear stories, it boasts systematic thinking of complex spiritual ideas. Instead of humans on every card, various forms of diverse deities, symbols, and colors offer a rich map of spiritual real estate. The RWS expresses the human experience. Thoth expresses the universe. The RWS illustrates the literal. Thoth symbolizes the abstract. The RWS was designed for divination. The Thoth was designed as an expression of the Qabalah and the universe.

Both tarot traditions can be traced to the Hermetic Order of the Golden Dawn, a magical initiatory society of the late nineteenth century. Both Waite and Crowley passed through this order, where they likely gained their foundational knowledge in tarot and Hermetic Qabalah. It was most likely Samuel Liddell MacGregor Mathers who was the mastermind behind the updated esoteric tarot of the Golden Dawn, which combined so many mystical traditions. The RWS did not explicitly uphold this modern synthesis. Luckily for us, the Thoth did.

You'll notice many of the previously mentioned artistic and functional differences in the following examples. One of the first things that may cause new readers of the Thoth to stumble is the court card system. In the RWS, we have a king, queen, knight, and page. This creates the typical nuclear family structure of father, mothers, son, daughter. More deeply, it illustrates four stages of life. Briefly, this can be summarized as mastery, maturity, adolescence, childhood.

The Thoth deck is different. The court card offices consist of a knight, queen, prince, and princess. Why the change? Instead of expressing human life stages, like in RWS, it expresses a cosmic creative pattern: The creation of something out of nothing through duality. This creative pattern has a more universal scale, and its four stages are expressed better through these updated offices (analyzed in chapter 3). This system maintains the original structure the Golden Dawn developed.

If you are coming from an RWS background, the truth is that the two systems are just different; there's no perfect way to transpose them. However, this is what I recommend for practical purposes: Attribute the RWS kings to the Thoth princes and the RWS knights to the Thoth knights. This may sound blasphemous to some readers as it forces a change in the order of offices in the RWS. I'll briefly go over my reasoning. If you compare all the descriptions from the Golden Dawn's *Book T* material (the material that greatly influenced both tarot traditions), you will find more similarities between the kings of the RWS tradition and the third office described in *Book T*, the princes. In fact, the titles used for this third office are both "prince" *and* "king." The first title is simply "knight." What's more, this solution works best for divination with the RWS deck. This way, the kings of the RWS can correspond to the element of air, the element of the mind, which is much more appropriate for a king who delegates and makes choices for their kingdom.

The next major difference is the fourth suit. RWS uses pentacles. Thoth uses disks. Crowley's reasoning for changing the symbol is that the disk is a whirling, universal emblem. It has a farther semantic reach, whereas the pentacles in the RWS represent coins and money. The whirling disks can suggest anything from atoms to planets to solar systems and beyond. This makes the element of earth include all of matter, not just money.

There are a few title changes for certain cards. Justice is updated to "Adjustment," again, to have more universal meaning. Justice, in Crowley's opinion, is too human, while Adjustment is cosmic. You will notice that Adjustment is number 8 while Justice is number 11 in the RWS. Strength in the RWS is 8 while its correlative, "Lust," is number 11 in Thoth. This switch is explained in chapter 2 under the Emperor. The name "Lust" is used instead of "Strength" to describe the "joy of strength exercised."[3] The name also offers a sexual connotation more apt to the symbolism and meaning of this card's associated deity. The World is updated to "the Universe" for reasons previously described. Lastly, Judgement becomes "the Æon," undoing the Christian iconography and replacing it with something Thelemic.

This leads us to Thelema itself, the religion Aleister Crowley developed. One does not need to be a Thelemite to use the Thoth deck. However, a general background can be helpful. *Thelema* is Greek for "will," and it refers to, among other things, its central principle, which is "do what thou wilt shall be the whole of the law" and "love is the law, love under will." These exact words come from the *Book of the Law*, *Liber Al Vel Legis*, the holy book of Thelema, which was channeled by Crowley in 1904 from an entity known as Aiwass.[4] The Thoth deck expresses many layers of symbolism and philosophy influenced by the *Book of the Law*.

ALEISTER CROWLEY

I am going to answer a question that often pops up in my students' minds sooner or later: "How do we deal with Aleister Crowley?" I'm going to encourage you, as I do my students,

---

3. Aleister Crowley, *The Book of Thoth (Egyptian Tarot)* (Samuel Weiser, 1991), 92.

4. Aleister Crowley, *The Book of the Law* (Red Wheel/Weiser, 1976).

to always make your own conclusions about everything. I can only offer my point of view, based on my experience and research. This is *especially* true with Aleister Crowley.

Some might see him as the Lord Voldemort of the occult revival—he was no saint. His biographies account for poor treatment of others, and there are places in his writing that suggest racist and anti-Semitic views. He criticized multiple ethnic groups (including his own) and yet, he also praised them, sometimes in the same paragraph. All this considered, his magical work and research has unquestionably altered and developed much of western esotericism, especially tarot. So what are we to do with that?

Luckily, no one has to study or agree with Crowley to use or succeed with the Thoth deck. I believe we can separate his lower character from his higher work and legacy and utilize his contributions in a way that corrects his shortcomings. That's part of the reason I started teaching the Thoth deck. The Thoth deck is an illustration of radical inclusivity and love. Crowley's major spiritual contributions far transcend his personal identity and prejudices, and he is not an outlier in this seeming contradiction. Many channelers and messengers of wisdom and other worlds have exhibited this. The *Book of the Law* (a major influence on the Thoth deck) was channeled *through* him. He just happened to be the mouthpiece.

At the risk of adding more perceived blasphemy to this exposition, what you will learn ahead transcends Crowley. Crowley is one messenger of many in the history of tarot and mysticism. In the same way that the RWS lived far beyond Arthur Edward Waite, the Thoth deck can surpass Crowley. I will do my best to honor the sources and stay accurate but will also frame this material in the context of other great mystical teachings and tools for growth, which promote love and radical inclusivity. In my experience, the iconography and philosophy of the deck and the Book of Thoth do not carry Crowley's lower prejudices. I believe we can enjoy the music without following everything the musician says.

Historically, I look at Crowley as an important confluence of western (and some eastern) esoteric ideas. I don't see him as a spiritual teacher, or guide, or inspiration like I do Ramakrishna, Plotinus, or my own teacher. I view him as a database of occult knowledge to support the exploration of the higher mysteries, in the same way as an iPhone can be used without following the example of Steve Jobs. For me, Crowley as a database is a means, not an end.

Regarding Thelema, like any religion, it can attract its fair share of ignorant people. Just like Norse Paganism has attracted neo-Nazis, Thelema has attracted the alt-right. But also, just as Norse Pagan groups have formed to correct this and disidentify with bigotry and hate, Thelemites have done the same. The Thelemites I have met (who were serious and high ranking in their orders) were extremely inclusive, loving, and supportive.

I believe the Thoth deck points to the universal. It's not concerned with race or sex because it's not even concerned with humans. It's concerned with consciousness. I find it peaks at the unspeakably blissful connection of all things in the same way as the Sufis, Neoplatonists, yogis, Hermeticists, and so on. The Thoth deck is an expression of cosmic love, a love so divine we can't even conceptualize it. It is the deck I have found to be the most explicitly esoteric, most radically ontological, and most hauntingly transformative. Crowley's definition of tarot is "an admirable symbolic picture of the Universe, based on the data of the Holy Qabalah."[5] This is as far as tarot can go because it's as far as anything can go. This book is not a case for Aleister Crowley nor an attempt to convert you to Thelema, nor even an introduction to the Thoth deck. You're about to learn one of the most powerful tarot decks and understand its connection to several mystical traditions, including Hermeticism, Qabalah, Neoplatonism, nonduality, and your own great work. You're about to learn tarot as a form of mysticism. So, what is mysticism?

MYSTICISM

Mysticism is the highest, largest scale of meta. What is meta? And what can be its largest scale? "Meta" comes from the Greek prefix μετά, meaning "beyond" or "transcending." The word can be used to describe that which transcends the subject in question, as in the word "metaphysical." Meta oftentimes deals with self-reference as well. For example, if an actor refers to the movie they are acting in, that is meta. Mysticism takes meta to the extreme. Mysticism is a unit of reality referring to reality itself. In the human scale, this is the human recognizing the infinite eternal reality he or she exists in, the unity of all things. This is consciousness becoming aware of itself. Truly it is an experience, or maybe a lack of experience. It's something that cannot be described because it contains the one describing it, the description, and the one listening. It is transcendent.

This book reveals tarot's ontological and mystical implications as a psycho-spiritual technology. It explores the loftiest questions asked by the philosophers, mystics, and sages: What are we? What is reality? What is God? And what can we do next? It also explores the practical: How can we live with less suffering, and more joy? How do these archetypal patterns of tarot show up in our daily lives? This book brings tarot beyond the context of divination, and into its majesty as a mirror of the self, and more deeply, the Self, the

---

5. Crowley, *Book of Thoth*, 92.

birthless mystery beyond all words and concepts. For convenience sake, I will call that "consciousness." The cards are examined in their connection with the Hermetic Qabalah as seventy-eight wardens of the one ineffable and awesome truth-mystery explored by all esoterica and mysticism. I will describe this "truth-mystery" as a mystical experience; a life-changing recognition of the unity of all things. The aim of this book is to provide the theoretical framework to facilitate that experience. It has fascinated the minds of humans since our updated frontal cortex could fathom such sophisticated modes of thought and symbol systems. Free from the confines of dogma and superstition, these pages curiously navigate age-old mysteries with a modern approach, which includes practical exercises, thought experiments, and remixes of occult ideas. I offer you an amalgamation of decades of research, professional practice, and personal experience of the esoteric tarot and its mystical insight.

The aim of the esoteric tarot, and perhaps, the occult as a whole, is not historical accuracy or academic rigor. Rather, the tarot is a means to an experience of knowing our individual self or our universal Self. The nature of the topics explored are not logical. They cannot be neatly expressed through facts and figures like scientific laws or historical time frames. At best, these deep spiritual mysteries can only be suggested, implied, and expressed through layers of metaphor, meaning, and conceptual frameworks. This cannot be stressed enough: The Mysteries are real but cannot be spoken. So what do we do? We speak about them. This is why card 0 is a fool. We begin a fool's journey.

I believe that all mysticism stems from an experience of truth. The ultimate reality, the absolute all-encompassing truth cannot ever be an idea because it includes and transcends the idea. One need only glance at the *Tao Te Ching*, the *Upanishads*, or the writings of Christian mystics to learn that the ultimate truth can never be put into words, because it transcends all expression. This is because all language is dualistic. All words and symbols can be broken into "signifier" and "signified." Any one thing that is signified delineates it from everything else. This creates a separation. The absolute truth is all encompassing, and has no separation. In the highest levels of mysticism, all language fails.

I believe we all want to experience this all-encompassing truth. We all have divine urgings. These are our intrinsic desires for union with the truth and the whole. It is our lust for another, our willingness to take part in nature, our drive to succeed, our predilection of social engagement. It can manifest in any number of ways. We will do anything that gets us out of our heads and into a feeling of connection with the world. A major aspect of this divine urge is our capacity to create. It is our insatiable curiosity, wonder, and awe. This is

Chapter 1

the *tathata* of Buddhism: The pure "suchness" of life, beholding reality. All tarot symbolism yields to this mystery.

For some, the divine urgings are so strong that their curiosity is insatiable. From them arise the deep questions that have danced through the minds of all sages and philosophers. These are the questions of the mystics. What are we? What is the universe? These questions, and their answers, are the engines behind mysticism. They are what spin the whirling dervishes. They inspire the complex calculations of the Kabbalists. They draw out the superhuman concentration of the yogis, and the short-circuiting riddles of the Zen masters. They fill the Christian mystic with unparalleled piety. They enthuse the choreography of the ceremonial magicians.

But you don't have to be a mystic or magician to take part in this curiosity. In a very literal sense, these existential questions drive the flow of the forty to seventy thousand thoughts you have each day. This will be made clear later on when I discuss the 22nd major arcana. The same curiosity that pinched the primordial nothingness into the big something of reality and our universe is the same curiosity that floods your awareness right now, your choices, your creations. Your body may be separate in space and time from the author of this book, but your consciousness is not. Notice how it continues, no matter what you do. The insatiable curiosity of pure awareness continues infinitely.

This work will not treat mysticism as a hidden doctrine that has traveled through only the most elite lineages of esoteric erudites. It will argue for something more awesome: That the existence of the Mysteries of all esoteric doctrines are inherent in your own mind, right now.

Mysticism is perhaps a not-so-rational approach to understanding the ultimate reality. I use the word "mysticism" to describe any method or discipline that facilitates the experience of oneness/the absolute. We might colloquially say that mysticism is a "race to meet God" before dying, and people have been on that race for a long, long time. Mysticism is nothing new, but the accessibility of its methods and traditions has grown drastically, as well as our openness and capacity to receive them.

Consider the earliest single-celled organisms. They could not fathom what it would mean to have control over their movement (mostly because they didn't have a mind). Sea creatures could not fathom what it would mean to walk on land. Early animals could not fathom what it would mean to grow dexterous hands and build tools. From agriculture to the Large Hadron Collider, life continues to surprise itself with its inventiveness, nerve, and capacity. Mysticism is one predilection of life that is becoming more recognized every century.

Mysticism is not a dogma or religion. Dogma and religion are a result of scavenging, hoarding, and repurposing the breadcrumbs left *by* mystics. It should be noted that mysticism is an experience which results in ideas and practices. Ideas and practices are used to reach the experience. This experience is our sovereign right as conscious beings. More accurately, the mystical experience is our natural state. It is the touching of the real, a singularity from which there is no return.

The approach of this book is to imply, suggest, and pontificate, in every way possible, this supreme reality of ourselves and the universe through the lens of tarot and its sister tradition, the Hermetic Qabalah (more on that later). The study of these seventy-eight cards provides a unique juncture of cultural and psycho-spiritual systems.

Realization of what we are through the tarot is not the end. We can also use the tarot, before even pulling a card, to manipulate meaning. The study of esoteric significance of these cards accelerates your ability to interact with symbols, and more deeply, transmute them. This in itself is already a form of alchemy. To manipulate meaning is to create your own reality. If we know anything about the human race, it's that we are meaning-making-machines. Many books on magick, self-development, and manifestation talk about the manipulation of meaning to create your own reality.

Most of this book may seem theoretical at first, but there is one life-changing practice that comes out of it: It is possible to manipulate meaning and symbol at such a fast rate that every symbol becomes every other symbol. It is at this moment you arrive at an ineffable mystical experience. This can provide a sort of "ecstasis" experienced by monks, sages, and the philosophers of antiquity. I have had several of these experiences. They have been labeled many different names by various teachers and researchers. What I can say with certainty is that the sheer immensity and effulgence of these experiences has made them my ultimate focus and life's work. After my first mystical experience, my life was changed forever.

These experiences are not logical or linear. They are divinely paradoxical because the awareness overrides any thought, description, or concept that attempts to capture it. Attempting to describe a mystical experience will sound insane. That is why the greatest card of the tarot, number 0, is the Fool. Folly and spiritual illumination are always positioned in close proximity by history and myth. That is because a mystical truth is oftentimes a complete reversal of the normal ways of thinking. This is why so many initiatory rituals require a metaphorical death and rebirth. One needs only think of Osiris, Buddha, or Christ.

Chapter 1

This book provides you with an elaborate and holographic template that suggests and maps out mystical realization. It combines multiple systems (most notably, tarot, Hermetic Qabalah, and astrology). Each symbol and idea ultimately contains every other symbol and idea, and each part suggests the whole. The reason for all of the symbols and ideas is to attempt to see the truth in as many ways as possible to increase the chances of … seeing it. By "seeing it," I am referring to a mystical experience.

If not an experience, this book will certainly provide you with a sound *dasarna*, Sanskrit for "right view." The logic of dasarna in tantra is to set up a philosophy of sorts for the seeker that draws them closer to the experience of a truth. This experience is some form of spiritual illumination (there are many stages of this with different names according to different traditions). At this illumination, the philosophy is discarded. The philosophies I provide you in this book are not my own. They are a remix of many esoteric ideas. I have only curated the expression of these ideas, which ultimately precede from an experience I couldn't even attempt to describe.

For convenience, and at risk of misleading the reader, I will use the symbol 0 to describe a mystical truth or experience. 0 is "the All" of the *Kybalion*, the Tao, the Atman, which is Brahman but also Shiva, the godhead, the absolute, the *sunyata* (the void), the ain soph. The 0 is the one consciousness, and what underlies it. 0 is not just the answer but also the question itself that started the whole universe.

I must reiterate an important point: All representations of occult mysteries share the curse embedded in the technology of language. In other words, all expression conceals. Language, symbolism, ritual, and even idea itself, are all masks that express truth but also conceal it. The tarot itself is not a literal map of occult science and the Mysteries, but rather a complex wardenship of ideas that have precipitated over countless years. Like any form of mysticism, the tarot and its framework of studying the universe was not created at one specific time for one specific purpose. It is in fact a complex amalgamation of cultural influences, or rather, a historical trainwreck. This does not nullify it as an authority of mystical technology. It supports it. The philosophical prowess of the tarot is due to its unplaceable birth. The myth of its ancient Egyptian origin enticed occultists of the last few centuries to synthesize it with other esoteric systems. That synthesis, ambitious as it may be, has brought it from a superstitious pack of cards to a syncretic system of mystical philosophy. And it is through this context I will be exploring the cards.

What is the purpose of studying this mystical philosophy? There are many. Before I go on about enlightenment, let's talk about the practical. From a divinatory standpoint, this gives the reader much more to work with. It also offers diviners higher sophistication with symbolism and association.

From a psycho-spiritual standpoint, the amalgamation of traditions in the mystical study of tarot creates a map of the subjective world I call the "youniverse." Deeper study or practice in mysticism may reveal to the seeker that the subjective youniverse encapsulates the objective universe, but we will take that phenomenological detour later. From a mystical point of view, this map can be used to traverse levels of consciousness. Numerous secret societies and organizations dealing with occult initiations have been built upon the frameworks I discuss in this book. Reading this book and seriously contemplating the ideas can bring personal initiations.

This leads me to the last major purpose of study: The prize won by the initiate is the knowledge itself. So lofty are the concepts embedded in esoteric tarot that the mere contemplation of them can lead to higher reward than any tarot reading or spread or prediction.

If life were a race, people might be attracted to magick or mysticism to win that race, or at least to get ahead. The truth is that if anything, high magick and mysticism slow you down. When done correctly, they force you to smell the roses and enjoy the journey. The mystical philosophy of tarot is one of engagement, not result. In the same way our brains and ears have evolved to register an average of eleven octaves, and our eyes have evolved to register the spectrum of visible light, tarot illustrates a rich spectrum of energies and patterns that were first unseen. The recognition of these energies and patterns in our life is only the first stage. The recognition of them within our subjective youniverse is the mystical question, what the mother of Krishna saw when looking into his mouth. He had the whole world in it. This is the pursuit of mysticism and the holographic nature of the universe: To understand the all through the one. It is the pursuit of true bliss.

CONSCIOUSNESS

You've heard it. You've tried it. And maybe, you are it: Present. "Be present." So many self-help books, spiritual teachings, and scriptures say this simple thing in different ways. Here are some of my favorite ways to say it: From the *Chandogya Upanishad*, we get *tatvamasi*, meaning "thou art that."[6] From Exodus, we get the Hebrew *ehieh asher ehieh*, "I am that I am."[7] From Buddhism, *tathata*, meaning "thatness." At the temple of Apollo, we read "know thyself." From Parmenides, we read "Come now, I will tell thee—and do thou hearken to my saying

---

6. *The Principal Upanishads*, trans. Swami Radhakrishnan (HarperCollins Publishers, 1953), 458.

7. Exodus 3: 7–8, 13–14. [All biblical references are from: *The Holy Bible, New International Version* (Zondervan, 2011).]

and carry it away—the only two ways of search that can be thought of. The first, namely, that It is, and that it is impossible for it not to be, is the way of belief, for truth is its companion."[8] A more modern one comes from *A Course in Miracles*: "Nothing real can be threatened. Nothing unreal exists. Herein lies the peace of God."[9] What do all these teachings have to do with being present? They are direct pointings to presence itself.

These phrases are what I call "mystical mic-drops." They point directly to reality. In modern spiritual nomenclature, this is called the "observer" or the "silent witness." I'm going to point out your observer now: Notice your mind reading these words. Notice how the words pass over your awareness. Now, notice that awareness. Notice that which is aware of the experience of these words. Stay with that over the next few sentences. We will revisit this later.

What is so profound about the teaching of presence is that there is nothing that falls outside of it. "Be present" not because you *should* but because that's all you can be. Anything that isn't present is a lie. The truth is presence itself. When we try to make change or differentiate anything apart from presence, there is unreality and oftentimes suffering. The lie is attachment. The truth, presence, is simple and needs no effort or justification. Lies need effort and justification. There is nothing but this present moment. Because of that, there is a sort of paradox.

The tarot is a symbolic expression of a paradox whose rectification has been the aim, mystery, and joke of all mysticism and truth-seeking. The paradox of beholding what is and what is not is the dilemma (and prize) of this work. Like I expressed before, the answer cannot be spoken. This isn't because it's a secret but because the answer is nondual, and all language and all symbolism is dualistic. So what do we do? We make a bunch of language and symbolism about it. This is the policy of tarot.

Reconciling what is and what is not, and all polarities for that matter, will be the red pill that gets you out of the Matrix, off the wheel of samsara, the hamster wheel of attraction and aversion that is all suffering. But don't worry, you can always go back into the Matrix. You can always have one foot on land and one foot on water like in the Star card.

In the alchemical crucible of tarot mysticism is a reconciliation of two truths. Really, there is just one truth, but the experience of a second truth emerges from the mysteries of the former. This can be labeled at this point as:

---

8. Poem taken from John Burnet's *Early Greek Philosophy, 3rd ed.* (A & C Black, 1920).

9. Foundation for Inner Peace, *A Course in Miracles* (Foundation for Inner Peace, 2007), 1.

1. Time
2. Eternity

By now you may have guessed this book is filled with philosophical side quests and theoretical tangents, but let me assure you that its powerful secret is its practicality. The most practical common denominator in most mystical traditions is this:

You suffer because of what you think you are, which is related to the world of time and/or ego. When you realize what you truly are, you won't even so much as blink! All difficulty stems from the illusion of what you are, a false identification with a small piece of yourself. We assume we are a brother, sister, mother, father, friend, lover, husband, wife, woman, man, cisgendered, nonbinary, heterosexual, homosexual, Christian, witch, morning person, night owl, able bodied, disabled, shy, confident, Aquarius, smart, stupid, and so on. But how many spiritual teachers have told us we are none of these things? How many teachers have told you: "you are not your mind, you are not your body"?

The spiritual quest is one of letting go of false identification. Usually, this starts with realizing we are not the body. Later on, we realize we are not the mind. Eventually, we realize we aren't even in the sense of "I." We eventually discover that we are simply presence itself. Ru Paul has said that we are born naked and everything else is drag. I would argue that from a spiritual perspective, being born is drag, the drag consciousness.

The question "what are you?" is existential. It is ontological. It challenges the very assumptions of our nature and of the scale of embodiment we believe we are confined to. Many *assume* we are bodies averaging at 150 pounds, 5' 7", made of bone, blood, and muscle. We assume we have evolved from apes with major evolutionary updates (most notably thumbs and fingers which allowed the creation of tools, and I'm sure I don't need to mention the whole "frontal cortex" update). Some assume we stem from a lineage dating back to a heteronormative nudist couple whose run-in with a snake bought them a ticket out of paradise (but even this classic story is a paradox: You can use numbers and letters to show that the snake was the Christ all along, but more on that later).

Whatever origin story you choose to believe about your self or the human race, I ask you to suspend it during the reading of this book, especially for the following exercise. You are much more than your body, much more than your mind, much more than your very sense of "I," and I can prove it.

Chapter 1

Measuring Me

I teach this exercise to students at the beginning of some of my courses. I want you to scan your body and measure it vertically. Bring your awareness to the top of your head and notice where your body begins. Now slowly work your way down the forehead, the eyes, over the nose and back of the head, and continue going downward until you reach the feet. Notice, when measuring the body, where it begins (the top of head) and where it ends (the bottom of the feet). Now do the same horizontally. Start with the right side of your right shoulder and slowly scan to the left side of your left shoulder. Notice where your body begins and where it ends. You can do this on any axis.

Now take your awareness and do the same exercise. Notice where your awareness begins and where your awareness ends.

What did you discover?

Almost all of my students have discovered that there is no beginning and no end to their awareness. The awareness is infinite. It's eternal. This is the essential realization.

You might argue that your awareness starts when you wake up in the morning and ends when you go to sleep. I would ask you to remember that moment when you weren't aware. Can you?

You might argue that your awareness ends at the farthest thing you can see. I would argue that that is a limitation of your sight, not your awareness. Sight exists *within* your awareness.

You will never find a beginning or ending to your awareness. It is *the One*, singular, all-encompassing non-thing through which we experience everything. It is the eternal, ever-present subject, the silent witness, the observer unto whom all objects are observed. The gnostic text *Eugnostos the Blessed* encapsulates this teaching using some of the exact same words as the *Upanishads* and the Neoplatonists: "The One is infinite, incomprehensible, and constantly imperishable. The One is unequalled, immutably good, without fault, everlasting, blessed, unknowable, yet it knows itself. The One is immeasurable ..."[10] Your true self is immeasurable.

Another key point is that consciousness is "unknowable, yet it knows itself." This is because consciousness cannot be an object to itself because it is the subject through which all objects appear. This paradox is very tricky. Eternity cannot be measured by time. Eternity is the one doing the measuring, which results in time. Infinite space cannot be

---

10. Marvin Meyer, ed., *The Nag Hammadi Scriptures: The Revised and Updated Translation of Sacred Gnostic Texts* (HarperOne, 2008), 276.

described by form. But it is within infinite space that form takes shape. In the same way, your experiences, thoughts, sensations, feelings, and ideas cannot be consciousness, but it is through consciousness that all experiences, thoughts, sensations, feelings, and ideas exist.

The exploration of this is called self-inquiry. The deeper you inquire, the vaster you will find awareness to be.

The infinitude and eternity of awareness is the other side of the coin of time. The marriage of time and eternity is the alchemical process illustrated in the tarot, echoed in the dance of Shiva and Shakti, nirvana and samsara, *purusha* (consciousness) and *prakrti* (nature), the above and the below, the formless and the form. All of mysticism is an attempt to reconcile what you just experienced: How is it that we experience ourselves as finite, yet our awareness is infinite? That is the business of tarot mysticism and what we will be exploring in depth.

I made this exercise after a mystical experience as a way to break down what I was trying to convey without sounding too insane. I later realized how similar the exercise was to a Qabalistic cross in ceremonial magic. I now believe rituals like the Qabalistic cross show the aspirant the relationship of the body to this vast awareness. When doing the Qabalistic cross, you are measuring the finite body in contrast to the infinite consciousness.

You do not have to believe you are infinite and eternal. I believed this for many years as philosophy, since so many spiritual books described it. But it wasn't until I began experiencing it directly that I had the empirical evidence to know it. The evidence is just being, watching, observing. What trips people up is that they look for a specific thing to be, watch, or observe. The evidence is consciousness itself. Consciousness is, in the *best* sense of the word, self-evident, or rather, Self-evident. It proves itself, because it is the one doing the experiment, the one through which all is proved. The knowledge of the reality of infinite consciousness can be developed through many methods: Meditation, contemplation, yoga, magick, or simply watching and being. There is a Greek word used to describe this objectless knowledge: *Gnosis*.

This brings me to a very important point on mysticism. All the great sages, philosophers, prophets, masters, and awakened beings have been trying to teach, through every possible poem, sutra, narrative, asana, and method, this one truth. There are many ways to experience different levels of this truth. Actually, there are infinite ways to experience this truth, because by definition, truth is universal. Here is just one of them:

CHAPTER 1

The Invisible Constants

We experience things because of wave-forms. An experience comes upon us, lasts, and then fades away. All experiences follow this pattern. You can compare this to the three modes of astrology: Cardinal, fixed, mutable. Cardinal is the onrush of energy, fixed is its apex, mutable is its fading away (covered later). What you must keep in mind is that all sensations happen in this way. You can only sense something because of its absence before and after sensing it. A light can only be on because it can be off. I was first introduced to this idea by Itzhak Bentov's "Stalking the Wild Pendulum."[11]

Something that is a constant might be difficult or impossible to notice. A constant is always "on." For example, it might be impossible to see the color of your cornea, the layer over the eye, or taste your own tongue. Do fish know that water exists? If there was a hum in the background of your life, you would never notice it. What constants are there in human life that we cannot notice? That we cannot even conceive of? What has always been that you never noticed? That one question can reveal some of the greatest mysteries taught by the sages (and I recommend meditating on it). They would actually argue that the invisible constant is more real than the very visible wave-forms of sensation in the material world. One way to experience the constant is to be the observer.

Being the Observer

One of the simplest and most profound spiritual exercises you can do is being the observer. Do you remember before when I asked you to be aware of the words passing over your awareness? All you have to do is connect to the part of yourself that observes. Let's return to the example of the light switch. You turn a light on and then you turn it off. You lose the sensation of the light. But what didn't change? What was constant? Your awareness.

The observer connects you to the infinite awareness—eternity—while also allowing you to participate in the world of time (although not really separate things; more on that later). Let's use the Wheel of Fortune to describe this. The Wheel of Fortune tarot card is samsara, the great chase! It is the card of going up and down, chasing our desires and avoiding your fears: Good days, bad days, attractions, and aversions. The good and bad is represented by the edges of the wheel, always moving with such violent and hasty centripetal force. The center of the wheel, on the other hand, doesn't move at all. The center of the wheel is still. "Be still, and know that I am God."[12] The center of the wheel is ... the

---

11. Itzhak Bentov, *Stalking the Wild Pendulum: On the Metrics of Consciousness* (Destiny Books, 1988).

12. Ps. 46:10.

observer. The observer is the constant that doesn't change while everything changes around it. This is the Buddhist nirvana versus samsara, the one versus the many, the purusha versus prakrti, shiva versus shakti, the ain soph versus the sephiroth (the list goes on).

The observer is what is watching your entire experience. The experiences always change; the observer does not. It is consciousness that connects every person, and even every unit of consciousness. It is the awareness that pervades all living things, and it has no agenda. We may compare it to the *atman* of the Vedanta, or the big mind alluded to in the *Hermetica*, or the Nous of Plotinus. It is the mind of the creator. Before I go deeper into this, please note this may sound like a philosophy—and it is—but it is also self-evident, or rather, Self-evident. To paraphrase the brilliant contemporary nondualist Rupert Spira, "there is no evidence that any matter exists outside of consciousness." Think about that: When has matter ever been proved to exist outside of awareness?

I recommend this exercise: For as long as you can, ask a question to all your thoughts, feelings, sensations, perceptions. Ask, "what is observing this?" and "what is aware of this?" Notice the difference between everything you experience, all of your thoughts, feelings, sensations, perceptions, and your awareness of them.

From a business perspective, this is the smartest investment you can make, as it is a state of mind that will never leave you. In fact, it might just be the only thing in this reality that will never change. It's quite worth your time, as it might be the only thing that is really timeless.

The Loops

After doing that for a while, you're ready for another exercise. Sit down, get comfortable and connect to your inner observer that you established in the last exercise. Notice that you are the witness to all your experiences as before. Now here's the twist: If you know there is an observer to all your experiences, who is observing that? Ask, what is observing that? And what is observing that? And what is observing that? It's quite a trip. This is one interpretation of the saying "it's turtles all the way down." This brings you into what Robert Anton Wilson has called "The Arena of Strange Loops."[13] I have seen this experience suggested in certain teachings and symbolism and even created a multimedia dance piece about it. It has been one of my favorite psycho-spiritual discoveries. It is definitely a cherished experience by psychonauts and mystics.

---

13. Robert Anton Wilson, *Quantum Psychology: How Brain Software Programs You and Your World* (Hilaritas Press, 2016).

CHAPTER 1

As a Matter of Mind

Hopefully you've already explored the previous exercises and they now have you question the difference between mind and matter. An advanced understanding of esoteric tarot invites us to dissolve the boundaries between the two, just like yoga. Much of the Hermetic literature and its many modern developments do the same. Mind is matter and matter is mind. There is no real duality.

Alan Watts describes this by pointing out the etymological connection between the word "matter" and "meter": Matter is just the mind measuring! For example, a table does not have an inherent nature as a table. A "table" is a table because our minds label it to be so. We "cut out" the frame and experience of the table with our mind to render it a separate object from everything else in the room. The table is not a table. It is a thought. This very capacity to discriminate sense data into "things" is the secret to the creation of the whole youniverse, the human experience, and is the secret of the suit of swords and the Lovers card in the tarot. The swords cut out and separate to create a diversity of existing "things." This *is* the creative process, the modus operandi of the human experience, the generative youniverse as a whole, and the secret illustrated by the tarot.

The punchline: It's still all the same. Mind and matter are not separated. Thought and the physical world appear to be separate realms but are actually the same. As taught in the Gospel of Thomas: "When you make the two into one, and when you make the inner like the outer and the outer like the inner … then you will enter [the kingdom]."[14] The separation between the inner and the outer might be the greatest illusion the cosmos has ever wrought, truly a divine play! This is how the Magician pulls a rabbit out of the hat or separates pure being into the four elements.

A personal anecdote: I was once very flustered at how my thoughts seemed separate from my physical reality (I was looking into this reality from a completely different plane). I mean, think about it: Why do we have an "inner world" separate from an "outer world"? Why not just one world? I couldn't shake the frustration of this. The universe/an intelligence finally told me what was happening: I was experiencing this strange frustration because I was believing a lie. The lie was that consciousness and matter are separate. The idea that thoughts are separate from reality is an illusion. This is what is meant in *A Course in Miracles* when it teaches that you cannot hide anything from God.[15] All your thoughts are of God. When I surrendered the idea that mind and matter are separate, I began to feel an immense ecstasy I could never begin to describe. I remember choosing to "come back"

---

14. Marvin Meyer, *Nag Hammadi*, 142–43.

15. Foundation for Inner Peace, *A Course in Miracles*.

to the duality of mind and matter, and the ecstasy left. I call this the "inside out" and even teach some of my students how to get there. It's the experience, or realization, that your mind is not separate from the world *at all*. This isn't to say that everyone can read your mind. It's much more existential than that. It's that nothing in your mind exists in a vacuum separate from reality, even though it may seem that way: Try to point to something that isn't in your mind. You'll never manage it. The mind is what does the pointing. The space between our ears is an arbitrary conventional border that anchors us into sanity and the conventional reality of the subject-object relationship.

My point is: Thought, sensation, feeling are all part of the universe, the one song we are all dancing to. You can look at everything and say, "That's God too, that's God too." Now is a good time to recall all the exercises taught in this book so far. Remember that you are infinite awareness that has no beginning or end. Remember that awareness is the one constant that doesn't change. And recall the past exercises of being the observer.

You can consider this philosophically or by extreme reductionism: The reality we experience runs at an average of forty to seventy thousand thoughts a day through about eighty-six billion neurons in the brain connected to a spinal cord. This includes every thought, sensation, and feeling. It all happens here: The spinal highway of human experience. Nothing in your local experience happens outside of this.

What does this have to do with tarot? Everything. I am only introducing you to the tip of the iceberg of tarot mysticism. The whole of tarot is a symbolic map of these realizations. The purpose of all of this is to give you insight and eventually, knowing. This is the best way I can invite you into an experience I can only describe as ineffable. There are no words to describe the state of being I am trying to share. It is not a philosophy, or religion, or method, or point of view, though all of those are (and certainly have been) made from it. It is what is, and if you know, you know. Once you experience this, or rather, realize this, there is no going back. But there is no rush. Such experiences happening too fast can make you feel like a stranger in your own home.

Ultimately, the one truth, the tao, cannot be named. All we can do, like the tarot, is create a sort of contemplative wardenship around it. We will soon ascend the great mystical heights of tarot, and discover that at the apex of all experience, there is only one unitive reality, and there is nothing apart from it. As said in Aleister Crowley's Gnostic Mass, "there is no part of you that is not of the gods."[16] There is nothing that is not this.

---

16. Aleister Crowley, *Gems from the Equinox: Instructions by Aleister Crowley for His Own Magical Order*, ed. Israel Regardie (Red Wheel/Weiser, 2007), 383.

CHAPTER 1

Conclusion of Suchness

To conclude with the madness of a modern mystic, let me echo all the great teachers before me by saying that "such" is the nature of things, tathata, beholding this moment. Presence. We are each an appendage of the creator in an elaborate dance. You are the universe expressing itself as you, a youniverse, on a stage of one dimension elaborating itself through many dimensions. You are the result of innumerable forces acting upon this moment through the vessel of "human."

The idea of the universe experiencing itself has become more popular than ever. This is represented in various symbols and stories. A common symbol of this is infinite eyes. I've seen this motif in the Bible, through the work of Alex Gray, in Enochian magick, and in my own personal experience. The youniverse is looking back on itself through all these eyes, through all these vessels, through so many localizations of consciousness. It's the same stuff! "Whatsoever you do to the least of your brothers and sisters, you do unto me."[17] "Behold, the kingdom of God is within you."[18]

The secret is, there is no secret, and there is no aim! If there is a point to it all, it is this moment, the original cosmic point, position, and monad which is the omnipresent point of view amidst infinite space. This is why compassion is so important. Compassion is not an ethical prerequisite of spiritual growth. Compassion is a cheat code. Compassion is knowing that whomever you are looking at is looking at you with the same consciousness. Their pain and joy is your pain and joy. It is the atman. If anything, the self. Compassion is a divine Self-ishness with a big, capital, ontological "S."

NUMBERS AND DIMENSIONS

Mystical philosophy is a series of concessions that lead to the ultimate ineffable experience of the absolute. What I mean by "concession" is a blind. The Mysteries have been kept secret for many reasons, but the most consistent is that they deal with paradigms of reality that are hidden from the view of most people. This level of knowledge is very difficult as it completely reverses the normal way of thinking. The early mystics and philosophers could not simply bring someone to the realization of truth. It was way too far a jump. To ameliorate the gravity of the teachings, they created concessions or steps or methods for the aspirant to inch their way up, until they finally arrived at the mystical experience.

---

17. Matt. 25:40.

18. Luke 17:21.

Here's an example using dimensions. Let's say we lived in a flat world. If we truly lived in a flat world, you and the other inhabitants would only be able to see a line, because to see a flat image requires us to be in a 3-D world looking at the x and y axis from the z axis. In a 2-D world, you and the other inhabitants can only see things in terms of varying lengths. Now, imagine one day, you experience something outside these two dimensions. You experience a 3-D sphere! It's a total mystical experience. You run to tell the rest of the 2-D inhabitants about this so-called sphere. They look at you like you're crazy and you are totally shunned. You realize you can't just teach them about the whole sphere. It's too much for them to comprehend, so you start breaking it down. Instead of describing the one sphere you experienced as one object, you limit your explanation to the second dimension. You start describing the sphere in terms of two-dimensional slices. You start with a super small slice, then you describe the next slice, which is slightly bigger, then the next slice, even bigger. The biggest slice you describe is the central slice of the sphere, the middle of your teachings. From then on, the slices get smaller and smaller until you've completed the sphere. It takes you a while, but the inhabitants of the 2-D world start to understand. Though each of the slices you teach are not the whole truth, by combining all of those points of view, an idea of a sphere may begin to arise in the minds of your listeners. Finally, one of your listeners imagines the sphere, and starts to transcend the second dimension into the third with you. You are no longer just a mystic, but a guru as well.

The mystics and philosophers were faced with the same challenges. However, instead of having to describe a sphere, they were attempting to describe … the absolute, the infinite all, everything. They had an experience that transcended this dimension. They couldn't possibly transmit all of it at once, so they broke it down. They made concessions to help different aspirants. One form of concession was number.

The Self-Continuing

Mystic philosophers such as Pythagoras saw numbers as sacred. I believe that is because at the highest levels of mystic realization, reality is so abstract, that it can only be communicated by numbers (perhaps this is a side effect of our overgrown prefrontal cortexes). I will go through the numbers from a mystical perspective. This isn't numerology. You won't get information about your life; this is mysticism. You're exploring your absolute existence.

At the level of enlightenment, duality becomes unity, two becomes one, and even unity can become a mystical "nothingness," one becomes zero (this is most famously expressed by the Madhyamika tradition of Buddhism). For any "thing" to exist, it must be defined.

CHAPTER 1

The definition of which separates it from what it is not. A thing can only be conceived by what it is not, which creates its boundaries and form. That is why duality is such a ubiquitous concept in all forms of spirituality. If a "thing" appears to be created in the universe, duality must appear to exist because there is something that is not that "thing." There is what it is, what it is not.

And just like the birth of one immediately renders two, two immediately renders three. The concept of duality can only exist by a third thing perceiving it (in this case, you reading this sentence). If duality is a line, and a line is all that exists, the only perceivable reality would be forward, one thing. But if the line exists, then it must have existence to something outside of it. It must be in the awareness of a third thing. What third entity is aware of the line? The plane. Thus the creation of duality immediately begets the idea of the trinity. This process unfolds itself. Numbers build dimensions. That is what you must keep in mind as we begin looking at the Qabalah. Remember that this is not a doctrine—we are investigating questions beyond our tools of investigation (our mind), and that is the point. This can be debated intellectually, but that invisible observer will always escape and transcend the debate.

To conclude, one can only exist if there is two, and two only if there is three. Each dimension renders the next dimension simply by existing, because to exist, something must be aware of it. This is why Brahman is titled *sat* (existence) and *chit* (consciousness) in the *Upanishads*. This is the meaning of Aleister Crowley's "Naples Arrangement," which we will look at below.

0 and 1: Being

The movement of 0 into 1 represents the highest mystery of all occult study: How does something come out of nothing? How does the Magician bring the universe out of the Fool and pull a rabbit out of his hat? The question is the answer itself. This mystery is the root pattern of creation and what was previously hinted at with the Self continuing itself (this will later be expressed Qabalistically by YHVH, the unpronounceable name of God in the Torah). This is the source code of all mystical philosophy. If 1 is truly the unity, it includes all things. If it includes all things, it is not one thing separate from anything else. If it is not one thing, it is nothing, 0.

Let's begin with 0. The *Brhadaranyaka Upanishad* describes Brahman as *neti neti*, "not this, not this."[19] The only way to describe the ultimate reality is through negation. This is

---

19. Swami Radhakrishnan, trans. *The Principal Upanishads* (HarperCollins Publishers, 1953), 194.

called "negative theology." The concept of nothingness is itself a paradox, because how can "no-thing" be conceptualized? If it is truly nothing, it can't be said to exist. And yet, it is a staple among many mystical traditions, appearing in Hermeticism, Kabbalah, middle and Neoplatonism, Christian mysticism, and Gnosticism. Here are a few examples: Probably the most radical of these is the Madhyamika tradition of Buddhism, with their *shunyavada* (doctrine of the void). In Qabalah, it is called *ain* (without). Meister Eckhart describes God as "in whom we must eternally sink from nothingness to nothingness."[20]

One of the most deeply philosophical upgrades to tarot was introduced by Aleister Crowley in his Book of Thoth.[21] It's called "0=2," a shorthand for $0 = +1 - 1$. The idea is that the universe is perfectly balanced and that all manifestation exists through a sort of disproportion stemming from a primordial nothingness. In this sense, if you combined every "thing" with its opposite, you would eventually get 0, "no-thing-ness."

Imagine the empty universe was a perfect plane of sand. The entire plane was covered in a layer of exactly one grain of sand. In order for this sand to reach any height, you would have to move one grain of sand onto another. You would then have one empty space and one grain of sand with a second on top of it. Now imagine this same thing happening with infinite complexity, with the grains of sand receding and adding to form all sorts of designs, but always under this law of gain and loss, positive and negative, under the strict jurisdiction of balance (the meaning of the Adjustment card).

From a physics point of view, this might not be so accurate a representation of the universe, but from a conceptual and psychological point of view, it does represent the youniverse, and it is important to investigate. From a mystic's perspective, this is essential. When you combine every "think" with its opposite "think" you arrive at a mental state of "none think." This is the method of yoga. Above cancels below, east cancels west, black cancels white, hot cancels cold, and so on. "No-thing-ness" or "no-think-ness" is the ability of the mind to be completely void of thought. This is a broad goal endeavored by all forms of mysticism. It is the point at which all things, or rather "thinks," are reconciled not into one, but into none. Yoga calls this *samadhi*.

All things balance each other out, and that makes the jazz of this universe. This is what the Kybalion mentions in several Hermetic principles. It is important to know that canceling out opposites is only one goal of the mystics and not everyone's goal. The opposites create the contrast that allows for all things, all experiences. This is the modus operandi of

---

20. Aldous Huxley, *The Perennial Philosophy* (HarperCollins Publishers, 2009), 32.
21. Crowley, *Book of Thoth*, 29, 54.

tarot. The Priestess balances the Magus, and they dance. The wands balance the cups, and they dance. The swords balance the disks, and they dance. The Fool balances the Universe, the knights balance the queens, and even the pip cards balance each other vertically and horizontally (which you will learn in chapter 4). From all these dances issue all forms.

It all comes from duality. When duality moves into unity, it is called mysticism. When unity moves into duality, it is called creation.

2: "I am"

The 2 is one of the most misinterpreted numbers. When people think of the number 2, they automatically go to the idea of duality. This isn't necessarily wrong, but it comprises the biggest mistake and invents the biggest hurdle to all mystical progress. When 2 represents duality, it excludes the most important part—you! If there is truly only 2, there is only the experience of one, because the other must be doing the experiencing. 2 is really the last possible moment of an experience of separation before absolute dissolution into the unity of the absolute. This most subtle division exists in the Hermetic Ennead with the idea of gnosis, the pure light of being. This is what Plotinus is talking about when he uses the word *nous*.[22] At this level, consciousness beholds itself. It is pure recognition of existence. "I am."

3: "I am this"

So what is the 3? Recall the exercise of the observer. If you have been doing the exercises, you are probably aware that there is a part of you, "the observer," that is always observing everything, but remaining untouched by anything. Some people call this the silent witness; I call it consciousness. What happens is consciousness descends from its absolute unity and splits itself into the subject and object of your experience. This adds two more characters to our divine psycho-spiritual play. Now we have the observer, the observed, and the original consciousness that precedes the whole show. Reality is the act of observing itself. This observation, or consciousness, is the zero that realizes itself through the observer and thing observed. We can look at this grammatically: There is a subject, verb, and object of that action. This is the triad; the subject and object create the fold of consciousness that is you.

One of the most sophisticated spiritual documents, the *Mandukya Upanishad*, expresses how this subject-object relationship arises. It uses *aum*, both a mantra of god and a formula of radical Self-inquiry. Aum represents four states. Three of these states are represented by each of the letters, and we experience them regularly. The fourth state is the higher truth

---

22. Plotinus, *Enneads*, trans. Stephen MacKenna (Penguin Books, 1991), 369.

that contains the other three and is represented by the silence that follows aum. I will break it down.

"A" is associated with the waking state. "U" is associated with the dream state. "M" is associated with the deep sleep state. These are, more or less, all possible states of our experience. The "fourth state," *turiya*, is the ultimate reality. This is what we actually are and all the other states within it. This fourth state is pure existence, consciousness, bliss: *Nirguna Brahman*.

The Advaita Vedanta tradition asserts that the world is unreal, and that Brahman (consciousness) alone exists. Shankara asserts further that ultimately, Brahman is the world. This is proven philosophically by nondualists like Gaudapada, who wrote a famous *karika* (commentary) on the *Mandukya Upanishad*. The work brilliantly argues how the waking world is just as unreal as a dream. This nondual tradition far exceeds the scope of the present work, and I will approach it more in depth elsewhere.

What concerns us is how the *Mandukya Upanishad* offers a model to understand the development of (at least an appearance) of duality. At the highest state, known as *turiya* (literally "the fourth"), there is no duality. It is represented by the silence after aum. Here, there is only consciousness, which transcends all ideas. It is "one without second" and thus can't be named.[23] One might compare this to the godhead, or "the One" of Plotinus. The next state down is the deep sleep state, the third state, called *prajña*. This is where consciousness is still undifferentiated, but has seeds of duality. It is the doorway into the next two states, which experience duality. This state is associated with Isvara, god as a creator. A creator god cannot transcend this state, because to be a creator, there must be something to create, and thus the potential for duality must exist. This is associated with the "M" of aum. It can be compared to the nous of Plotinus, as well as the first three sephiroth of the Tree of Life (more on that later), and all creator gods. This is the fulcrum point where "something" starts coming out of divine "no-thing." This fulcrum point is not so much a departure from unity, but a mutually arising and even identical process with unity. It is the mystery of the ouroboros, and something I can only begin to explore in this present work. This is the beginning of separation between the observer and the observed. The actual experience of being an observer with something to observe exists in the second state: *Taijasa*. This is the inner world and dream, where consciousness appears to be separated out into a world, yet is still all just you, happening in your head, the dreamer and the dream. This is associated with the "U" of aum, and can be compared to what Plotinus talks of as the soul. What

---

23. Radhakrishnan, *The Principal Upanishads*, 447.

CHAPTER 1

happens next is very interesting. The first state, *viśva*, is the waker, who acts in the world as we know it. This is where we experience physical duality. This is associated with the "A" of aum. You can compare this to what Plotinus calls "nature." The argument of Gaudapada is that the experience of a physical, dualistic world is no different than the experience of the dualistic dream world, and that the dreamer of it all is really one unitive reality: Birthless, infinite, and unchanging consciousness.

What does this have to do with tarot? Literally everything. At its highest level, tarot, like the *Upanishads*, and all other mystical tools, help recognize the Real. Aleister Crowley and Gaudapada both write from such a peak level of mystical awareness, that the style actually contradicts with their other work. At the level of absolute unity, or 0, one can only speak in paradoxes, and even the most sophisticated use of philosophy can only hint at the vastness of the absolute. When you understand tarot as a mathematical expression elaborating on the canceling out of opposites for this divine 0, every card becomes a symbol of the ineffable whole, which is consciousness, the highest level of truth, which is you.

The number 3 is a good place to start. You can experience it directly. There is you, there is this book, and there is action of reading it. But look closer. Are these three really separate? Where does one begin and one end?

The triad is not always used to express something so existential, and is seen in many other traditions as well. Yoga finds a triad in the body: There are three channels that lead from the base of the spinal cord to the brain. They are called the *pingala*, *ida*, and *sushumna*. These are the three major nadis, which are funnels of energy in the body. There are 72,000 in total. (It may be worth noting that there are 72 angels of the shemhamphorash in the Kabbalah.) The following is of particular importance: The ida is associated with the left side of the body, the color white, thought, and the moon. The pingala is associated with the right side of the body, and is described as fiery, activating, and associated with the sun. These two channels are the essential wiring of the nervous system. Through them are channeled two types of signals. Afferent signals are sensory information from the outer world to the brain. Efferent signals contain motor information from the brain to move the body. The central channel is called the sushumna. Methods of mysticism like yoga can raise an energy coiled up at the base of the spine through the sushumna to reach the brain to bring about spiritual illumination. Occultists call this energy the kundalini, or "serpent power." These three channels are symbolized in the caduceus of Hermes.

We find a similar trinity In Qabalah and the Tree of Life: Three mother letters created the Hebrew alphabet. They represent the three spiritual elements—air, water, and fire. Fire is the thesis, water is the antithesis, and air is the synthesis or space in between. We see this trinity in the supernal sephiroth of the Tree of Life: Kether (air), Binah (water), and Chokmah (fire).[24] These three supernals manifest the three pillars of mercy, severity, and neutrality.

This triad is also reflected in the modes of astrology (cardinal, fixed, mutable), the three alchemical properties (mercury, salt, and sulfur), the three Vedic gunas (rajas, sattva, and tamas), and the Christian holy trinity (father, son, and holy spirit), amongst many others.

We can draw all of these trinities to the infinite observation, the observer, the resulting "things" observed. The trinity is the prism of consciousness. It's where the infinite unitive light of consciousness becomes a rainbow of diverse experience through a localized point of view.

However, the observed and the observer are not quite as real as observation itself, pure awareness. The step from consciousness into the duality of observer-observed is the first step toward what Crowley describes in his *Book of Thoth* as "the phantom show of time and space."[25] The trinity is the first step out of the dual threshold guarded by Jachin and Boaz, the pillars of Solomon's temple. This is the first step into the *may* of Indian philosophy, the world of illusion. Observation itself is like a perfectly flat paper. The emergence of the observer and subsequent object observed together make the first fold in the cosmic origami of manifestation. This is the bending of the infinite nothingness into dimensions, into some "things" … this is the secret of how something comes from nothing. As Lao Tzu says:

> *The Tao produces one, one produces two.*
> *The two produce the three and the three produce all things*
> *All things submit to yin and embrace yang.*
> *They soften their energy to achieve harmony.*[26]

The Tetractys: 4 Through 10

One folds into two, which folds into more and more. Consciousness bending itself into the observed and the observer is one of the highest mysteries expressed in so many mystical

---

24. In the original Jewish Kabbalah, Chokmah is associated with water and Binah with fire.

25. Crowley, *The Book of Thoth*, 29, 54.

26. Lao Tzu, *Tao Te Ching*, Barnes & Noble Classics (Barnes & Noble, 2005), 42.

CHAPTER I

traditions. I believe Pythagoras conceptualized this with his tetractys, one of his most sacred symbols. It represented God, creation, and the universe coming into manifestation. It may be considered to be an analog or prototype of the Qabalistic Tree of Life, which is itself cognate with the Holy Tetragrammaton, YHVH, the name of God. The tetractys is expressed as what an occultist might call the "theosophic extension" of 4: 1+2+3+4=10.

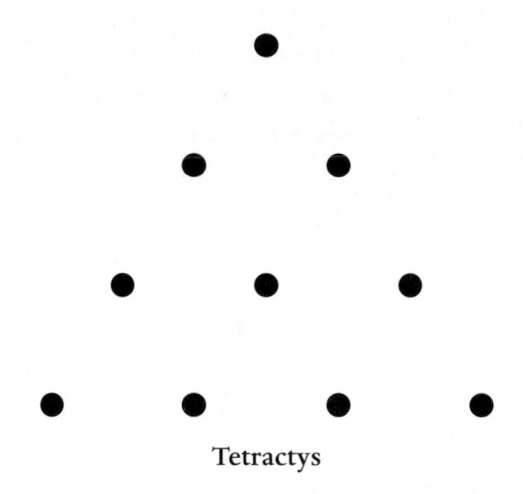

●

● ●

● ● ●

● ● ● ●

Tetractys

The first dot can be interpreted as the unity. This is the monad, God, the supreme mind that contains all expressed as circular. The second two dots can represent a duality. Pythagoras considered odd numbers masculine and even numbers feminine, with their origin in the number two. The first two rows of three dots in total can represent the triad, and function similarly to the supernal sephiroth on the Tree of Life that will be discussed later. These are our thesis, antithesis, and synthesis, or observer, observed, and observation. You can experience this right now. Notice yourself. Notice these words. Notice the awareness pervading both.

Through the interplay of the observed, observer, and faculty of observation above, the sensible world below is created. This is symbolized by the last two rows of seven dots in the tetractys. The third row consists of three dots. Manly P. Hall describes them as "the spiritual nature of the created universe" as well as the primary colors.[27] This can be thought of as the ego, the experience of a self. This self is the space we experience between our ears. It's the localization of consciousness. It's the ability to say "I am this or that." One dot represents "I." One dot represents "am." One dot represents "this or that." This simple state-

---
27. Manly P. Hall, *The Secret Teachings of All Ages* (The Philosophical Research Society, 1928), 258.

ment, "I am this," may bring to mind the mystical mic-drops already introduced. When the Guru tells you, "you are God," it is a concession. That teaching is on the level of the third row of the tetractys, one word per dot. The highest teaching is one dot, unity, to which the sages can only offer silence. To give it a word, you could simply say "being," but even *that* is a concession. The closer downward we go from unity, the easier the mind can understand it but the further it is from truth. Let's continue.

If the mode of the third row is "you are that," then there is something that you are not. That which you are "not" combined with that which you are creates the "circumstances" of the material world. These circumstances are represented by the last row of the tetractys, consisting of four dots, the four elements and seasons, while the row of three represents the three modes of astrology. The seeds of time in the triad bear the fruit of circumstance in the tetrad.

Hall notes that this last row represents the "inferior world" to Pythagoras.[28] This is matter. The last two rows together consist of seven dots representing the seven classical (visible) planets. Astrologically, these seven planets represent seven aspects of our psyche that govern our experience in life.

The profundity of this symbol is in the relationship between the rows and what the proportions suggest. Musically, the proportions are thus: 1–2, 2–3, 3–4. When reversed and used with pitch, the proportions become 2–1 (octave), 3–2 (perfect fifth), 4–3 (major third), creating a musical arpeggio. The relationships between the rows also indicate important doctrines, explained here.

The mystical implications of this symbol are the self-perpetuating qualities of dimensions and consciousness. Understanding this will lead you to the highest spiritual peaks of tarot and Qabalah. In the tetractys, the 3 introduces time. The 4 introduces space and difference. The 5 brings about the experience of both as agents of change and limitation.

Let's start with the 3. As mentioned earlier, the 3 is the dance between the observer and the observed in the act of observation. What this allows is the potential for time. Time only exists if there is a change in the relationship of the observer with the observed. If there is no change at all, there is no evidence of time. If you can see the clouds moving across the sky, you experience time. If you can see the sun rising and setting, you experience time. A more subtle example is your body, an object of your observing consciousness. You can only feel your body because it is constantly changing as energy runs through it in different ways, or as it senses the outside world. Time requires a present state that is different from a past state

---

28. Hall, *Secret Teachings*, 258.

CHAPTER 1

and future state. The 3, past–present–future, is the potential for that change. The 3 is connected with Saturn, the planet of time. Time and the number 3 are also associated with the *spiritual* (not material) aspect of the dying god, who has 3 phases: Life, death, and rebirth. Christ, Buddha, Osiris, and many others follow this formula.[29] They all accomplished their spiritual triumphs because of time. They lived one way, had a transformation or death, and lived a new way that contradicted the first, helping others with that transformation. Transformation, by definition, requires time. This includes the spiritual transformation.

Before we move onto the 4, we must understand the subtlety in the 3. The 3 is only the spiritual aspect of the dying god, not the *material* aspect. That lies in the 4. Though the 3 is related to time, it is not the experience of time. It is only the potential of time that is experienced as change and differentiation by the 4, 5, and subsequent numbers.

When 3 meets 4, interesting things start to happen. Incarnation, life, and death is a potential of the 3 but a product of the 4. The 4 is an attempt of the harmonious 3 to see itself from outside itself. The attempted cosmic voyeurism results in an invention of a false self.

To understand this, imagine you are observing a candle flame. You and the candle are perfectly still. No change can be detected whatsoever. The 3 shows up like so: First we have the observation itself (the experience of the flame). Then we have you, the observer. Third we have the candle flame, the object of observation. Notice how tightly linked these three are. From the perspective of the yogi's nirvikalpa samadhi, there is no "you" separate from the experience of the flame. That unity becomes a duality through the subtle differentiation between you and the flame. The trinity is that division linked with the original unity (which is formless consciousness). What happens when the candle flame is snuffed out? That's the number 4, the change of circumstance. The number 4 is the material basis for change in time or space to create circumstance. That material experience allows for the invention of an ego. When the candle was burning, there was no experience of change. When the candle is snuffed out, there is an experience of change. What doesn't change is our awareness, which is our true reality, the monad, the Self or macrocosm. However, there is another self that doesn't appear to change: The mind. Even though the mind is always changing, we fall under the illusion that we carry the same mind with us through changing circumstances. When the candle goes out, you can think *"I can light a new candle."* In the 3, there is only a subtle difference between you, the observer, and the candle, the observed. In the 4, *difference* makes elaboration. Now there is the possibility of a different candle, a

---

29. In the Hermetic Qabalah, this formula is associated with the sixth sephirah, Tiphareth, which is the theosophic extension of the number three.

different time, and difference in space, organized by the gravitational center of your mind. The change of the candle going out precipitates a desire, a direction, a possibility, and variation all rendering an individual "self" taking its own action upon a world of diversity and causality. The key concept is this: "Difference makes circumstance."

One way to understand 4 is through space. Space includes three dimensions projected by the observer that has been developing in our story. In the 4, we know that situations can exist because of differences in space. To understand this, we must first understand that 3 is a localization of consciousness. The original unity, pure consciousness, finds itself localized through an observer, and observed, acting through observation. This localization is an individual "self." When we add a fourth point of view, that individual, localized "self" can be experienced from outside itself. With a fourth axis added to the matrix, the original triad of an individual self (observer, observed, observation) now has a choice of what to observe. Let's use our example of the candle flame. In this stage, the main character, the observer, must choose if they will light another candle or not. This allows for all possible situations.

Without the 4, the 3 is a pure, individual self. It has no desire because there are no circumstances of concern. It is simply observing. If you were to stare at a candle, and completely let go of the invention of time and space, your sense of self would begin to soften, and eventually dissolve (compare this to the yogic dharana, dhyana, and samadhi). The impure self, or "ego," arises in the 4, which allows the original trinity to be viewed from the third person. This creates the possibility of circumstance to be projected or interpreted from the original triad. This is where we can view ourselves as a "self" separate from everything else because of significant perceived differences that make for a situation. When the 4 comes, the 3 is demoted from its place as an existential, direct reality by being viewed from another point of view. This objectifies the harmonious triad (the universe observing itself) into an identity. To put it in more colloquial terms, this is when a "story" is projected onto or interpreted from reality. Here is one of the most profound teachings: The fourth point of view was invented by the original triad. Why do you think that is?

When 3 becomes 4, we reach what's called the centipede's dilemma. The centipede has a hundred legs all working in harmony. Luckily, she doesn't have to consciously move them, that is, until you ask her *how* she moves them. When she begins to *try* to move them, she gets in her own way, and the harmony stops. Can you remember a time when you got in your own way from overthinking or trying to hard? This was one of the first lessons I learned from my mentor: There is no try. There is only do or don't do. There is only choice. The centipede represents our three O's (the harmony of the observer, observed, and pure observation). This harmonization is the centipede simply being. It's all Zen! But when asked how she does it, she becomes interrupted, confused, disconnected. The very question forces her to objectify herself and then disconnect from the natural flow.

Self-objectification is the killer of possibility. It's when the self tries to be anything else but the observer of its objects. It's when the self tries to push up against reality, as if that self is something other than the reality it's trying to push up against! It's like water trying to wet itself, a knife trying to cut itself, or a snake eating its own tail. From a Tantric perspective, it may be described as the play of the universe. But on the personal life scale, it's the treadmill of samsara, hopefully burning off karmic calories.

The self we invent that pushes up against circumstance is an invention we make, an illusion. It's our ego that we conceptualize. It's our effort to find ourselves from outside ourselves. In doing so, we are allowed to interrogate existence and attempt to find some sort of purpose outside of the Real happening in the Now. It divorces our idea of ourselves from our actions, and further, from the consciousness that it all takes place in. All suffering comes from the illusion of this separation, and this illusion is in no place more emphasized than in the 4.

That is why the 4 is attributed to the demiurge. In Gnosticism, the demiurge is an entity who believes it is god, but is not god, and has trapped humanity. The 4 is associated with matter. As you will learn, the fourth sephirah represents the demiurge. It is the ability of the one single unitive reality to fantasize itself into the third person.

I'd like to make a quick point here for those that want to jetpack up the Tree of Life and attain instant enlightenment. Just as the 4 is an illusion, or invention, of the original triad, the original triad is an illusion, or invention, of the original duality which is really a unity. But the "one" is really a "none." In a way, the original unity or "no-thing-ness" came to be realized in duality by questioning itself and creating its own divine ego or point of view. One might say that this point of view is the *point* of it all, points of view created within points of views, ad infinitum.

But there's more! Next up is 5. The number 5 explains your current experience, especially as it contradicts the more abstract spiritual reality described above. The number 5 is the actual experience of time and change. You can interpret this in the tetractys by the bottom row of 4 points being added to the top row of 1 point. The relationship of the top and the bottom express the change that is the full creative process of the whole design. Another way to find the 5 in the tetractys is by adding the second and third rows together. This is where the macrocosm shifts into the microcosm, where the above begins to identify with the below (as in the Emerald Tablet). If the 4 is consciousness identifying itself in time and space through difference, 5 is that identification endured. The 5 suffers the illusion of the 4. Remember that in the 4 there was an attempt to interrogate the Real from outside of itself, which created the illusion of a separate self, the ego, through difference. The result of that is the experience of time in the 5. The potential of time existed in the 3, but only in the 5, through the fall of the 4, do we experience our localized consciousness moving from a literal past into a literal future, always through change, on the carousel of samsara. Any identification with any*thing* (in time or space) is, by definition, contrary to the unity "no-thing-ness." In the 5, we perceive a difference between our identification below and the unitive truth above.

Opposite to the 5, the 6 is a remembrance of our connection with the divine unity. This is expressed on the tetractys in two ways. The first is by the theosophic extension of 3 (1 + 2 + 3 = 6). Six is counted by going through the first three rows. The third row is three points, which reflects the three-point total of the first two rows. You can relate this with the Hermetic axiom "as above, so below." The third row is like a reflection of the first two, but on a different level. Another way to experience the 6 is by counting the second and fourth rows (2 + 4 = 6). This shows two levels of duality, and how the material results of duality below are a result from the divine seeds of duality above in the first split of the universe observing itself (2). If the 2 is the ouroboros, the serpent eating its own tail, the 4 is that ouroboros getting tangled (similar to our centipede above) and making a lemniscate. The lemniscate is an infinity symbol. Compare that set of symbols to the first *Tao Te Ching* quote earlier.

The number 7 is the bottom half of the tetractys, and represents many profound formulas that share the same source code: 3 acting upon 4. This is the branding of the Hermetic Order of the Golden Dawn, and is symbolized with a triangle surmounted by a cross. Traditionally, this symbolizes light coming into darkness in order to redeem it. It is the purity of the individual self (observer, observed, observation) coming into the material and impure circumstances of the world (4) and bringing salvation by demonstrating its purity. Remember that the 3 is the result of the unitive consciousness separating into the observer and observed, and that the 4 is the illusion of difference in space or time that can result from this. The 3 helping the 4 overcome this illusion is the formula of the dying god. Tarot decks like the Rider-Waite-Smith and Thoth decks symbolize this in the hanged man. The Hanged Man is number 12, which is 3 x 4, the multiplication of the last row of the tetractys (material 4) by the third (spiritual 3). Adding 3 to 4 gets 7, the number of Venus, love. It is through love that God incarnates as a 3 (the avatar/dying god) and enters the world

Chapter 1

of 4, humanity. If you reverse the number 12, you get 21, the number of the World/Universe card. This is a symbol of the *shekinah*, the feminine aspect of god in matter, and also humanity's salvation. Another equation worth noting is 3 x 7 = 21. Seven is thus a divine self (3) acting through space and difference (4) to create circumstance. This circumstance is multiplied by the original triad to create the universe (3 x 7=21). The meaning of this is the participation of the logos in the shaping of the material universe. This logos is also the supernal sephirah on the Tree of Life. We will explore this in greater detail later on the court cards.

The number 7 has way too many associations to list, but some important ones are: Stages and metals of alchemy, colors of the rainbow, and the biblical days of creation. When an ego is moving through time and space and acting on circumstance, it gathers a story. This is the Chariot card. Seven is also the number of classical (visible) planets and 3 x 4 is 12, the number of signs, which contain three modes and four elements, bringing us to the system of astrology.

The number 8 is the material logos and shaping power of the universe. It is conceptualized on the tetractys by counting all the rows except the second row. As I have previously stated, the second row is the most important part. It is the very first seed of separation that allows pure, undivided consciousness to separate. When we focus on the symbol without the second row, we direct our gaze to the universe itself *as* that second row. From this perspective, the dyad is disregarded as an ontological phenomenon so we can praise it as a direct experience: The universe. The 8 is 2 cubed (2 x 2 x 2). This is the ouroboros realizing itself threefold, where the serpent becomes a figure eight eating its own tail. Multiplying 2 by 4 also emphasizes the material universe below energized by the dyad above. I recommend Plotinus's *Enneads* to really understand this relationship.

While the 8 is 2 to the third power, the 9 is 3 to the second power. The 8 is the logos realized in matter, while the 9 is the microcosm or the separate self entering matter. Conceptually, this is the whole tetractys counted without the first point. This is where we begin to forget our divine origin. And in doing so, we create a blueprint for a world of separation. This blueprint is suggested by counting the tetractys without its center piece, showing a vacant triangle. Adding that center piece would bring us to 10.

It is important to note that 10 is not the end. 10 is the beginning that results from the end. At 10, the process starts over again on a different scale. The tetractys becomes one point on a larger scale.

The Tetractys Meditation

The tetractys can be used as a meditation that traverses four stages of spiritual unfoldment. This is a huge undertaking. The curriculum I teach my students at Tarot Mysticism Academy is over a year long and, through many different courses and exercises, accomplishes this. However, this exercise is a sort of summarization of the levels of evolution. The meditation consists of four steps, three affirmations followed by one boundless silence. Each one is loosely attributed to a row on the tetractys, one of the four elements, a court card, and a letter of the Holy Tetragrammaton and you will see parallels in the four quarters of aum and the Vedic koshas previously mentioned. Additionally, they correspond to the levels introduced in the beginning. Each one goes deeper into the reality of your pure being and corresponds to a major phase in spiritual growth:

1. "I am (experience, location, or context)." Example: I am sitting in my bedroom.
2. "I am myself," or "I am (name)." Example: I am Joe.
3. "I am."
4. (Silence)

Let's begin. First, be still, close your eyes, and relax. You must relax deeper and deeper until your brain moves from the beta state into the alpha state. The beta state is like being on the top of a pond when it is rained on. The rain is all your thoughts. It's pretty noisy. When you move into the alpha state, you begin to submerge. As you sink underneath the waterline, the noise from the rain (your thoughts) gets muffled and quieter. They are still there, but not as sharp. The pitch goes down and all your sensations and thoughts begin to soften. This can sometimes take up to ten minutes or more. We experience this alpha state when we are drifting to sleep or daydreaming. One way to help you get there is to see every thought as a subtle effort of the mind-body system and invite it to "surrender the effort."

Once you are completely relaxed, you can begin the first step. Say to yourself "I am ____." In the blank, say where you are physically in space or what you are experiencing. For example: "I am in my bedroom." "I see my books." "My muscles slightly ache." "I feel enthusiastic." Take a moment to really notice your experience of your body in space and time. Notice the edges of your mind-body system, and its relationship to the physical world. You might, for example, notice the edges of your body from shoulder to shoulder, or from head to toe. Notice the differences, diversity, and change of sensation and thought. Notice the temperature, breeze, tastes, smells, sounds, and the visual experience of the eyes closed. This is the tetrad and the outer world, and the annamaya kosha.

Chapter 1

Next, we will move to the third row of the tetractys and say "I am aware of myself" or "I am (name)." Notice how everything you noticed above is only an object to your localized consciousness. Notice how no physical thing or sensation has ever been shown to you outside your observation. Notice the subject-object relationship of all experience. And notice how you are the center of your universe. Notice how you are aware of your local awareness, your own mind. This is the triad, the third row and the vijñanamaya kosha. This is sometimes called the microcosm. As it moves closer to the pure sense of "I," we get closer to the next step.

The next row is only two dots, which represents reality beholding itself. Say in your mind "I am." At this point, the subject and object occupy a much grander scope. You are going to merge the subject and the object together through radical surrender. This is a big step and can take time. Yogis work on this their whole life! One way to start is by trying to find the difference between the experience of an object and the object itself. You will find that there isn't. This can get very epistemological, but don't philosophize it during practice. Notice how all your experiences are not separate from you experiencing them. The point is recognizing that the object "outside" of you is not separate from your inner experience. You then apply that to the experience of yourself in the last step. That very sense of "I" that you have, if it is a sense, must exist in an awareness greater than that "I" to sense it! This is the bliss of being, the dyad, and the anandamaya kosha. It is the love affair between pure awareness and your own self existing.

But that love affair requires distance for the partnership to take place. In the last step, the distance between "I" and the awareness of that "I" is totally collapsed. Duality becomes unity. The two dots become one. Unlike the triad, which was your localized consciousness observing objects, the dyad (in the context of this meditation) is the absolute consciousness observing your entire experience as an object. In the monad, the distance between the awareness (Hermetically expressed as "above") and the objects of awareness (Hermetically expressed as "below") is collapsed. The important part is to recognize how the local cognition is an object of a nonlocal consciousness. Experiencing this will elucidate the symbolism of "the sacred marriage." The last step transcends all visualization and idea, so we won't be priming it with part of the tetractys or a phrase. It is simply a profound silence. The monad is the absolute reality with no form. Some call it the observer or the silent witness. I prefer to conceptualize it as that very existence-conscious reality that allows for all to be, and is the formless substance and infinite space for all.

These numbers and ideas may seem very abstract and impractical, but understanding them will connect you to the highest wisdom of tarot. I would challenge you to find anything in this reality where these four stages aren't at play. They are the very building blocks of all possible experience. They are the very intelligence and shaping power of the universe, or at least the neuro-youniverse. This system shows us what we are made of and how to unmake ourselves in mystical ascent. To echo Plato, this is the practice of dying. But in mysticism it's not dying—it's knowledge of a greater reality.

A MYSTICAL APPROACH TO ASTROLOGY

Early humans lived with absolute clarity. They had a pure point of view, unobstructed by the restrictive net of so many names, forms, and functions that they would eventually self-impose. They looked out into space and saw not only the reality of space, but knew it directly. They *were* space. Have you ever experienced a moment of peace, where reality simply was, uninterrupted and unobstructed? Have you ever felt the flow and ease of being connected with your purpose, what was right in front of you, and the sentient beings around you? The early humans were always in this state. They were consciousness, unobstructed by today's clinging, averting, pinching, wincing, stitching, typing, hurting, abstracting, hacking, paying, loaning, debting, owing, and "oh-no"-ing. They simply *were*. They recognized their eternity. In this single conscious eternity, there was only one.

Then they became ambitious. About thirty to seventy thousand years ago, one human said something to another. It was the first communicated idea. The humans started speaking to each other, and more dangerously, conceptualizing. This came about because of a sudden evolutionary update. The overgrowth (that they would later call a "prefrontal cortex") started to create an "inner world" that was "separate" from the "outer world" and everything started to become "separate" and "in quotes"! They developed a capacity to interpret, conceptualize, and imagine a world "within" and made efforts to separate it from the world "without." This process overflowed from their inner subjective experience into mouth movements. Words developed and then developed some more.

At a particularly impressive evolutionary moment, someone conceptualized a circle, or a sphere (whichever came first). The sphere seemed most appropriate to fit the subjective (or objective) experience of a conscious observer localized in human form. It was regarded as divine and projected onto reality. This was the beginning of the end.

Chapter 1

They wanted to measure eternity and infinite space, and so they did. They invented time, and projected degrees onto the immeasurable. Space was differentiated from earth. A sun was conceptualized, and then a moon. They measured life between "birth" and "death," cutting it off from immortality. Simply being became "coming and going." They analyzed the infinite into every possible idea. Out of one immeasurable perfection arose all the names, forms, functions, and ideas. Something big started coming out of nothing. Things came about within things. Many things were being made, done, differentiated, or changed. The noise of it all roared amidst a humble, quiet backdrop of infinite space, infinite consciousness.

The humans took this to the sky. All the many things that could be made, done, different, or changed became marked in space and time. They divided all "things" into "here or there." The humans reduced eternity into time and divided the infinite space. Out of the one infinite space arose two: The sky and the earth. One added to two is three. And three arose as the knowing-knower-known relationship.

This manifested on a lower plane as the three modes of astrology: Cardinal, fixed, and mutable. The cardinal signs commence the energy of their element. The fixed signs maintain the energy. The mutable signs release and spiritualize the energy. The Vedic analog to this is rajas, tamas, and sattva. The alchemical analog is sulfur, salt, and mercury.

After three arose four. The four elements were fire, air, water, and earth. Four added to three is seven. The seven classical planets (including the two luminaries) came into the communal consciousness: Mercury, Venus, Mars, Jupiter, Saturn, the sun, and the moon. These seven expressed many "things" that could "come and go" when the three (knowing-knower-known) acted upon the four (the world of difference and circumstance).

Multiplying three by four we get twelve—the signs of the zodiac. Each sign is given one of the three modes and one of the four elements. Each sign represents a constellation in the sky. If the seven planets expressed the "coming and going" of three acting upon four, the twelve signs expressed the "here and there" of three acting upon four. The "here and there" further divided the space around the earth into twelve houses.

The early humans wanted to divide further. They had many ways to do it, as it was the nature of their prefrontal cortexes. One way they divided the sky was into 360 degrees. Each sign governed thirty degrees. Each sign was further divided into three sections of ten degrees each. These are called decans.

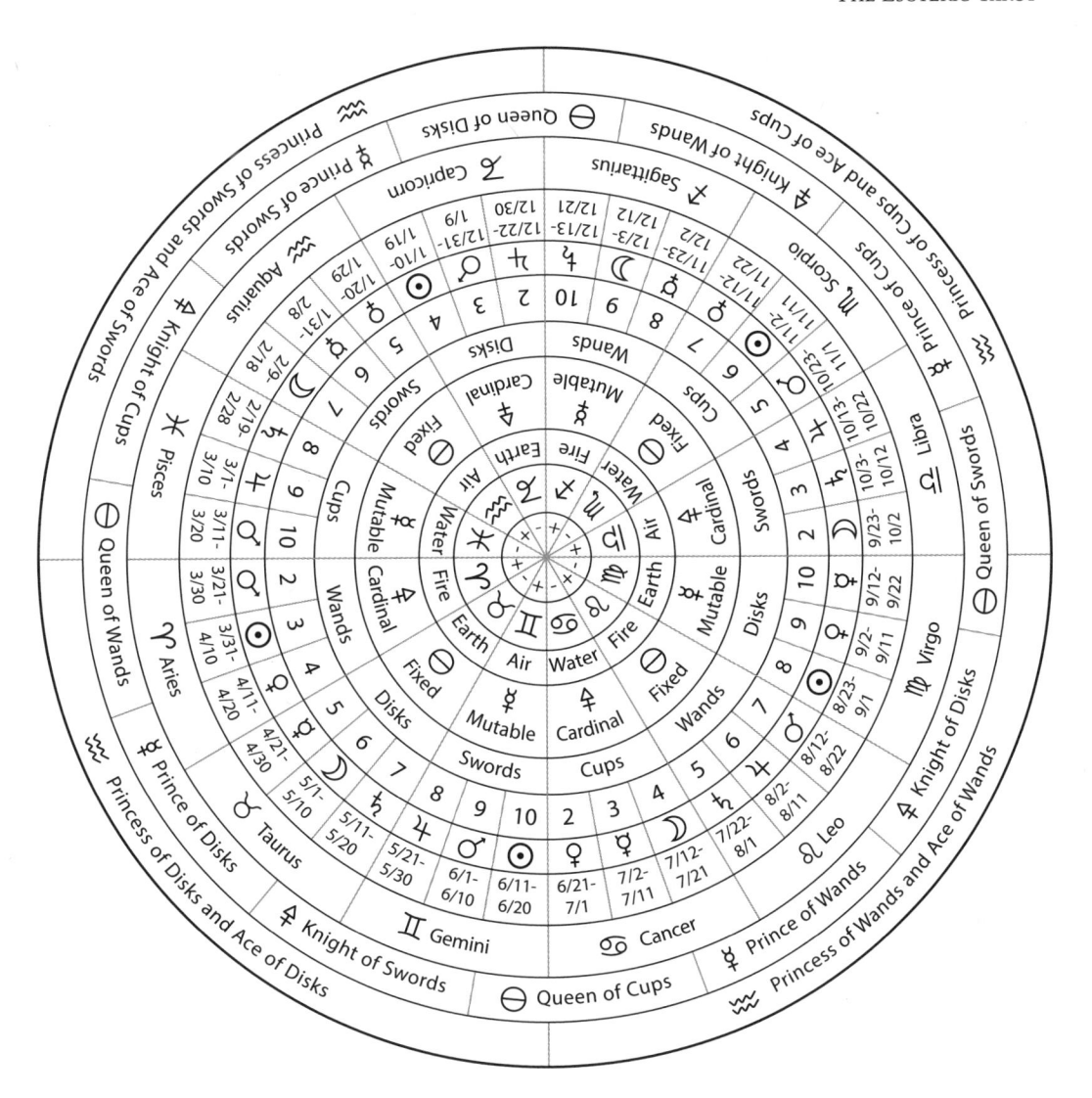

Zodiac Wheel with Full Tarot Deck

The early humans interpreted relationships between the planets and the signs. Each sign (a "here" or "there") was ruled by a planet (that "came" or "went"). They also interpreted each decan to have a ruling planet in addition to the planet ruling the sign.

The humans were so proud of their invention of time that some of them started to forget they were timeless. As they elaborated their methods and concepts, they lost their immortality. The rules of "coming and going" and "here and there" first projected onto the sky now ruled the early humans. Eventually, there was a matrix of things that were made, done, different, or changeable, coming and going, here and there. This matrix pinned time and space into a virtual reality where all things were abstract, separate, and under the illusion of lack.

The humans had fun, but they suffered. They tried their best to regain immortality. There were countless reconstructions of the earlier systems: Countless reinventions, permutations, and syntheses. Gods, goddesses, codes, doctrines, angelic and demonic systems, spiritual hierarchies, exoteric and esoteric practices all came and went like the planets themselves. Occasionally, a human would glimpse immortality and help others do the same. But these "prophets" were often killed. The humans were too hypnotized by all the "coming and going," all the "here and there."

As you can see above, the tarot is only one of the latest updates to these systems. It expresses everything above. However, even today, most humans are pulled into the rule of "coming and going," "here and there," uninterested in the quiet backdrop of the undifferentiated Real. If you're reading this book, perhaps you are one of the few interested in the quiet, undifferentiated Real. To understand that, we will climb the Tree of Life.

QABALAH

Qabalah, which means "to receive," is a Jewish mystical tradition and essential system when studying tarot. It has become the backbone of the western esoteric traditions.

I will provide only a very brief history. Like other mystical traditions, Kabbalah (with a "k") has been passed down orally for at least a thousand years. Some Kabbalists claim it was first received by Moses on Mount Sinai. Others claim it was first written down by Abraham, or given to Adam by angels. Kabbalah stems from Merkava mysticism, a form of mysticism where one would travel to higher realms (or "lower"), pass guarded thresholds, meet angels, and hopefully have a vision of God's throne chariot. Much of this stemmed from apocalyptic literature such as Ezekiel's vision. In 332 BCE, the founding of Alexandria gave birth to Hellenic culture, which fused Egyptian, Greek, and Jewish forms of spirituality. The mathematical emphasis of Neo-Pythagoreanism fused with the linguistic genius of Hebrew and Jewish mysticism. It was around this time that the legend of Hermes Trismegistus, father of Hermeticism, first appeared. This cultural fusion developed through to the third century, where the *Corpus Hermeticum* appears, a soteriological text attributed to Hermes. This nondual philosophy held that the world was a living being, consciousness expanded beyond the body, imagination was real, and that there was a corresponding relationship between larger entities (the macrocosm) and smaller entities, us (the microcosm). Hermetic philosophy was a major influence on Renaissance esotericism and thus tarot.

It was around the time of the *Corpus Hermeticum* that the Neoplatonists, starting with Plotinus, remixed Plato's ideas into that of emanation. Emanation is the idea that the universe/god poured itself outward from higher forms of itself to lower forms. The Jewish mystics and Neoplatonists may have influenced each other in approaching this big question: If God is infinite, why do we experience ourselves and things as finite? The idea of emanation closes the gap between the two realities: Our experience of being finite and our intuition of the infinite (remember the Measuring Me exercise?).

Qabalah made its appearance as distinct from earlier Jewish mystical traditions, around the thirteenth century with the *Sepher Bahir*. This commentary on the Torah introduced the idea of ten emanations, which likely had their origin in the mystical text *Sepher Yetzirah*, which itself was possibly influenced by Neo-Pythagoreanism. Kabbalah continued to develop with various updates and deeply mystical texts such as the Zohar and brilliant minds like Isaac Luria, who further systemized the tradition.

In the fifteenth century, the Kabbalah fused with Christianity and occult traditions to mutate into what would be known today as the "Hermetic Qabalah" in the western esoteric traditions. Its merging with tarot took some imagination. It may have started with the French occultists, like Antoine Court de Gebelin, who believed the tarot to be originally written by Hermes Trismegistus in ancient Egypt. His friend, Comte de Mellet, claimed the tarot was the Book of Thoth, and suggested the trump cards (major arcana) were connected to Hebrew letters. Etteilla then developed these ideas further. Though these pioneers of esoteric tarot may have been historically inaccurate, their experimental synthesis started to stick, and provided fuel for the fire of the nineteenth-century occult revival.

In 1888, the Hermetic Order of the Golden Dawn was founded by three freemasons who claimed to be working from a mysterious document known as the Cipher Manuscripts. This initiatory order further synthesized Qabalah with tarot and other systems, including astrology, ceremonial magic, Enochian magick, Tantra, Egyptian mythology, Christian mysticism, geomancy, and Hermeticism. Hermetic Qabalah became the backbone. The two most popular tarot decks today, introduced earlier, come from this tradition. They are both implicitly and explicitly qabalistic.

Tarot and Qabalah just fit. The tarot is made with four suits of ten pip cards each, twenty-two major cards, and a four-office court card system. The Qabalah describes existence in four worlds, ten sephiroth, twenty-two paths, and four aspects of the soul. It's hard not to see a connection.

CHAPTER 1

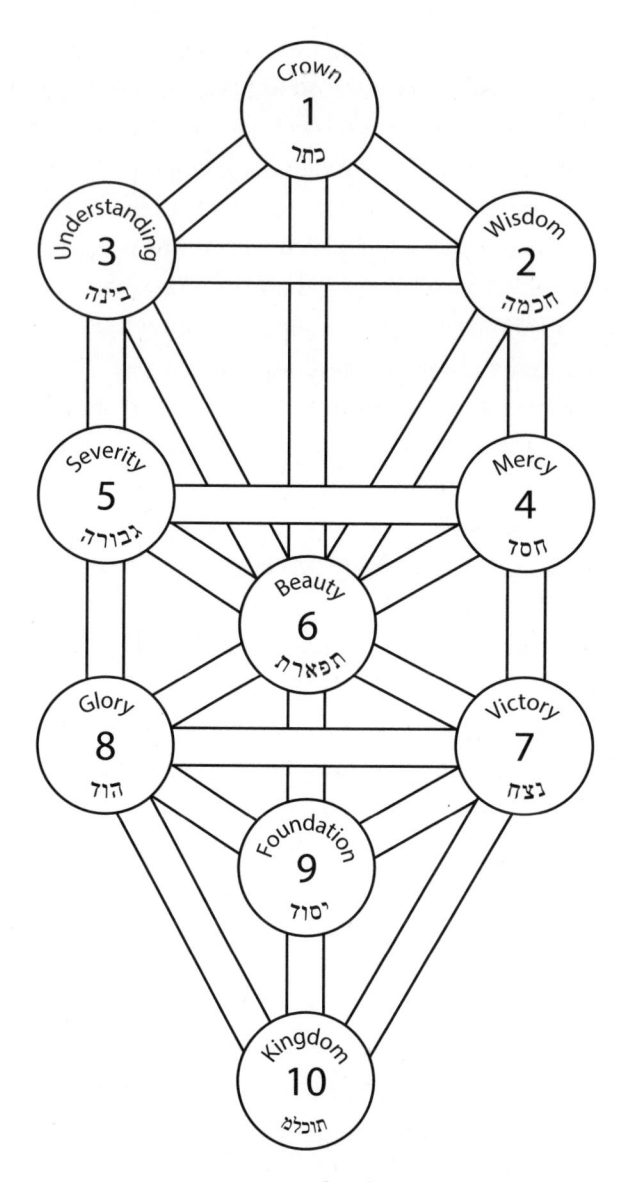

Tree of Life

Many historians agree that there is no solid evidence of this common origin of tarot and Qabalah. However, the ideas that have traveled between the two share uncanny similarities with mystical and esoteric traditions running throughout history. To me, the common threads underlying these traditions are more impressive than a shared historical birthplace. The commonality testifies to the perennialism of this knowledge.

THE ESOTERIC TAROT

The tarot, through the blueprint of the Hermetic Qabalah, becomes a complex illustration of a beautifully deep mystical tradition that explores what we are: The universe, and the youniverse. No tarot deck is more explicit in its qabalistic content than the Thoth deck, a direct expression of the Tree of Life:

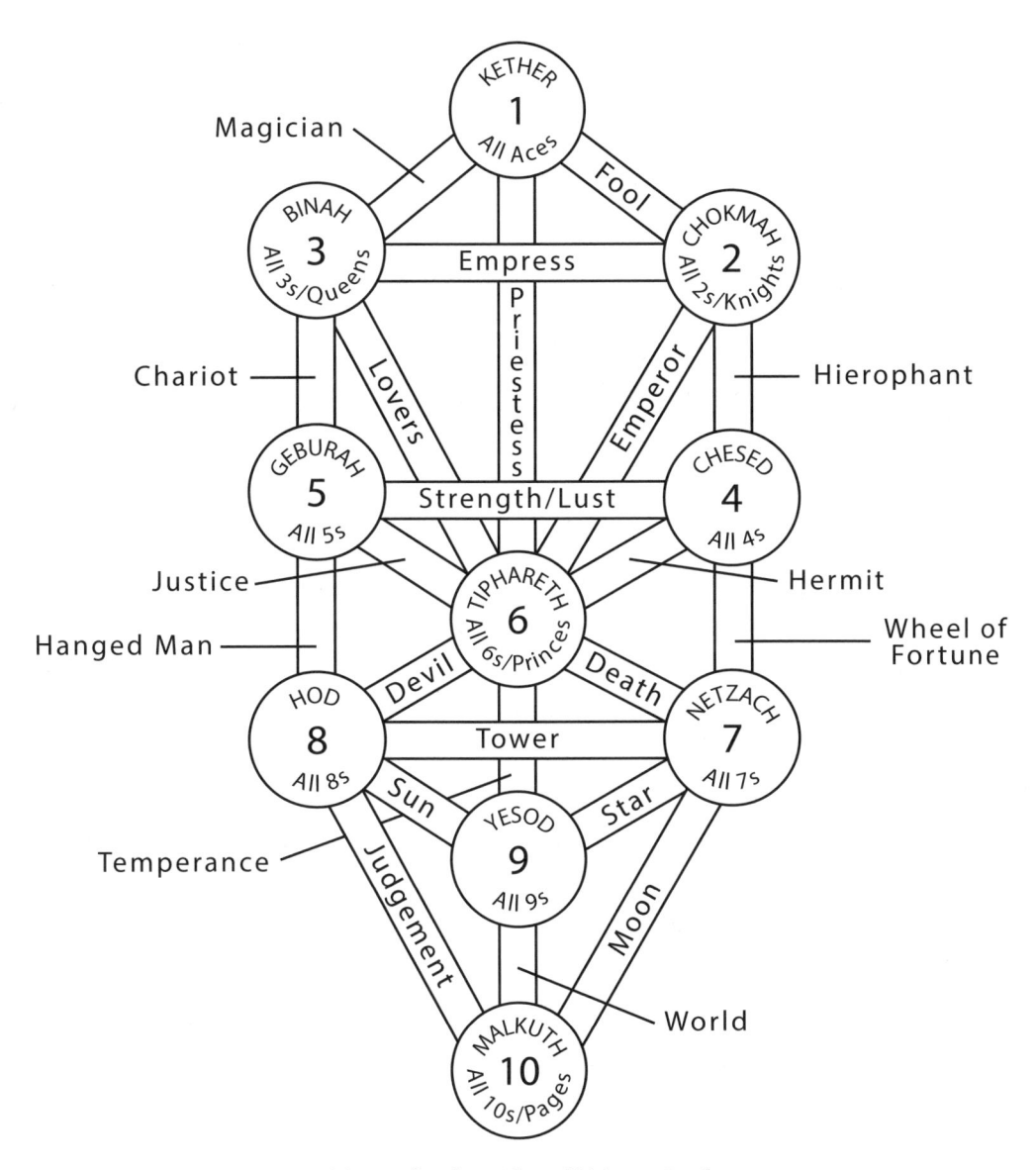

Tree of Life with Full Tarot Deck

CHAPTER 1
MAPPING THE TAROT ON THE TREE OF LIFE

I strongly recommend arranging your cards according to the Tree of Life on the previous pages. It is the backbone of western esotericism and thus one of tarot's biggest influences. It maps out the tarot as an expression of pure being and your true nature. Simply placing the cards accordingly forms the blueprint for all the knowledge (and perhaps gnosis) ahead. If possible, I recommend keeping a Thoth tarot deck in this arrangement as you progress through this book; it's a perfect tool for reference, integration, and contemplation. Be warned, though, this spread may take up a bedroom floor! I have even seen students use bulletin board paper on their walls to tape the seventy-eight cards and other correspondences on the Tree of Life together, resulting in a perfect mystical mind map.

The Tree of Life

The Tree of Life was a visual update to the Kabbalah. Its origin is obscure. Many mystics were building all sorts of conceptual ladders to God, such as the Neoplatonic hypostases, which may have influenced the Tree of Life. The tree itself may have originated with Isaac Luria, the "Holy Ari," the great Kabbalist and pioneer of modern Kabbalah.

This cosmic diagram can be considered fractal or holographic: The design of the whole is similar to the design of the parts. As you zoom in, you eventually see the same idea. Each part contains the information to create the whole, and that whole is the universe, pure being. At its most mundane, the glyph acts as a magician's filing cabinet for all experiences, ideas, archetypes, and correspondences in consciousness. Used for loftier means, it is essentially a ladder to the Divine.

It is imperative we apply Alfred Korzski's caution not to mistake the map for the territory. The tree is only a map which has surfaced from thousands of years of Qabalists exploring the highest peaks of wisdom and understanding.

The Hermetic Tree of Life is composed of ten *sephiroth*, a word that has been translated as "spheres," "emanations," or "shining sapphires" (*sephiroth* first appears in the *Sepher Yetzirah* and has no clear translation). Think of them as emanations of the Divine descending into matter. The highest sphere, Kether ("crown"), is the godhead, the source, while the lowest sphere, Malkuth ("kingdom"), is our material experience. Recall the Hermetic axiom "that which is above is like that which is below" from the Emerald Tablet of Hermes Trismegistus.[30] The Tree of Life shows the relationship between god and human, eternity and time, truth and falsehood, and in so doing, explores some of the loftiest questions mys-

---

30. Hermes Trismegistus, *The Emerald Tablet of Hermes* (Merchant Books, 2013).

tics ask. The Tree of Life, like Plotinus's great chain of being and other maps, attempts to show us a bridge between our immediate experience of the finite and our intuition of the infinite. It solves the problem presented to us in the "measuring me" exercise.

I offer two metaphors to understand how the Tree of Life is a bridge between ourselves and the Divine. The Tree of Life is itself a creative act and represents ten stages of creation. One way to understand this is through the fountain metaphor. The fountain pours the waters of life/consciousness/energy/reality. These waters are first poured into Kether, the first sephirah. They overflow and pour over into Chokmah, the second. This continues until the water fills the last sephirah, Malkuth. Each sephirah is a container with a unique quality and energy that gives the infinite form. This paradigm is similar to that of the earlier Hermeticists and Neoplatonists, with their cosmological or hypostatic levels of the being.

A more contemporary metaphor is that of a video game. Imagine that God, the infinite, wanted to have fun and know itself. God decides to play a video game. This game is called Kether and is the first sephirah. The game is so fun that God gets lost in it and forgets its own reality. In the video game called "Kether," the avatar of God decides to play a video game called "Chokmah." So now, God is playing a video game in a video game. This continues until Malkuth. And it is here, in Malkuth, the kingdom, we are consciousness playing a video game, and our bodies and minds are the avatars.

Let's explore the structure of the tree. The ten sephiroth are arranged in three columns. The central column is called the pillar of neutrality; it is generally considered hermaphroditic and is associated with air. The right column is called the pillar of mercy or pillar of force and is generally considered masculine and associated to the element of fire. The left column is called the pillar of severity or pillar of form and is generally considered feminine and associated with the element of water. So what about earth? That is attributed to the last sephirah, Malkuth. Recall the doctrine on the trinity: Duality is the nature of consciousness to split itself into a subject-observer and object-observed. The tree does the same. Neutrality becomes positive and negative, masculine and feminine. With the original unity, this duality becomes the triad. The tree is further arranged in three triangles or triads with a remaining sephirah at the bottom, Malkuth. The first triad is called the supernal triad. The second is called the ethical triad. The third is called the astral triad. The tree repeats the idea of three coming into one, splitting into three, and returning to one. This relationship has a powerful connection to the four elements as well and the Holy Tetragrammaton, explored later.

You're about to learn the ten sephiroth. But before we begin, we have to talk about *nothing*. The tree begins before it "begins," with the three *ains* or veils. Before the first sephirah is "no-thing-ness." This is called *ain* in Hebrew, translated as "without." From ain comes *ain soph*, which can translate to "without limit," meaning infinite nothingness. From here comes *ain soph aur*, or "light without limit," limitless light. Tarot master and author T. Susan Chang cleverly describes this as the "lights, camera, action" of the universe. These three veils (as well as the first few sephiroth) are so high on the Tree of Life, that normal human consciousness cannot conceptualize them. If you find them confusing, that's okay. It is common for Zen masters to use paradoxes and riddles to push a student into a new spiritual awareness (they are called koans). The third sephirah and above are purposely contradictory, as the spiritual nature of things becomes divinely paradoxical and irrational, or rather, suprarational. It is important to note that every*thing* below ain is only a play of ain, only a fold in the cosmic origami of pure nothingness. Let's explore the folds of existence.

The Sephiroth

The Tree of Life shows the creation of the universe, as well as our own human creations. You can map any creative process onto it, as creation is the universal process of being. The method of creation is a dance between extremes. The divine energy above is manifested below through a gradual exchange between force and form, masculine and feminine. By tracing the ten sephiroth in the order of their emanation, you will see a lightning bolt. This is the lightning bolt of creation referenced in the tarot, as well as what magicians call the "path of the flaming sword." This can be compared to the flaming sword held by Michael, guarding the entrance of Eden.

Some Qabalists would argue that the Tree of Life is the fall from Eden, but I prefer a different teaching. It is said that "Kether is in Malkuth" and "Malkuth is in Kether." This teaches that spirit is in matter and matter is in spirit. I've been teaching tarot and mysticism for many years. I've met so many great aspirants and seekers. Most of them (including myself) were, at least at one point, looking for something outside of themselves. People will find God in anything but themselves. Why? Because God *is* everything. There is nothing that can escape the pure quality of being. The irony is that the truth of pure being is closer to you than anything. There is nothing that is not in Kether besides nothing itself.

These three veils of nothing emanate into *Kether*, the first sephirah, translated as "crown." This is the monad, the primum mobile, or "first mover" of the universe. It is the original point of view and also the ubiquitous point of view. This sephirah realizes itself by emanating into the second sephirah, Chokmah, and the third sephirah, Binah. These three are manifested in the fourth sephirah, Chesed, which in turn develops further into the second triad, containing Geburah and Tiphareth. This second triad descends into Netzach, which further manifests itself in the third triad through Hod and Yesod. These three triads find themselves fully realized in Malkuth, the tenth sephirah. The pattern is one understanding itself as three and then integrating back into one. This is also the secret to the court card system, which we will look at later. The following paragraphs will go into the details of each sephirah.

Kether is our first sephirah, the crown, the source of all. A crown sits atop the head, just as Kether transcends rational thought. It is called the macroprosopus, the great face. Here lies the infinitely small but omnipresent point of view, the godhead, the monad. The first three sephiroth—and Kether especially—are impossible to describe in words. They make up the supernal triad. At the level of Kether, there is no "thing" because there is absolute unity. It is literally the emanation of nothingness. No "thing" can exist separate from it as total unity. Thought can only exist in duality. Kether is often symbolized by a diamond, the purest crystal. We can compare Kether to "the one" of Plotinus and Nirguna Brahman of the Vedantic tradition. The mode of consciousness attributed to Kether by the *Sepher Yetzirah* is "admirable" or "hidden intelligence." It is hidden because it is borderless and edgeless, and thus cannot be the content of experience, but rather, the infinite "experiencer." The entire universe is hidden in its potential in the unity of Kether. Kether marks the highest macrocosmic world, Atziluth. In the tarot, Kether is represented by the four aces.

The absolute is so absolute, it is absolutely *something*. Kether is something coming out of nothing, which becomes the source pattern for the Tree of Life and reality. The first germ of a "thing" to be begins to exist separate from Kether's unity of "no thing" through our next sephirah, Chokmah, meaning "wisdom." This is the ontological/cosmogenic moment that all sages, mystics, and philosophers are looking for. This is when one becomes two and is expressed in tarot by the Fool, the knights, and the aces' movement into the twos. Zero, the three veils of nothingness, were not definable before one. However, Kether, one, has potential of definition by its *being*. But its *being* arises mutually out of its own reflection. If it *is*, who's to say that it *is*? Its being requires an observer. This mystery is the highest mystery of tarot and is symbolized by the ouroboros. It is the most important paradox and the glory of the nondual understanding.

This paradox expresses the mystical mic-drops and other ontological affirmations introduced earlier. However, I would like to bring up a few more examples to really emphasize the profundity of Chokmah's departure from Kether. This one departure echoes the source pattern, how something comes out of nothing. It literally reflects how Kether came out of the ain soph. And, it will be reflected below in each emanating sephirah. If you understand this, tarot and all mystical technology will take on a whole new level of meaning. Every unit of reality is this one ontological surprise.

I'm going to introduce a few quotes to help explain how one becomes two simply by existing. Let's start with the mystic philosopher Plotinus. Keep in mind that the Qabalistic correlative to the "intellectual principle" he speaks of is Chokmah and Binah. He states, "at that, the object known must be identical with the knowing act (or agent), the Intellectual-Principle, therefore, identical with the Intellectual Realm. And in fact, if this identity does not exist, neither does truth; the Principle that should contain realities is found to contain a transcript, something different from the realities; that constitutes non-Truth; Truth cannot apply to something conflicting with itself; what it affirms it must also be. Thus we find that the Intellectual-Principle, the Intellectual Realm, and Real Being constitute one thing, which is the Primal Being… The intellectual object is itself an activity."[31] This is more than an epistemological problem of knowledge (as seen in the sephirah Da'at below). It's an ontological paradox. How can something exist separate from what is aware of it? If there was nothing aware of it, it could not be said to exist. You might argue that something's existence does not depend on one's awareness of it. This is true. The nondual philosophy would agree. Nothing's existence depends on one's awareness of it. However, everything's existence depends on awareness itself. You don't have to be aware of the moon for it to continue to exist, but never has the moon been shown to exist outside of awareness.

When you leave your home for work, and forget about it, it still exists, yes? But how do you know it exists? It exists in your awareness. When you come home, and your home is still there, it only ever remains *in* awareness. If that home existed in a void, with no awareness or relationship to anyone or anything, it could not be said to exist. This is not to say that reality is loading up to us like some sort of video game. The point is that consciousness precedes—or is—reality.

To summarize, all objects can only be said to exist by the consciousness that is aware of them. Conversely, anything one is conscious of can be said to have some form of existence (this is why *sat*, existence, and *chit*, consciousness, are two words used in the *Upanishads* to describe Brahman.) Simply put, there is no difference between this book and your awareness. You can never point to this book without pointing to your own awareness. This applies to everything called a "thing." Remember that "things" are all that can be made, done, different, or changeable. They are here or there, coming or going, and most importantly, have

---

31. Plotinus, *Enneads*, trans. Stephen MacKenna (Penguin Books, 1991), 369.

some sort of beginning or ending, some sort of edge in time, space, or dimension. "Things" are experienced by the thing called "nothingness" of consciousness. Consciousness is not a thing in this context. It is not made, done, different from anything else, or changeable. It is both here and there, neither coming nor going, and has no beginning or end. At the highest spiritual revelation, there is no difference between the nothingness of consciousness and the "things" of its experience.

These same spiritual revelations are reached in the fourteenth book of the *Corpus Hermeticum* when Hermes Trismegistus teaches that there is ultimately no difference between the maker (God/consciousness) and the made (its objects): "We must understand these two things: What comes to be and who makes it. Between them there is nothing ... If the maker is nothing other than the making–solitary, simple, uncomposed–then necessarily the making happens of its own because the making that the maker does is generation ... Without the maker, the begotten neither comes to be nor is, for the one without the other completely loses its own nature from deprivation of the other. Thus, if one agrees that there exist two entities, what comes to be and what makes it, they are one in their unification ..."[32] The relationship between zero and one, one and two, is thus described as maker and made.

One of my favorite ways this is taught is from the Vedantan sage Gaudapada, progenitor of the Advaita tradition. In his commentary on *Mandukya Upanishad*, he refutes a series of theological arguments. He concludes with a radical statement that the world is not created or dreamt by God, but is God's very nature: "With regard to creation some have the firm conviction that creation is a mere will of the Lord ... Some others say that creation is for the enjoyment (of God), while others say that it is for (His) disport. But it is the very nature of the Effulgent Being, (for) what desire can One have whose desire is ever fulfilled?"[33] The radical nonduality of Gaudapada and the Advaita Vedanta tradition collapses the distance between maker and made altogether. It reveals the "is"-ness that destroys all separation between subject and object, like in the samadhi of yoga. That which is, is. That level of "is" is the same as anything else that "is." What we must learn now is that not only is the "is" the ultimate reality of things, but that this "is" can be experienced and interpreted as the ultimate creator. It is through an eternal self-beholding of "is" that the ouroboros devours itself. In this infinite dance, Kether "becomes" Chokmah, its word,

---

32. Brian P. Copenhaver, trans., *The Hermetica: The Greek Corpus Hermeticum and the Latin Asclepius in a New English Translation, with Notes and Introduction* (Cambridge University Press, 1992), 56.

33. Swami Gambhirananda, trans., *Eight Upanishads with the Commentary of Sankaracarya* (Swami Muktidananda, 2019), 196–97.

and the word speaks the universe into being. However, from a higher perspective, like that of Gaudapada, we might say that the nature of Kether *is* Chokmah. The immediacy of this *self-beholding* contrasts with the appearance of its *becoming*. When we say something "becomes," we fall into the illusion of time. When we are aware that something "is," there is no time, only the Real.

Chokmah means "wisdom." It is the first departure from the Real and is the wisdom behind the shaping power of reality and its becoming. It follows that this second sephirah represents the will, the logos (the word), and the intelligence of the universe to be, which is ultimately, the same "is"-ness. This manifests (or is conceptualized) in its expansion. Chokmah is also the supernal father and divine masculine. I like thinking of Chokmah as force. This force drives the creative process. If Kether is "no thing" by being the unity of "everything," we might call Chokmah the movement of that no thing. The movement of the infinite circle with its infinite degrees twists into the glyph of infinity, the snake eating its own tail. When the infinite unity moves, it creates the possibility for relationship, which is introduced in the next sephirah, Binah. The sephirah Chokmah and its movement is also expressed by the yod of the Holy Tetragrammaton, and by extension, the knights of the tarot. The twos are also attributed here, and express the movement of their aces' potential. This is how consciousness illuminates itself, through its own movement. It is fitting that the mode of consciousness attributed to Chokmah is "illuminating intelligence." Astrologically, Chokmah is attributed to the zodiac, which illuminates the sky. The attribution to the zodiac also emphasizes the expansive nature of Chokmah.

The force of Chokmah would return to nothingness unless it is given form. That form is Binah, meaning "understanding." We can think of Binah as the relationship that mutually arises from the movement of Chokmah. She is the divine feminine and supernal mother to the divine masculine and supernal father of Chokmah. If Chokmah is the purusha, Binah is prakrti. She is the shakti to shiva, and Kali, the divine mother of Hinduism. She is form itself, in all its horror and glory, the gate into incarnation, and also time. Astrologically, she is attributed to Saturn (Chronos). She is the prism between the white light of the supernal triad and the many colored sephiroth below. She gives birth to all phenomena through division and duality. Being the matriarch of diversity and multiplicity, she is the engine creating all "things." She is all possible border, boundary, and edge, which make all "things" appear amidst the ultimate "no thing." Recall that for something to be, there must be the contrast of what it is not. This mystery of duality is found in Binah, the third sephirah, because a third entity must exist to recognize the division into two. Binah corresponds to the heh primal of the tetragrammaton. In the tarot, she is expressed by the queens and the threes. The *Sepher Yetzirah* attributes "sanctifying intelligence" to this sephirah. To sanctify is to set apart. In so doing, Binah (and the queens and threes of the tarot) set apart one aspect of consciousness from another to offer duality to the movement of Chokmah. If Kether is a circle, Chokmah would be the twisting movement of that circle, and Binah would be the resulting figure 8. In that figure 8, the original circle now touches itself. The point of contact is the duality. You might argue that the second sephirah should be duality, being the number two, but it is not so. Duality can only exist by the consciousness experiencing it, and so it requires three. In Chokmah, there is no object, but only the movement of consciousness. Consciousness is always in the first-person perspective. The duality of Binah is emphasized in its associated world, Briah, the creative world. This is the first major separation between creator and created. Binah is the last sephirah of the supernal triad which represents ideal reality, as opposed to actual reality, represented by the following seven sephiroth. These two aspects of reality are separated by "the abyss," an unfathomable chasm between Binah and the fourth sephirah, Chesed.

Before we go into the abyss, I would like to make a comparison between the three supernal sephiroth and three very powerful words. The *Taittiriya Upanishad* attempts to subtly indicate Brahman (the ineffable absolute) through three words (this method is known as *lakshana*). They are *satyam*, *jñanam*, and *anantam*, translated as "truth," "knowledge," and "infinite/limitless." Truth is the unchanging is-ness of the Real. If it is, it is. Knowledge is its all-knowing aspect. This is the intelligent design of the universe and its shaping power. In this sense, every form is an object of the knowledge of the absolute. Every form is an expression of the intelligent shaping power. The edges of any form or "thing" come about through knowing it. Lastly, anantam is its limitless nature. Each of these words leads to the other two. If something is true, it cannot be outside of the infinite by definition of the infinite. If something is known, it must be true, having an existence to the knower. That which is infinite must encompass all the known things. In the same way, that which is known is true and is contained in the infinite. And lastly, the infinite, by including everything, makes everything known and true. These three lakshanas suggest each other, and are meant to point to the absolute through which they all derive existence. To use the metaphor introduced earlier, these three lakshanas are like three slices of a sphere used to describe the sphere they make up. In the same way, we might approach Kether, Chokmah, and Binah. Kether is the Real, the unitive existence. Chokmah is its infinitude. Binah is the knowability of it and its contents. That which exists can only be said to exist in some form of its knowability within the infinite. At this level, knowability, existence, the absolute, the truth, all merge into that which transcends the mind. It is here we find the *nous* of Plotinus and the Hermetic tradition before him.

Just under Binah, there is a mysterious eleventh sephirah called Da'at, translated as "knowledge," which sits in what is known as "the abyss." The *Sepher Yetzirah* explicitly says that there is not an eleventh sephirah and that there are only ten. I will offer one interpretation of Da'at. Being knowledge, we must ask, "knowledge of what?" There are two things to know in mysticism: The apparent reality of matter and the reality of the Divine. These manifest in two ways. In the unreality of matter, there is a *real experience* of something. In the reality of the Divine, there is an *experience of the real*, which is "no thing." In a real experience of something, there is an object of knowledge. You are having a real experience of this book, an object of your knowledge. This is the type of knowledge that Da'at expresses when crossing over the abyss downward into manifestation. However, it is also possible to have an experience of the real. In this case, there is no object of knowledge besides the real. Transcending all objects, it is non dual. This is the knowledge Da'at represents when crossing over it into the supernal triad above. It echoes the paradox of Chokmah carrying the logos out of the absolute into manifestation. Honoring the *Sepher Yetzirah*, I don't see Da'at as a sephirah. It is rather a fulcrum point that turns our ontological stance inside out. And thankfully, it does so. It is that very dramatic shift that allows the unitive consciousness above to know the many delicious objects below in the world of matter. In doing so it creates space and materialization. There is a meditative technique to get to this inside-out fulcrum point, but I can only teach this to students directly.

Chesed, meaning "mercy," is the beginning of materialization. This is our fourth sephirah. It receives all the energy from the first three supernals and translates it into materiality. Just as Chokmah was the paradoxical being/self-beholding/becoming of Kether before it, Chesed is the same being/self-beholding/becoming of the supernal triad above it. He is the nerve and mercy of the ideal supernals to actualize in material coordinates. He represents loving kindness, compassion, comfort, and structure. Chesed takes the expansive quality of Chokmah and the forming function of Binah and emanates them into three dimensions. Though it is on the masculine pillar of mercy, this sephirah is attributed to water. This is where the sephiroth start to exchange gender qualities as the universe complicates itself. An important thing about Chesed is that it is the first sephirah below the abyss. That makes it the highest sephirah that can fully experience separation. Because of this, Chesed represents the illusion of rulership. This is why he is so easily attributed to ruling deities like

Zeus, Amoun, and Indra, rulers who believe they are at the highest peak but are not. His watery quality attributes him to Poseidon. Astrologically he is attributed to Jupiter. Chesed is represented by the fours of the tarot. If the four Qabalistic worlds were attributed to one Tree of Life, this would be the beginning of Yetzirah, the third world attributed to the air element and blueprint of material reality below. The *Sepher Yetzirah* attributes "cohesive or receptacular intelligence" to this sephirah. As a receptacle, it receives all the divine energy from the supernal triad and emanates it into materialization, creating cohesion for the blueprint of the formative world, the next phase of creation. But this divine receptacle, the universe in three dimensions, is about to hit some turbulence.

Chesed's comfort and stability is balanced by the interrupting force of Geburah, translated as "strength," "severity" or "judgment." Though a feminine sephirah on the pillar of severity, she is attributed to the element of fire—the polarities are beginning to mix and complicate themselves. She applies motion to the three-dimensional world of Chesed, giving it experience. The motion she applies comes through receiving the emanation of time from Binah above her. This fifth sephirah is one of challenges, change, friction, trials, and even war, but also of editing, refining, and perfecting. Because of this, war gods are often associated here. Geburah is attributed to the planet Mars and the god Ares. It is the war and conflict of Mars that overthrows the Jupiterian ruler in Chesed. Chesed tells us "you can have it all!" Geburah tells us "you can have none of it." This is a good thing, because if we had it all, there would eventually be nothing left to have. The fives of the tarot express Geburah as they each show a disruption or challenge. The *Sepher Yetzirah* attributes "radical intelligence." We could interpret this as the intensity of the universe to continuously change and challenge itself through destruction and recreation. After Chesed builds things up, Geburah breaks them down. This creates a perfect balance that emanates into the next sephirah.

The combination of the previous two sephiroth realizes a harmony in the sixth sephirah, *Tiphareth*, "beauty." This is the heart of the tree, the midpoint between spirit and matter. It is fitting that the *Sepher Yetzirah* attributes "mediating intelligence" as the mode of consciousness, since Tiphareth mediates the above with the below, the masculine with the feminine. As the center sephirah on the middle pillar, this is our true center, compassion, the "self." Tiphareth is connected to every sephirah except Malkuth, including the three supernals. The hexagram/hexad around Tiphareth includes Chesed through Yesod. This is considered the microprosopus, the "lesser face." Here in the microcosm is where we first really experience ourselves as a localization of individual consciousness, the ego. This is the space between our ears. Because of that, here is where we first experience time, having a past, present, and future. The time experienced by an individual is represented mythologically by the "dying god" archetype. This is Christ/Buddha consciousness. It is the first sense of a personal self, but it is not distorted by desire, which comes in the next sephirah. It is pure individual consciousness untainted by false identifications. As the microcosm, it is called "the son." This son is attributed to the vav of the tetragrammaton (its father is the yod and Chokmah, and its mother the heh primal and Binah). In the tarot, this is attributed to the sixes and the princes. Not only is it the son but it is the sun. All sun gods, such as Ra and Apollo, are attributed here. The sun is very much like the localization of our consciousness, our egos. The sun is the gravitational center of the solar system while also its illuminator. In the same way, our egos are the gravitational center of our lives and the illuminator of our personal experience. When the pure, localized, individual consciousness of Tiphareth slips lower into Netzach, interesting things start to happen.

As we descend the Tree of Life, things get more familiar. The pattern of descent is one of sacrifice. Consciousness is the nerve to become (as emphasized in Chokmah), and in so doing, it continues to trade its connection to the whole for its fascination with its parts. This always requires a sense of lack. This first happened in the paradoxical emanation from Kether into Chokmah. It happened again when the supernal triad emanated into Binah. Now, the ethical triad (Chesed through Tiphareth) will emanate into Netzach to form the astral triad. Netzach holds the same "nerve" as Chesed and Chokmah above it. This last triad is the dance between feeling (Netzach) and thinking (Hod) that makes the choreography of the subconscious mind (Yesod) and the astral world.

We begin with Netzach, translated as "victory" or "eternity." This sphere departs from the middle pillar into the pillar of force. Crowley notes that Netzach is a degeneration because it is both low on the tree and off the middle pillar. This is a sphere of ambition, independence, self-sovereignty, motivation, rhythm, desire, and motility (the ability of organisms to move on their own). She manifests the liberative qualities of Chokmah and the materializing qualities of Chesed into the personal volition below. She very much connected with feelings and emotions. Netzach is said to express the masculine aspects of the feminine. She is considered feminine because of her feeling and emotional prowess, but masculine because of her activity. She is a fiery sephirah, drawing from the fires of feminine Geburah only two stops away behind. This fiery feminine beauty makes her a lover and an artist. Goddesses of love and beauty are often attributed to this sephirah, including Aphrodite and Hathor. It follows that she is attributed to Venus, the planet of love. In the tarot, she is expressed by the sevens and is attributed "occult intelligence" by the *Sepher Yetzirah*.

If life was a film, Netzach would be the motion of the film, zipping across the light of the projector from Kether.

Hod, on the other hand, would be the individual frames of the film. Our next sephirah, Hod, is said to express the feminine aspects of the masculine. Hod translates to "glory" or "splendor." He is the submission contrasting and balancing the ambition of Netzach. He submits to the trials of Geburah above him. As a lower emanation of the pillar of form/severity, Hod takes the dualistic nature of Binah and Geburah and manifests it in the human mind. He is intellection, patterning, math, language, communication, use of symbol, reason, and thought itself. This perfectly balances the emotional nature of Netzach. Hod is the reasoning and choice that follows the raw desire of Netzach. This sephirah is the home to deities of communication and magick, like Thoth and Hermes, and is attributed to the planet Mercury.

I was asked once in class, "What is the relationship between the submissive aspect of Hod and its connection to the intellect?" It's a very good question, much bigger question than you might think. It questions the very nature of omniscience. A common interpretation of omniscience is the "all-knowing" God comparable to Santa Claus keeping track of who is naughty and who is nice. However, when we graduate from this lower, guilt-driven paradigm, "all-knowing" omniscience becomes not a quality of judgment, but one of intelligent design. The omniscience of consciousness is its natural ability to form into all the intelligent forms that make the universe, from quarks to superclusters. This is the shaping power of the universe. If you compare this to the logos, you are correct. Mercury is the planet often used to symbolize the logos, the word. It is through this intelligent design that the universe communicates with itself. But notice how this intelligent design does not happen with effort. In fact, there is no effort at all. Forms just appear. In this sense, Hod shows us the submission of the universe to its own design. In this submission to complexity, simplicity and complication find identity with each other (imagine the astronomically high number of molecules that go through chemical change during one breath). This is what the *Sepher Yetzirah* means by "absolute or perfect intelligence," the mode of consciousness attributed to Hod.

The relationship between the thought of Hod, feeling/emotion of Netzach, and the body (which will emanate next) is well researched in psychology, healing, and kinesiology (see David Hawkins).[34] When doing deep healing work, you'll notice that a feeling (Netzach) is often accompanied and sometimes hidden by a swarm of thoughts (Hod). It would

---

34. David R. Hawkins, *Letting Go: The Pathway of Surrender* (Hay House, 2012).

behoove the student to compare the relationships of Netzach and Hod with that of Chesed and Geburah as well as Chokmah and Binah. Understanding these nuanced relationships below in our direct experience through the abstract relationships above is part of our aim. It will be discovered that our very thoughts, feelings, and sensations below are direct reflections of the subtle dynamic patterns introduced earlier in the tree. Investigating these conceptually and somatically is part of the great work.

Hod descends into Yesod, which translates to "foundation." Yesod is the subconsciousness, the foundation of who we are. The subconscious is the hidden interface underlying all thoughts (Hod), feelings (Netzach), and sensations (Malkuth). Here we find the astral plane. Many cultures talk of a tenuous substratum of matter, from the Chinese *qi*, to the Indian *prana*, or Éliphas Lévi's "astral light," or the "fohat" of theosophy. There is a rhythm to this substratum that echoes the repeating opposition of the whole tree. In this elusive fluid which animates or emanates into matter, there is changeability. But because of that changeability, there is stability. Yesod is the funnel of divine energy from all other sephiroth. The active expansive pillar of mercy is perfectly mixed with the passive and contractive pillar of severity, balanced by the pillar of neutrality. This brings creation and destruction into a stabilized flow of subtle experience, constantly in flux to ensure its continuation. Yesod is often attributed to dreams and the akashic records. It has been called the "storehouse of images." Yesod's changeability and connection to dreams and the astral are further emphasized by its astrological attribution to the Moon. The *Sepher Yetzirah* attributes "pure or clear intelligence" as the mode of consciousness. In tarot, Yesod expressed by the nines. As the subconscious mind, Yesod is also the autonomic nervous system which governs the body's activities. This perfectly bridges it to our next sephirah.

Out of the funnel called "foundation," comes Malkuth, "kingdom." This is this moment, the manifest world. It is everything you can sense. It is your body. Malkuth is all matter and thus meter, since all matter is really measurement. This is everything we can measure, everything with edges, in all its high-definition glory. Everything measurable can be measured by an immeasurable measurer, which is consciousness (refer to the "Measuring Me" exercise). This is why it is said that Malkuth is in Kether. This is the grand result of maya, all the names, forms, and functions that have developed through the tree. It is the final masterpiece, and is thus called "resplendent intelligence" by the *Sepher Yetzirah*. In the tarot, this is the tens and also the princesses. The last letter of the tetragrammaton, heh final, is attributed here.

We must briefly talk about the pattern of three in one. The three veils of nothing found emanation in Kether. Then, Kether and the other supernals found emanation in

Chesed. Then, Chesed and the next two sephirah of the ethical triad found emanation into Netzach. Finally, the last triad finds emanation in Malkuth. Compare that to the triad introduced earlier on the section on numbers: Observation, observed, and observer find itself in circumstance through the invention of difference to create the world, and there you have it! Congrats, you've arrived!

The Paths

Number is a great way to express the movement of the absolute unity into the diversity of our direct experience, but it's not the only way. Speech has been used as a metaphor by mystics of many cultures to express the relationship between the infinite and the finite. Speech carves out ideas with conceptual form from formless awareness of the listener. Many traditions have compared speech to the creation of "things" and voice or breath as the life, consciousness, or raw material that creates them. The idea is that words and letters are how divinity articulates infinite potential into finite form. Words become the "something" that comes out of the formless "nothing" of voice and breath.

The sacred sound of aum, for example, is the most important word, mantra, and invocation in Hinduism. The *Mandukya Upanishad* starts by declaring that aum is everything. Aum is a syllable that is supposed to include all possible sounds, in the same way as Brahman is the absolute reality that includes all possible "things." When meditating on the all-inclusive sound aum, we can meditate on the all-inclusive reality that is Brahman.

The *Sepher Yetzirah*, one of the earliest textual influences on Kabbalah, has a similar reverence for speech. This obscure document teaches the reader how the universe was created by God through thirty-two paths: Ten sephiroth and twenty-two letters. Remember earlier how we explored the way language both expresses and conceals. Each letter is an articulation of the Divine that takes the formless into form.

You've been introduced to the ten sephiroth, but what about the paths? These twenty-two paths are attributed to the twenty-two letters of the Hebrew alphabet, and the twenty-two major arcana cards of the tarot. They connect all the sephiroth. The paths on the Tree of Life draw the divine energy between the sephiroth. They are the shaping powers of consciousness, just like the mouth shapes sound through the voice and breath. Alongside their Hebrew letter attribution and other correspondences, the major arcana cards express these divine articulations. Some would say that the paths are masculine while the sephiroth are feminine. We will go into detail with each major arcana card later on.

Chapter 1

Dimensions and the Naples Arrangement

Crowley made his own remix of the Tree of Life called the Naples Arrangement, on which I will provide a bit of commentary that further elucidates the core concepts introduced in the section "Numbers and Dimensions." First, you must understand that to be in one dimension means to experience reality through the dimension under it. For example, if you were in a flat, two-dimensional world, you would not see shapes. You would only see lines. Your vision would be squished into that flat plane and looking in any direction would only yield the one-dimensional experience of the two-dimensional forms. To use a classic video game reference, Super Mario never actually sees a goomba. He only sees its height.

There is one more thing to know about the Naples Arrangement: Gematria. Gematria is the esoteric art of finding numerical values of words and connecting them with other words of the same value. If you've ever watched or read a parody of a crazy conspiracy theorists trying to predict the end times through a bunch of weird numbers and calculations from the Bible, they were probably doing Gematria. It is actually a very deep aspect of Kabbalah and far exceeds the scope of this present work. However, it is the tool Crowley uses for the numbers in the beginning of the Naples Arrangement.[35]

$61 = 0$.

$61 + 146 = 0$ as Undefined (Space).

$61 + 146 + 207 = 0$ as basis of Possible Vibration.

1. The Point: Positive yet indefinable.
2. " " Distinguishable from 1 other.
3. " " Defined by relation to 2 others. The Abyss-between Ideal and Actual.
4. The Point: Defined by 3 co-ordinates: Matter.
5. Motion (time)—Heh, the Womb; for only through Motion and in Time can events occur.
6. The Point: Now self-conscious, able to define itself in terms of above.
7. The Point's Idea of Bliss (Ananda).
8. " " " " Thought (Chit).
9. " " " " Being (Sat).
10. " " " " Itself fulfilled in its complement, as determined by 7, 8, and 9.

I will now break down this table and go over each line:

---

35. Crowley, *Book of Thoth*, 32.

61 = 0

The Naples arrangement starts with our three veils of nothing. The gematria value of ain (nothingness) in Hebrew is 61. 6 and 1 mark the path of the High Priestess, who descends from Kether (1) to Tiphareth (6). It is through the Priestess we reach the divine nothingness. She guards the threshold between "things" and "no thing." She is boundless, oceanic consciousness (Kether) poured into the mental space between our ears (Tiphareth). In boundlessness, there is no edges, and there can be said to be no "thing."

61 +146 = 0 as Undefined (Space)

But nothing is in love with everything, as Shiva is Shakti. Being nothing, it allows for everything. The second veil of nothingness is ain soph, meaning without limit. This is the same nothingness, but now it is limitless, because limitation is included in the nothing (or rather, nothing "cancels out" limitation). Crowley introduces this as undefined space. The gematria of soph is 146. That added to ain makes 207. This is the same value as aur, "light," which is our next veil of nothingness. One might say that the nature of infinity (ain soph) and the nature of light (aur) are the same. They suggest each other instantly. They are mutually arising. This pattern of dependent origination will continue throughout the Naples arrangement, Tree of Life, and tarot in general. I would call this the logos.

Another note on 146 that suggests the emergence of light: 1 is Kether the macrocosm. The number 4 is Chesed, the demiurge. The number 6 is the microcosm. It shows the descent of light into our experience. The path that connects 4 and 6 on the Tree of Life is attributed to the Hermit. The Hermit represents, on one level, the all-inclusive nature of the infinite, the absolute, standing alone (ain soph). If something is truly infinite, it can only be alone in itself since there is no second thing apart from its infinitude. This is the esoteric meaning of the Hermit in the Rider-Waite-Smith deck, a full visual expression of God. The Hermit is also the source of revelation and light, which comes next.

61 +146+207=0 as basis of Possible Vibration

The next level of nothingness is ain soph aur (limitless light), which has the same gematria value as ain soph before it, 207. Since Ain is true nothing, it nullifies limitations to create everything and nullifies everything to return to nothing. In nullifying all possible limitation, its nature is elucidation and revelation of all possibility. The nondualist would call this the simple light of consciousness. Spiritual traditions from all cultures have described light as a spiritual experience and metaphor for awareness and truth. It's almost as if the awareness of

CHAPTER 1

the original nothingness shed light on itself by canceling out its own voidness. This brings us to the purest substance from which reality is made, which the alchemist called "azoth." The gematria value of this word is 414, the sum total of ain soph aur.

1. *The Point: Positive yet indefinable*

One could say this point brings us to pure observation. Out of nothing comes a concentrated point which is the first primordial idea of position. On the Tree of Life, this is Kether. In the Pythagorean tetractys, this is the first point, the monad. Being the true monad, there is *nothing* else. The value of "Kether" in Hebrew is 620. The number 620 reduces to 8, the number of Adjustment, the feminine expression of the dynamic balancing act of the Holy Tetragrammaton (see chapter 2). The number 620 is the same value as "Torah" and also the combined value of the next three sephiroth, "Chokmah, Binah, Da'at." From this, we can surmise that the very nature of Kether is Chokmah, Binah, and Da'at.

2. *" " Distinguishable from 1 other*

Now enters the observer through the number 2 and Chokmah. Without the relation of the line, could the point, being only position, exist? The very existence of a position suggests the possibility of distance. The mutually arising pattern continues. "Position" begets "distance" here in the same way as the awareness of nothingness begets its own light. The point begets the line. Awareness begets an observer. The logos is the enthusiasm of one dimension saying to another "I exist so you can exist," and reality pours itself from sephirah to sephirah. This is the most important teaching, and one of the higher interpretations of the ouroboros and what Plotinus calls the nous.

3. *" " Defined by relation to 2 others*

Now, for the observed. We have a line but if the universe was a line, no line would be experienced. If only a line exists, all reality would be experienced as points. To experience a line, the first plane is formed, and so the point can be defined by two references (two-dimensionally). The appearance of the line, which mutually arises from the appearance of a point, also creates the mutually arising plane. This is symbolized by the third sephirah, Binah. This plane, symbolized by a triangle, is a powerful shape. It is architecturally sound not only in buildings and engineering but also in our chakras. This is also the first triangle created in the tetractys of Pythagoras. The next three steps are represented by the third row of the tetractys.

The Abyss–between Ideal and Actual

The Abyss is what separates the ideal from the actual. The ideal world consists of the three supernals on the Tree of Life: Kether, Chokmah, and Binah. The actual is everything below, starting with Chesed and ending with Malkuth. The abyss is the last possible moment the ego can last before absorption into pure being.

4. The Point: Defined by 3 co-ordinates: Matter

If the plane exists, a fourth point must exist to experience it, which brings us into three-dimensional space, the sephirah of Chesed. Let's welcome the cube. This is materialization, the solid, and matter. This is the first moment where reality starts to be recognizable, as we all experience ourselves in space. But could space be experienced without motion?

5. Motion (time)—Heh, the Womb; for only through Motion and in Time can events occur

Motion and the sephirah Geburah are applied to this space so things can happen. This is because three-dimensional space can only exist if it is known by more than one perspective. We have to move to experience space. Space is defined by some sort of motion. This implies time, and also allows for sensation. Recall that sensation requires an "on and off," a sense of time, and comes in a wave-form. What is Heh, the womb? The gematria value of the Hebrew letter heh is five. Heh is the feminine letter of the Holy Tetragrammaton and has been symbolized as a womb in the same way as the first letter, Yod, is symbolized by the seed. The womb is also the literal gateway for consciousness. On one side, before incarnation, there is eternity. On the other side, after incarnation, there is time.[36] Coming into being through the magical sexual act is a central theme of the Thoth deck.

6. The Point: Now self-conscious, able to define itself in terms of above

If time can be said to exist, there must be something other than time to experience it. The answer is localized consciousness. When consciousness experiences time, it separates itself from eternity by divorcing reality into a past and future organized around its present point of view. This is in some sense the microcosm, the human mind, and the ego: The illusion of a separately unchanging "self" maintained through change (time). Now that our point has motion in three-dimensional space, it can have a past, present, and future, and thus, a

---

36. Whenever you see an archway in the Rider-Waite-Smith tarot, it is a reference to the womb and the letter heh, a threshold between life and death, time and eternity.

"self." Crowley goes as far as to say that atoms maintain a memory, so that as the universe continues to combine and separate its smaller parts, the memory of the particles' journey is maintained, allowing the universe to grow. This alludes to the popular paradigm "the universe experiencing itself."

7. *The Point's Idea of Bliss (Ananda)*
The next four steps correspond to the last four sephiroth on the Tree of Life, as well as the last row of dots of Pythagoras's tetractys. Crowley applies the Vedantic ideas of sat, chit, and ananda. At the risk of blaspheming the Book of Thoth, I find this a poor attribution. As they are taught in the *Upanishads*, sat, chit, and ananda would more accurately describe Kether, since they describe Brahman, the nondual absolute. Duality is introduced in Chokmah and developed in Binah. We will explore it nonetheless. Ananda is the idea of bliss. According to Crowley, this is the bliss of going through reality as a self. This is Netzach.

8. *" " " " Thought (Chit)*
Chit is consciousness, Hod.

9. *" " " " Being (Sat)*
Both of them flow into Yesod, which Crowley attributes to sat, "being."

10. *" " " " Itself fulfilled in its complement, as determined by 7, 8, and 9*
This is reflected in 10, Malkuth, the point's idea of itself through all the previous levels.

Notice how the whole process was self-continuing. Each step had dependent origination from the previous step. The tarot cards will continue the patterns introduced here in symbolic form.

CHAPTER 2
THE MAJOR ARCANA

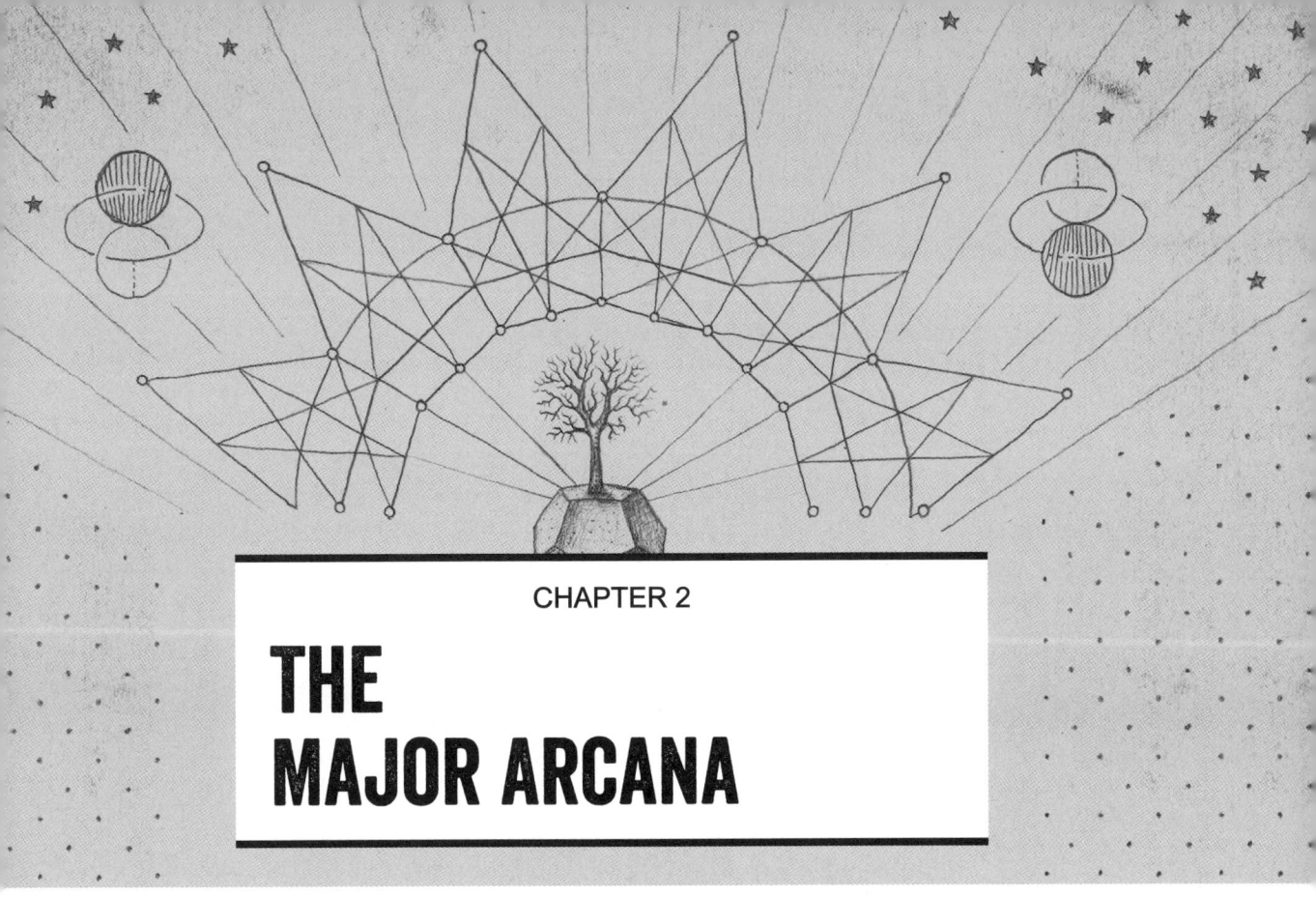

Now that you understand the general theory of qabalistic tarot, we can move onto the cards. As discussed, the Tree of Life is made up of thirty-two paths. The first ten paths are the sephiroth, which act as vessels for the Divine. The remaining twenty-two paths connect all of the sephiroth. They show how their energies move into one another and create reality.

Each of these paths is associated with a Hebrew letter. The letters represent articulations of energy. One could say they express how God spoke the universe into existence. Speech is a common metaphor in many mystical traditions to express how "things" come out of "nothing." The "nothing" can be thought of as vast consciousness and is symbolized by the breath. The "things" of reality are the words that God speaks into being, the literal articulation of divine breath into meaningful sounds.

Each of these paths and Hebrew letters corresponds to one of the twenty-two major arcana cards. An advanced understanding of the majors will show how they express the same self-continuing pattern discussed in the last chapter. Each path is a further expression or development of the initial ontological event where nothingness nullifies its own voidness to create everything. Each path is an advancement from something subtle to something gross. Each letter is an articulation of divine breath, shaping the formless into form through names and functions. This is the word, the logos.

These paths, letters, and major arcana cards all represent the relationships of divine emanations, the sephiroth. Traditionally, the Tree of Life is thought of as a system of emanation. However, there are actually three other paradigms to understand its divine relationships: Creation, becoming, and being. The paradigm of creation is dualism. This is the view from the mechanical plane. Here, God is seen as creator and thus separate from the seeker. In this understanding, Kether creates Chokmah, and Chokmah creates Binah, and so on. Each sephirah is separate. Next, there is the paradigm of becoming, which one might call pantheism. Here, God becomes the seeker and everything that is. This is the view from the subtle/causal plane. Applying this view to the Tree of Life, Kether would become Chokmah, and so on. Lastly, there is the paradigm of direct being: Nonduality. This is the highest view, where nothing exists but God, void of differentiation: "Let there be no difference made among you between any one thing & any other thing."[37] This is the mystical plane. At this level, the Tree of Life would collapse in total unity. "I am alone."[38]

There are further correspondences: Each tarot card is associated with an element, planet, or zodiacal sign, among a selection of deities from various cultures. Certain cards express Thelemic deities or philosophies. Some express alchemical, sexual, or magical practices. As you explore these various symbols and associations, you will build up a deeper understanding of the subtle/causal plane.

The subtle/causal plane includes the paradigms of creation and becoming. On this level, each major arcana card will represent how one energy (or sephirah) creates or becomes another. However, there is a deeper level of work: The mystical plane. To explore the mystical plane of tarot, the distance represented by each major arcana card must be collapsed. At this level, there is no creation or becoming, only pure being. This is something I teach my students directly. For now, study the material ahead. Eventually, each symbol and idea will melt into every other symbol and idea until the subtle plane begins to suggest the underlying, all encompassing unitive being.

---

37. Crowley, *Book of the Law*, 21.

38. Crowley, *Book of the Law*, 31.

THE FOOL

The Fool knows nothing. The Fool is the cosmic joke, which is both the point and divine pointlessness of it all. The truth of the Fool reveals that the universe was not made out of purpose or some grand scheme or teleology. The Fool teaches us that the universe comes out of a question, and in its most primordial level, does not "know" itself in the way we normally think of self-knowledge. It has no objective to know itself, because as we have discussed, there is ultimately "no thing" to know. The Fool is the Qabalistic 0. The point, Kether, arises from three veils of "no-thing-ness" previously discussed. The Fool is the paradox of a point knowing "no thing," in the form of a question. That question starts the entire creative process. The creation of the universe, in its infancy, shared the curiosity, naivete, and awe of a baby. It is this curiosity that underlies the truest forms of art, untainted by the lust of result or the confines of conclusion. I will remind you that we are using tarot as a psycho-spiritual technology to investigate the nature of the subjective youniverse, rather than the objective universe. But, at the higher levels of consciousness, there is no difference.

Another aspect of this "cosmic joke" is "something out of nothing." This answers the question asked of the universe, "what's the big idea?" The Fool is consciousness in search of experience. "Something coming out of nothing" is madness. Madness has an archetypal proximity to spiritual illumination. Various mystics throughout time were considered mad, as reaching the higher levels of the Mysteries requires a total reversal of one's paradigm. One need look no further than Diogenes or the paradoxical writings of Parmenides. The strange and sometimes irrational testimonies of these awakened thinkers are oftentimes filled with riddles. But they aren't trying to trick us. The realm of paradox is the realm where all things cancel out in divine nothingness, and pure peace. This is symbolized by the Fool's attribute Hebrew letter aleph.

Aleph is the mother letter of air, in this case not the terrestrial air of the four elements but the primordial air we can conceptualize as a vacuum, pure space. Aleph is connected to the idea of the *ruach*, meaning "spirit," and what the Greeks called *pneuma*. This is etymologically connected to the word "pneumatic," suggesting a device powered by invisible air. In the same way, our bodies are powered by invisible pneuma, prana, qi, the Human Energy Field, or whatever you want to call it.[39] Many spiritual teachers have described the nature of the universe and our energy bodies as spiral. Crowley compares aleph to the shape of a swastika, claiming it symbolizes this spiral nature of the universe in its creative process (the +1 and -1 come out of 0 through a spiral force). He notes that this contrasts the last letter of the Hebrew alphabet, *tav*, which was originally written like a "+" sign. The "+" symbolizes the universe stilled and completed, the opposite of the whirling aleph. Aleph is the first sound made by babies, and oftentimes the first letter of major god names, such as Adonai, *Ahih* ("ehieh"), and Aum.

One god name of particular importance is El, transliterated as "Al." When reversed to "La," it means "not." Crowley reveals a doctrine here in the relationship of "God," Al, and "Not God," La. The letter "L" in Hebrew is lamed, connected to the Adjustment card. Adjustment is thus the fulfillment of the Fool, representing manifestation, which is the +1 and -1, "not god." We can infer here that an aspect of God and spiritualization is a resolution of opposites, a return to "no thing," symbolized (and even at times embodied) through

---

39. Barbara Ann Brennan, *Hands of Light: A Guide to Healing Through the Human Energy Field* (Bantam Books, 1988), 41.

folly and ignorance. Below the abyss, we experience contradiction as division, but above the abyss, this contradiction is union.

This is also why the Fool is connected with the Devil card. The Fool, aleph, is phonetically similar to ayin, the letter attributed to the Devil. The deity Pan is connected to the Fool, but also to the Devil. Pan means "all," think "panorama." Crowley notes that the Devil is the full establishment of the Fool in a material sense.

The symbol of the letter aleph is "ox." One interpretation of this is that the ox is a symbol of agriculture, itself a symbol of the birth of civilization. The ox is used to plow the fields. By bringing air and space into the soil (remember, aleph is the mother letter of air), the land becomes more fertile. The plowing of the land through the use of oxen is a metaphor for the descent of spirit into matter, intelligence into the gross, and specifically, the human experience.[40] Anthropologically, agriculture was probably the biggest cultural update of our race, engendering all concepts of ownership.

Crowley sees the plowshare as a masculine symbol, the divine lust to create. He connects many masculine, lustful deities to this card, such as Pan, Bacchus, and Dionysus, but these attributions should not be confused with a lower nature, but rather their higher, more cosmic significance as creative, generative processes. It is important to note that Crowley's interpretation of lust and desire often implies the higher aspects of the human capacity to create rather than the lower aspects of attachment to matter.

Each major arcana card is attributed to a mode of consciousness through their path on the Tree of Life.[41] The mode of consciousness attributed to the Fool is fiery/scintillating intelligence. So many mystics and scriptures compare God to fire. Some examples include the burning bush appearing to Moses, the fiery form of Krishna revealed to Arjuna in the *Bhagavad Gita* and even the primordial fire in the *Divine Pymander* of the *Corpus Hermeticum*. This mode of consciousness alludes to fundamental subatomic processes beyond my understanding. Light will be a major symbol and can be used literally in an ontological approach to this material, or metaphorically, for a psycho-spiritual approach. Light can also be interpreted as the logos, which we have explored earlier as the nature of reality to continue itself.

---

40. This is the esoteric meaning of the symbols in the Rider-Waite-Smith tarot's major arcana. Each card expresses in its own context how spirit becomes matter. In the same way, each path on the tree of life leads from a spiritual place above to a more material place below. Each symbol on each card can also be reduced to this creative movement, which mirrors all mahavakyas and mystical mic-drops mentioned later. The collapsing of each movement expressed by every symbol of the tarot is the goal of mysticism.

41. The earliest record of the modes of consciousness is the *Sepher Yetzirah*.

Chapter 2

The Fool is path 11, connecting our first sephirah Kether to our second sephirah Chokmah. Recall in the Naples arrangement the idea of dimensions. A point can only be known if there is distance. The appearance of that distance to render the point is the path from Kether to Chokmah (and is itself a prompt for meditation). Spirit can only be known by its movement into Chokmah, a force, in the same way that it is expressed through the yod of tetragrammaton and the movement of the knights. Remember that Kether is the primum mobile, the first cause, and through the Fool, blind curiosity and impulse, it becomes the zodiac of Chokmah.

The symbolism of the Fool in the Thoth deck illustrates all manifestation from nothingness through the equation $0 = +1 -1$. You can see analogous symbolism to the Tree of Life (connecting to the small cards) and more specifically, the tetragrammaton (court cards). In this context, the Fool is the "wandering prince" who, according to the myth proposed by Crowley, wins the princess in marriage by murdering the old king, thus becoming the king and making her the queen. They procreate, and a new wandering prince starts the process again. The four characters, king, queen, prince, and princess, represent the four offices of the court cards and the tetragrammaton (knight, queen, prince, princess). Using this myth, Crowley expresses the tetragrammaton as an infinitely revolving loop. We will cover this in a later chapter on the court cards, but know that the Fool (being 0, but also Kether) is the backstage to this play.

Because the Fool represents all the court cards, and is the number 0, he is androgynous (I use the pronoun "he" because of his association with certain deities). He is "parthenogenetic," meaning he is not born of parents. This is symbolized by the vulture who was thought to take birth parthenogenetically. The dove as well shares both genders: It holds the masculine aspect of the holy spirit but also the feminine aspect of Venus. This card, more than any other in the Thoth deck, has contradicting symbolism, as is appropriate to the Fool. It is through contradiction that we arrive at the equilibrium of 0 and silence. The Fool is connected with the god of silence, Harpocarates. In Crowley's theogony, Harpocrates is one of the two aspects of Heru-Ra-Ha.

Now, how does all of this occult philosophy show up in your life? Aleph is the "AH!," the yawn in the morning before you begin the day. It is also your first conscious inhale of the day, and the first breath you took after being born (in the same way as it is said to be the in-breath before the first letter, B, of the Torah). Path 11, the shift from the position of Kether into the direction of Chokmah, is your first movement and thought of the day or of any creative process. It is the primum mobile, the first cause of any creative action, from writing a symphony, to brushing your teeth. It is motivation before motivation is conscious. This is also why this card is connected with Pan, Bacchus, and Dionysus: They all represent the raw desire in us to happen to the world. These are mysterious, almost crazy forces, that urge is to take the first step in a direction to become ourselves. In a reality where most are comfortably confined to a matrix, the first step in becoming yourself is often viewed as crazy, even foolish! The aleph, "ox," symbolizes the plowing of our fields to grow our desires. It is the readying of our fields of possibility, connecting, however crazy, to the quantum foam that answers when we ask questions. To plow the fields is to soften the fields and make fertility. We soften ourselves, or rather, the illusion of our "self," as we surrender our egos to the creative process and the flow state (compare this to the first chapter of the *Tao Te Ching*). Inspiration feels like something out of nothing! It comes from silence and trust. This can be compared to Harpocrates, the god of silence, as the observer. It is the consciousness that is watching all that we do, but that makes no noise. It is what we can always return to. That is why, in a reading, the Fool can signify spirituality, idea itself, thought, a light bulb. More mundanely, new beginnings, a new journey, impulse, folly, lunacy, inexperience, and eccentricity. In love, this could be foolish love, a positive breakup/reset, a skydiver or going too fast. In work this could be a new field, impulsive spending, or a spiritual career.

THE MAGUS

Meet the Magus, card number one of the tarot. They are mind itself, the same mind reading this book, which it has also written. Take a moment to know that, experiencing consciousness as you read these words. This consciousness is the same one that experienced so much grief, so much joy, so much pain and pleasure and desire, in all the high and low moments, ups and downs of the rhythms of ambitious brain waves. It's all been here, in this awareness. The Magus is the human capacity and predilection for idea making, including the production and reading of this book, and all books, and all words. We are meaning-making machines.

Let's talk about words (the meta here is intended). If anyone knows the words of the verse that is the universe, it is the Magus, who is our emcee and disc jockey of the cosmic song. If the Fool is a question, the Magus answers with a word (these two create the binary code of reality, 0 and 1). Crowley notes that the Magus represents "the wisdom, the will, the word, the logos by whom the worlds were created."[42] All this is to say that the Magus

---

42. Crowley, *Book of Thoth*, 69.

is the intention behind the creation of the universe. As the will of the universe, this is the Greek *logos* or "divine reason." Biblically, this is the word John told us about in his gospel. It is through the Word that eternity becomes the screenwriter of time. A word is an idea, thought, concept, data point. Words create everything—everythink! Each think can be a word. Words themselves do not have meaning—they trigger meaning in you. The words are vehicles for ideas, which are the "plus ones" and "minus ones" of manifestation. Words and concepts makes up the psycho-spiritual code of the matrix, the world of edges.

The discriminatory capacity of the human mind is revealed in the beautifully but ruthlessly sharp technology of language, which creates things by carving them out from everything else. Words carry ideas that separate and divide the unity that is God, chaos, or the tao. Words and ideas make things what they are, and that's fun! As the *Tao Te Ching* says: "The Tao that can be followed is not the eternal Tao. The name that can be named is not the eternal name. The nameless is the origin of heaven and earth. While naming is the origin of myriad things."[43] Who doesn't love myriad things? The Magus is the naming process and origin of myriad things.

The Magus is Mercury, both the alchemical ingredient (one of three, the other represented by the Empress and the Emperor) and the planet. As the planet, he is connected with the Greek Hermes, Indian Hanuman, and Egyptian ibis-headed Thoth, in addition to all messengers, tricksters, or psychopomps. The ibis was a symbol of concentration due to the observation of its one-legged balanced posture.

Here is the great secret of the Magus: The function attributed to the letter bet in the *Sepher Yetzirah* is "attention." This single-point focus is the essence of the Magus that creates the myriad things of the Tao through sensory discrimination. From this discrimination, binary codes flood the amorphous world to create form, and eventually our virtual realities. The reverse of this is also true. The Magus can resolve these binary codes of opposition through a perfect balance that is single-pointed focus. This is the goal of all mystics and is related to what has been contemporarily called the "flow state."

The Magus corresponds to the twelfth path on the Tree of Life, linking Kether, the crown, to the third sephirah, Binah, the great mother, whose cosmic birth allows the joys and sorrows of separation. Binah is the engine of the binary code of our youniverse. Binah is the prism through which light is separated into our rainbow existence. The Magus, therefore, is the primum mobile (first movement of the universe) acting upon understanding and form (Binah) through Mercury (transmission).

It follows that their mode of consciousness is "transparent intelligence." The transparency is the relationship between our human experience and the Divine, which one could describe as the logos and light. This is the light of God/consciousness shining through to us transparently which is refracted and separated by our minds.

This separating power of the Magus is their shadow, which takes the form of a gnarly ape: The Cynocephalus, or Ape of Thoth, a creature of ambiguity, deception, and confusion. In this domain of the Magus, we fall for our own powers to discriminate reality, and turn our brilliant faculties against us. This is the trickster archetype. Note that the original Magician cards were street magicians, whose cleverness and dexterity create illusions and trick the mind in the blink of an eye. This is the illusion of separation that brings us so much suffering. This is the illusion of lack, described in *A Course in Miracles* that includes

---

43. Lao Tzu, *Tao Te Ching*, 1.

feelings of loneliness, guilt, shame.[44] In one reality, this is the cost of the myriad things in the universe and our lives. This ape also symbolizes the faultiness of language, which, though a tool of expression, has the side effect of concealment and ambiguity.

For now, it is important to understand that the bliss and suffering spraying off the comet of consciousness is the unbiased nature of the Magus and your own mind. They are beyond any human idea of good and bad. They are continuous impartial creation and don't blink at the appearance of ambiguity and falsehood that complements their gift of language. They are the big bang, after all, the pantomorphic and infinite thrust of God, the logos itself.

So, can we surrender ourselves as the scribbles of the Divine's pen? Can we be willing to receive all of our superpowers?

You bet! *Bet* is the Hebrew letter attributed to the Magus. Bet is also the first letter of the Torah, and is connected to the logos, the word of God. When you say "you bet," you are saying "word … and the word was with God." In Hebrew, *bet* means "house." It is the house of God that is built through the faculties of universal mind, which is the Magus. The tarot is highly influenced by Hermetic philosophy, which states that the universe is mental: We build our realities, our "houses," by adaption, through thought, word, and deed. We can use the power of the Magus to create entire virtual realities.[45]

Remember that the Magus, as mind, is so high on top of the Tree of Life, they are beyond morals. In our reality, they do have a dark side, which is the *citta vritti*, Sanskrit for "mind modification" in yoga. They are like ripples in the lake of our consciousness. They include anything that disturbs our peace. The first sutra says "the restraint of the mind modifications is yoga."[46] The goal of yoga is to free the *citta* (mind stuff) from the *vrittis* (modification).

Every great mystic and sage has said, in one way or another, "you are not your thoughts." As the Magus you are an infinite being. According to Crowley, the Magus represents ain soph, limitlessness. Try this: Envision ten feet ahead of you. Now envision a thousand feet ahead of you. Keep going. You can envision forever. Your awareness does not stop. You can always imagine more. You are infinite. Review the *Measuring Me* exercise in connection with all the ideas of the Magus and ain soph.

---

44. Foundation for Inner Peace, *A Course in Miracles* (Foundation for Inner Peace, 1992), 13–14.

45. *The Kybalion*, attributed to Three Initiates, is a modern text that claims a Hermetic origin. It teaches that the universe is mental. The Hermetic tradition, according to the *Corpus Hermeticum* by Hermes Trismegistus, did not share in this teaching. However, in its cosmology, the highest spiritual level, second only to God, was called the nous, comparable to intellect or consciousness.

46. Swami Satchidananda, *The Yoga Sutras of Patanjali* (Integral Yoga Publications, 2012), 3.

Here is another exercise to explore this. Begin by closing your eyes and focusing on your breath. Begin to imagine your body expanding, slowly at first, but increasing in speed, until it fills the room. Then imagine your body expanding past the corners of the street, then the city, the country, continent, earth, solar system, galaxy, and so on. Feel this massive awareness growing until "you have galaxies at your fingertips," as my mentor would say. When you expand your awareness larger and then to infinity you will see the smallness of any one thought or feeling or sensation. Compared to boundless awareness, every "thing" in life is infinitely small. Anything done, made, different, or changeable is nothing compared to the quality of existence-consciousness including and transcending it.

But it is the nature of that boundless consciousness to do, make, differentiate, and change. This, one might say, is the logos, the nous, the ennead, the very nature of omniscience. In some sense, consciousness is a creative act, a magical act of the Magus. On the local human scale, this is how easily creativity can work for us… or against us. Every*thing* is a *think* of the Magus. You are everything until you use a word and make a thing with a think. All things are thinks at the end of the day. Things are rendered by the thinking you put on them! When you were a newborn, there were no things. Simply a blur of unidentified experience. The things became things with thinks over time and the phantom show of time and space was carved out of raw consciousness. This is how you and the Magus can play and create all realities. It is through the mind that the Magus does (fire), makes (water), differentiates (air), and changes (earth) reality to their will.

In the body, the Magus corresponds to the cerebral and nervous system. The neurons act in a binary. They turn on or off. This further carries the symbolism of the dual nature of Binah, and also the double nature of bet: The Hebrew letter bet is a double letter, meaning it has two pronunciations. Each double letter has two meanings assigned to it by the *Sepher Yetzirah*; the double meaning of bet is life and death. The mind creates both. We choose death when we become ignorant of our infinite nature and identify with something finite. When we choose death, we confuse ourselves with something we created (a lie, a memory, a fantasy, anything small thing that eclipses the awareness of our infinite selves). The coming and going of these finite forms we've identified with create the Hermetic principle of rhythm that has its origin in the Magus (1) but its full manifestation in the Wheel of Fortune (10).[47]

There is another death—the reverse. The finite forms we identify with (our job, our relationships, our mind, our body, etc.) also die and in so doing return back to the infinite consciousness. In the RWS Magician card, the ouroboros and lemniscate (the sideways

---

47. Three Initiates, *The Kybalion: A Study of The Hermetic Philosophy of Ancient Egypt and Greece* (Rough Draft Printing, 2012), 75.

number 8) both hint at the infinite loop of life and death that creates the rhythm of incarnation as part of the will of the universe, going between the infinite and the finite.

If the universe was produced in the manner of origami, the Magus would be the first fold, the initial bifurcation that allows the universe to experience itself in further geometric complexity and further dimensions. They are the source of the linguistic separation of subject and object that we have previously explored in the number 3 (notice his path terminates in the third sephirah).

What does all this mean in divination? The Magus indicates all matters of mind and manifestation. Metaphorically, they are the bet, house, that we chose to build for ourselves, what we chose to manifest, and all the skill and craftsmanship required for it. As Mercury, they indicate cunningness, speed, elasticity, messages, communication, and impulse. As the word, they are wisdom and ultimately mind itself.

THE HIGH PRIESTESS

Recall the idea of the invisible constants: There has been an awareness your entire life. Perhaps you've never noticed it, because it has been constant, silent, alert behind all experience, like an ambient hum you've never recognized. It has always been. I challenge you to experience it now. By investing in this, you may never again be swayed by the external world. This is the meaning of *"when the complete comes, what is in part disappears."*[48] I call this underlying nameless truth the "lidless eye," and it is my quest to find her. The lidless eye is like the silent observer that is always watching, even when we shut our physical eyes. It silently remains aware, waiting for our return. Changeless and birthless, the lidless eye is immune to the treachery of the Ape of Thoth (see the last section on the Magus). The lidless eye is what we've always known but pretend to forget in the phantom show of our valid but virtual realities. The Magus has gifted the ability to name, and these create what the *Tao Te Ching* calls the ten thousand things, Maya, the world of illusion. All the unnamed, all the forgotten, all the things unpinned to time and space in our virtual realities, are in the domain of the Priestess. If the Magus folds the origami of dimensions, the Priestess is the space between the folds. From her humble perseverance flow the waters of the unconscious, the akashic records, and memory itself.

The moment the Magus decided to concentrate was the moment that the infinite separated into thoughts, which created an "above" and a "below." The bridge of the two became the real estate of the Priestess. The Magus and the Priestess are mutually arising. She is the

---

48. 1 Cor. 13:10.

infinite underlying reservoir of possibility that complements the Magician's thought-events. She is the blurred background to the clear focus and concentration of the Magus.

Her path connects Kether, the crown, the Godhead, with Tiphareth, the son, the highest aspect of humanity, through the Moon, her planet. Crowley notes that she is the one connection between the supernals and the hexad, making her the essence of God in form. This path brings the infinitely small point, and source, to the reflection of itself in the self-consciousness of Tiphareth. On the soul level, she connects our intellect (Ruach) with the highest part of our soul (Yechidah). This means that the Priestess works on our discerning, rational minds all the way from the source (Kether) through the fluctuating mysteries of the Moon. She is the highest aspect of the Moon, which waxes and wanes as she oscillates between the above and below. Her duality is not so much that of the illusion-matrix introduced in the Magus, but rather that of a threshold between two worlds: Form and source.

Chapter 2

She is the number 2. She connects all "separate" forms below to the infinite truth of the lidless eye above, in Kether, and that is her lunar rhythm.

From the lidless eye flows the collective unconscious and the personal subconscious, which mutually arise from the Magus's choice to focus consciously. The unconscious is what unites all humans, and so the Priestess corresponds Qabalistically to "uniting intelligence," the mode of consciousness attributed to her letter, gimel.

Gimel means "camel," which was the method of societal connection in ancient times, connecting people through travel and trade. The symbolism maintains ideas of connection and traveling between.

The Moon is a symbol of the subconscious: It reflects, fluctuates, and pulls at earth's waters (our emotions). The Moon is our intuition, giving us information about others, connecting us, like the camel, to the rest of society. The subconscious, symbolized by the Moon, is the space of our telepathy and psychic work, where we discover our sameness. This is why the Priestess is so often linked with intuition. All these symbols can be summarized through one main idea: The reconciliation of duality into unity through connection, the nature of which is extreme subtlety.

The Priestess's waters symbolize humanity's reflective capacity that allows all sensation to be rendered as experience, and logged in memory, having been named by the Magus and recorded with the stylus of Thoth. There are many Buddhist teachings that describe the mind as a mirror to be cleaned or a pond to be stilled to reflect the Moon (the Divine). This is the superpower and bragging right of the Priestess. She is the Queen of borrowed light, the Moon, and reveals the doctrine that the ability to truly see is to reflect. The Moon reflecting the light of the Sun symbolizes the microcosm (us and Tiphareth) reflecting the macrocosm (source and Kether). It also represents how +1-1 reflects 0.

Scientifically, everything we see is reflected light. Everything we see, therefore, is within the domain of the Moon. We all see, and are seen, in this same borrowed light from source, literally and figuratively, amidst all the fluctuations within us and our environments at the lower scales of reality. Aleister Crowley associated the Priestess with *ain soph aur*, "limitless light," the third Qabalistic veil of nothingness.

We can compress all these ideas in the number 2, which must exist for 1 to know itself. The Priestess, the Moon, and the number 2 introduce us to the law of polarity.[49] This is the idea that everything has poles, from forces, to sensations, to experiences. The Priestess allows for this polarity by being the passive response to the active initiation of the Magus.

---

49. Three Initiates, *Kybalion*, 71.

Their relationship exemplifies the doctrine of $0 = +1 - 1$: The existence of one thing is rendered only by its opposite. We experience all things not through a static sensation but a dynamic rhythm between one sensation and its absence. It is the lack of a thing that allows us to experience it, to reflect upon it. The lack of the experience, which engenders the reflection of it, is the function of the Priestess, and the creation of memory. As mentioned earlier, all experience is a wave-form, like the waves of water and the lunar cycle.

The Priestess is the space between notes that lets us hear the music of the universe. Without this space, gifted to us by the silence of the Priestess and the waning moon, we would not have the noise. This is why she is considered virgin and the first mother, first matter, and prima materia of alchemy. She is untouched until she hears the *word* of the Magus, which makes her the fertile Empress. She represents the virgin subconscious that is impregnated by the self-consciousness of the Magus to create the fertile imagination, which is the Empress. It follows that she is connected with all virgin deities such as Artemis, Diana, and Virgin Isis.

What does she mean in divination? Her association with the Moon ties her to ideas of fluctuation, rhythm, and alteration. The descent of Kether into Tiphareth can indicate a pure, spiritual influence on the matter, which may be the cause of fluctuation. The caution here is not to be led astray with awe or too much enthusiasm, but to stay grounded in this deeply intuitive, spiritual experience.

THE EMPRESS

The Empress is love, in all its aspects, diversity, and meaning, through passivity and the natural flow of consciousness. Existentially, she is the source of all shape and color, and all mutually arising characteristics between them. More broadly, she is the relationship of all things, all that is done, made, differentiated, or changeable, whether here or there, coming or going, in time, space, or any other dimension. She is relativity, relatability, relationship. Recall the creation of dimensions in the Naples arrangement. Each stage immediately generated the following stage to exist in itself. This is the nature of the Empress, which is love: To behold the self is to be experienced by another. She is the mutually arising relationship between zero and one, and so her path connects Chokmah to Binah, bridging the Fool to the Magus crossing the Priestess. This path unites the supernal father with the supernal mother, force and form, the sacred masculine to the sacred feminine. This marriage germinates Binah to produce the multicolored world below in all its divine diversity.

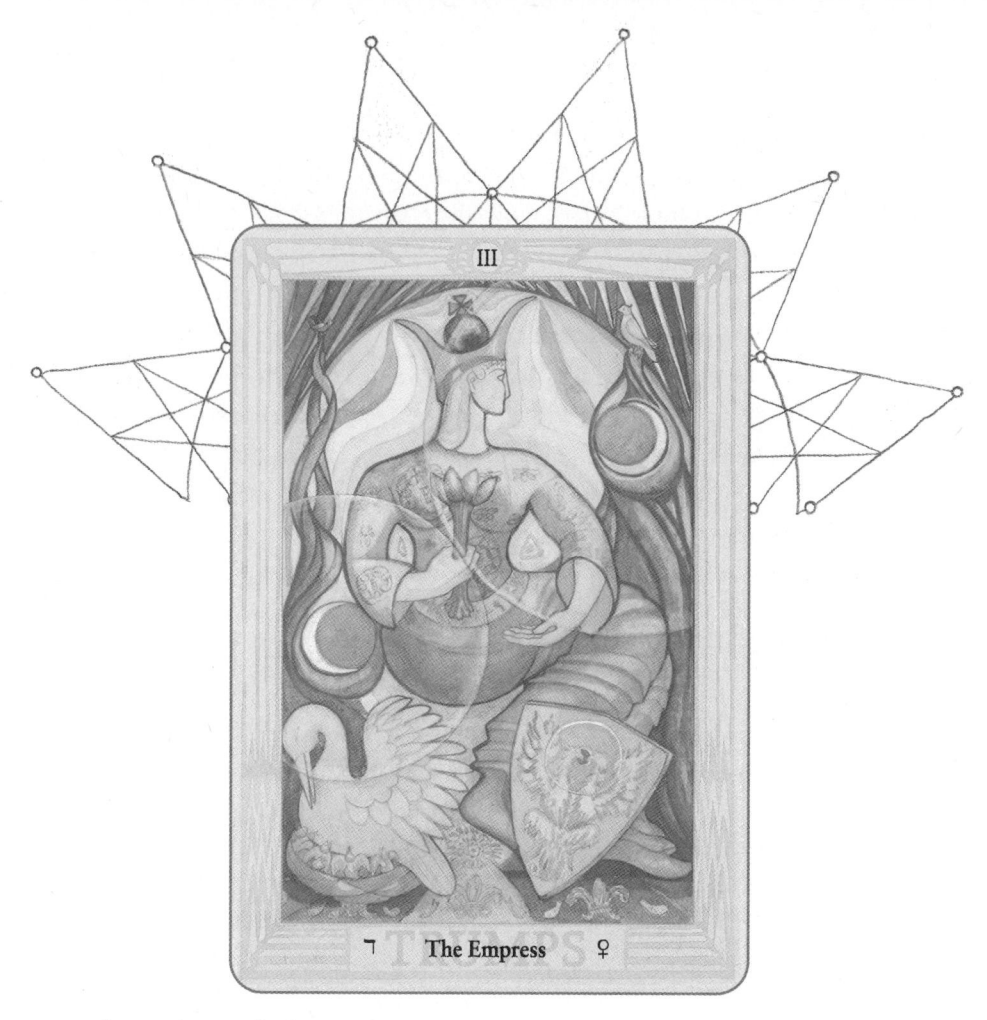

Her relationship with the Emperor is unique. She represents the universal scale as he represents the personal-material scale. Her power is natural, inherent, and spontaneous while his is imposed, self-generated, and framed out of personal volition. The marriage of the two shows us another angle of the relationship between the macrocosm and the microcosm. Keep this in mind as we consider her alchemical import.

    She is the alchemical salt, the second of our three alchemical ingredients. The glyph of salt is formed by her arms and posture. According to Crowley, salt must be energized by sulfur, represented by the Emperor, to maintain the equilibrium of the universe, mercury, represented by the Magus. We can rephrase this by saying that the universal forces (Empress) are energized by humanity's (the Emperor's) adaptation of them and participation with them through humanity's personal volition, which continues the cosmic transmission of mercury, which is the word, the Magus, and omniscience itself. That in itself is a whole worldview. Understand that salt is the passive ingredient in the process, and so love, in the context of the Empress, is a passive state, in the same way that shape begets color and color begets shape without imposition or effort (Crowley notes that more so than any other card, this card should be studied as a whole instead of its separate symbols). In an alchemical context, salt represents stagnation (salt preserves) and death (salt corrodes). The idea of death is very important to Binah, as it is the gateway between the supernal triad and the abyss below. Leaving Binah is a death of unity into diversity, incarnating downward through the abyss into manifestation. Leaving Chesed, going into the abyss to reach Binah, is a death of the self and diversity required for a merging with the unity of the supernal triads. Arriving in Binah is what occultists call the "land of the pyramids."

The Empress is attributed to the letter *dalet*, meaning "door." This is the door to life, the cosmic, and literal, vagina. This is also the psychological door; the function of dalet is imagination. Not only is the Empress the existential marriage of force and form, but the mental marriage of the +1 and -1, from which arise all images. She is, as Paul Foster Case says, the "generatrix of mental images."[50] She is the subconscious of the Priestess (memory) penetrated by the conscious experience of the Magus (attention) which germinates and forms imagination. From this arises wisdom and folly, which is the double meaning attributed to the letter dalet. The mode of consciousness attributed to dalet is "luminous intelligence," the light revealing all the divine creations of mind and the earth, which are mutually arising in their diversity from the source of light itself. This is another form of the ten thousand things of the Tao Te Ching. As Waite puts it, she is the "refugium peccatorum, the fruitful mother of thousands."[51] Dalet also means to "move in/move out," which is the nature of traveling ideas from one mind to another, as well as the function of a door. The door is also the threshold between our inner world (our house, bet), and the outer world.

Astrologically, she is Venus, the planet of love. Venus governs all relationships. These go beyond human relationships, and include the relationships and harmonies of all sensations and conscious experiences. Crowley notes that the Venus glyph is the only glyph that can connect all the sephiroth on the Tree of Life, suggesting that the fundamental formula of the universe is love.

---

50. Paul Foster Case, *The Tarot: The Key to the Wisdom of the Ages* (TarcherPerigee, 2006), 61.

51. Arthur Edward Waite, *The Pictorial Key to the Tarot* (U.S. Games Systems, Inc., 1977), 80. Originally published in 1911 by William Rider.

What does this mean in divination? How can we possibly compress the source of all images and sensations? The secret is beauty, which is harmony. Beauty is the balance and organization of sensation in proper proportion as a reflection of the Divine. Consider that the marriage of Chokmah and Binah, like the marriage of the +1 and -1, does not return to the Qabalistic 0 but creates its equivalent in manifestation through a divine harmony of diverse elements. The prince in the tarot is the combination of the knight and queen, in the same way that the suit of swords (our minds) is the result of a divine marriage of fire and water. It is through our minds, the element of air, that we behold the earth. Practically, this is the creation or experience of beauty through the organization of sensation and experience. This includes all forms of artistry, fashion, design, and creativity, but also the nurturing of others. The Empress is the mothering of ideas or humans. She is sexual and creative fertility and growth. She is pleasure, success, completion, elegance, luxury, friendship, delight, beauty, and ultimately, love.

THE EMPEROR

The luminous intelligence of the Empress, derived from the borrowed light of the High Priestess and the moon, delivered in the blink of a brainwave from the attention of the Magus, which flowed forth from the primordial "no-thing-ness" of the Fool, finally reaches a personal awareness in this universe in the Emperor. This is the dawn of the self and the source of ego. If you have an ego, you must take care of it.

According to Manly P. Hall, the ancient mysteries used the lyre as a symbol of the body: The body of the instrument represented the physical form, the strings were the nerves, and the musician was your soul.[52] Playing your body like an instrument was normal functioning. Compare this to Crowley's philosophy of the true will, "Do what thou wilt shall be the whole of the law." This does not mean do what you want, but do what you are meant to do, your higher purpose. The idea here is that flowers should blossom, because that is their natural course, and they do so beautifully. They shouldn't try to buzz like a bee. The Emperor is the dawning of the self, the source of ego, personal volition, self-sovereignty, rulership, and will.

First we must discuss the changes of attributions. If you lay out the zodiacal major arcana cards in their original order (by "original," I mean in the order of the Marseilles tradition), you will notice that they are in the proper zodiacal order except for two cards. Justice, associated with the sixth sign Libra, is numbered 8 while Strength, attributed to

---

52. Hall, *Secret Teachings*, 250.

the fifth sign of Leo, is numbered 11. This creates a loop on the wheel of the zodiac. When Waite instructed Pamela Colman Smith on the creation of their deck, he changed the placement of Justice and Strength to maintain the zodiacal order. When Crowley channeled the *Book of the Law* in 1904, he was instructed that the Hebrew letter tzaddi is not the star.[53] This puzzled him for years. Eventually, he discovered that by returning the order of the major arcana to their original placements (which included a loop on one side, with Justice as number 8 and strength as number 11), he could balance that loop with another loop on the other side by switching the Hebrew letters heh and tzaddi. This would satisfy what he channeled while also maintaining the original order of the trumps. Further details

---

53. Crowley, *Book of the Law*, 26.

CHAPTER 2

on this switch can be found in Aleister Crowley's *Book of Thoth* and Lon Milo Duquette's *Understanding Aleister Crowley's Thoth Tarot*.[54]

I will begin our discourse on the Emperor with Crowley's Hebrew attribution: Tzaddi. The mode of consciousness attributed to tzaddi is "natural intelligence," which I believe may refer to the natural course of action of a unit of consciousness when self-possessed, which is the main theme of the Emperor. Crowley argues this attribution's legitimacy by connecting the Hebrew letter etymologically to words like *tsar*, *tzar*, *Caesar*, and so on. The letter's symbol is a fishhook; though not necessarily phallic, it is a masculine symbol nonetheless. The fishhook may allude to humanity's interception of natural processes and rule over ecosystems. More deeply, it represents the quest into the waters of the subconscious to pull out truths. The fish captured by the fishhook is a great secret. The fish is the symbol of the Hebrew letter nun, attributed to the Death card. The Death card is number 13, which reduces to 4, the Emperor. The doctrine here is humanity's reconciliation with death, or rather, the illusion of it. The Emperor and Death suggest both the illusion of rulership (emperor) and the illusion of mortality (death). These are two illusions that mutually arise with incarnation, and mutually fade away in mystical revelation.

More abstractly, fish and the fishhook suggest the contrast between humans and the rest of nature. Our updated forebrains have allowed us to project a sharp matrix onto the soft natural flow that is the earth. This matrix is our illusion of ownership, architecture, and may even extend to geometry and math, if you conceive of those things being born in the human mind instead of inherent in nature. Modern technology is only a material reflection of the psychological technology that has accelerated in human evolution, a matter discussed by anthropologists. The evolution of thumbs and the creation of tools were the catalyst that further developed our abilities to intercept nature. The carving out of angular kingdoms from the soft curvature of nonhuman ecosystems became ubiquitous, and the human race grew to the rhythm of the rising and falling of civilizations. Unlike the sharp fishhook—inanimate, manmade, threateningly seductive—the fish is alive, moving, born of nature. This is not to critique the morality of the human race, but to present the striking contrast we've brought to the earth, as this stark and forceful mode of operation is the domain of the Emperor. The predilection of our species to interfere with natural processes is ironically its own natural process, which circles back to the idea of natural intelligence. There is a more sophisticated related doctrine that will be hinted at in the Death card.

---

54. Lon Milo DuQuette, *Understanding Aleister Crowley's Thoth Tarot* (Red Wheel/Weiser, 2003).

Following one's nature is no more characteristic of any sign than Aries, whose mode is cardinal and whose element is fire. The Emperor is our first zodiacal major, being the first sign of the zodiac. This may suggest the meaning of the Emperor's esoteric title, "Son of the Morning." The motto of Aries is "I am" (note that this is also the translation of the Hebrew god name Ehieh, attributed to the Fool). Aries is ruled by Mars, the planet of adrenaline, war, and the will to live. The Sun is exalted, which is the ego. Crowley comments that the Emperor is a combination of energy in material form with the idea of authority, because Crowley attributes Mars to gross matter. Aries is represented in the Thoth deck both through the horns of a wild ram, but also a docile lamb. The former suggests the mode of the new æon, which is to rule, while the latter suggests the passive approach of the old æon, which is to be ruled. This is a major theme and choice for Aries reflected in the symbolism of the fishhook and the fish.

The Emperor represents the third of our alchemical ingredients, sulfur. This is the male, fiery energy of the universe and can be compared to rajas in the Hindu system. This is swift and creative energy that takes initiative. Sulfur's active nature complements the passive nature of salt, the Empress, which is balanced in the equilibrium of mercury, the Magus. These three energies will be suggested again explicitly in the Fortune card, and implicitly in the Lovers, and Art card, among others. Crowley notes in the Book of Thoth that the Emperor represents a "generalization of the paternal power...sudden, violent, but impermanent activity, if it persists too long it burns and destroys."[55]

Compare these qualities of alchemical sulfur to the path of tzaddi. This 28th path leads Netzach, a fiery sephirah of motivation, independence, and ambition, into Yesod, a watery sephirah connected to the subconscious mind, the Moon, and change. Yesod could be the waters pierced by the fishhook from Netzach. Ambition (Netzach) applied to change (Yesod) echoes the symbols of fishhook and fish.

I will now examine the Emperor's original attribution: The Hebrew letter heh. Heh's symbol is called the "window," and is used as the article "the." Both of these suggest framing and distinction. The mode of consciousness attributed to heh is "constitutional intelligence," which refers to the ability of consciousness to constitute itself in certain dimensions, parameters, and definition, which is certainly the realm of the Emperor. The window suggests a frame or opening of light, symbolizing the incarnation of light into separate units of egoic consciousness. The window symbolism also connects the letter to its associated function, which is sight. Note that Aries corresponds to the face and head on the

---

55. Crowley, *Book of Thoth*, 78.

human body. All these symbols—the window, sight, the face, the head—connect to ideas of exposure, visibility, wakefulness, watchfulness, protection, and surveillance. The great mystery of the Emperor is the infinite awareness of the Fool confined—or rather, embodied—in a separate unit looking outward. This is the consciousness beginning to localize between our ears and behind our eyes. This is why the path of heh connects Chokmah, the will and expansion of the universe, to Tiphareth, the organized unit of consciousness with definitive parameters. Remember, Tiphareth is the point's idea of itself, the novelty of self-consciousness. This is the dawning of self-constitution.

What does this mean in divination? The fishhook symbolizes any influence the querent has on others. It can represent conquest, victory, strife, or ambition. Aries, with its Mars rulership, could signify war, anger, quarreling, struggle, but also confidence and authority. The number 4 and the window symbol allude to law, rigidity, power, and protection. Seeing light through a window, or fishing for truth, both suggest a level of self-realization in the querent, new energy, and originality. Beware of stubbornness, rashness, and too much use of force.

THE HIEROPHANT

With an inner authority now established as a "separate self" in the Emperor, a connection to the higher reality of oneness (or rather noneness) mutually arises. The threshold that appears between self and source is the Hierophant. His office symbolizes the ability of the new "self" to manifest outwardly the Mysteries of its origin and truth, in any form of expression, explanation, experience, or idea. Religion is only a byproduct of this human faculty.

The Hierophant gives us the use of symbol as well as the powerful technology of metaphor and semiotics. Entire experiences are collapsed in compact and portable symbols. Eventually, entire realities are compacted into symbols systems. We could confidently say that language, as we know, comes from the Hierophant. He has carried oral traditions throughout the human race, and then eventually writing, and then books, including this one.

The Hierophant is our spiritual Wi-Fi. He keeps us all connected in culture, history, belief, language, or otherwise. Spiritually, he is the initiator of the Mysteries and one of the thresholds of the microcosm to the macrocosm. Crowley notes that the main arcanum of this card is "the essential of all magickal work: The uniting of the microcosm with the macrocosm."[56] This is why there is a pentagram in the center of his card, representing the microcosm, surrounded by a subtle hexagram, representing the macrocosm. This idea should be studied with this card's juxtaposition with the Priestess and Chariot, as these

---

56. Crowley, *Book of Thoth*, 78.

three cards represent the three vertical paths connecting the supernals to the sephiroth below them.

    The main theme of the Hierophant is connection, which is emphasized by his Hebrew letter *vav*, meaning "nail," "joining," and the word "and." You can see nails above the card. There are nine of them to refer to the Moon which is exalted in Taurus, the sign of the card. The moon connects us, as we've learned in the Priestess. Nails connect things and crucify. The Hierophant connects spirit and matter, as well as people. In the Thoth deck, the major connection is the old æon of Osiris to the new æon of Horus. A Christian mystical interpretation of the card may link the nail symbol to the crucifixion and the number five to the five wounds of Christ. The mode of consciousness attributed to this letter is "triumphal/eternal intelligence," a reference to the pleasure of glory and the garden of Eden prepared for the saints. I interpret this as referring to the doctrines revealed in the path of vav.

CHAPTER 2

In the Tree of Life, Vav is attributed to path number 16, leading from Chokmah to Chesed. This path delivers the wisdom of Chokmah, to Chesed, mercy. One could think of this as the mercy of wisdom. This is the materialization (Chesed) of the word (Chokmah): The Hierophant manifests the Mysteries of the universe (Chokmah) in physical reality and three-dimensional space (Chesed). This card thus represents all possible ritual, method, and *upaya*, the Buddhist concept of means. The Hierophant is the means through which something is done. It is the means through which the directionality of Chokmah becomes the space of Chesed, and the means through which the logos is echoed in matter, the word made flesh. It is also the means through which we can hear the logos in our physical reality. Channeling, intuition, and the inner voice may be just some examples. "He that hath ears, let him hear."[57] It is fitting that the function attributed to vav is hearing.

Astrologically, this card is connected to Taurus, the fixed/kerubic earth sign, which represents earth in its strongest and most balanced form. Taurus governs the throat, which further emphasizes the idea of the word being spoken, heard, and transmitted. The throat is also what connects the head to the rest of the body. This symbolizes the relationship of the word, and the universal mind, becoming embodied. The head is attributed to Aries, whose motto is "I am." Taurus's motto is "I have." Taurus represents the sophistication of the five senses leading to affinities with such fields as cooking and music. Manipulation of the senses is important in all ritual. The method of magick itself is the manipulation of sensory experience in combination with ideas and mental imagery to create change in accordance with the will. Taurus is ruled by Venus, the planet of artistry, attraction, values, harmony, and the relationship of the senses: All things undertaken in the office of hierophant as manifester of the Mysteries. The Moon is exalted in Taurus, suggesting the fluctuation central to the strength and assured continuation of the firm earth. The stability of Taurus is due to its flexibility, not brittleness. Recall that Venus is attributed to the Empress and the Moon to the Priestess. The numbers of these cards, 3 and 2, add to 5, the number of the Hierophant. It is therefore suggested that the Hierophant bridges the unconscious mysteries and spiritual memory of the Priestess to the consciousness imagination symbolized by the Empress. I would argue this is the aim of high magick and ritual.

Crowley's version of the Hierophant has some significant updates. This is our first introduction to the symbols of the snake and dove together, which allude to the *Book of*

---

57. Matt. 13:9.

the Law: "There are love and love. There is the dove and there is the serpent."[58] The dove is what Crowley describes as the "sublimated phallus," the descent of spirit into matter going down the Tree of Life (the logos). The serpent is power that can be considered the kundalini energy force, which rises. This represents going up the Tree of Life. Most importantly, this card represents the shifting of the office of hierophant from Osiris, who is the main figure, to Horus, who is the dancing male child in the pentagram. The woman before the Hierophant is Venus, Babalon and Isis, who represents the age before Osiris.

Crowley writes about a unique formula of divinity made flesh. He refers to Pasiphaë, the Greek goddess who was cursed to lust after a bull. She had Daedalus build her a wooden cow she used to disguise herself and seduce the bull. It worked and she gave birth to Minotaur, whom Crowley states is the prototype of all bull gods. Crowley compares this divine impregnation to that of Mary being impregnated by the Holy Spirit. The main idea is an abnormal but spiritual conception and birth, the word made flesh, the path of Chokmah to Chesed.

How can we compress all this occult symbolism into divination? This card is about what we actualize in matter, in our bodies and in our sensations, and how that mirrors our will. This includes manifestation and the rituals, rhythms, and endurance of any practice, work, or effort that ensures that manifestation. The symbol of the office of hierophant suggests learning something new, study, explanation, education, teaching, transmission, tradition, goodness of heart, help from superiors, patience, organization, and occult force voluntarily invoked. With Taurus, we get ideas of stillness, stubborn strength, toil, endurance, and placidity. This card can indicate any practice, ritual, meditation, or means to arrive in a new awareness, state of mind, or experience, including the tarot itself. The darker aspects of this card can include dogma, narrow tradition, and conformity.

THE LOVERS

If the Hierophant holds the vertical mystery of creation, that of the meeting place between macrocosm and microcosm, the Lovers card examines the horizontal mystery, which is the method the macrocosm uses to become the microcosm. This method is one of the most creatively expressed occult secrets: The splitting of any entity into more entities only to eventually merge once again into one. These entities could be ideas, the cells in our bodies, or exploding stars—it doesn't matter. The general method is the same and leads to the same result: The creation of more experience, and more information. The philosophy here

---

58. Crowley, *Book of the Law*, 26.

is that though energy cannot be created or destroyed, information can. Crowley, along with some quantum physicists, would argue that particles maintain some sort of record of their experiences of their cosmic journey, including their combinations and separations. The descent of spirit into matter through division increases information by creating more units to experience the whole.

Imagine a delicious pie. The pie is a certain volume and surface area. By cutting the pie into eight slices, you now have eight units of pie with eight surface areas. The total volume of the pie is the same, but the total surface area has increased when you total the surface area of each slice. Perhaps a similar pattern occurs on a cosmic level: As any unit continues to separate and recombine, the sum total of information in the universe increases. Like particles, our minds are units that have been divided from the infinite mind, the big mind, in order to more fully experience it, and increase information. In a way, our minds are hosts of information. We are like folders on the desktop of consciousness, in a constant exchange of files that we pick up from everywhere.

The Lovers corresponds to the Hebrew letter *zayin*, which means "sword." It symbolizes the division of consciousness into more units to experience itself. What does a sword do? It divides. It cuts. It is the antithesis of vav, the nail of the Hierophant, which brings things together. The mode of consciousness attributed to zayin is "intelligence of disposition," suggesting a level of distinction, character, and specificity. The sense function is smell, suggesting sagacity and discrimination. All of these ideas suggest the split required for the beloved to behold the beloved.

The sword represents division for the chance of ecstatic union. This is a lower form of the 0 becoming +1 and -1, for which the +1 and -1 recombine for something equivalent to 0 but evolved, something greater. This is expressed in the court card system in the merging of the knight and queen to create the prince and princess. This secret has been expressed in the Lovers card of older "exoteric" tarot decks where the common interpretation was that of a man's choice between the vice or virtue represented by two women.

Psychologically, this card is about opposition. Division is a major characteristic of the mind. The creation of any one idea immediately suggests its opposite. Up begets down. Hot begets cold. It is through this formula that worlds are created. Remember, everything is really a "think."

In this card, Crowley introduces us to the concept of *solve et coagula*, "analysis and synthesis." The Lovers card is the analysis, the separation, and the Art card is the synthesis, the recombination. Crowley says that the "question asked by science is 'of what are things composed? How shall we recombine them to our greater advantage?' This resumes the whole policy of tarot."[59]

All these concepts are summarized in zayin's path, number 17, from Binah to Tiphareth. This is the great mother, Binah, who is duality, form, and the gateway of incarnation descending upon Tiphareth, the son and higher consciousness of humanity. This is the queen, having been impregnated by the knight, transferring energy to the prince. No other path could best express the relationship of duality divinely flowing into the human experience.

The path from Binah to Tipareth is especially important since both represent letters from the Holy Tetragrammaton. Binah is connected to heh primal and Tipareth is connected to vav. These represent two parts of the soul, the intuition and the intellect respectively. Thus, this path shows the relationship of the neshama, intuition, descending upon

---

[59]. Crowley, *Book of Thoth*, 82.

the ruach, the intellect. The intuition is a single united flash that pulls together the many diverse thoughts of the mind and its faculties. The thoughts embrace and unite like lovers in one powerful, connected realization.

Rudolph Steiner describes intuition as the tenuous, elusive data in the inner world created by all contact with the outer world, a very appropriate process to the mystical philosophy of this card. The intuition is the part of the soul that rises out of the maze of life to see the escape instantly, whereas the intellectual brain will stay in the maze trying to figure out the right way to go at every intersection. The esoteric title is "Children of the Voice Divine." The voice may refer to the intuition. I believe the other esoteric title, "the Oracle of the Mighty Gods," refers to the transmission of the influence of the supernals through the path of zayin.

Astrologically, this card is attributed to Gemini, mutable air. Their symbol, the twins, certainly suggests duality and division, following the themes already presented. Gemini governs the lungs, collarbones, shoulders, arms, and hands, all being in pairs. A major characteristic of Gemini is their inquisitive nature, and more deeply, their desire to perceive. That is their ultimate joy and talent. They are the most curious sign and are always searching for more information. If we approach it through a phenomenological lens, perception is a creative act, as all data comes from the discernment we project onto the one reality. Perhaps perception is the creation of the universe itself, or the engine behind its creation. That doctrine would fit astrologically, because Gemini is ruled by mercury, the Magus, mind itself, and the word. So, the point of it all, the will of the universe (Mercury and the word) is perception of itself (Gemini).

This doctrine is hinted at in the Thoth deck, which represents the Lovers as the Hermetic marriage being initiated by the logos, the word, which is both Mercury and the Hermit, who wills the universe into manifestation through the splitting and marriage of opposites. The design is as follows: The Hermit is the will to create, inspired by the desire of Eros (the cupid above him). He creates through division, which is the will and the logos. The Lovers are the result, and they inherit the same will to create as the Hermit/logos but now through sexual desire, procreation, and union with each other. This can be taken literally and metaphorically. It refers to the pure desire, unassuaged of purpose, that happens to the world. It is union and division happening at the same time, *"for I am divided for love's sake, for the chance of union."*[60]

---

60. Crowley, *Book of the Law*, 22.

These three major characters of the Thoth cards can be compared to the three major nadis of our energy body: Ida, pingala, and sushumna, as well as "oberservation-observer-observed" idea mentioned earlier. This is also the general pattern of the Tree of Life and the tetractys.

One will also note the symbols of the Gnostic Mass of the O.T.O. This public ritual enacts the order's most sacred secret of sex magick. One could interpret the ritual and the Lovers card as the method of procreation. This includes but also transcends the human scale, and expresses the method for the creation of the cosmos itself and all beings. Further details on the ritual and its secrets are known only to certain higher-ranking members of the O.T.O.

All these occult ideas of otherness and division create a wide array of topics to be looked at in divination. Some more obvious interpretations include relationships, friendships, and self-love. More deeply, the Lovers is about choice, decisions, and multiplicity. It is the choice to create from the perspective of the logos. It is also the choice to love from the human perspective. Thus, we have universal desire reflected and refracted into the smaller desires of the particulars. It is the multiplicity of creation from the dividing sword, and the many paths to choose. This card could suggest the awareness of a great process, patience but also frivolity. From the symbols we can surmise the idea of disposition, choosing one thing over another, and our ability to discern. It is the curiosity of Gemini and all the information they want to perceive. On the soul level, this card is about intuition because of the path of zayin on the Tree of Life, which draws the intuition down into the intellect. For the same reason, this is also a card of inspiration, as it is the flow of the completed supernal triad to our higher mind.

The Lovers card represents explicitly what so many other majors imply: Creation through separation and thus choice, resulting in creation again. This is how every "thing" is done, made, differentiated, or changed to create the world. The resulting diversity ornaments the human experience with all kinds of "good things" and "bad things," especially in relationships. Relationships, whether interpersonal or interstellar or intermolecular, show you energetic charges.

Interpersonally, what we see in others is a reflection of ourselves. However, to make what we experience in others positive or negative is to limit our infinite being. When judging someone else, we project the aspects of us we don't like and subconsciously identify with the illusion of finitude. We say "they are bad because they are x" and assume that "I am *not x*." The truth is, you are x. And you are y and you are z, by virtue of your recognition of them. You would not be able to know x, y, and z if you didn't share in their identity. Your neural choreography *makes* them. Pretending you are not something by trying to see it outside of you is a defense mechanism. Here, the illusion is the separation of our self from the external. This works for both negative and positive judgments. In a positive judgment, such as idolization, the ego yearns for union with what it invents to be separate, and thus ignores the completeness of the self. Only by ignoring the completion of reality can there be the illusion of choice. But that's okay—look how much fun we're having.

Both are the illusion of separation. Both compromise the truth. This is a lie mended through mysticism, through a complete surrender to the only real underlying common denominator of all things: The quality of pure being, the business of "isness." This is done by recognizing that you are indeed everything. Whether your path is yoga, knowledge, devotion, magick, or otherwise, the realization that you are everything requires deep integration and discipline for adepthood. This brings us to the Chariot.

THE CHARIOT

In the same way that the bridge to the Divine in the Hierophant immediately followed the formation of a "self" in the Emperor, by the splitting of consciousness into multiple units through the Lovers card, the parameters of each unit appear in the Chariot card. The Chariot is the vessel of life, a glyph of the personality-soul complex in its efforts (or non-efforts) to reflect the Divine. The esoteric title, "Child of the Triumph of Light," gives us a clue to the process expressed in the card. The "light" refers to the separation of things revealed only in light, coming from the unconscious waters/light of the Priestess. In darkness, all is void; all is 0. In light, all is many. This, like many other cards, refers to what the *Tao Te Ching* calls the "myriad forms": Multiplicity of manifestation.[61] This was catalyzed and expressed to its maximum degree in the previous card, the Lovers, where the creative hunger of the divine sword separated unity infinitely, making it the engine of creation. This may also be the fiery sword guarding the entrance to Eden after the fall. The Chariot then is the result of the separation. What do chariots do? They battle. They race. They compete. All these activities require an "other." Who will the Chariot battle, race with, compete against? The gift of the Chariot is the acceptance and integration of the "truth" of separation. More specifically, this integration manifests itself for our species through the relationships between our body and soul, and our lower and higher selves. We now have wheels of personality to

---

61. Lao Tzu, *Tao Te Ching*, 4.

VII The Chariot

play with in the race of life... can we get them to go in one direction? Or will we literally drive our souls apart?

Being in *agreement* with the self is the key to the Chariot. We will return to this idea many times. Let us first look at the astrological attribution: Cancer, which rules the stomach. We don't physically feel the stomach, unless we have a stomach ache, when our body doesn't *agree* with something we ate. The same rule applies to the mind. When focused on something fun, in creative fervor, on our true will, the buzz of our rapid firing neurons never occurs to us. But in drudgery, mental anguish, or straining to piece together logic or experiences that don't agree with us, those thoughts make themselves known, such as memories that hurt or projections of the future that worry us. These thoughts do not agree with our minds in some way, and so they are digested clunkily, harmfully even, down the mental sewage system of our subconscious. Sometimes it leaks. When the darker subconscious leaks we don't get the crab of Cancer—we get the crayfish or kephera, who lives in the Moon card (more on that later). But the subconscious has a major role in the Chariot as well.

Cancer rules the fourth house in astrology, which contains our home and childhood. What will we find hidden in the attic? In the basement? What have we forgotten about, or are secretly protecting? The fourth house is where the archetypes of the hero and the shadow live. The Chariot is both the hero that protects the city and the shadow hidden behind the armor, deep in the shell of the crab. If these two can be in agreement with our higher self, the wheels will be in alignment. The duality is further suggested in the black and white horses of the Rider-Waite-Smith deck.

Cancer is ruled by the Moon. Cancer is the sign of emotions, motherhood, protection, nurture, child development, all things which shape our personality and form our metaphorical chariots. The Moon is the Priestess, our cosmic memory and the subconscious. Notice in the Thoth deck how the Chariot is meditating on top of a crescent moon. The secret here is that all occult work and development has for its foundation the subconscious, and in some ways, our evolutionary past as a species and development as a child in this life. Jupiter is exalted, suggesting that its expansive nature is complementary to the reflective, internal nature of Cancer. The power of the external journeys of Jupiter allows for the depths of the internal journeys of Cancer and the Chariot. The Chariot adventures outside superficially but esoterically is a race within.

The Chariot is driven by you, your authority, your intuition, which in turn is controlled by a higher authority. Above the mind, there is the spirit. How many times in your life have you said, "I knew I shouldn't have chosen that." How did you know? The Chariot integrates intuition, just as it integrates the mind, and the body. However you want to divide the human entity, the Chariot expresses those divisions (let's say, body, mind, and spirit) as containers of the source, the Divine. The shell Cancer the crab is a container, a protector. Cancer is also a mother, who protects. The Chariot protects the city as well as its rider's pride. Whatever the Chariot protects becomes the gravitational center, pulling and integrating all its assets: Mind, body, personality, and so on. It's like Russian nesting dolls. The Chariot is the ability of consciousness to pour itself in a vessel and emanate lower. It is this very function that allows the mystical plane to become the subtle/causal plane, and for the subtle causal plane to become the mechanical plane.

Historically, the Chariot card stems from Plato's chariot, a metaphor for the soul. He divided the soul into three parts: The soul of appetite (black horse), the soul of will (white horse), and the soul of reason (rider). More information on that can be found in Plato's

Republic. For our purposes, let's consider the horses. Are the horses of your soul pulling you in one direction? If that were the case, would there be any esoteric secrets left in the tarot to discover? It is the dissonance between our karmic horse power that creates the fun, bumpy ride.

Esoterically, the Chariot exists on the 18th path: From Binah (form and understanding) to Geburah (strength, judgment). In the human body, Geburah is connected to metabolic processes, the breaking down of molecules in the body. Does the food agree with us? This path is about consciousness descending into life through the path of water. The ideal supernal triad emanates itself into the actual human experiences in several ways on the Tree of Life. On the pillar of form, this is through one specific ingredient: Life. The symbol for life is blood, and that's what the Chariot holds in his holy grail.

The mixed and matched attributes of the sphinxes are the fractal personalities below which reflect the archetypal personalities of YHVH above, made possible by division (the Lovers).

The Hebrew letter attributed to the Chariot is chet, the letter of life. Chet and Yod together means living. *Chayot* are the "holy living creatures" in the Chariot of God in Ezekiel's vision. The symbol of chet is "fence" or "field." This symbol alludes to our body, our aura, our field of awareness, our personality, our soul. It is that which makes us a distinguishable unit of consciousness amidst the truth of boundless, oceanic consciousness. Our energy bodies are like those Russian dolls: One encapsulation in another. Refer to the last chapter where you learned about the koshas. The main idea is vehicles within vehicles: The body is a vehicle to the mind, which is a vehicle for the Divine. This is why a major theme of the card is "authority under authority."

The function attributed to chet is "speech." We can connect this idea to the word, the will of the universe, which we might say is our highest authority after the absolute. This also creates a relationship to its parallel path, the Hierophant, whose function it is to hear. The Chariot speaks through life itself. The Hierophant hears through tradition and record. The other parallel path is the Priestess (the Moon, which rules Cancer) whose function is memory, which is fitting. All speech comes from memory. Meditate on these ideas and these parallel paths.

According to Paul Foster Case, the card is connected with "the House of Influence," something Case describes as our real personality, an area where universal forces are at work. He teaches that personal will doesn't exist and that volition is a synthesis of innumerable cosmic influences within us. The idea here is we are a reflection of God. This idea may seem deterministic for some, but it can also be enlightening for others. Think of how a Zen master teaches students to be as still as water to reflect the moon. Can we be still enough to reflect the Divine? Notice that the Chariot, in esoteric decks, is oftentimes not moving. In the Thoth deck he is meditating. In such stillness, we become an encryption of infinite virtual mantras of this holographic universe. All of this aligns to the path of chet, connecting Binah to Geburah.

Aleister Crowley offers us the word *Abrahadabra* in his description of the card. The numerical value of this word is 418, the same value as Chet spelled in full. This formula represents the five elements and microcosm through its five vowels and macrocosm with its six consonants, the higher self. In ceremonial magic, the pentagram would be visualized alongside a hexagram symbolizing the union of the lower self with the higher self. Abrahadabra is the formula to invoke this higher self and merge the elements with the planets. Doing so would bring the aspirant into adepthood. We could say this is the fancy nomenclature of the occult which translates to "being in agreement with yourself."

Another unique update in Crowley's Thoth tarot is the use of sex magick symbolism and his deity Babalon. I am going to simplify these advanced concepts into a more broad understanding of the cosmic forces. In the center of the card there is the cup of Babalon/the holy grail. Babalon is Crowley's divine feminine deity who symbolizes all form. Her cup contains the "blood of the saints."[62] Every "saint" or Magician must give the last drop of their life's blood to that cup. This is the price for magick but by "magick" what is meant is a form of enlightenment, not a sacrifice to an apocalyptic demon. This juncture is probably the most misunderstood aspect of the occult mysteries. There is death in certain high levels of spiritual awareness, but it is death of the ego, of illusion. By offering our "blood," we give up the illusion of ourselves for full awakening. By crossing the abyss, our ego dies, and we end up in Binah, the city of the pyramids, where the reunion with the whole is symbolized by the merging of our blood, our life, into the cup of Babalon in a sort of divine sexual ecstasy. This will later be consumed by the beast, chaos, in Chokmah. This is just a set of symbols to express a deep mystery of attainment. Remember, the esoteric real estate of Babalon is Binah. This card's path stems from Binah to Geburah and it represents life. Thus, the central symbol of the card is the cup of Babalon above, the vessel of life from which we all aspire to return to but also from which we descend from (note also that the Lust card, which is expressed as Babalon, terminates in Geburah as well). The symbols also refer to an act of sex magick which is beyond the scope of this book.

---

62. Rev. 17:6.

In divination, it is triumph and conquest. It is the success of a working apparatus on any plane to deliver the will of a higher intelligence. This apparatus is the field or life that chet symbolizes. We can describe this card as the interface of spirit and matter. Practically, this is our personality and the success of our character to deliver and exact our higher goals. This is what is meant by "authority under authority." From Cancer and its lunar relationship, we get the meaning of memory and digestion. The symbol of the Chariot offers us ideas of violence, obedience, protecting what we believe is right, following our own traditions. This is our will, courage, action, and determination.

The first seven majors illustrated the creation of the universe, or consciousness as we know it. It brought us from the supernal triad into the rest of the tree. In the second row of the majors, every card has a snake, which is generally a symbol of life and death, and specifically, a symbol of DNA's double helix, the kundalini, rhythms, and change. All these things are echoes of the logos, which the serpent also symbolizes.

In the next seven cards, we are questioning the rhythms of life and death as they weave the fabric of reality (the matrix) created by the first seven. We begin centering on how those cosmic patterns operate in ourselves, and our relationship with them. The orphic egg enters its final stage in Art, and then we don't see it anymore! I see the orphic egg as the operation of fractalization/separation. The great work accomplished is the reconciliation of all opposites in spiritual union, samadhi. This is the hidden air above fire and water that is the Fool, the great 0, which is realized in the lower air, the suit of swords, our minds, the microcosm, itself the union of father and mother as the prince. This union is perfected in the physical world, the earth, in its divinely unscrupulous nature, the Princess. Here it signals for redintegration back into the 0. This is the Thoth deck's lunacy or spiritual profundity.

ADJUSTMENT

Adjustment is what Crowley calls the "phantom show of time and space."[63] Cosmically, this card represents the manifest world in the Newtonian sense of action and reaction. This is expressed in the Thoth deck as the harlequin, the fulfillment and complement to the Fool, because she is the divine dance of the manifest universe. Her every movement, shake, jump, and spin is recorded and counterchecked as action and reaction, +1 and -1. Crowley says that "nature is scrupulously just. It is impossible to drop a pin without corresponding reaction in every star."[64] She is the dance of 0, the Fool, into the disproportion that is sensation,

---

63. Crowley, *Book of Thoth*, 87.

64. Crowley, *Book of Thoth*, 87.

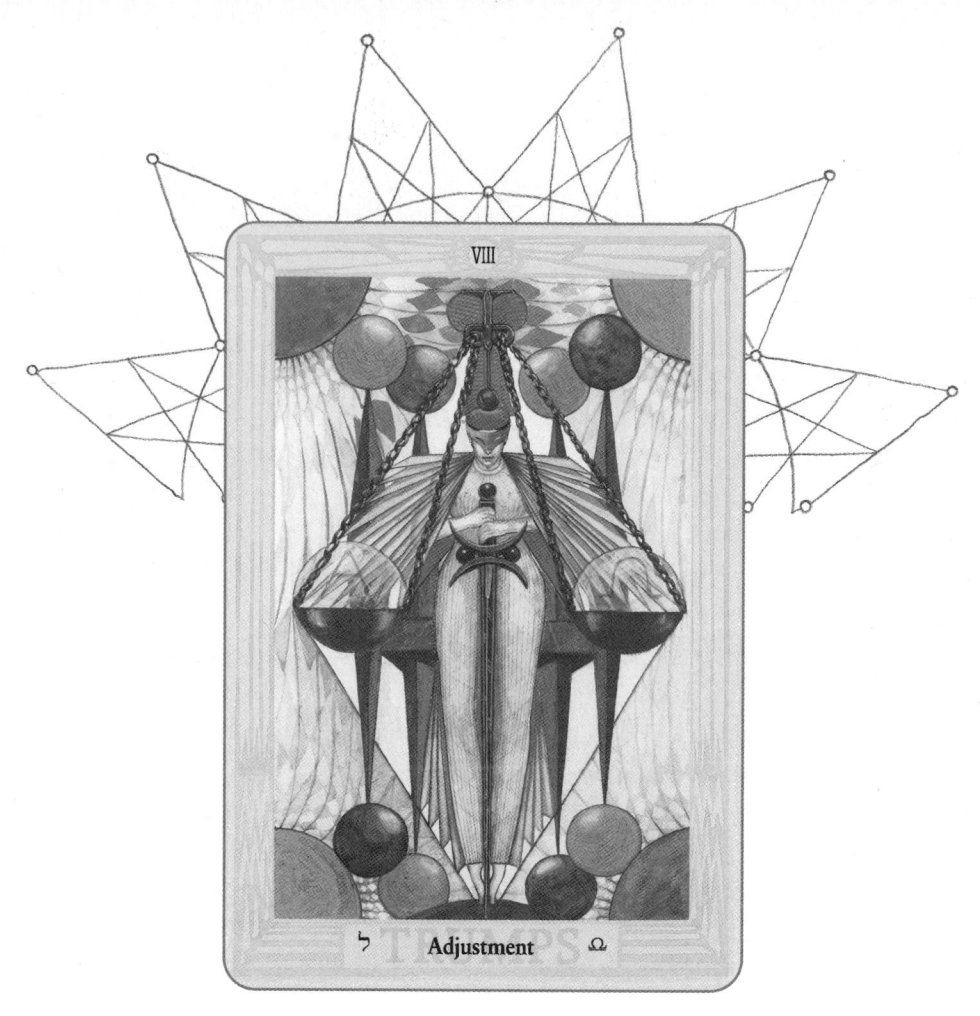

experience, and harmony. The name "Adjustment" suggests the universal principle instead of "Justice," a human invention.

The Hebrew letter attributed to this card is *lamed*, Hebrew for "ox goad" or "to instruct/teach." Compare this to the Fool's letter, "ox," the ox being goaded. The doctrine here is that there is an inherent quality in the Fool to guide and goad, which is the creative process of the cosmos, and is related to karma. Adjustment is the manifestation of this intelligence that balances the universe into its duality and diversity. The function attributed to this letter in the *Sepher Yetzirah* is work or action, which is the meaning of karma. The moment the Fool moves from something into nothing, he is greeted by his consort, the harlequin in adjustment. This is the folding of the fabric of consciousness, the ripples and "mind modifications" that makes life what it is.[65]

---

65. Swami Satchidananda, *The Yoga Sutras of Patanjali* (Integral Yoga Publications, 2012), 3.

Karma doesn't have to be a moral multi-incarnation game. It can be an immediate game. It's actually happening right now. Every word you read has no meaning. Each word is a carrier of meaning. The meaning exists in you. It's your own neural choreography. Recall in the Lovers card that every possible charge, positive or negative, is you. All the meaning you give everything is, in a way, karma. It's the landscape of the mind. At the scale of one life, one could consider karma a rehearsal of neural pathways, for better or for worse. The dance of those pathways is the dance of the harlequin in the Adjustment card. Karma is also the connection of our brain to the rest of our body, and in that way, we can say that karma runs at 270 miles per hour.

Karma is also the subconscious mind keeping track of our faith in ourselves. This is a great lesson I learned from my teacher: For every promise we keep to ourselves, we gain self-esteem. The reverse is true for promises we break to ourselves. Keep a promise to yourself, gain a point. Break a promise to yourself, lose a point. We are faithful to our subconscious score of ourselves. Perhaps this is why the mode of consciousness attributed to lamed is "faithful intelligence." This subconscious record keeper is our internal scales. These scales secretly weigh our chances of success and manifest the level we trust ourselves.

The scales are the symbol of Libra, the sign attributed to this card. Libra is cardinal air and rules over all things balanced and harmonized. She is ruled by Venus, which is love. Saturn, time, is exalted. The doctrine here is that the manifest universe of cause and effect is ultimately love, and the conditions of its phenomenon (the harmony of the many relationships between sensations) is time.

Compare all these ideas to the path of lamed, which begins in Geburah and descends upon Tiphareth. This is the gift of motion (5) that allows for self-consciousness (6). Recall that Geburah is a sephirah of challenges, trials, friction, and severity. It is this sephirah that edits the merciful materialization of Chesed to create the perfect harmony in Tiphareth, our higher self, and the heart of the tree. Just as lamed goads the ox, Geburah goads the tree for a balanced issue of energy.

We must now further examine the doctrine underlying the word *al*. In Hebrew, *al* (sometimes transliterated as "el"), *aleph lamed*, is a root word for God. Think of all the angelic names ending in "el." When we reverse the letters, we get "la," meaning, "not." As we have already explored, "God" and "not" are two sides of the same coin. One can be said to represent the ain, "no-thing-ness," and the 0, while the other can be said to represent the Tree of Life, the +1 and -1, and world of manifestation. There are two ways to interpret this: One is to see "not" as the 0 and "God" as that which comes from it, and the other way is to see "God" as 0 and "not God" as the illusion that comes from nothing's departure into something. I believe both are true, and that is the koan. As Meister Eckhart said, "Thou must love God as not-God, not-Spirit, not-person, not-image, but as He is, a sheer, pure absolute One, sundered from all two-ness, and in whom we must eternally sink form nothingness to nothingness."[66]

The Egyptian goddess of justice attributed to this card is Ma-at, symbolized by vultures (hence the plume of Ma-at on the Thoth deck). Vultures were thought by ancients to reproduce by themselves (parthenogenesis) which matches our philosophical stance on 0 (refer to the Fool).

How do these cosmic, conceptual ideas show up in divination? Balance is not static, but dynamic. This card represents an adjustment in the literal sense of the word. On the surface, this card can indicate legal matters, marriage (from its Libra attribution), social or political matters, or a suspension of action to make a decision.

More deeply, this card is a change in our patterns. Balance is active participation and is a conversation between us and the rest of the world. It is the ability, best exemplified by Libra, to work with and balance any energy. This is what creates poise. This is a card governing all the transactions of energy, in thought, word and deed. This card asks us to look at all these transactions. What are we bringing into our life, energetically, culturally, socially, nutritionally, and what reactions in our physical, energetic, and mental bodies do they produce? What output results from our input? Adjustment is a change in these patterns. Oftentimes, it can show a change in priorities, which shift our patterns, our stance on life, and where we invest our time (Saturn) and energy. Any change in the pattern will create a different result. We are not static selves but whirlpools of patterns in the ocean of consciousness. Change the pattern, and you can change your life. This is the glory of the scales of Libra, and the power of the ox goad. It's up to us to direct the course of the creative energy and what mathematical wonders come from 0. But the equation will always be balanced.

THE HERMIT

The Hermit is the secret creator of the whole tarot deck and the universe. He is its origin, its method, and its result, because he is the word revealed. This will make it difficult to describe in linear writing as every symbol in this card becomes every other symbol. But such is the aim of tarot and how we can merge with the youniverse.

---

66. Aldous Huxley, *The Perennial Philosophy* (HarperCollins, 2009), 32.

He is the will of the universe and the youniverse maintained throughout all its many processes, from potential, to conception, to birth, to death. The Hermit, number 9, is, in a way, the aged wisdom that is inherent in the innocent fool, number 0. Nine is the completion and goal of zero. The Hermit is the miracle and mystery of consciousness and incarnation symbolized by and encoded within a seed. This is why the Thoth deck includes the symbol of a homunculus in a sperm cell. This suggests the holographic nature of the universe as the youniverse.

The homunculus is a small human, originally drawn in 1694 by Nicholas Hartsoecker. Though biologically inaccurate, it expresses the universal/magickal doctrine "as above so below." The message here is that the object of any operation must be fully formed within the mind before entering ritual, and ultimately manifestation.

Chapter 2

The seed is the Hebrew letter yod, attribution of the Hermit. The actual figure of the hermit in the Thoth tarot is in the shape of a yod. The letter means "hand," and its design is the foundation of all the other Hebrew letters. I see the design as a divine apostrophe, hinting at the owner of the universe, and the youniverse. The yod is the flame that God blew to create the Hebrew alphabet. It can be compared to a seed or a spark. Yod is also the first letter of our tetragrammaton, connecting the Hermit to the father, Chokmah, wisdom, the word, and the logos. He is thus a form of the Magus. The mode of consciousness attributed to yod is the "intelligence of will," through which Qabalists understand the essence of the original will and structure of all reality. Connect this with the homunculus and the idea of a holographic universe. It thus represents the divine shaping power and intelligence of the universe from the subtle to the gross. Yod is also the first letter of Yechida, the supreme part of the soul that unites with the one true consciousness.

The hand symbolism suggests creativity. It was the evolution of thumbs that allowed humans to make tools and start civilizations. One could think of the yod's hand as the hand of God creating the universe. Hands suggest ideas of skill, dexterity, and work. All these ideas relate to the Hermit's zodiacal attribution, Virgo.

Virgo is mutable earth, the flexibility of earth allowing it to flow in the alchemical process leading to perfection. Mutable signs are also the spiritualization of the element, and so Virgo is the spiritualization of earth. Virgo is the virgin and her symbol is wheat, suggesting the pure and fertile potential of earth to receive the seed of the yod. Virgo is the most receptive and spiritual aspect of matter and is thus the crust of the earth covering Hades, a metaphor for incarnation, itself the great work. Virgo is the sign of perfection, the aim of mysticism and Hermetic philosophy. Virgo governs the intestines, the organs that discard waste. The discarding of mental waste is the method of mystics and high magick. Virgo is ruled by Mercury, suggesting that this process is guided by the self-consciousness of the Magus but also cosmically by the word—perhaps in addition, the very process is the word and the will of the universe.

Another way to look at this is that grand teleology is the word, masculine Mercury, acting upon the feminine virgin earth, Virgo, from the source, which is the sun. This is metaphorically sexual. This is why the function attributed to yod is sex and the sense-function is touch.

And so in the Thoth tarot, the masculine Hermit adores the feminine orphic egg. He lusts after it. The orphic egg represents the material universe made by dual gender. The Hermit himself is a sort of divine intelligence and desire. It is through his lamp, the sun, that energy is transmitted. This image and set of symbols bear a resemblance to the *Divine Pymander* of the *Corpus Hermeticum*.[67] You can also compare the earth, the sun, and Mercury/the Hermit to the three alchemical ingredients shown in the next card.

Mythologically, the Hermit is Mercury, a psychopomp (one that guides souls between worlds) who rescues Persephone (a virgin) from the underworld (incarnation). The myth can be interpreted to represent our connection with Mercury as the will, which when realized, frees us from the bondage of illusion in the underworld, the projected matrix of matter.

The ultimate mystery of concern for this card is that of the will that is ultimately one and of the cosmos of which you are part. The entire will of the universe can be experienced and understood trans-rationally within your subjective youniverse. We can express it through every possible symbol, commentary, and scripture, but it is ultimately ineffable as the Hermit is quiet and the Tao is nameless. This may appear to be some lofty philosophy but the truth of it is revealed in the most mundane daily expressions, here on earth itself, in the always changing mutability of matter and Virgo. All events, however loud, occur amid a background of vast silence. It is that vast silence that is most characteristic of the Hermit, and by extension, the logos. This silence can further be interpreted as the lack of reason, the lack of "because." "May Because be accursed for ever! If Will stops and cries Why, invoking Because, then Will stops & does nought."[68]

How does this show up in divination? When we apply the idea of a holographic universe whose will can be understood through its parts (as above, so below), we get the general meaning of illumination from within. This card is our secret impulse from within, esoterically the will of the universe, but divinatorily, and desire to make something or move forward with practical plans, an affinity of Virgo's. This may also involve a retirement of sorts, or a removal from society and current events. This is a very deep card that can also indicate effort, patience, and a process of perfection and guidance, all ideas related to Virgo.

FORTUNE

In the Hermit, we uncovered cosmic law through introspection, discovering universal volition. This is mirrored externally in the Wheel of Fortune. This card is the machinery of the external universe that reflects the machinery of our internal nature. As number 10, it

---

67. Brian P. Copenhaver, trans., *The Hermetica: The Greek Corpus Hermeticum and the Latin Asclepius in a New English Translation, with Notes and Introduction* (Cambridge: Cambridge University Press, 1992), 1.
68. Crowley, *Book of the Law*, 33.

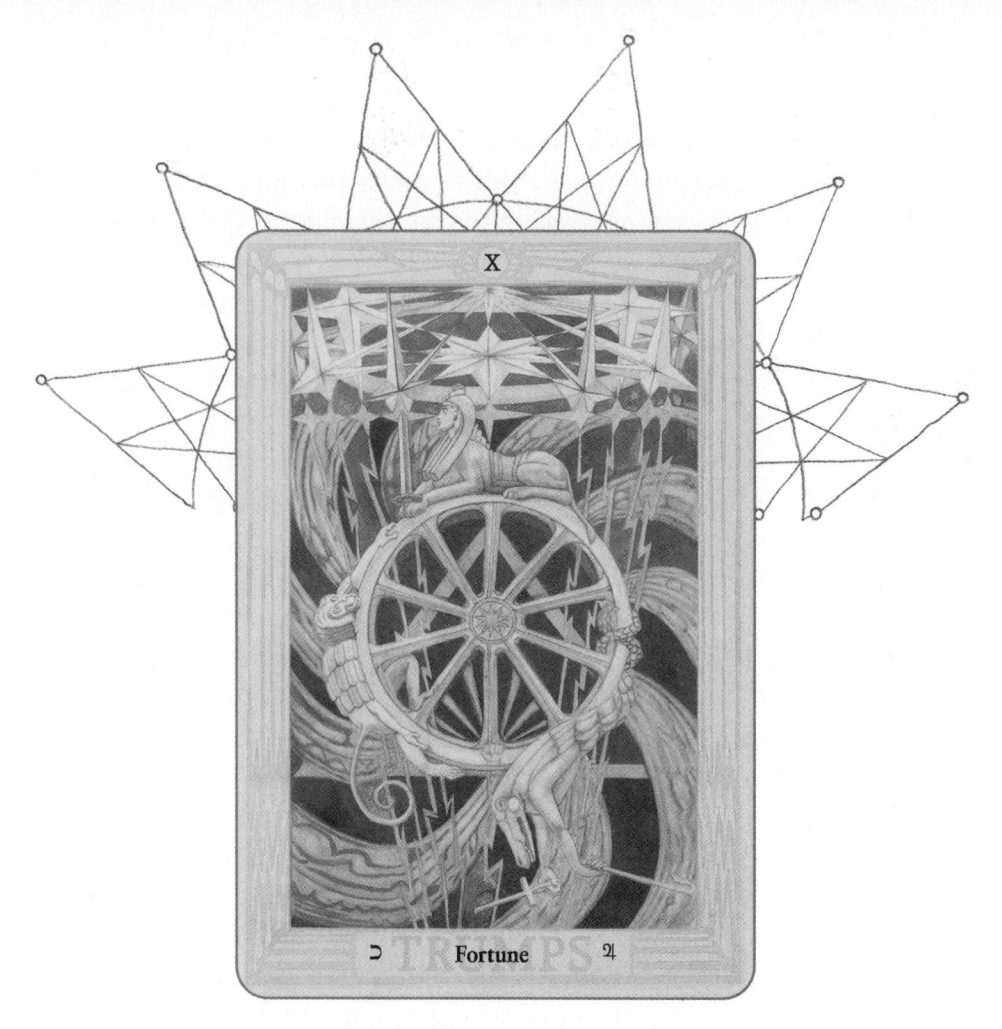

reduces to number 1. This card illustrates the manifestation of mind and will that was initiated in the Magus, personally realized in the Hermit.

The Hermit was yod, symbolized by an open hand either creating or giving, but the Wheel of Fortune's letter is *kaph*, which also means "hand." However, this is the closed hand—a fist or a hand in the act of *grasping*. This reveals to us a number of doctrines. An exoteric teaching here is that of cautioning the seeker against the temptation of the external world, represented by the Wheel of Fortune and a hand grasping. *Dukkha*, Sanskrit for "suffering," can be more accurately translated to "grasping." Kaph is a double letter with the two meanings, wealth *and* poverty, the extremes of fortune. Conversely, the opening hand of the Hermit is a common mudra in mysticism, often suggesting the letting go of illusion, release, or the reception of the Divine.

A deeper doctrine here is that the Hermit is at the center of the Wheel of Fortune. The center of the Wheel of Fortune is what Joseph Campbell describes as the world navel.[69] It is also the eye in the triangle. The wheel represents samsara. Samsara can be interpreted metaphysically as the continued incarnation into this world of suffering based on our karma and desires, or it can be looked at psychologically as the chase. Any incarnated being is always chasing something, whether it be love, money, sex, pleasure, or something else. The chase, this grasping of the hand, leads us around the hamster wheel of samsara. This is the rhythm of pleasure: Having and then losing.

Compare this with kaph's double meaning: Wealth and poverty. It is the goal of all mystics to arrive at the center of the wheel, or axle, because it doesn't move. There is no wealth or poverty there, only a truth. Compare this to the general doctrine of the *Corpus Hermeticum* that the big mind of the universe is immortal, but all the "things" that issue from it are not.

The Wheel of Fortune was a popular concept in medieval and Renaissance literature and philosophy often accompanied with the words *Regno, Regnavi, Sum sine regno, Regnabo*: "I reign, I reigned, my reign is finished, I will reign." The Consolation of Philosophy by Boethius declared that the unpredictable and changing nature of fortune was part of the providence of God. Intentionally or not, this work, a major influence on medieval Christianity, aligned with much of the philosophy of the age-old mysticism; that the coming and going of fortune is indeed in God's plan. It is the rhythm of God! This very rhythm, which appears to humans as chance, is actually law. And so, the "Intelligence of Conciliation" or "Rewarding Intelligence of Those who Seek" is the mode of consciousness attributed to the letter kaph. This is an intelligence of being in accord with natural law, being in agreement with change, and being in communion with the cyclicity of circumstance. This is the explanation of the popular phrase "find your center." In the *Upanishads*, the center is called the "heart." The word "heart" in much of eastern mysticism does not refer to the emotional or anatomical heart, but the secret center of being.

We may compare this to the observer, the silent witness at the center of all your experience. But remember: There is an observer observing that. This continues infinitely. The waking up of the observer of all observers could be said to be Shiva. The opening of Shiva's eye is the destruction of the universe. The fortune card of the Thoth deck illustrates Shiva's eye.

---

69. Joseph Campbell, *The Hero with a Thousand Faces* 3rd ed. (Novato, CA: New World Library, 2008), 32. Originally published 1949 by Pantheon Books.

CHAPTER 2

It is here we arrive at the third and deepest esoteric doctrine revealed in the relationship between the ninth and tenth arcana. They are actually the same. The same hand that opens in the Hermit and aligns with the cosmic will is the same hand closing, grasping, and attaching to fortune.

Astrologically, this card is attributed to Jupiter, the "greater benefic." This giant planet has so much mass that its gravity rivals that of the sun. In fact, the sun and Jupiter rotate around each other. This supports its correspondence to Chesed, the demiurge, the highest god below the abyss. This is a creator god known as "Mind the maker" or "craftsman" in the *Corpus Hermeticum*.[70] It was an intelligence created by God to create the universe. However, this creator god thinks he is the supreme deity.

Compare this to another god coterminous with Jupiter and Chesed: Zeus. He is the king of the gods, but he was not the first. Recall the myth of his father, Chronos, who is time, and Binah. Chronos ate his children (the seven classical planets) so he would not be overthrown. Eventually, Zeus and Gaia tricked him by feeding him a stone, causing him to regurgitate his swallowed children, the sephiroth under Binah, and give birth to the cosmos.

Jupiter governs Sagittarius and Pisces. These two signs excel in higher understanding and broadening of experiences. Jupiter is exalted in Cancer, the sign of the vessel. This intimates that vessels and vehicles (the chariot) we create to be embodied are not unlike that of the demiurge. This is a secret beyond the scope of the current volume. Hints of it may be found in the *Bhagavad Gita*. Jupiter governs the circulation of blood held in the holy grail of the Chariot.

All the previously mentioned ideas will be found in the path of Kaph. This path brings the materializing and merciful energy of Chesed to the ambitious, desiring movement of Netzach. Chesed is merciful allowance, giving desiring Netzach the fortune it wants. We might say that this path creates the bliss (Netzach) of three-dimensional space.

The three agents of change in the machinery of the material universe are often depicted in this card. Different occultists will have slightly different attributions, but always, the three will be some sort of analog to the three alchemical ingredients and the three gunas of the *Bhagavad Gita*, which may be seen as a lower manifestation of the three mother letters of the Hebrew alphabet and the three spiritual elements: Air, water, and fire. Compare this also to the three supernals, as well as the $0 = +1 -1$ formula. In the Thoth deck, the sphinx with the sword represents rajas from the Samkhya philosophy, the alchemical sulfur, temporarily exalted (introduced to us in the Emperor). Hermanubis represents sattva, alchemi-

---

70. Copenhaver, *Hermetica*, 2.

cal mercury, and the Magus. Typhon represents tamas, alchemical salt, and the Empress. The lightning in the card is the lightning of Zeus, which destroys, but also begets by hailing the coming of life-giving rain. Remember that the Thoth deck in general, and these middle 7 cards of the atu especially, explore the identification of love with life and death.

It should be noted that surface layer concepts of this card are still valid and can be successfully used in divination. This card can indicate any form of a cycle, chance, luck, or a change of fortune. Usually, this is a positive change of fortune. More deeply, this card could indicate the need to let go of control. It could also mean momentum, highs, and lows, but generally, a direction that is improving. It cautions against the intoxication of success.

The Wheel of Fortune is the manifest universe emanating from infinite space (which is the ain soph of the Qabalah, or the Thelemic Nuit). This infinite space is symbolized in our species' history as a circle because a circle has infinite degrees. At any time, you stop what you are doing and walk in any direction of these infinite degrees and start a new life. All you have is choice: You could leave behind everything. You could gain everything. You could come back or not. The point is you have a full circle of possibility. This is the freedom of Chesed, mercy, descending upon Netzach, victory. This is the freedom of the hand that can grasp. This is expansive Jupiter, and Zeus rebelling against his father. This is the freedom and reward of the number 10, and a secret to the Pythagorean tetractys. This is the ten thousand things of the Tao.

LUST

Originally titled Strength, Lust is the nerve force of the cosmos. If God is the musician, and matter is the instrument, the Strength card signifies the vibrations of the strings, the music. Exoteric interpretations of the card include self-control and the virtue of fortitude. Esoteric interpretations of the card include ideas of manipulation of energy in general, or the kundalini energy force specifically. The broad doctrine under the card is simply the play of energy itself, which can be conceptualized on the Tree as the energetic tension between above and below, right and left. If the Tree of Life was a cosmic kite, the strength card would represent the hidden forces of energy, and play, that keep it taught in four directions to be picked up by the air of aleph. Crowley updated this card's name, symbolism, and even mythology.

A great deal of eastern mysticism is concerned with the manipulation of the kundalini force, a flow of energy which begins at the base of the spine. Various practices can bring this energy upward to the brain to unlock *ojas* for higher spiritual awareness. The energy is drawn up by using three major nadis, the ida, pingala, and sushumna. These can be interpreted as analogous to the Tree of Life and the caduceus. An elaboration on this process is beyond the scope of this work but can be researched elsewhere. Swami Vivekananda explains it in *Raja Yoga*.[71]

The Hebrew letter *teth* is attributed to Lust. When spelled out in full, it means "snake" (which it resembles in form), "to knot," "twist" or "coil." All these words can refer to the nature of the kundalini force that occultists call the "serpent power." This one symbol has become almost pantomorphic in its meaning. It has been used to describe so many things in the occult. In the Thoth deck, it appears on every card of the second septenary (atu 8–14) and many of the others.

The beauty of the snake symbol is most appreciated when all its associations merge into one. It is a symbol of the word (the concept introduced in chapter 1 and elaborated

---

71. Swami Vivekananda, *Raja Yoga*, (Ramakrishna-Vivekananda Center, 1980).

in the Magus and the Hermit), but also of life, death, and the rhythms in between. The serpent is change but also our evolution. More specifically, the serpent represents our DNA and our desire. DNA is the code of our apparatus of incarnation, which is itself the desire of the earth, which is itself a result of the desire of the universe, stretching as far back as the logos, the Hermit, and the Magus. The serpent is the desire of the Lovers whose marriage is officiated by the word. Recall that the nature of sensation is always a wave-form (see the section on the number 3). This wave-form is again symbolized in the serpent. As Alan Watts had taught, life and death are different coils of the same snake.

Crowley says that the Lust card is marriage as it occurs naturally in nature. We see his deity Babalon, symbolizing Binah, riding the beast, represented by a lion serpent, and symbolizing Chokmah in divine ecstasy. We will explore Babalon below. For now, notice the serpents above the card on the Thoth tarot. They create and destroy the universe. This rhythm of creation and destruction is best expressed in the popular alchemical symbol of the ouroboros, a snake eating its own tail. This could be interpreted as the constant cycle of incarnation (consider the idea of samsara discussed in the previous card) or as the infinite nature of consciousness to reabsorb itself.

The function attributed to *teth* is digestion, and its sense is taste. The mode of consciousness attributed to this letter is "Intelligence of the Secret of all Spiritual Activities," which alludes to the dynamic vertical and horizontal undulatory rhythms on the Tree of Life. These same patterns exist in the body with the kundalini. I will explain these rhythms further.

It is here I would like to share a popular use of gematria to elucidate the nature of the serpent of Genesis. The Hebrew name for the serpent of Genesis is *NChSh*, transliterated as "Nacash," with a numerical value of 358, *also* the value of the word *MShICh*, "Messiah." We could interpret this as suggesting that the salvation of humanity is ironically in its fall.

The doctrine of the fall of humanity coming from the same source as its salvation should be explored. It is conceptualized as the Tree of Life being a two-directional, spiritual freeway: Going below allows for going above. Manifestation allows for mysticism. Birth allows for death. This is the policy of tarot and a major point of interest in esoteric circles. One of the biggest mysteries concerning incarnation and awakening is hinted at by the symbol of the serpent. We will revisit this in our discussion on the universe card.

Crowley uses the symbol of the snake to indicate upward movement on the Tree of Life, an ascent back into oneness (or rather, noneness, zero). The opposite of which is symbolized by the dove, what Crowley calls, the "sublimated phallus," the holy spirit that descends from spirit into matter. These two symbols indicate the two opposite directions on our spiritual freeway. They were revealed to Crowley in the *Book of the Law*, "for there are love and love. There is the dove, and there is the serpent. Choose ye well! He, my prophet, has chosen, knowing the law of the fortress, and the great mystery of the House of God."[72] Notice how both directions are described as love. The two forms of love indicated are self-love and Self-love. While Self-love is love of the universal which is mysticism, self-love is love of the particulars, which is magick or manifestation. The "House of God" may refer to the Tower card which perfectly parallels the Lust card on the Tree of Life below and represents the creation and destruction of grosser forms through the same love.

The lowercase self-love is the downward path into incarnation. It is loving the self as a distinct entity from the All, the absolute, which is a sort of death of unity. This is not evil—it is play! It is the joy of assuming a role in the cosmic theater of experience through dimensions. It is the Naples arrangement; the point becoming aware of itself.

Conversely, Self-love is loving the supreme Self, the All, the absolute, and in so doing, there is a sort of death of the small self. The dove and serpent symbolism may have a connection with the verse "be ye therefore wise as serpents and harmless as doves."[73]

This idea of multidirectionality to create experience is not just vertically on the tree, but horizontally: In the same way that Tiphareth is the heart of the Tree of Life, this path of *teth* can be said to be the central path on the Tree of Life because it is balanced horizontally and (for the most part) vertically. This path is also part of and symbolic of what is known as the "path of the flaming sword." These are the paths that trace the order of the sephiroth as they were created from nothingness. This path is known as the lightning flash of creation, and this same lightning flash appears in the Tower (the path that parallels this card). You could metaphorically trace the lightning flash through all the majors, beginning with the wand or stylus of the Magus. This flaming sword is also what guards the Gates of Eden, the exit into matter. This exit from paradise also symbolizes manifestation downward on the Tree of Life from above to below. Notice the card's esoteric title, "Daughter of the Flaming Sword."

This is the nineteenth path which leads from Chesed to Geburah, mercy to strength. Crowley calls this card Lust because it expresses "the joy of strength exercised…the rapture of vigor, expressed in this path."[74] These two sephiroth create the dichotomy of building up and breaking down. We see this in the rising and falling of empires, as well as in our

---

72. Crowley, *Book of the Law*, 26.

73. Matt. 10:16.

74. Crowley, *Book of Thoth*, 92.

bodies' metabolic and catabolic processes. It is the dance of chemical compounds forming and breaking apart.

Astrologically, this card is attributed to Leo. This fixed fire sign rules the spine in the body, which is the home to the serpent power, as well as the back and the heart. Note this card's order in the major arcana makes it the "heart" of the series. Its path, as previously mentioned, is the "heart" of the twenty-two paths. The glyph of Leo also resembles that of a serpent. The superpower of Leo is magick (in the literal and performative sense) and creativity. This sign has an uncanny ability to create experiences in the external world that mirror their internal world. These experiences can draw a crowd and offer to people the recognition of deeply shared human experiences. This is what makes Leos such great speakers, performers, entertainers, and leaders. They become the heart of an experience. They pull energy around them and offer themselves as a canvas to express the hidden feelings and mysteries of the previous sign. This is their creativity. It is a form of play. It is fun. Leo symbolizes our natural state as creators. Leo governs the fifth "house of joy" where astrologers look for sportsmanship, creativity, sexuality, and fun. Leo is ruled by the sun, the ego.

It is now time we look at Crowley's Thelemic updates to the card. We must first begin with chapter 17 of Revelation, where we meet "Babalon, the Great, Mother of Prostitutes and of the Abominations of the Earth."[75] The woman in this vision rides a scarlet beast of seven heads and ten horns, and she holds a golden cup of the blood of saints and abominable things. She represents adultery. Her guest appearance as Babalon in Crowley's *Book of the Law* gives her a modern remix: The symbols of whoredom in this context are no longer evil but instead symbolize the propensity of the cosmos to participate with every single thing. There, she personifies nature's willingness to become everything and anything. She is the pure joy of the diversity of the cosmos, in all its horror and glory. Crowley states in the *Book of Thoth* that this is "the original marriage as it occurs in nature, as opposed to the more artificial form portrayed in Atu VI: There is in this card no attempt to direct the course of the operation."[76] The original marriage is thus divine lust or divine play as opposed to the order of business expressed in the Lovers through separation and fertilization. This may be the divine desire underlying all operations of the universe, naturally, without function or reason, whereas the Lovers is ruled by Mercury, having a sense of purpose or reason. Babalon can be compared to the Tantric Shakti.

---

75. Rev. 17:5.

76. Crowley, *Book of Thoth*, 93.

The name "Babalon" consists of *Bab*, meaning "gate," *Al*, meaning "God," and *On*, meaning "Land of Pyramids." Babalon is attributed to the third sephirah, Binah, where occultists say is home to the Land of the Pyramids. This is the first sephirah we arrive at when crossing the abyss. In Thelemic symbolism, this is the giving up of your blood to her cup of abominations, and merging, ecstatically, with the Divine. It is not selling your soul to a demon—it is enlightenment.

Compare these qualities of cosmic diversity represented by Babalon to our discussion of the Empress card, which signifies the mutually arising nature of experience, sensation, but also, imagination, which is all ultimately love. The path of the Empress card parallels Lust and the Tower. Furthermore, the other editions of the Empress card, such as that of the Rider-Waite-Smith deck, illustrate an earlier scene in Revelation, chapter 12, where a woman is seen "clothed with the sun, with the Moon at her feet, and a crown of twelve stars on her head."[77] The twelve stars could represent the twelve signs of the zodiac, the firmament. From a classical view, the Sun would be below that, and the Moon would be below that, above the earth. This is the cosmic order of things on the Tree of Life.

The marriage of the Sun and Moon is a deep symbolic connection. The path of the Lust card, Leo, is ruled by the Sun and passes through the path of the Priestess, ruled by the Moon. Below this intersection on the tree, we have the Sun represented in Tiphareth, and the Moon represented below that in Yesod. The relationship here has so many possibilities but some worth noting is the connection of light and its reflection, consciousness and subconsciousness, masculine and feminine, ida and pingala. The elaborate polarities referenced by the Sun and Moon are like the game board of a pinball machine. They create the borders for the ball to bounce around. The back-and-forth movement of the ball is the dance of the Lust card, life, and play.

So what does this card have to do with divination? How do these show up in our life? A surrender to play, lust, desire, and creativity. On the surface, it may seem to oppose the card's older meaning or suggest self-control. But when you look deeper, it is the same: The card indicates the relationship with your creative energy, how it is aligned with yourself, united with love, lust, or passion. The major urge here is to love yourself, not as the illusion of a fixed identity but as a whirlpool in a sea of consciousness constantly creating in rhythms and cycles. Being the center of the tree, the Lust card is the dynamic rhythms happening vertically (incarnation and ascent) and horizontally (building up and breaking apart) being played out. This happens cosmically but in our own lives in all our creativity.

---

77. Rev. 12:1.

Whenever we create something, we transmute material from one to make up another. That material could be paint on a canvas, or information, or food in the oven. The Lust card is the serpent of transformation which is a death and birth in any creative process. Getting lost in our creative passion is giving up our blood to Babalon, our creative state which is ecstasy. The surrender required is dealt with in the following arcanum.

THE HANGED MAN

The Hanged Man is the mystical misfit, the personification of a reversal of ordinary ways of thinking. Esoterically, this is a card of initiation, a surrendering of one reality for another. This is a stage in the spiritual quest and also a pattern expressed in the mythological formula of the dying god. This theme is shared by the preceding and following card. As previously mentioned, all cards suggest the same truth, the same source code, through different angles, as the Tree of Life is a holographic design. Lust, the Hanged Man, and Death show this source code through one of its unique expressions: Radical surrender. In the same way as nothingness surrenders itself to its own voidness to *be* everything, the Hanged Man surrenders himself to the logos.

The Hebrew letter attributed to the Hanged Man is *mem*, "water." This is our second of the three mother letters. This is the most passive of the mother letters, in the way that the element of water passively fills its container. This is the metaphor of incarnation and is the secret of the Hanged Man. Life surrenders itself to incarnation by pouring itself into units and populating the earth. The life force illustrated in lust finds its embodiment in the Hanged Man in the way that water spreads itself out to reach the borders of its container. The essential idea is extreme allowance.

Before the developments of the Hermetic Order of the Golden Dawn, water was considered the third element (the order was fire, air, water, earth). This was likely the order of elements considered by the transmitters of the *Sepher Yetzirah*, which reads "Three Mothers, AMSh, in the Universe are air, water, fire. Heaven was created from fire. Earth was created from water. And air from Breath decides between them."[78] The idea here is that space/air separates fire from water. Kabbalist Anthony Noa teaches how we see this in the solar system as the Sun separated from the earth by space.[79] We see this in our faces as the eyes, which register light, being separated from the mouth, which takes in solids and liquids, from

---

78. Aryeh Kaplan, *Sefer Yetzirah: The Book of Creation* (Samuel Weiser, 1997), 144.
79. Antony Noa, *The Book of Yirah*. Self-published, n.d.

XII

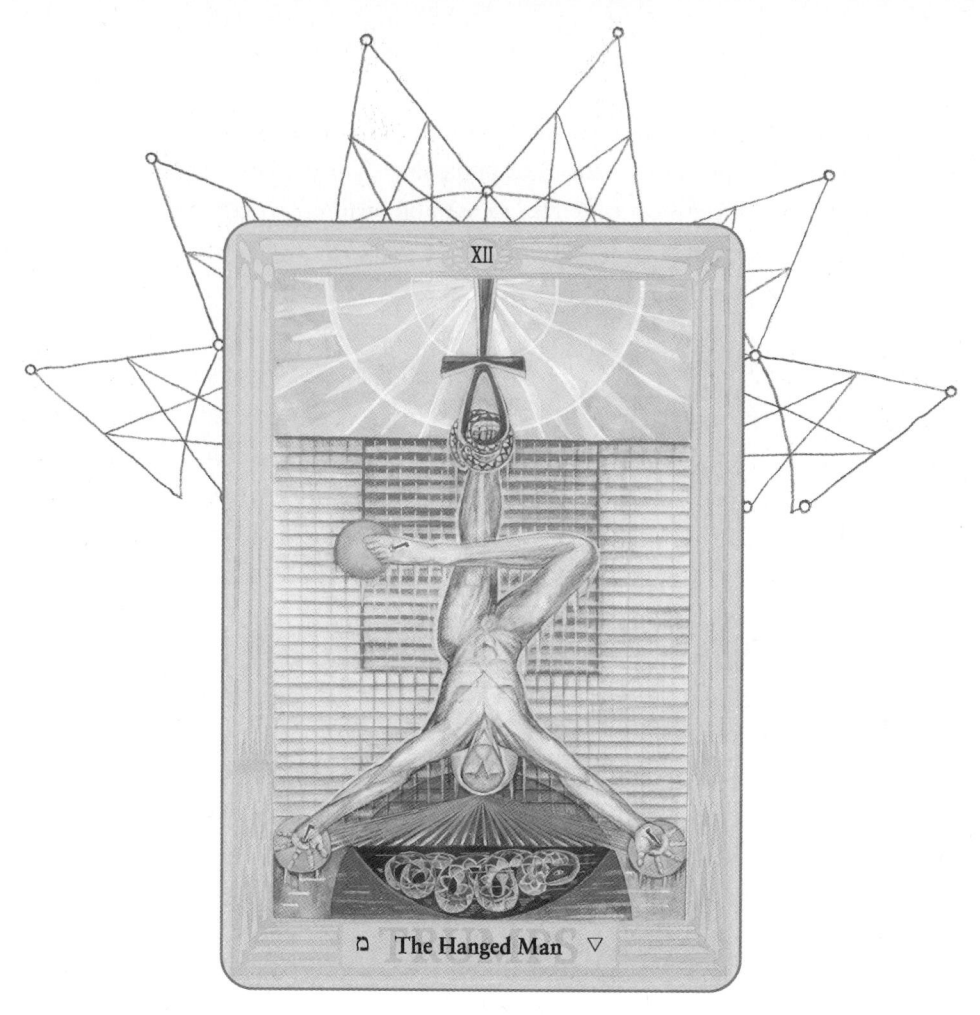

מ **The Hanged Man** ▽

the nose, which breathes in air. On the Tree of Life, Chokmah, fire, is separated from Binah, water, by Kether, air.

Concerning the mother letters, *mem* was traditionally associated with earth as well as water. This creates a three-tier hierarchy of emanation. The source is fire above; this is the subject, and the result is water and earth below. This is the object. The means and action itself *is* air, the space that lies between both. In the same way, the Hermit stands between the sun and the earth. Similarly, in the *Divine Pymander*, Hermes Trismegistus sees a light (spiritual fire) which acts upon darkness (spiritual water/earth) through the "word" (spiritual air).[80] By doing this, the word separates out four elements: Fire and air are separated from water and earth (a separation also illustrated in the Lovers and the Sun cards). These

---

80. Copenhaver, *Hermetica*, 1.

latter four are the more terrestrial elements expressed in the minor arcana, and they are slightly different from the three spiritual elements (fire, water, and air).

What follows next in the *Divine Pymander* is the creation of a so-called workman mind that fashions the seven planets that create the reality of sensation and fate. So, our numbers so far are 3, 4, and 7. Note that we have three spiritual elements acting upon four terrestrial elements. Remember that three and four make seven (the number of Venus and the classical planets). Multiplied they make twelve, the number of the Hanged Man. Reduced numerologically, twelve becomes three, the number of the Empress, which is the Hanged Man's mother. Reversing the digits of twelve, we get twenty-one, the Universe card—the world he is born into. The general shape of the human figure in the Universe is the same as the Hanged Man but flipped.

Generally, the figure on the card is a cross surmounted by a triangle. It represents three acting upon four (comparable to the last two rows of the tetractys). This symbolizes consciousness as observer-observation-observed, or subject-object-action, acting upon the sensory world of the world elements. This is the Empress (card 3)—the universal harmony of mutually arising diversity—acting upon the Emperor (card 4), the personal constitution of a separate self as interceptor in the material world.

As Paul Foster Case explains, "The correct geometrical figure concealed by the Hanged Man is a cross, surmounting a water triangle. It signifies the multiplication of the tetrad by the triad. This is the number 12. The door, dalet, is the vehicle of the tetrad, for it is the Great Womb also; the head of the Hanged Man reflected therein is the LVX, in manifestation as the logos. He is Osiris, Sacrifice, and yod-heh-shin-vav-heh—Yeheshua."[81] *Yeheshua* is the transliteration of the Hebrew word for "Joshua," the name of Jesus. This is thus a card of salvation through sacrifice. Crowley says that the cross surmounting the triangle is a symbol of "light descending into darkness in order to redeem it," beautifully paralleling the vision in the *Divine Pymander*.[82]

LVX is Latin for light. The enumeration of the Latin letters is sixty-five, which is also the number of the Hebrew word ADNI, *adonai* (lord). The six and five together represent the macrocosm and the microcosm. The formula of abrahadabra, (discussed in the Chariot card) echoes this relationship (note that the Chariot card is directly above the hanged man on the Tree of Life). It is also the number of HIKL, *haikal*, meaning "palace" or "temple," which refers to our bodies, our "sanctum sanctorum." Our bodies are the passive containers

---

81. Paul Foster Case, *The Tarot: The Key to the Wisdom of the Ages* (TarcherPerigee, 2006), 136.
82. Crowley, *Book of Thoth*, 96.

filled by the life-giving waters of mem. Surrendering to the fact that we are only a container for this life energy is the secret of the Hanged Man. This is what is meant by the LVX in his head, the manifest logos.

Furthermore, LVX represents three ritualistic signs in the adeptus minor ritual of the Golden Dawn. L is the sign of the mourning Isis, who mourns the death of her partner Osiris. V is the sign of Typhon/Apophis who kills Osiris. X is the sign of Osiris Risen. This shorthand of these deities is IAO. It represents the rhythm of life and death, the two sides of the undulating snake coiled at the foot of the Hanged Man and in the darkness below his head. Recall the many meanings of the serpent introduced in the Lust card. The content of the symbol will bleed into all the cards of the tarot as they all begin to express the logos.

Consider now the element of water (mem) as a symbol for the sea of consciousness. This sea is first introduced to us by the Priestess, who is the deep waters of the collective unconsciousness. She is the origin of the personal subconscious which flows to us through her function of memory, and reflection, symbolized by the Moon. The three water signs are as follows. First, Cancer, the Chariot, shows the pouring of life/water into the literal vehicle, the holy grail (in Crowley's deck, this source of life is the cup of Babalon). Scorpio is the Death card that holds the doctrine that change and death are requirements to ensure everlasting life. Lastly, Pisces is the Moon, the gateway back into the sea of consciousness through the memory (priestess) of all our incarnations and through death. In this threshold of the eighteenth arcanum, light, LVX, is removed because the microcosm begins its absorption into the macrocosm.

The major themes of this card are thus the surrendering to the many rapids of life and its surprising movements, which include death. This is what is meant by the esoteric title "Spirit of the Mighty Waters." It is the beautifully capricious and enthusiastic flow of energy. In deep healing work, the most effective course of action is surrendering to the feeling of something, which allows the stuck energy to move through the body. This has been a huge area of research by psychiatrist and mystic David Hawkins. It is through surrender to the rough waters of life and death that there is stability. The mode of consciousness attributed to mem is "stable intelligence." It is only through radical surrender to the illusion of instability that true stability is found.

The idea of surrendering, whether in occult initiation or healing is further expressed by the path attributed to this card. Path 23 runs from Geburah, severity, to Hod, glory. It is thus the severity of Geburah that pushes us to submission in Hod. Hod is also the sephirah of mind, which is turned upside down through the hanged man by the influence of Geburah. You can imagine the Hanged Man's head in hod while his feet are tied to Geburah, the cause of his perceived instability. In terms of our dimensional blueprint using Crowley's Naples Arrangement, this is motion being applied to thought.

In traditional decks, this idea of surrender was contextualized by the title "the traitor." It is worth noting here the sociocultural impact of occult works. Occult means hidden. This is because the truths explored are hidden to normal states of consciousness, and in many traditions, could only be understood by a select few, making them "esoteric." Another reason for hiding these mysteries was persecution. I believe the betrayal implied by traditional decks was a betrayal of the status quo. This is a betrayal of dogma, religion, and any predominant "reality tunnel" (a term coined by Tim Leary). This is the role of mystics, who, through reflection on the waters of consciousness (mem) suspend their mind (Hod) on its path to Geburah (strength, severity, judgment) and go against the norm.

Crowley was not a fan of this card. According to him, we are in the Æon of Horus, which is one of fire, making the Hanged Man an obsolete arcanum. Crowley urges that the formula of the sacrificed god is no longer needed. Much of Crowley's philosophy is based on direct connection with truth as opposed to using another entity as a bridge. Symbols of particular importance are the snakes above and below. They represent the logos but also its faculty of redemption through sacrifice. The ankh above is another form of the rose cross, symbolizing the macrocosm and microcosm, from which is coiled the serpent. Note that this card and the universe card both have a serpent under a foot. This symbolizes our relationship to our DNA and life cycles. The Hanged Man represents humanity as direct results from those rhythms. In the Universe card, we conquer those rhythms with the collective consciousness of our species.

How does this card and its energies show up in life? It is the act of surrender. It is a reversal of your normal ways of thinking (symbolized by the influence of Geburah on Hod). It is also about being different, being a traitor to the norm, so to speak. In a way, all that is mysticism, the act of surrendering to a will higher than "I." It is certainly misfitism, surrendering to a point of view outside the status quo. In the Thoth deck, it is a card of enforced sacrifice, considering the less optimal context of the element of water in a deck based on an æon of fire. In this way, it may be interpreted as loss, suffering, and failure. It is also a card of suspension, being in between two worlds, which has been expressed by the card's esoteric implications of our cosmic positions as appendages from spirit (fire) reaching into matter (water and earth, represented by mem).

DEATH

Traditionally, this card has been the most feared. It was surrounded with such superstition that older decks did not include its name on the card. As typical of occult investigation, the esoteric significance of this card is actually much more auspicious and complex. It *is* a card of death, yes, but death as a method for life. The recurring theme of tarot, especially expressed in the Thoth tradition, is the mutually arising relationship between life and death, which coils the snake of wisdom as an expression of love.

The Hebrew letter attributed to Death is *nun*, the fish. The ancients brilliantly intuited our marine origin and thus employ the symbol of the fish as our source. The Egyptians expressed the cosmic, formless beginnings as a vast water. One of the earlier signs of Christ was a fish. Oannes, a deity of Mesopotamian myth who taught humans wisdom, came in the form of a fish. The Egyptian Osiris, god of the underworld, was sliced up by his jealous brother Set and scattered around the world. Isis, his wife and lover, had to find all the pieces to bring him back to life, and the last she had to find was his penis, which had been swallowed by a fish. In all these stories, the fish has become a symbol of the germ of life.

As the germ of life, the fish is a symbol of coming and going. It relates to the formula of the dying god (Christ-Osiris), the symbol of the age of Pisces. The function attributed to nun in the *Sepher Yetzirah* is motion. It is the motion that has traveled through the unconscious waters of the Priestess that allowed for life as we know it. Nun has linguistic connections to the words "descendants," "propagate," and "growth." The doctrine is that of freedom through life, which itself is change but through the engine of death. In older decks like the Marseille, Death was illustrated reaping a field of body parts. The field symbolized the fertility ensured through disembodiment. This is the reaping of what is sowed by the ox of the Fool, perfectly ordered by the ox-goad of Adjustment.

The fish was also sacred to Venus. The Greek Orphic hymn to Venus is filled with deep sea imagery. The idea here is that the imagination, symbolized by Venus and the Empress, (the mutually arising diversity of experience), is fulfilled through the agent of change (fish) swimming to us through the waters of the subconscious (the Priestess).

It follows that the mode of consciousness attributed to nun is "imaginative intelligence" or "apparitive consciousness." Aryeh Kaplan notes that this is what provides appearance to apparitions.[83] It could be interpreted as ghosts (fitting for the card) or more deeply, the psycho-spiritual complex of mind that renders this reality in the garments of fixed form, "matter" as we call it, which ultimately breaks down. This psycho-spiritual complex is itself imagination. The doctrine is that death is a human invention.

The invention of death comes about when consciousness descends from Tiphareth into the lower triad. Crowley notes that the next three paths, 24 (Death) 25 (Art) and 26 (the Devil) show how idea manifests as form. This first happens in path 24, from Tiphareth to Netzach, with nun. Pure self-consciousness, which is ultimate Self-love and Christ consciousness, descends through the path of the fish to Netzach, the sphere of desire, movement, and motility. The purity dies for the desire. The depth of this path can be understood by comparing it to its higher parallel equivalent, that of the Fool. In path 11, the ox, the plowing of the fields, is nothingness becoming something as the godhead (Kether) reaches out as a force (Chokmah). The Death card is ultimate self-consciousness (Tiphareth) becoming realized as a desire (Netzach) through the path of the fish, motion. It is this descent into desire and ambition of Netzach that creates the illusion of death.

---

83. Aryeh Kaplan, *Sefer Yetzirah*, 299.

CHAPTER 2

Similar logic is argued by the great Indian philosopher Shankara: Death results from birth. Birth results from karma (literally action). Karma results from desire (if you desire something, you take action toward it). Desire results from ignorance. Ignorance is the lack of knowledge of your own completeness, the illusion of lack.

Another interpretation of this path is that it is through death (nun) that desire (Netzach) is reconciled by our higher self (Tiphareth). A very important relationship here is that of Venus, Netzach. This further emphasizes the idea of love begetting death, a philosophy so familiar to the Thoth tarot. Venus is also the letter dalet, the great door to life, the Empress. The irony is that the ultimate desire of Netzach is death, the path toward Tiphareth. "In love the individuality is slain; who loves not love? Love death therefore, and long eagerly for it. Die daily."[84]

The serpent in the previous arcanum represented the logos as the source of humanity, hung between above and below, implying that we all hang from a divine intelligence, ultimately dangling from the Tree of Life. In Death, the serpent is an aspect of Scorpio, the fixed watery sign attributed to the thirteenth arcanum.

Scorpio is the sign of intensity, transformation, mortality, death, and sex. All of these have the common denominator of finding an extreme, braving toward the edge of something and then going beyond. This is the nature of "growth," one of the meanings of nun. Scorpio is symbolized by three animals to represent its three stages of change. The scorpion represents its lowest form, a solid. It was believed to commit suicide when in danger, or put in fast heat for cooking. The Serpent is the middle form, a liquid, the main theme of the sign, which symbolizes the undulation between life and death. Recall the serpent in Genesis, NChSh, as having the same enumeration (358) as *MShICh*, messiah. This is the snake that will be conquered in the universe card. The eagle is its highest form, gas, exaltation above solid matter. Alchemists considered gas to be the most spiritual, the most subtle.

Scorpio is ruled by Mars, attributed to the Tower. Mars is the will to live as well as the god of war, matter, the gross, just as it is friction (the sephirah attributed to Mars is Geburah, motion). Fiery Mars is a hot planet, and this is the heat that incubates the orphic egg that finds its final form in the following card.

What is dying in this card? A lie, but the lie is not just any we tell ourselves or others. The lie that is dying is the lie of the self, the ego. The ego is like a bubble in the ocean. When it reaches the surface, it joins the rest of the atmosphere. This process of the bubble

---

84. Crowley, *Book of Lies*, 42.

is seen in Crowley's Death card, where souls dance in their bubbles rising upward. The card also depicts the fish, the scorpion, the snake, and the eagle.

Crowley notes that "this card is in a strict sense, a completion of atu XI–Lust through the dissolution or solution of hanged man."[85] It is the destruction of the self in the beholding of the beloved. Orgasm was called "the little death" in the Renaissance. Remember the idea that "to die is to beget," a notion revealed to us in the symbol of the letter nun and the dying god. The Thoth deck depicts Osiris in the dance of death, creating bubbles that represent the chemical change from a lower state to a higher state.

But death in this context is from heaviness to lightness. This is not just expressed in the mythologies of dying gods, but also in our bodies. David Hawkins discovered that the body weakens around information or material that is harmful to it or false. Conversely, the body strengthens around healthy material or true information. The subjective feeling of this is heaviness in the body around a lie, and lightness around a truth. Even a slight kinesthetic awareness will reveal to you this universal reaction. The evolution of Scorpio represents a process of becoming lighter. Many believe this is what happens when we die—the heavy matter is left behind so the lighter essence is freed.

When death concerns this sort of evolution, it is the death of a lie. The lie can be anything including our identification with our circumstances, with our bodies, minds, or egos. There are so many lies from which we may evolve. There are lies spinning within lies (the Wheel of Fortune). The removal of a lie isn't always easy. A lie is like a splinter. It enters us, and sometimes we forget it, but it often stings whenever we touch it. Removing it is the most painful part. But once it's gone, we can start to heal.

In divination this is a sort of death, but to leave it at this single interpretation is an error. Like the fish, nun, the card is the natural flow of things; to surrender to it is to join the dance of Osiris, who typifies the formula of the dying god, Christ, Joshua and other incarnated beings flowing in and out of life along the coils of wisdom that is the serpent, and our DNA. Love is a form of death. Death diversifies consciousness, as it is one side of the door of incarnation, the Empress.

Ultimately, death is an invention of the mind. As our invention, it is up to us what we do with it. In a reading, this indicates not so much a loss, but our relationship with a perceived loss. The perception is itself a very real thing. Now is a time to let go. "Die daily."

---

85. Crowley, *Book of Thoth*, 100.

ART

In the same way the Chariot sums up the occult forces generating consciousness in the first septenary, the Art card summarizes the second septenary. In this card, the forces of life and death, which is also love, are reconciled in a deep alchemical process. Crowley emphasizes that this is the complement of the Lovers card. The Lovers represents the dance of opposites whose marriage is officiated by the divine word-hermit-will-logos-mercury-magus. If the Magus was our cosmic DJ, the Art card is the perfected mix of the one verse that is the universe. In this card, the splitting and fractalization of consciousness that occurred in the Lovers, represented by the alchemical word *solve*, finds its full harmony as art, *coagula*.

This resolution is symbolized by the Hebrew letter attribution, *samekh*, "tent peg" or "prop" with linguistic connections to "training" and "to trust." A prop is used to keep something standing. When you are creating art, you are surrendering yourself to a state of creativity. There is a level of spontaneity, curiosity, and openness that softens the mind and allows a more fluid and natural approach to problem solving. This is the flow state, when the mind and body are united in one creative direction. This is a required state of all serious magick. The mind is "propped up" in a way to divine intelligence.

Let's explore the metaphor of a tent peg. Imagine setting up a basic tent. You lay the tent out. It is flaccid and takes the form of the flat earth. It isn't until you extend the tent with the pegs that the tent takes on three dimensions and becomes a space to inhabit. The pegs create one single tent space by directing its shape in two directions. The prop or tent peg works because of the resistance of the earth. Resistance is the law that allows us to walk and governs all motion in general. Remember that the previous card, nun, had motion as its function. Motion requires resistance. Walking requires muscular activation and the resistance of the earth. This is the secret of Art: The combination of forces to create something greater as a whole. This doctrine repeats on many levels and is expressed in all the card's symbols.

On the Tree of Life, samekh is literally the support, corresponding to the central path (25) from Tiphareth to Yesod. It draws the solar influence of Tiphareth, the higher self and consciousness, onto the lunar influence of Yesod, the subconscious nature and automata of the body. The relationship between consciousness and subconsciousness is a key element in normal mental functioning and is the psychological tent peg holding up our psychic home (Cancer/the Chariot) or our house (bet, the Magus). After learning to walk, you no longer need to *try* to walk, you just walk. It is a simple command the brain gives the body. But this simple command contains vast amounts of racing neurons (the Magus) working with afferent and efferent signals to keep dynamic balance (Adjustment). The combination of all this information allows the body to walk. The Art card represents the harmonization of opposing forces for a more complex experience.

This is also the realm of synchronicity, meaningful coincidence, explored by Carl Jung. Is coincidence divinely orchestrated? Is it an interpretation of the psyche originating in the mind? Or does the psyche orchestrate the external coincidence from the inside out? In the lens of mysticism, all of these are true. In the lens of the western mystery traditions, they are especially true because they are governed by the higher self. The idea is that the higher self directs the lower self from the above sephirah Tiphareth. When in connection with the higher self, you are one, and can accomplish so much more. This is having the "support" (samekh) of the universe (Tree of Life) at your back, which is also your psyche. Practically speaking, this is where meaning, symbolism, and communication with the universe blurs the boundary between what is "inside" and "outside." Through integrating the inner with the outer, we achieve further spiritual heights.

This concept of progress through the integration of opposites is heavily emphasized by the sign of Sagittarius, mutable fire, the arrow. An arrow is shot first by pulling it against a tight bow and then releasing it. This opposing relationship of potential and kinetic energy accomplishes its goal. There is also the symbol of the centaur. The centaur is half equine, half man. Recall the previous example of walking. Sagittarius governs the hips and thighs. Its motto is "I see" or "I go." The legs support (samekh) the body by pressing energy into the earth while the earth resists. This basic principle orients us in space. Sagittarians are archetypally students, travelers, and philosophers. All these roles share a persistent desire to explore, physically or mentally. It is the integration of their minds that draws all their faculties into one direction that allow them the freedom of the arrow to explore. Sagittarius perfectly opposes the Lovers card. Sagittarius alchemically unites all the facts, figures, and oppositions curiously perceived by the Hermetic marriage of the Lovers card and integrates it into one forceful beautiful movement.

It is like the uniting of colors in a rainbow. The rainbow is another symbol of Sagittarius. It is also a symbol of the promise of God not to destroy the world again (it was destroyed by fire and water, which are being merged in this card). It may also signify the promise of attainment to the higher self, which I will describe below. Zen masters have spoken of a rainbow body and Norse Pagans speak of the rainbow bridge. The last three paths of the tree are the letters qoph, shin, and tav. Together they make the word *QShTh, qeshet*—Hebrew for "rainbow."

What died in the Death card was only a part and thus an illusion that is now sacrificed for the working of the whole in the Art card. This is true on any scale. You only need to look at the natural world and its many species to see how the destruction of an organism on one means the health of an ecosystem. Beholding the beauty of the harmony on higher scales is the domain of Sagittarius—ruled by Jupiter—seeking the big, beautiful picture. To do so is to integrate all your opposites in order to behold the vision of the Wheel of Fortune, Jupiter, the cosmic work of Art. This is a lofty goal of philosophers and mystics. Glimpses of such truths such as Ezekiel's vision are often described as terrifying.

But to even arrive at such a broad state of consciousness requires an alchemical process, hinted at in the original title of the card, "Temperance," a tempering and modifying of the self. This is the reconciliation of our opposites, and ultimately, reconciliation with ourselves in the vision of our higher self. The higher self sits upon Tiphareth, which is where the path of samekh leads.

The *Sepher Yetzirah* attributes this letter to "intelligence of probation/trial and error." It is through curiosity that we try, err, and learn, in the slow path of attaining what is called "knowledge and conversation" with one's holy guardian angel. In Thelema, this is also the discovery of the True Will.

The lion and eagle refer to the paths on either side of path 25: The Devil and Death. These are also the adjacent major arcana. The doctrine here is the balancing of the material world, which is symbolized by the Devil, and the truth of the flux of reality, which is death. This is represented in the Rider-Waite-Smith deck as the archangel Michael having one foot on land and one foot on water. The cups being poured into each other are the conscious and the subconscious.

In the Thoth deck, this is represented as an androgyne, the black and white lovers are combined and their colors exchanged. The red-blood lion has become white and the white-gluten eagle has become red. This is the joy of counter-exchange. This suggests Crowley's sex magick and the body's ida and pingala energy channels. The androgyne as a whole is the many-breasted version of Diana the huntress, a moon goddess. The inclusion of the moon goddess refers to the two lunar attributions flanking the path. The path of Samekh leads from Tiphareth to Yesod. Yesod is attributed to the Moon. On the other end of the path, we find Tiphareth, which begins the path of Gimel, the Priestess, also associated with the Moon. The Priestess also expresses Diana, but in her virgin form. The elevation from "many-breasted" Diana to "virgin" Diana exoterically intimates the practice of chastity in many spiritual traditions. Esoterically, it suggests the increasing distance away from manifestation, something practically described in the *Yoga Sutras* as the transferring of sexual energy from the base of the spine upward through the chakras. This virgin form, whose path is above the many-breasted form, may symbolize the transferring of sexual energy from the base of the spine into Ojas at the head as described in the *Yoga Sutras*.

A broad interpretation of this can be thus: The reconciliation of opposites within leads to the integration of the self with the higher self. This delivers the soul in Tiphareth at the threshold of the Priestess, the next major stage, another death through the abyss. The raven on the skull is a *caput mortuum*, an alchemical symbol of what is left over from the previous card. The arrow in this card is of Sagittarius but also the same one held by Eros, divine lust, in the Lovers card. It directs the divine will and the logos. The card also shows the orphic egg, now in its complicated but matured and completed form.

CHAPTER 2

Written above is "Visit the interior parts of the earth: By rectification thou shalt find the hidden stone." On one level, the statement is about the merging of the two lovers, sulfur and salt, with mercury, the will. This is thus the merging of the observer with the observed in pure observation. This is the gold of the alchemists.

What does this card mean in divination? As all the symbols suggest, it means the bringing together of any opposites or parts, to allow for progress and integration. It is the ability to be in full agreement with yourself to proceed in any direction, similar to the Chariot card. However, in this card there is more subtly in combination, reconciliation, and assimilation of forces. Balancing a personal and work life, different relationships, or contradicting points of views within yourself, are all examples of making the proper support (tent peg). The alchemy is any series of elaborate maneuvers to get something, to release your arrow, your will. It is the combination of the Sun and the Moon to meet your higher self.

THE DEVIL

The middle septenary illustrated for us the rhythm of life and death issuing from the logos established in the first septenary. The third and final septenary concerns transcendence of earthly life and the awareness of cosmic forces. One could argue that this contradicts the sequence of the Tree of Life: Shouldn't the last septenary lead *toward* earthly life since these seven cards are lowest on the tree? Yes. However, we must remember that the creative process expressed by the tarot (and all technologies of mysticism) is holographic. The same creative pattern expresses both the descent of spirit into matter (manifestation) and the ascent of matter back into spirit (mysticism). It is at the lowest that we reach the highest. It is consciousness becoming you that allows consciousness to be appreciated. Perhaps no better card better deals with this apparent contradiction than the Devil.

The Devil is the divine impulse for and by the particulars of reality experienced independently from the whole. The Devil is the material universe. Like every other card, it represents the arising of boundaries amidst a boundaryless consciousness. It shows how limitations arise amidst the limitless divine to create more and more experience. The Devil's limitations are the most indulgent yet.

The Hebrew letter attributed to the Devil is ayin, meaning "eye." Representing sight, it becomes a symbol of all the senses. More specifically, it symbolizes visible light, the frequency we can sense, which is only a part of the whole light spectrum. The idea of partial vision is a main theme of the card, as the Devil represents the visible, material world, but not the spiritual.

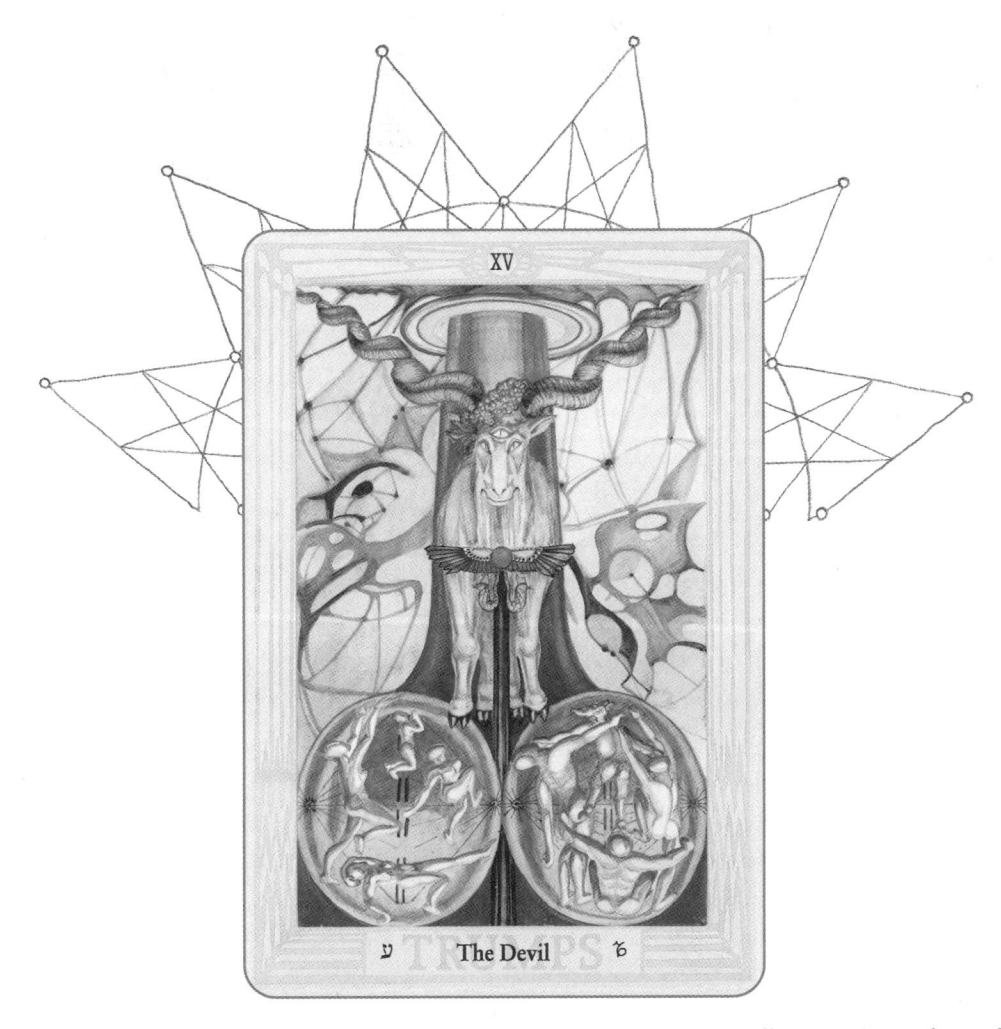

The mode of consciousness attributed to ayin is "renewing intelligence." It is through the realization that sensation and matter, as we know it, are only part of the whole, that we can renew our understanding of our true nature. "Renewing" may also refer to the renewing quality of spring in particular, and the natural world as a whole.

Spring, and the deity Pan Pangenitor, the "all-begetter," are attributed to this card. Pan symbolizes the lust, impulse, and play of the natural world. He would frolic in the fields of Arcadia in Greek myth. There is an archetypal "outside world" beyond the borders of civilization. This symbolizes the wild natural world, but also ourselves, our own impulsive nature to lust and desire. We might compare this to Freud's id, our internal child that is only concerned with itself, which must be balanced by the superego to be controlled.

Crowley says that this card represents "creative energy in its most material form."[86] Consider creativity in all its horror and glory. Creative energy is sexual energy. It can be used to create worlds, but also, as evidenced by the past few cards, destroy.

Éliphas Lévi redrew the card using the deity Baphomet, an idol of the Knights Templars symbolizing the rising force of the kundalini through the ida and pingala. This is a form of yoga, mentioned in the Lust card, that draws sexual energy from the base of the spine to the top of the head for enlightenment. This opens up the chakras including the third eye. This leads to another interpretation of ayin.

The eye of ayin is not just the eye of the sensory world and our attachments to it, but the eye of revelation. This is symbolized in the Thoth card by the third eye being opened, which is also the eye of Shiva, the destroyer, in the Tower card, as well as the one in the universe card. This could also be the eye of Horus, and the eye in the triangle. This would signify the awakened self in the Self. Crowley says, "in every symbol of this card there is the allusion to the highest things and most remote."[87] "If I lift up my head, I and my Nuit are one. If I droop down mine head, and shoot forth venom, then is rapture of the earth, and I and the earth are one."[88] The idea here supports the paradoxical interpretation of ayin, the deeper mystery. God *is* the immediate of what you see, but the truth of the immediate world of the senses alludes to the highest spiritual world. Crowley describes Pan as lusting for and uniting with all things, all textures, in the same way as Babalon is a divinely cosmic whore, participating with the adultery that is love with all forms. Compare this to the teaching Ramana Maharshi added to the Advaita Vedanta tradition: The world is unreal. Brahman alone exists. Brahman *is* the world.

A more exoteric version of this doctrine is in the Rider-Waite-Smith deck: The chains are big enough for the fallen Adam and Eve to escape. It is the awareness of the chains that give cause for their removal, hence "renewing intelligence." It is through reaching the bottom of the Tree of Life that the top is realized.

It is the joys of the lusting upon the earth that exhausts Pan to eventually sleep in what is called the "night of Pan." This is another way of saying "crossing the abyss," and it means leaving behind the actual, manifest world of Chesed and below for the ideal unmanifest world in Binah and above. This is what is described by Dionysius the Areopagite: "Here we take away all things from Him going up from particulars to universals, that we may know

---

86. Crowley, *Book of Thoth*, 105.

87. Crowley, *Book of Thoth*, 107.

88. Crowley, *Book of the Law*, 32.

openly the knowable, which is hidden in and under all things that may be known. And we behold that darkness beyond being, concealed under all natural light."[89]

The night of Pan is the passage upward from Chesed, which brings us to Binah, Saturn, which rules Capricorn. Capricorn is the cardinal earth sign and is attributed to the Devil. Capricorn is the lust of the earth, its ambition and desire to create. The lofty goals of Capricorn lead them to the very top of the zodiac. More exoteric interpretations of the Devil card can be easily connected to the negative characteristics of Capricorn: Greed, desire for power, attachment to reputation. The esoteric interpretation is the mountain goat climbing the mountain: A symbol of the earth reaching into the heavens. It is through the earth that spirit declares itself, such is the word made flesh.

Consider now that the path of ayin runs from Tiphareth, the dying god, to Hod, which is Mercury, a lower form of the word. This path expresses the "word made flesh." It is higher consciousness entering the world of thought through the materializing powers of Capricorn. Note that this card's number is 5, the same numbers as YH, Jah, a god-name associated with Chokmah, which is the higher form of the word and Mercury. The lower form of Mercury, and its traditional attribution on the tree, is Hod. In this sense, it represents the logical, sharp matrix we project onto the natural flow of things to make order. Remember Hod is the splitting up of the film of life (Netzach) into frames, or thought-events. This is the invention and application of language which carves out space and time through a system of labels. Hod casts an intellectual net over matter to measure it and render it into individual objects, moments, spaces, and conventional designations for civilization to prosper. Such conventional designation was the knowledge acquired by Adam and Eve, recognizing their nudity, projecting their separation, and divorcing themselves from Eden.

Another interpretation is that civilization is the rejoicing of spirit in matter to experience itself, and that the falling of the Gnostic Sophia (wisdom) into manifestation was not an accident, but a dance. And Pan loves to dance.

Capricorn is ruled by Saturn. Saturn is time. Time is one of the inventions inherent in civilization. Saturn is also form, and how we carve out designation. Mars is exalted in Capricorn. Mars is the will to live, which it shares with the Devil card's lust for life. Mars is also the destroyer, which is the Tower card and the open eye (ayin) of shiva. Crowley attributes Mars to matter, especially in its aspect as continually changing and being destroyed.

In this card, all the symbols continue to suggest each other. One may even argue that, as we try to become gods, the gods try to become incarnated as humans, the word made flesh.

---

89. Huxley, *Perennial Philosophy*, 34.

Pan, the flesh, is the son of Hermes, the word. The function attributed to the letter ayin by the *Sepher Yetzirah* is "laughter." Laughter is a sort of "zooming out." It almost always comes from zooming out to the larger picture of things, and taking the particulars, including the self, less seriously. In comedy, laughter is almost a delight in a shared experience of a "smallness" in the human condition. The Devil is the opportunity to zoom out and recognize the smallness of a particular aspect of yourself, within the wholeness of your true Self.

In a reading, the Devil indicates all desire operating upon the material world, for better or worse. More characteristic of this card is the blind impulse of Pan, the leaping goat of Capricorn upon the earth. This is a card that asks the question "what are you looking at?" Where are your eyes (ayin), fixated? What do you see? It is the will to live (Mars) in the world of time (Saturn) that is ultimately ambition (Capricorn). There is temptation and obsession, but also hard work, obstinance, and endurance, all qualities of Capricorn. The card indicates creative fervor, especially materially. It depicts a phallus and testes. The humanoids/demons within the testes are itching to get out to happen to the world. They will be released through orgasm, shown in the next card.

THE TOWER

"Love never fails. But where there are prophecies, they will cease; where there are tongues, they will be stilled; where there is knowledge, it will pass away. For we know in part and we prophesy in part, but when the perfect comes, what is in part disappears."[90] The Tower shows the destruction of the particulars for the whole, and sometimes, destruction of the whole for the particulars. Continuing our themes, the Tower identifies creation, with destruction, as revelation.

The clearest example of the descent of truth into illusion, or the sacrifice of the whole for the particulars, is in language. The Devil card introduced us to the application of language, which separated out reality into its diverse ayin-grabbing forms. On the Tree of Life, the Tower is the creative and destructive aspects of language. Its Hebrew letter, *peh*, means "mouth," from which flows language. In the bottom of the card, the mouth of the Roman Hades, Dis, breathes flames onto the scene. This is the destruction of language, and any presupposed synthetic truth. In traditional decks, this was called the "house of god." This may have referred to the destruction of exoteric religion, which supports the biblical verse above and the general theme of this card.

---

90. 1 Cor. 13:8–10.

It may be clear at this point that the general pattern of the Tree of Life, and therefore the youniverse, is that of the cost of holistic truth for the reward of elaboration in relativity: Analysis is the descending path, while synthesis is the ascending path. Compare this to Schopenhauer's will to live and the will to die.

This is what is symbolized in the Thoth card by the dove and the serpent. In the Tower, the mouth of peh is the symbol of language, which sacrifices truth in an attempt to express it. What is more awesome is the reverse: The destruction of language in the face of truth. Some call this grace. Consider the pentateuch. *Peh* is a double letter whose two meanings are "grace" and "sin."

The symbol of lightning is one of destruction, creation, and revelation. It creates fire but often hails the coming of life-giving rain, and sometimes a rainbow, a QShTh (see the Art card). Qabalists describe the creation of the Tree of Life as a "lightning flash," wherein the lightning shoots through the sephiroth, one through ten. This order is known as the

Chapter 2

"path of the flaming sword," whose connection to this card is one of love. The lightning flash also runs mysteriously through the major arcana, starting at the spiral force of aleph (lightning is a spiral force), and continuing through the antennae of the Magus onward. It has notable appearances in the Wheel of Fortune (connected to Zeus and his lightning), among others.

The idea of creation, destruction, and revelation is one of love. The lightning flash of the Tower and the "path of the flaming sword" in the Lust card are two directions of the same order of sephirah, the former descending, the latter, ascending. Both the Tower and the Lust card are on this order of paths. This upholds our concept of the destruction of unity through the creation of particulars in materialization, versus the destruction of particulars for the creation of unity in ascension. Notice that the path of the Tower and the Lust card are parallel. They are also parallel to the Empress, universal love, imagination, the marriage of the supernals. The doctrine here is that these three cards show love on three different levels of consciousness. In the Death card, we introduced the idea that tragedy on one scale was harmony on another, and that the laughter of the Devil was the zooming out to behold the smallness of one's shortcomings to appreciate oneself in the harmony of the whole. In the Thoth deck, the Lust card is symbolized by the serpent, and the Empress is symbolized by the dove, two symbols mentioned together in the *Book of the Law* and the Bible. They both appear in the Tower.

The Path of Peh connects Netzach, desire and emotion, to Hod, submission and intellect. One interpretation of this is that the ambition of Netzach is being surrendered in Hod. Another interpretation concerns Hod as the lower form of the word, being attributed to Mercury. With this in mind, the descent of the Devil card, the eye, into Hod from Tiphareth, creates the matrix of civilization that engenders the more sophisticated desires and attachments we are aware of (money, fame, sex, love, et cetera). In the Tower, this matrix in Hod is arrived at through its opposite, Netzach. Netzach is a sephirah of flow, rhythm, desire, and the movement of the film of life. Hod is the logical, sharp, organized, and fragmented mental interpretation of life, the frames of the film. These two forces combine in a violent illustration of the Tower. Remember how the Tower is a much lower expression of the same marriage illustrated by the Empress, the diversity of experience. The doctrine here is that neither the bliss of movement in Netzach nor the glory of thought in Hod is altogether the one reality. The one reality is something greater than both. This same doctrine appears in the path of samekh, which this path runs through. In samekh, fire and water are combined through patient alchemy to bring the aspirant to the higher self in Tiphareth. This intersection of the tree deals with a sacrifice of the small self for the higher self, a concept occultists call the Veil of Paroketh.

In this concentrated intersection of fire (Netzach), water (Hod), and air, (Yesod and Tiphareth), the Tower acts as a point of revelation. This can be a psycho-spiritual crisis, or an ego death, a true annihilation of the self. Spiritual illumination can be intense, and can be symbolized by lightning. Many spiritual visions in the Bible are described as "awful" because of the sheer greatness of them. In the *Bhagavad Gita*, Krishna says "Of weapons, I am the thunderbolt."[91] Pymander reveals himself to Hermes as a magnificent fire. How many times must angels say "be not afraid"?

In the Thoth deck, the true reality being revealed is symbolized by the eye of Shiva, whose opening hails the destruction of the universe. This same eye is suggested in the Wheel of Fortune. This is the eye foreshadowed in the previous card when reversing the symbol of the eye to its more esoteric meaning of spiritual sight, like that of the third eye. Waite says of this card "it is idle to indicate that it depicts ruin in all its aspects ... It signifies the materialization of the spiritual word."[92] This concept leads back to the one of creation by destruction.

This idea of creating and revealing by destroying is a sound concept in the planet Mars, which is attributed to the Tower. Mars is the will to live but ironically also the planet of war and struggle. It governs the muscles, and rules Scorpio, the sign of death, and Aries, the sign of self-perpetuation. Mars is exalted in Capricorn, the sign of the desire of matter to generate. These astrological associations all concern the idea of living and dying as forms of desire. Remember, Love begetting death and vice versa are major axiomata in tarot and mysticism, especially the Thoth deck.

Here are some technical examples of the doctrine of "destruction begetting creation." The first and the last decan of the zodiac is ruled by Mars. The beginning of the *Sepher Yetzirah* opens with "With 32 mystical paths of Wisdom engraved yah."[93] The word "engraved" suggests removal. Also in the Qabalah is the idea of *tzimtzum*, which is where the infinite consciousness of God contracts itself, removes itself from infinitude into a small point. All these ideas suggest that to create, space must be made. Something must first be destroyed or removed.

---

91. A. C. Bhaktivedanta Swami Prabhupada, *Bhagavad-Gita As It Is*, (Macmillan, 1972), 423.

92. Waite, *Pictorial Key*, 80.

93. Kaplan, *Sefer Yetzirah*, 5.

CHAPTER 2

Crowley views Mars as a planet of matter. He states that this card is the "manifestation of cosmic energy in its grossest form." He says that this card is the quintessential quality of the new fiery Æon of Horus destroying the old æon.

In his explanation of the card, Crowley alludes to the doctrines of yoga and the god Shiva by saying "the ultimate reality (which is perfection) is nothingness. Hence all manifestations however glorious, however delightful, are stains. To obtain perfection, all existing things must be annihilated."[94] Consider this quote in the context of the previous discussion on the creative, flow state. In the face of the beloved, there is a death, and we return to oneness, or rather, noneness.

In a reading, this is the sudden destruction of anything. We could interpret this as a destruction of a lie, including the ego in ego death, but it could be as simple as a car breaking down. Crowley emphasizes the "grossness" of the card implying its low materialization, so it can definitely signify a physical loss. The spiritual doctrines of this card find divinatory meaning in the ideas of a structure being undermined and the very foundation of something being destroyed. It is ultimately a realization of truth, a lesson in humility, and/or a dramatic realization. In the context of Mars, it can indicate war, adrenaline, danger, and destruction, the aftermath of which is almost always more valuable and worth the ordeal.

The Tower offers us a "de-pixelization" of life. When the Tree of Life is used to depict the parts of the soul, the ruach, the mind, is represented by Chesed (4) through Yesod (9). The seat of the ruach is Tiphareth. Hod is our thoughts, which have the illusion of fixity, but fly by through the motion, and emotion, of Netzach. Moving beyond thought in Hod is the beginning of the removal of the matrix that we project onto the natural flow of things. It's like taking the rules of Tetris out of the game, and instead of reacting to the falling pieces, you can build whatever you want.

THE STAR

The Tower destroyed the illusion of the particulars. The Star is the resulting realization of the whole, the perfect. This card shows our relationship with the firmament, a symbol of infinite space. Space is the key concept here, a very sophisticated concept of God. On the Tree of Life, space as we, exists in three dimensions through the sephirah Chesed. However, that space, which is also connected to the demiurge, is a manifestation of a deeper, more abstract space that can only be penetrated above the abyss by the most advanced mystics and magicians. Let us consider this space as our relationship with the complete

---
94. Crowley, *Book of Thoth*, 108.

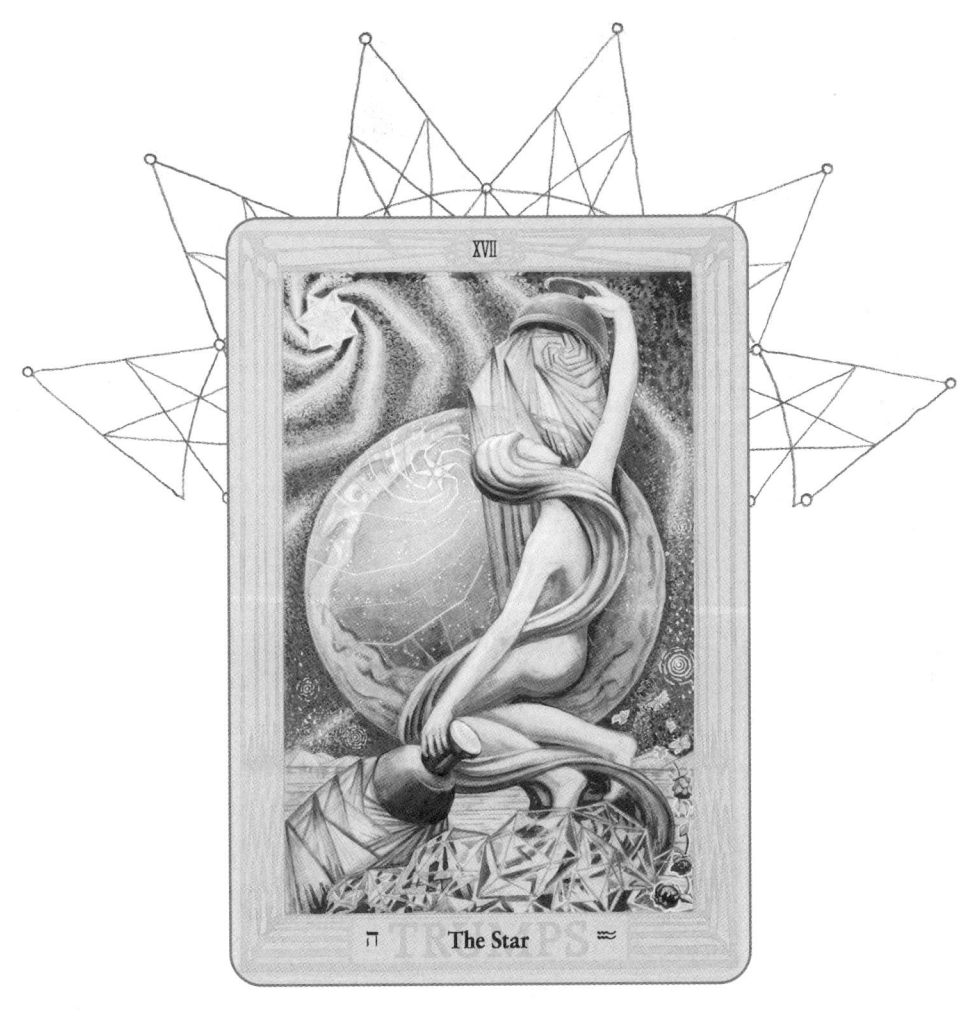

zero from which flow forth all miraculous stains of manifestation. The Star is the washing machine of the universe, and also ourselves. It is the secret to all healing and renewal, which is ultimately space, which we experience as what I call consciousness. The Star continues the doctrine introduced by the Tower (and ironically hinted at by the Devil) that nothing that is *truly* true can ever be lost.

I will begin our discussion on the Star with the traditional associations and then move to Crowley's important developments. The Golden Dawn attributes the Hebrew letter t*zaddi* to the Star, which means "fishhook." In this context, the fishhook symbolizes a penetration into the waters, which symbolizes the unconscious. The goal is to pull out a fish (nun), the Death card, change. This is an allegory for meditation, the function attributed to tzaddi according to some versions of the *Sepher Yetzirah*. The mode of consciousness attributed to tzaddi is "natural intelligence." This is a quest of our internal nature, the truth. As explained by Paul Foster Case, meditation is a patient method (fishhook) to enter the subconscious (water) and provoke some sort of change (fish). The change symbolized by the Hebrew letter nun is the Death card, the end of the old paradigm.

The major theme of the Star is progress, and progress is a key characteristic of Aquarius, the water bearer, the fixed air sign corresponding to the Star. The path of Aquarius is one of uniqueness, genius, and advancement. This sign is obsessed with finding and honoring the truth of one area or another, especially if it goes against the status quo. This is the path of the mystics and meditators. In a microcosmic sense, this is the search for a truth within one's own mind that may go against its idle assumptions. In this way it is a breaking away from what neuroscientists call the "default mode network" in order to reach higher states of consciousness. The meditation function of tzaddi is not only echoed in Aquarians' inner search for truth but also their contemplation on problem solving and collective advancement.

Aquarius is classically ruled by Saturn. The doctrine here is that invention and progress flow in the world of time. Furthermore, this progress is derived from the world of matter/matrix the results from projected measurement and a superimposition of limitation, which is represented by Saturn's card, the Universe. Saturn was considered in classical astrology to be the farthest planet in the solar system. The idea presented here is that the quest for truth leads the Aquarian far and wide, and often encapsulates whole systems at work, in the way that Saturn circumscribes the solar system. This is why Aquarius rules the eleventh house, governing groups of people and social influence. This book was written in the age of Aquarius. At this time, social media is one of the largest arenas of communication, business, and civilization as a whole.

Modern astrologers consider Uranus as its ruler, a planet of revolution. The truths uncovered in Aquarius are often ones of rebellion, and they renew the whole system, whether that's one person renewing themselves or an entire civilization in a paradigm shift. This prepares the system to behold the truth on the other side, represented by the threshold of the Moon card, and Pisces.

The idea of searching the subconscious for renewing truth is expressed in the path of tzaddi, which runs from Netzach to Yesod. This is the motivation and desire of Netzach acting through Aquarius upon the subconscious mind of Yesod. The fishhook is cast by the fiery aspiration of Netzach into the flowing subconscious waters of Yesod, which is also the automata of the body and nervous system. Hopefully, the seeker can catch a fish. That fish is the path that leads to Tiphareth and the higher self.

The Major Arcana

The number 17 reduces to 8, Adjustment, where Saturn is exalted. The doctrine of renewal revealed by the Star and its associations is one that requires Adjustment. Adjustment, the ox goad, is a symbol of causality. Its function is work, and action, which is our karma. The relationship of the cards suggest that genius (the star, the brilliant lightbulb) comes through constant Adjustment. In the same way a baby learns to walk by falling over and staggering, we learn the higher truths of the cosmos by exploring and making the most beautiful of philosophical errors and wrong hypotheses. This is the philosophical angling of the fishhook, searching for its fish. This is happening on a collective scale on the species. From our perspective, the progress is slow, but it only takes a quick peak to the last thousand years to see how far we've come. Such is the influence of time (Saturn) on Aquarius. I would agree with the alchemical philosophy that everything is becoming better, more refined, more complex, and more beautiful, however slowly. Statistically, this isn't a line going straight up, but I believe the mean complexity, and sum total of information on the earth (as well as conscious units to receive and interface with that information) is increasing.

In some forms of mysticism, the progress of the Star is seen spiritually in the human body by the rising of the kundalini, or "serpent power." Many have compared the seven chakras, the signposts along the way, to seven metals of alchemy and the seven classical planets. For example, Saturn and lead are connected with the muladhara chakra. These seven energy centers may also coincide with the bottom seven dots on the Pythagorean tetractys, as well as the seven colors, and seven seals in Revelation.

Let's consider Crowley's updates to the card. First and foremost, he depicts this card as a manifestation of Nuit. Nuit is the first entity we are introduced to in Crowley's channeled *Book of the Law*. She is the lady of the stars, space itself. She herself is a personification of the Qabalistic ain soph and her lower manifestation is Babalon, situated in Binah.

In the Thoth deck, this card is attributed to the letter heh. The reason for the change was explained in the description of the Emperor, but another argument for this attribution is that heh is the feminine letter of the tetragrammaton. Since Nuit expresses the highest aspect of divinity in feminine form, it would make sense that her letter is the single feminine letter of the Holy Tetragrammaton. In this way, she represents not just ain soph but its manifestation in heh primal and Binah (as Babalon) and its manifestation as heh final and Malkuth (as the shekinah). Thus, Nuit and the star are "Nothingness with twinkles…but *what* twinkles!"[95]

---

95. Crowley, *Book of Thoth*, 109.

Furthermore, a window suggests the outside, which is the firmament, the stars. I view this as the indwelling space/Nuit/consciousness that peeks out of all of our eyes, our bodily windows. Recall that sight is the function of heh. Nuit is the stars that lights up space. She is what makes sight possible.

In this card she pours over herself milk, water, blood, or wine, depending on the interpretation. This is the "milk of the stars" that may hint at what Robert Anton Wilson, calls the biosurvival circuit (commenting on the work of Timothy Leary).[96] The theory here is that we form an idea of what the world is like based on our beginning relationship with our mother through breastfeeding. Our spiritual mother is Nuit, as she is constantly renewing us with consciousness itself which is inexhaustible love. From her cups flow light and life, two cosmic agents described in the *Corpus Hermeticum*. This card is the washing machine of cosmic consciousness, constantly cleaning, renewing, and surprising itself. The life we get from a mother is the same life swirling infinitely within itself in every cosmic body. It is the closed system through which all of our creations flows and comes from. There is nothing done, made, changed, or differentiated outside the infinite space of pure consciousness, pure existence, and pure bliss. There truly nothing (ain soph) apart from it. As Krishna says, "Whatever you do, whatever you eat, whatever you offer or give away, and whatever austerities you perform–do that, o son of Kunti, as an offering to Me."[97] And Nuit echoes, "To me! To me!"[98]

This card is also very connected to healing because it is a card of space and allowance. The healing process of so many conditions is often delayed because of denial, repression, suppression, or expression. These four strategies take an ailment or issue and attempt to push it away or enlarge it when the fastest way to heal something is to experience it. Working with an expert healer for years, I've found that the fastest mode of healing is to observe and let pure awareness into the wound (physical or psychological). This has been researched in many circles of body-centered therapy and energy work. Mystically, this is being in allowance and complete surrender. It allows one to see everything in its highest quintessential quality. No matter the experience, good or bad, all experiences share in this quintessential quality: The quality of simply being. When you can see the quality of "being" in everything, you see God in everything. In this way, Nuit stretches infinitely and

---

96. Robert Anton Wilson, *Prometheus Rising*, (Hilaritas Press, 2016), 27.
97. Prabhupada, *Bhagavad-Gita*, 385.
98. Crowley, *Book of the Law*, 28.

includes all with pure love. To really understand this card, it is recommended to read chapter 1 of the *Book of the Law*.

Thus is this a card of renewal in divination. The fishhook searches the depths and pulls out change. It is a card of letting go, as the water of consciousness is let go into the cosmic washing machine, poured over the body of Nuit. This indicates letting the light shine through the window of heh: Insight, inspiration, new ideas, new sight. It is meditation, but also the results of meditation: Bettering oneself which raises one's energy and attracts people of the same frequency energy. Like Aquarius, this card attracts progress, hope, and new clarity, within the self or the collective.

THE MOON

Every symbol and attribution of the Moon is connected to the subconsciousness below that creates a link to the superconscious above. When following the order of the major arcana, this is the last major trial of the soul before it begins fusion with The All. When looked at in the order of the Tree of Life, this card is one of the first major thresholds of reconciliation with our wild nature and nerve force working secretly in the backstage of conscious reality. The Star was the fishhook that penetrated the subconscious waters. The Moon reveals what is hidden in the deep. It is all of our fears; personally but also existentially. It is the hunt of the subconscious mind, Diana the huntress. It is the dark night of the soul. It is also the illusion of lack and the illusion of unworthiness amidst an influx of natural influences, percolating sinisterly as the nervous system.

The Hebrew letter attributed to the Moon is *qoph*, "back of the head," which is where the cerebellum and medulla oblongata are located, an anatomical featured shared with many lower species. This part of the brain is heavily connected to the subconscious and is said to stay awake during sleep. It follows that sleep is the function attributed to the letter qoph in the *Sepher Yetzirah*. Sleep is symbolized on the Thoth card as waves, sleep patterns, or as Crowley puts it, "graphs of abomination."[99] Certain mystical experiences will guarantee a new appreciation for sleep and its mysteries. The *Mandukya Upanishad* profoundly teaches how deep, dreamless sleep is closer to our true nature than waking or dreaming. This is because there is no subject-object relationship, pure "zero." We already know from the previous cards how important 0 is in our mystical ascent and the Thoth deck. While qoph is the back of the head, the following letter, *resh*, is the front. Qoph is thus the unconscious mind.

---

99. Crowley, *Book of Thoth*, 112.

The Moon

No other sign is more familiar with the unconscious than watery, mutable Pisces, attributed to the Moon. This is the last astrological sign. Pisces is the most psychic of signs, being the most predisposed to mystical thought and transcendental experience. Their abilities lie in the subjective youniverse to understand the objective universe. This is an ability experienced during the dying process. Pisces governs the last house, the house of sorrows, considered in traditional astrology as the last chapter of life and the threshold of death. This may be one reason why Anubis is depicted on the Thoth tarot card. Jupiter and Neptune rule Pisces. Jupiter is the Wheel of Fortune, the planet of expansion. It expands Pisces awareness beyond itself psychically by bleeding out the waking, localized awareness (the space between the ears) into transpersonal consciousness and even beyond that. It also expands Pisces evolutionarily, which will be discussed later. Neptune is the Hanged Man, the surrender of self that allows for the transcendence of the small self which is both the terror and beauty of the Moon card. Pisces is the fish, another link to the previous card's fishhook. The glyph of Pisces represents the sea. This is the sea of the collective unconscious, or "objective psychoid" explored by Carl Jung. It is the same sea flowing out of the High Priestess. The Moon accesses this sea but through a dark threshold.

The subconscious nature of the Moon is also concerned with the personal and psychological level above the body. The Moon reveals to us that our deepest fears are in fact our hidden strategies: Our malfunctions are really our functions. In a therapeutic sense, this is identifying behavior patterns that manifest recurring results. Working professionally in healing and self-development has taught me that everything in someone's life is created for a reason. Ron Kurtz, therapist and founder of the Hakomi institute, uses the amazing example of grunion, which has symbolic as well as practical relevance to the eighteenth arcanum. Grunion are fish that lay their eggs on the beach during high tide so that the eggs will be undisturbed until the next high tide, a strategy the species developed unconsciously through its evolution in reaction to the Moon. How many unconscious strategies do you think have been developing in the human race to get to where we are now? And how many subconscious personal strategies have you developed?

The Moon card illustrates 3.7 billion years of subconscious development of life strategy, starting with the earliest microbes in the sea. This broad scope of maturing consciousness, from the depths of the waters through the various kingdoms, into the human species, is symbolized as a path in the Rider-Waite-Smith and other tarot decks.

All of these qualities are reflected in the path of qoph, path twenty-nine: The desiring nature of Netzach descends through the sign of Pisces onto the physical world of Malkuth. Remember that Netzach is motility, which is the ability of an organism to move by itself. It's almost as if the artistic desire of Venus, through the powers of the subconscious Pisces, beckoned matter into moving independently. Netzach is also called "eternity" and is a sephirah of continuation. The doctrine here is that through a subconscious influence (Pisces) on the body (Malkuth), continuation (Netzach) of the self, or human race, is ensured. This path illustrates the mysteries of the tides and the lunacy attributed to the Moon. But this is only lunacy in some cases. The madness of the Moon includes the psychosomatic strategies we have learned over 3.7 billion years. The threshold of the Moon is a reconciliation of all these strategies. It is the karma of the human race. It is the nerve of consciousness to continue its flow and spill into the complex form that is human. Note that this is the first path of ascent that leads to the pillar of mercy. This pillar began with the Fool. The madness of the Fool and madness of the Moon share in the cosmic joke of creation which is the theme and secret to the pillar of mercy. What are you most guilty about? What has embarrassed you the most? Can you see that all of those events were an automatic reaction based on subconscious strategies that are billions of years old? It's all part of the lunacy of the Moon and the divine madness of the Fool.

The Moon as a general symbol is seen more on the Tree of Life than any other astrological entity. It is both a path, a sephirah and a tarot card, independent of its path. This reveals the importance of the subconscious in the achievement of the great work. Remember that the adept in the Chariot card meditates on the Moon. The versatility of this symbol is the neuroplasticity that makes magick and intention work. It is the quality of our psyche that is flexible.

The Priestess, attributed to the astrological Moon, is a higher form of this card but in some ways occupies the same psychological space. She is the divine virgin unconscious represented by Diana and Artemis reflecting the light of consciousness. She is a threshold from consciousness of self into consciousness of Self across the abyss. It is through her subconsciousness we connect to the Divine. Such is a path of advancement.

The Moon card is the reverse. It is a path of devolution and psychic history. However, going backward far enough will lead to the same mystical unity. The moon is not so much transcendence, but immanence. Divinity is manifested in matter through the lower, waning moon, in the eighteenth arcanum. Here is the threshold of the body and its subconscious programs of automation. The Moon card is the subconscious that keeps us breathing, and our heart beating, in the same way as the back of the head runs our sleep simulations. It is what keeps our very cells alive. It follows that the mode of consciousness attributed to qoph is "corporeal intelligence."

The Moon card is thus a threshold between a normal sense of self and a transcendental experience but through a unique method: The identification with life patterns pulsing through the body that are very, very old. In this sense, we go into the darkness of our personal subconscious but even more so the collective unconscious of the human species.

In the Thoth deck, the Egyptian Kephera bears the sun through the threshold of midnight, the darkest hour. Crowley says that this moon is "poisoned darkness which is the condition of the rebirth of light."[100] Consider this in relationship to the hanged man and general idea of redemption through spirit descending into desire and via our DNA. Mystically, this is a surrender to the cosmic forces influencing the terrestrial and biological patterns of our human experience.

---

100. Crowley, *Book of Thoth*, 112.

In divination, this is a threshold we fear. It is going into the unknown with pure trust and no logic. The Piscean influence gives us intuition and psychic awareness. The Hebrew qoph suggests matters of the subconscious level, or things unknown. "Corporeal intelligence" and "sleep" indicate processes in the body outside the light of the conscious mind. Now is a good time to move forward but cautiously. It is easy to get led astray by fantasy, or frightened into hysteria by illusion.

THE SUN

The Moon is the epitome of the subconscious while the Sun is the epitome of the conscious. This is the liberation of the big mind through the small mind, which is ultimately divine creativity. This is the creative edge of the life force, which we experience as the "flow state." The Sun card can be thought of as illustrating the monad of the tetractys realized in our own minds. This is cosmic liberation realized in personal liberation, where the point (literally the monad and figuratively the purpose) of the tarot is realized within us.

The Sun card is attributed to the Hebrew letter *resh*, "head." Esoterically, this is the frontal cortex symbolizes consciousness, as opposed to the back of the head (qoph) in the previous card. Resh refers generally to the human brain, the self, as a reflection of the Self. This is expressed in many ways, such as the rose cross, which will be explored later on.

Both the card's numerology and its path express its essential theme: The function of the localization of consciousness (the space between your ears), especially in interpreting the world. The number of the Sun, nineteen, reduces to ten, the Wheel of Fortune, and one, the Magus. The Magus is the mind itself which created the universe through naming. Consider Michelangelo's depiction of God as a brain in the creation of Adam. Consciousness holds the capacity to name things and create the world, as seen in the Magus and as Adam in Genesis. This capacity is also suggested in the path of resh, which brings language and thought (Hod) upon the foundation (Yesod) of the world. In this sense, the world is revealed by the light of the sun, which is the thought-capacity of Hod. When light is shed on the world, we see the differences between all its shapes and colors. The mind of Hod and subconscious of Yesod interpret the differences.

Resh refers literally to the point in the brain called the pineal gland. As energy rises through the chakras, it can eventually reach this region of the brain, activating what mystics call the third eye. This brings the aspirant to new levels of spiritual illumination. There is actually a channel of energy running up the spine that you can physically feel. Put two fingers of one hand on your perineum and two fingers of the other hand on top of the head.

Breathe, relax, and focus on the central channel. What do you experience? When I discovered this, I called it my antennae. It wasn't until later I heard it was called the Hara line.

Aside from its mystical implications, the Hebrew letter resh symbolizes the organizing body of any system. Think of the way the brain organizes the body through afferent and efferent signals. The esoteric significance of the glyph of the Sun is infinite space contracting itself into a point. From a macrocosmic scale, this was the birth of the monad of Pythagoras, or the contraction of infinite divinity into a point, Kether, called the *tzimtzum* (contraction) in Lurianic Kabbalah. On the human psychological scale, this is the ego, our gravitational center, what we call "I." In the same way, the physical sun is the gravitational center of the solar system, and also, what elucidates it. The light itself is a symbol of local consciousness.

The idea of a gravitational and illuminating center is reflected in the mode of consciousness attributed to resh, "collective intelligence." It is the Sun's ability to collect cosmic material, through its gravity, that ultimately orchestrated the solar system. It is the function of our ego that collects our mind-body system to organize us as a "self."

The Sun is exalted in Aries, the sign of self-assertion. The Sun rules Leo, a sign often associated with ego, but also esoterically, with the kundalini and its path to the brain.

It is important that this gravitational center, of the self or the solar system, stays at the appropriate balance of pulling in and expanding out energy, otherwise the system revolving around it will not sustain. This is why the double meaning attributed to resh is fertility and sterility, two extremes that can be caused by the sun's light and heat.

These two extremes are mirrored in the twin-deity of the Sun, the main character in Crowley's theology, Heru-Ra-Ha. Heru-Ra-Ha comes in two forms. The first is Hoor-Pa-Kraat/Harpocrates. He is the passive nature. Harpocrates was the Greek god of silence. He is represented as a baby with his finger to his lips, comparable to Kether. The second form is Ra-Hoor-Khuit/Horus, the active violent aspect. This is the hawk-headed god depicted in chapter 3 of the *Book of the Law*. Why twin suns? Lon Milo DuQuette brilliantly compares these two to the two forces keeping the Sun in balance: The active thermonuclear reactions expanding the Sun perfectly balanced by its gravity.[101] The personification of these two forces is seen in several of major arcana. Crowley says of these twins, "They are dancing in the light and yet they dwell upon the earth. They represent the next stage of mankind where the cause and result of freedom is new access to solar energy on earth."[102] Quite a solarpunk prediction.

Crowley notes that this is an advancement of the formula of the rose and cross. The rose and cross depict the microcosm, us, the youniverse, symbolized by the five-petaled rose, realizing itself in the macrocosm, the universe, symbolized by the cube. The rose cross is a design that reconciles humanity with divinity. We see this in practice in the Lesser Banishing Ritual of the Pentagram (4 pentagrams, with us in the center, with the "hexagram in the column") unites the 4 elements of the physical world (pentagrams) with the seven planets (hexagram). Also called the rose cross, it is a symbol of Christian mysticism stemming back as far as Mark the Evangelist. It was adopted by the Rosicrucians and later by the Hermetic Order of the Golden Dawn which elaborated the symbol. It is the back of the Thoth card.

The Sun card of the Thoth deck is meant to symbolize an advancement of this formula, which itself holds the philosophy of Thelema. Instead of a lower entity being linked

---

101. Lon Milo DuQuette, *Understanding Aleister Crowley's Thoth Tarot* (Red Wheel/Weiser, 2003), 149.

102. Crowley, *Book of Thoth*, 113–14.

to a higher entity, there is direct connection. Notice how the sun's rays extend directly into space, into Nuit, without any need of a cross. Here lies the doctrine of the new æon: Direct connection with spirit, with no need of an intermediary. The idea here is complete emancipation of the human race, the central theme of the card. Crowley mentions an established connection with celestial forces in the new æon.

This card shows a new relationship with the Sun that is also a new relationship with ourselves. Esoterically, this new relationship is formed by the philosopher's stone. The old method is as follows. As Paul Foster Case teaches "stone" in Hebrew is *ABN*, "Ahben," formed by the words AB, father, and BN, son. Now consider the verse "I am the way the truth and the life. No one comes to the Father except through me … Believe me when I say that I am in the father and the father is in me."[103] Here, Christ, who is the son of God and the Sun, shows us the path. It is through the Sun, the flesh, the brain, the microcosm, that we meet the father, the macrocosm.

Anatomically, this is the rising of the kundalini force to activate the pineal gland in the brain. This brings a state of spiritual illumination where the small mind, microcosm, is linked to the big mind, microcosm, in holographic fashion. This is the relationship of Tiphareth, the sun, pure self-consciousness, and Horus, with Kether, the primum mobile, Harpocrates. This exemplifies the Hermetic axiom "as above, so below." This is the alchemical process, the great work, the goal of all mystics.

In divination, the Sun is any form of creativity and liberation. God is a creative principle, and this card is the microcosm of this creative principle—our mind. Like the sun, this card is one of radiance, vitality, creativity, life. The card can tell of success, recovery from sickness, self-knowledge, candor, and shamelessness. It reveals truth in the manner of the sun. The egoic aspect of the Sun can also indicate vanity. It says "yes" in every way.

THE ÆON

Originally called Judgement, the penultimate arcanum represents the merging of the self with the true awareness of the Self and the "I am." It is the last possible moment of personal distinction from the whole before such distinction is dissolved in pure being. When looked at in the order of ascending the Tree of Life, this card is a stage of fiery aspiration that burns away unneeded elements in the seeker's life and reveals inner knowledge for further growth. The Æon card is Crowley's unique update and illustrates his mythology. The general theme of this card is that of a singularity, in a spiritual life or of a collective paradigm.

---

103. John 14:6–11.

The singularity in question is expressed by the Hebrew letter attributed to the Æon, *shin*, meaning "tooth" and "to devour." The teeth are used in the first stage of metabolism, as the path of shin is the first path that directs us to the metabolic pillar of the Tree of Life. The teeth break down one form so the energy can be transferred into another form, and such is the main theme of this card. The many boundaries of Malkuth are broken down by the fiery aspiration toward the knowledge in Hod. Shin is the third and last mother letter of fire. Crowley attributes both the elements fire and spirit to shin, as it is known by Qabalists as the holy letter. This may be due to its enumeration of 300, which is also the enumeration of the god name *Ruach Elohim*, "holy spirit."

In Acts 2, the holy spirit descends upon the apostles in the form of fiery tongues, which allows them to speak in tongues and understand all languages. This suggests a unification of mind. Recall our discussion on the Tower and the subject of revelation as both graceful

Chapter 2

ascent and terrible destruction. In the Tower, whose letter is peh, the mouth is the inverse: Language is destroyed, fractured like in the Tower of Babel. In the Æon, tooth, fire, and language are unified.

The general role of fire in symbolism is to unify through destruction. Aries does this through self-assertion and the war waged by the personal interest of the Emperor claiming his distinct existence from the whole. Leo does this through creativity in the Lust card, which is on one level a death of the self for the created art by surrendering to passion. Another level is the death that arises with the rising of the kundalini force represented by the lion serpent and Babalon. Finally, Sagittarius reveals a death through alchemical transmutation of opposites. God is described as a powerful, sometimes consuming fire by various mystical texts including the *Corpus Hermeticum* and the *Bhagavad Gita*. We might compare this fire and more specifically, its light, to the ain soph aur, the limitless light that contracted itself into the monad. This is the same light called LVX which descends down the Hanged Man in order to redeem the darkness. The destruction, creation, unification, and separation of this light is relativized through the essential function of the Æon card. The light becomes glory (Hod) descending upon the kingdom (Malkuth).

Modern astrologers attribute this card to Pluto, the planet of death and collective change. This is the planet that signifies major changes in the zeitgeist of the human race and major historical movements. Both the Æon card and its correlative in other decks (like "the Last Judgment") represent these major collective shifts.

The mode of consciousness attributed to shin is "perpetual intelligence." This implies the promised continuation of consciousness ensured by symbolic fire, the agent of our rebirth. In his *Pictorial Key to the Tarot*, Waite says, "let the card continue to depict, for those who can see no further, the Last Judgment and the resurrection in the natural body; but let those who have inward eyes look and discover therewith. They will understand it has been called truly in the past a card of eternal life."[104]

The path of shin draws thought (Hod) into matter (Malkuth). Reversed, it is the leaving behind of normal, materially focused consciousness (Malkuth) for the consciousness, language, and philosophy of the occult (Hod) which is illuminated by the passion and aspiration of the holy letter, and thus holy spirit, shin.

Shin is also the teeth of the serpent eating its own tail. This symbol, the ouroboros, represents the infinite universe in its "perpetual intelligence." Another interpretation is that it represents the chase of samsara, which was discussed under the Fortune card.

---

104. Waite, *Pictorial Key*, 151.

The Thoth deck depicts Lady Frieda Harris's beautifully abstract remix of the Stele of Revealing. This image was discovered by Crowley and his wife Rose in 1904. Rose was picking up on an entity and instructed Crowley that he would be channeling something soon. What he channeled was the *Book of the Law*, which illustrates three main characters of the Stele of Revealing. First is Nuit, who is voiced in chapter 1 of the *Book of the Law*. She is the starry sky of infinite space and infinite potential depicted in the Star card. Ultimately, she is love. Philosophically, she is the Qabalistic veil of nothingness, ain soph aur. In chapter 2, the voice of Hadit is heard. He is the solar disc. Philosophically, he is the infinitely small point, or rather, point of view, which is the inverse idea of Nuit, comparable to Kether and the Pythagorean monad. Their son is Horus, whose true name Crowley states to be Heru-Ra-Ha. This is the dual god depicted in the Sun card. I see his passive form as an aspect of Kether, and his active form as an aspect of Tiphareth. It should be noted that these are not Egyptian deities—they are Thelemic deities with Egyptian influence.

The three of them present a whole new paradigm. Crowley predicted the Æon of Horus to come with scientific advances, use of solar energy, and major developments in communication and transportation. This is also the Æon of the "child," where spiritual progress is attained freely by the seeker without need of any intermediary (as expressed in the previous card). I interpret the new Æon as a paradigm of radical self-love with an emphasis on personal sovereignty and connection to one's higher purpose, what Crowley calls the "true will."

In divination, this is the devouring (shin) of the old for the new. This is being swallowed up by the serpent of wisdom into a new way of thinking. This is illumination by the fire of shin and arrival at new knowledge in Hod. The card can indicate major changes on a collective scale. It is a good time to consider the relationship of your efforts to the changes being undergone by humanity as a whole. Ultimately, this is a card of a singularity. This is positive progress. It is a final decision in respect of the past, a new path toward the future, a renewal within you or the collective. There is no going back. "My left hand is empty, for I have crushed an universe; and nought remains."[105]

THE UNIVERSE

The last card, like the first card, reveals a mystery through a paradox. It is the punchline which resolves the whole buildup. The universe answers the deepest question asked by all philosophers, sages, and mystics: Who am I? Practically, it answers the question: What

---

105. Crowley, *Book of the Law*, 49.

would it take to feel complete? What would I need to feel whole? The answer to these questions is the voice asking them. There's no twist at the end of time. The end is the beginning. Time itself is only the play of eternity, and its play is the point, the figurative point of it all, and also the point at the top of the tetractys, which is Kether, where we find ourselves all the way down from Malkuth.

The Universe is the answer that points to our divinity, infinitude, completeness, and something else that cannot be put into words. The truth is not an idea. It is an experience. And it's not even an experience—it just is. All mysticism comes from experiences, or direct apprehension of the ineffable better communicated as "experienceless experiences." These non-experiences are translated into ideas, methods, philosophies, all sorts of psycho-spiritual and somatic recipes and ideas. From there, they are further complicated into myths, stories, and eventually religions and philosophies. It is important to note that most mysticism, which is at the core of every religion, leads to the same non-experience if it is truly mysticism.

There are many ways to achieve mystical experience. There are direct, knowledge-based methods, like that of the Vedanta. There are meditative and somatic methods like yoga. There are magickal methods such as ceremonial magic. And there are philosophical and contemplative methods, the aim of this present work.

The universe card illustrates the result of these methods, which is an ineffable experience. Paradoxically, this card represents the fully crystalized world as we know it, in full manifestation. This card occupies the last path of the Tree of Life, which takes consciousness from the subconscious or astral layer of Yesod, the foundation, and brings it into concrete matter, Malkuth. This is the final manifestation, so why does it deal with mystical experience?

The Universe is the same "no-thing-ness" as the Fool, but fully realized in matter. Similarly, Zen art often contained so much detail, but only to suggest its emptiness, the spaces in between the detail. No-thing is the essence of the universe, and definitely the youniverse. When the mind is fully quiet enough, the mystic destroys the duality of the subject-object relationship. This is known in yoga as samadhi, gnosis by the Greeks, Nirvana by the Buddhists. But the bodhisattva comes back from their enlightened state, back into the world. Similarly, Ramana Maharshi teaches that although the world doesn't exist, and the Brahman alone is the world (the central philosophy of Advaita Vedanta), Brahman *is* the world.

Qabalistically, this is the shekinah, the female God dwelling in matter, illustrated on the card. If the Fool was nothingness issuing into manifestation, the Universe is that manifestation, returning to nothingness. Cosmically, this might be compared to the theory of "heat death." This is the idea that eventually, through entropy, the Universe will exhaust all its energy throughout space, that there will be no heat left, but rather cold blackness. This sounds morbid, but to the mystic, whose concern is the subjective youniverse, this is a goal.

The Hebrew letter attributed to this card is tav, which is etymologically connected to the following ideas: Mark, cross, seal, ownership, join, bind, or signature. It is the seal of the work accomplished. The original way to write this letter was like a plus sign (+), a symbol of extension in four directions. What is being extended is the four letters of the Holy Tetragrammaton into the four fixed signs of the zodiac, representing the four terrestrial elements and four seasons. Crowley notes that this quarter-armed cross is the aleph (fool) stilled, frozen in crystalized matter, whereas aleph is spinning.

CHAPTER 2

Since the end begets the beginning, it would make sense that the two letters, aleph and tav, spell *ATh*, meaning "essence." The essence of our youniverse starts with the Fool and ends with the Universe. The cards in between illustrate for us the great work, the alchemical process. If you are alive, you are part of the great work. In the same way as consciousness continues to become more elaborate and sophisticated, we too learn and grow in our personal lives.

The planet associated with the Universe is Saturn. Saturn is the planet of time, and so this card's esoteric title is "Great One of the Night of Time." Saturn (attributed to Binah) was the Greek Kronos. As discussed previously, Kronos ate his children as they were born from Gaia to prevent being overthrown. Eventually, Zeus and Gaia tricked Kronos into eating a stone, causing him to regurgitate the other gods. Zeus and these other gods made up the planets below the abyss and the rest of the Tree of Life. The doctrine here is one of absorption (Saturn swallowing) into the whole. This is what Crowley means by "redintegration." This term is used to describe the signal given by the completed universe to return to its beginning.

Saturn, like the other planets, corresponds to two places on the Tree of Life: Path thirty-two, which leads to Malkuth and Binah. These two places mark the journey of the princess in Crowley's doctrine of the revolving tetragrammaton: The princess of the tarot symbolizes the final heh of the God name YHVH and also Malkuth. She meets her higher self, symbolized by the prince, the vav of tetragrammaton, and Tiphareth. This higher self is the "wandering prince" who kills the old king and wins the daughter in marriage. In this marriage, she becomes queen, which is the first heh of YHVH, and Binah. As queen, she awakens him as king, the yod, now the Knight of the court card system. Together, they procreate and the process repeats. The woman in the universe card of the Thoth deck depicts this princess, who, now fully manifest, can ascend spiritually by uniting with her higher self, the wandering prince, and continuing the process. She will become queen, Binah, and awaken Chokmah. In their divine love-making, they will return to 0 in orgasm (in this case, a metaphor for enlightenment, samadhi, the great work accomplished). The end begets the beginning. This four-character play is represented in the equal-armed cross version of the letter tav. The wandering prince, in this case, is the Fool! This is how both the major arcana and court card system reveal the infinite journey descending into incarnation, and ascending into spirit. This is the cosmic play.

The Universe card is attributed to both the planet Saturn and the element of earth. This was originally because of a supply issue with the esoteric tarot, but as you will see, there is an underlying secret. Let's start with the supply issue. In the *Sepher Yetzirah*, there are only three elements: Fire, water, and air. Spirit and earth were added later. As you've learned, the twenty-two major arcana attribution consists of twelve signs, seven planets, and the three original elements. When spirit and earth were added to the system, they were attributed to the cards whose attribution held the most similarity in quality and hierarchy. Spirit, for example was added to the Judgement card, since its first attribution, fire, is spiritually the highest element in the Hermetic tradition. Earth is added to the World card, since Saturn represents materialization and inertia and shares in the qualities of earth (coldness and dryness), while also being the closes major to earth on the Tree of Life. Crowley argues that this attribution of symbols follows the same logic to how the tip of the yod, which is attributed to Chokmah, starts in Kether. But there's something deeper going on: In all three cases, the associations allude to either the highest high (like the yod originating in Kether and Judgement's attribution to fire and spirit) or the lowest low (like the Universe being attributed to earth and Saturn). I will use a metaphor to explain the overpacking of correspondences. Because they are either the highest high or the lowest low, they can accrue more symbolism for a needed U-turn. You see, there is an occult U-turn of sorts at both the highest high and the lowest low of spiritual work to continue the journey. At the lowest low, we turn around through redintegration, where the fully crystallized manifestation, fully formed, recognizes itself in its formlessness. Conversely, at the highest high, at the peak of spiritual attainment, "Brahman *is* the world," we come back! This can be compared to the logos. There are techniques I give my students to explore this, but I can only teach them directly.

As the most manifest of the majors, this Universe expresses the fully functioning matrix, which includes the world of time, that is projected onto reality to create life as we know it. This matrix is the abstract net of boundaries, concepts, and edges that carve out reality into civilization. This is why the double meaning of *tav* is "dominion" and "slavery." They are the two possible extremes of working in the world of time (and other limitations) imposed on eternity. Colloquially speaking, this card represents "working the system." Esoterically speaking, it is about the view of cosmic order and how we work with it that enables our domination, or how we work against it, resulting in slavery. The invention of agriculture, for example, is a form of domination by working with natural law. It follows the patterns of the Sun to best support the species. This is why "administrative intelligence" is attributed to tav. This is the awareness of how the cosmos is administered, and the order of things. It is the goal of occultists to work with the natural order. Compare this to the philosophy of the Tao.

CHAPTER 2

As discussed in the Hanged Man, the number twenty-one reduces to three, the Empress. Reversed, it is twelve, the Hanged Man. This is the darkness that is redeemed through the Hanged Man, born out of the Empress. The redemption is not one of consequence, but one of realization and completion. The Hanged Man forgets he is complete and so he changes his perspective in order to advance. He surrenders himself as an appendage of God. The secret of the Universe card is that there is no other perspective besides God. The idea of advancement is a lie, because all is complete. This is the mutually arising relationships of all things in the Empress, which is ultimately love, fully manifest in the Universe card. The Empress is the first three dots of the tetractys, while the Universe is the full symbol. Waite says this card is "the perfection and end of the Cosmos, the secret which is within it, the rapture of the universe when it understands itself in God. It is further the state of the soul in the consciousness of Divine Vision, reflected from the self-knowing spirit."[106]

There are some symbols worth noting. First, the ellipse is a common symbol in this card. It represents "squaring the circle." The Greek philosophers believed that if they could make a square from the same area as a circle, they would find divinity due to the circle's infinite degrees symbolized as the Divine and the square with its four sides, a symbol of matter. The Venn diagram is the womb of life, which is Binah but also the meeting of matter and spirit. In the Universe card, there is a circle made of seventy-two squares. The squares represent the seventy-two angels of the *shemhamphorash*, a series of angels in Kabbalah known as the "divided name of God." Each decan of the zodiac is assigned two of these angels. The maiden represents the final letter of tetragrammaton, manipulating the active and passive forces of Heru-Ra-Ha. She stands on a snake. I interpret this as consciousness stepping on top of life and death, which is literally DNA but generally desire, and transcending it by integrating it. In this sense, the redintegration is integrating NChSh, the serpent of wisdom, as the messiah. This is the canceling out of sin and salvation in divine zero, the Fool.

The Fool was the Universe attempting to see itself through your eyes. The Universe is you seeing yourself through the eyes of the Universe. It is the hide and seek game of "I am that I am" spoken to Moses. It is the supreme self beholding the Self, and vice versa, infinitely. It is, as Swami Vivekananda so eloquently said, "Consciousness becoming aware of itself." It is knowing that there is only ever one true Self, in all its infinite multitudes. This is the reward of mysticism: Knowing what you are.

---

106. Waite, *Pictorial Key*, 156.

In divination, this is a total completion of something. It gets the seal of completion, tav. As the last card of the majors, it is the last stage of development. Like any conclusion, it can be slow and patient. Saturn brings about meanings of delay and inertia. But the reward is always worth it. There is total completion and synthesis of the particular within the whole. Opposites cancel out. All rests in the naked, boundless quintessence of pure being. Thus, the major arcana illustrate, with their eloquent symbolism and fluid associations, this mysterious quality of pure being. The court cards will do the same.

CHAPTER 3

THE COURT CARDS

The four court cards express pure being through the Holy Tetragrammaton, transliterated in this book as YHVH, "yod heh vav heh." *Tetragrammaton* is a Greek word meaning "four-letter name." This is the Hebrew name of God and the formula of creation. The transcendental nature of the name makes it unpronounceable (remember, the absolute is beyond all possibility of name or form). The word ADNI, *adonai*, is often used as a substitute.

The etymology of YHVH hints at its supremely mystical meaning. It is believed to be derived from the Hebrew word HYH, *hayah*, meaning "to be." This reflects the becoming and self-existent aspect of god. When Moses asks God for his name, God responds with "*Ehieh asher ehieh*" (I will be what I will be / I am that I am).[107] Another way we can interpret God's answer is "I am that which is." Here we arrive back at the "business of isness" reminiscent of other profound sayings in the history of mysticism. I call these the ontological

---
107. Exod. 3:13–15.

affirmations or mystical mic-drops and have listed several in chapter 1. These mystical mic-drops point out the ultimate reality as directly as possible with words. A paradox always arises from these ontological indicators. They point to that from which everything arises, which must include the pointer. This is the "meta" nature of mysticism: To be radically, cosmically, ontologically self-referential. It attempts to show that which *is*, including that which is doing the showing.

To reiterate, "to be" is the "is"-ness of the universe. This "is"-ness is the highest spiritual reality uncompromised by any idea, form, or word. It is not a "thing" (something done, made, different, or changeable, here or there, coming or going, with edges in time or space or other dimensions), yet all things arise in and through it.

However, "to be" does have a nature. The Buddhist would argue that this nature is emptiness. The Vedantic would argue that this nature is fullness. Are they really different? That would take a whole different book to discuss. Regardless, it will be helpful to think of both absolute emptiness and absolute fullness as a creative act, especially to understand the mysteries of YHVH and the court card system of tarot. In the case of emptiness, true emptiness will empty out its own emptiness. True nothingness, like the ain soph of Kabbalah, will void its own voidness and become everything. True fullness, like the *purnam* concept of Vedanta, will be so full it is everything by definition. In the same way, YHVH is past being and is thus everything. As a concession, one could say it is a creative act. Conceptualizing God as a creator presses God into time, which is easier for our brains to understand. This is actually one of the deeper functions of tarot. So, for our purposes, let's imagine YHVH as a creative act, singular and all-encompassing, where nothing exists apart from it (just like the Tree of Life and the major arcana we've explored).

More traditionally understood, each of the letters of YHVH corresponds to a specific world on a ladder of emanation (there is good evidence that Kabbalists and Platonists/Neoplatonists influenced each other, sharing in the idea of emanation). The yod represents the transcendent masculine and the archetypal world, known as Atziluth. The primal heh represents the immanent divine feminine, and the creative world, Briah. The vav represents the link between spirit and matter, the formative world, Yetzirah. The final heh represents the feminine aspect in matter, the world of action, Assiah. Each world emanates into the next one, getting denser, more material, and more detailed until we arrive at our current state, a finished product. This is the creative act.

THE COURT CARDS

BRIAH
Creative World
ה

ATZILUTH
Archetypal World
World of Emanon
י

YETZIRAH
Formative World
ו

ASSIAH
World of Action
ה

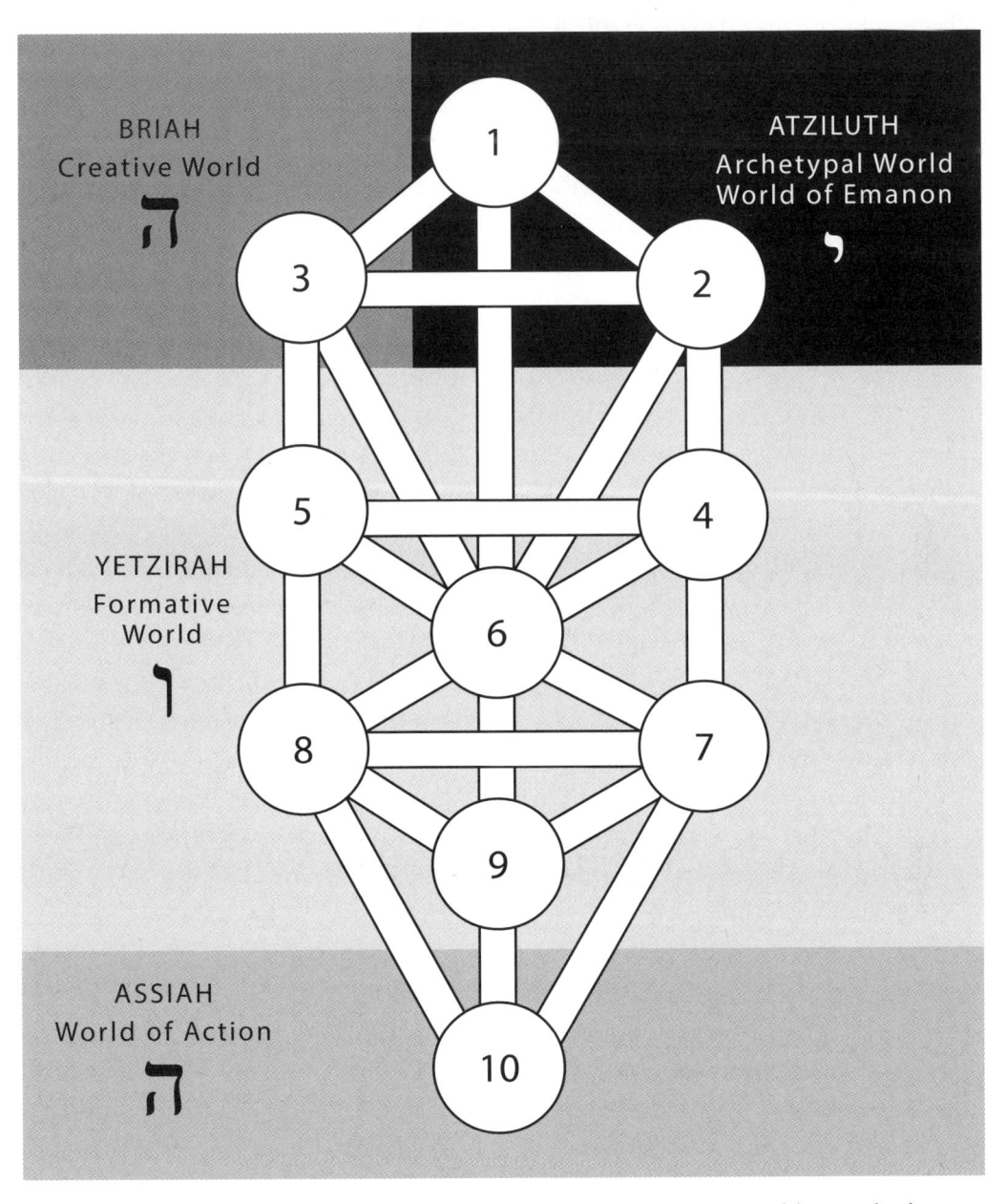

Holy Tetragrammaton on the Tree of Life with the Four Worlds Overlaid

YOUR CREATIVE ACT

To best understand this, let's do an exercise. Write out your recollection of something you created that you cared about. This could be something you manifested, a work of art, or any idea you brought into fruition. Write it in four stages. In stage one, describe the initial inspiration. In stage two, describe how the idea formed in your mind. In stage three, describe how you planned it out. In stage four, describe how you carried it into materialization.

I will share a personal example to illustrate these four ideas and how they connect to the four worlds. I was first inspired to write this book over six years ago. I didn't even think it was going to be a book. I simply felt called to write out my ideas about some of the major arcana cards to help teach some of my clients at the time. This was a sort of "Atziluth" stage, a sort of formless inspiration.[108] Years later, the idea of a book came to me. It wasn't written, but the motivation was there. This is Briah, the creative world. In Briah, there must be something to *create*. I wanted to *create* a book. I continued writing with the intention that it would one day be a book. After that, I stopped for another couple years. Then finally came Yetzirah. My amazing friend and colleague Ethony Dawn recommended I finish the book. Thanks to her support and inspiration, I finished the manuscript that was the blueprint of the book. This is Yetzirah. The last world is Assiah. If you're reading it now, it has been successfully published into manifestation, the world of action. This process shows how an inspiration emanates into an idea, which emanates into a blueprint, and finally, a physical action and result. We will explore this fourfold emanation deeper as we analyze the court cards. For now, it is important to note that this creative act is the nature of being in a qabalistic sense. Furthermore, everything follows it. We are all part of this creative act not just as created beings, but as creators, reflecting the divine creator. Let's now explore how Crowley taught this.

YHVH IN THE TAROT

As explained, YHVH represents a creative act starting with yod and ending with heh final. However, Crowley abandoned the idea that YHVH has an end. He interpreted it as a self-perpetuating process, where the final heh triggered a return to the first letter yod to start the process again. In this way, the end becomes the beginning. Crowley used the court card system of the tarot to express this profound doctrine. When you understand Crowley's use of the tetragrammaton and the court card system, you realize that there's no part of you

---

108. Atziluth is described as a nearness to God in the same way that "inspiration" has etymological connections to "spirit."

that is separate from the divine creative process (manifestation) and the reverse of that process (mysticism). Eventually it all leads back to an ecstatic 0—no one is left out.

It all starts with the Fool, 0. Remember how we explored the creation of the universe as a divine split or disproportion coming out of 0, nothingness. To review, Crowley expresses this as 0 = +1 - 1. In the general tarot, this is how the Magus comes out of the Fool. In Qabalah, this is how Kether (and the whole Tree of Life) comes out of the three veils of nothingness, ain soph. In Taoism, this is how the Te comes about from the Tao. In the Samkhya philosophy (the philosophy of Patanjali and the *Yoga Sutras*) this is the prakrti to the purusha. In Hinduism, this is the great mother, Kali, and Shiva. In the Vedanta, this is *saguna brahman*, "god with form," and *nirguna brahman*, "god without form." In the Thoth deck, the formless god is the Fool and expresses 0, while the formed god is Adjustment, harlequin, who expresses +1 - 1, which we covered previously. All of these express how some "thing" comes out of no "thing." Remember my definition of a "thing": Anything made, done, different, or changeable with edges in time or space. All these traditions show how form comes out of the formless, and this expresses a sequential creative process. This process shows how spirit becomes matter, and how the one is measured into the many.

The path of the court cards represents a two-way street. Downward, they move into manifestation. But upward is the path of mysticism: The reverse of this process is how matter realizes itself as spirit, the absolute, returning to 0.

Returning to 0 is the peak of mystical realization. At this level, there is no difference between the form and the formless, no difference between samsara and nirvana, no difference between feminine and masculine. This is the "sacred marriage" of many traditions. In the *Corpus Hermeticum*, this is expressed in a lecture to Asclepius by Hermes: "No maker can exist without something that comes to be. Each of the two is just what it is; therefore, one is not to be parted from the other <nor> from itself."[109] Ultimately, you cannot separate the maker from the made. This is nonduality. The direct experience of this might be considered *gnosis* (direct knowledge).

And yet, we experience duality. Though not an experience of the Real, duality is still a real experience. Gender is used in tarot and mysticism to express this arising experience of duality from unity. Before I continue, please note that I use the word "gender" in an archetypal and symbolic context used to express a greater mystery. It is not my intention to confine any sex, gender identity, or gender expression to these ideas. It is simply that mythological gender plays a huge part in the cultural matrix of the tarot and mysticism,

---

109. Copenhaver, *The Hermetica*, 56.

however antiquated or outmoded it may have become. A mystical understanding of these symbols on an ontological, philosophical scale transcends all sex, gender identity, or gender expression, though anyone may incorporate the ideas into the above.

Historically, the feminine is often attributed to an object observed while the masculine is attributed to the subject observing. In my earlier studies, I thought this was due to some lingering forms of outmoded misogyny related to the concept of the male gaze. Though this may be true, I realized later what this was really about. So many feminine deities are connected with form, duality, and immanence while so many masculine deities are connected with formlessness, unity, and transcendence. I believe the pattern can be explained by one of the deepest feminine mysteries: The biological female sex gives birth. The biological male's participation in the procreative process is much less visible and may have been invisible to ancient cultures. Historically, the female deity was then connected with matter and incarnation while the male deity's associations concerned the immaterial. This is an oversimplification and by no means a rule—we can choose to replace the associations of masculine and feminine with active and passive.

This dichotomy is pertinent to Aleister Crowley and the Thoth deck. Crowley conceived of three æons. The first was the Æon of Isis, a matriarchal society where female mysteries were at the forefront of spiritual work and the earth was worshiped. At this time, childbirth was not connected to male participation in the collective understanding. When the male participation was realized, the spiritual paradigm shifted from the goddess and earth to the god and the sky, and the social structure shifted from matriarchy to patriarchy. The formula of the dying god became the main one, and the sun became the main object of worship. The sun expressed the dying god with its rising and setting and seasonal changes. According to Crowley, the latest æon of Horus began in 1904, that of the child. In this æon, there should be balance.

The dichotomy of the divine feminine in matter has been associated with form and the divine masculine in spirit associated with the formless. This dips into a big theological conversation: Does god have form or is it formless? Sri Ramakrishna taught multiple times the difference between worshiping god with form and without form. He taught that the path of knowledge, *jñana*, like Vedanta, approached the Divine as formless. This path concerns direct knowledge of the ultimate reality without an intermediary to focus on. Conversely, the path of devotion, *bhakti*, worshiped god in some form. Sri Ramakrishna achieved enlightenment through both methods, but always urged devotion, claiming that it was much easier than the path of knowledge for our time.[110]

Against Ramakrishna's insistence, we will be exploring the formless, as that is the structure of tarot and Hermetic Qabalah. To understand the court card system and deepen your understanding of tarot in general, it is important to keep in mind that at its highest level, tarot expresses a balanced equation that can be reduced to 0. I explained it earlier, but this matter cannot be overlooked. No "thing"-ness represents the ultimate reality which, being infinitely all-encompassing, cannot be named and thus cannot be "thinged." It can only be realized directly (perhaps Ramakrishna would have considered tarot mysticism a path of knowledge). If I was a Zen master, I may be able to bring you there tactfully with a koan, a riddle that breaks down your logical mind. If I was a guru of the Vedanta, I may be able to bring you there with the *Upanishads* and divine instruction. However, the path that concerns us is tarot, and so we will approach it with concepts that cancel each other out.

Everything in the tarot, and the universe (according to Crowley), is balanced in one way or another to express this divine 0 represented by the Fool. As described earlier, every "thing" can be canceled out by its opposite "thing." Remember that things don't really exist except as "thinks." Something comes out of nothing by nothing separating itself into opposite "thinks." Those opposites are the first two letters of the tetragrammaton, yod and heh. This is the +1 and -1 coming from 0. These are the knights and the queens of the tarot. At this stage, they can either unite and return to 0 in ecstatic sexual union (a metaphor for enlightenment in general and perhaps samadhi in particular) or they can combine and produce a third thing. The former is mysticism. The latter is manifestation. If they choose the latter, they give birth to a prince and a princess. The prince is the vav of the tetragrammaton and the Princess is the heh final. The heh final and the princesses represent us. The princess is sleeping, like us, unawakened by divine origin. But don't worry, because this tetragrammaton is a two-way street.

The good news is we can reverse the process and return to 0 and realize the absolute. To understand how this is done, we must know the coterminous relationship of the tetragrammaton to the Tree of Life. The yod and knights are attributed to Chokmah. The heh and queens are attributed to Binah. The princes and vav are attributed to Tiphareth. Lastly, the heh final and princesses are attributed to Malkuth. As a princess, unawakened to our divinity, we are sleeping in Malkuth, the kingdom.

---

110. Swami Nikhilananda, trans., *The Gospel of Sri Ramakrishna: Abridged Edition*, (Ramakrishna-Vivekananda Center, 2015), 148.

CHAPTER 3

The sacred name, and the court cards, map out major points in our mystical or magickal ascent back to union with the absolute. We start in Malkuth as the princess. The prince represents our higher self. In Crowley's system of magick, this is known as the holy guardian angel (HGA) and is the first major goal. By magick, I mean high magick. Unlike low magick, in which achieves lower desires tangible results, high magick is a pursuit to know the absolute truth. Known as the great work, it can be compared to mysticism for our purposes. Attaining what is known as "knowledge and conversation with the holy guardian angel" is the union with our higher self. It is analogous to the princess uniting with the prince. This would signify the aspirant arriving in Tiphareth. The prince then sets the princess on the throne of the mother, meaning the aspirant reaches Binah on the Tree of Life. This requires the aspirant to "cross the abyss," a major threshold in the Tree of Life where the identity is totally destroyed. As the queen, from the position of Binah, the aspirant can "awaken the eld of the all-father." This means the entrance into the second sephirah, Chokmah, and becoming the knights of the tarot. The knight and queen have children and the process continues. However, to procreate, they get lost in sexual union, and cancel each other out. This returns them to 0 (compare this path of ascent to the yoga sutras of Patanjali).[111]

Notice how the sexual union that will start the next creative process is also the last step of the return. In both directions of the two-way street, the universe comes to know itself. To know its reality, it manifests. And to know its reality again, the manifestation returns back to its unmanifested origin: 0.

THE WANDERING PRINCE

So now we're back at 0, the Fool, and it's a good thing we are, because Crowley expresses this formula in another way. In the Thoth deck, the Fool represents the wandering prince in a divine play expressing the creation and continuation of the universe. Crowley describes a time when the succession of rule of a kingdom was not done through lineage, but through battle. In this age, the new king was always a stranger who conquered the old king and won his daughter in marriage, making her the new queen, and himself the new king. This process repeats. A new conquering stranger always comes.

On the Tree of Life, this new conquering stranger is the Fool, on path 11, which connects Kether to Chokmah. The nerve of this fool to disrupt itself from 0 into manifestation is symbolized by the knight. The knight that the Fool will become is the yod, connected to Chokmah, which is where the Fool's path leads. It is said by Kabbalists that the tip of the

---

111. Swami Satchidananda, *The Yoga Sutras of Patanjali* (Integral Yoga Publications, 2012).

yod begins in Kether though it sits in Chokmah. Notice how the aleph of the Fool and the yod of the knights occupy very similar esoteric real estate on the Tree of Life. In this way, both the knight and the Fool express the divine nothingness becoming something through divine impulse. That divine impulse hints at the logos, the intelligence, will, and shaping power of the universe. This logos is fully personified on the other side of the Tree of Life, directly opposite from the aleph and yod, in path 12, the Magus. The Magus, and the logos, both express the DJ of the cosmic turntable, whose record scratch disrupts 0 into a rhythm of manifestation.

Crowley's story of the strange "wandering prince" emphasizes a state of continuous change which ensures the stability of the universe. In the original teaching, the formula of the tetragrammaton was a creative act with a final result. In Crowley's reinterpretation, it is a creative act that repeats itself within itself.

Thus, the court card system of the Thoth deck explains the creation of all things in a repeating process, but also the path to return to the creator (and even the nothingness that precedes it). The creation of all things is manifestation. The return to the source is mysticism. Divination is a passive approach to understanding the former. Tarot mysticism is an active approach to the latter.

For now, I'm going to focus on how this sacred name expresses the creation of the world as the court cards personify it. This will illustrate the meaning of "to be" and the "is"-ness of the absolute. Recall what the *Corpus Hermeticum* told us earlier, that there is ultimately no difference between the maker and the made. This notion is quite a leap ahead of antiquated conceptions of God as an old white man who created the world. We are playing with mysticism. This approaches the Real.

Before I begin, I would like to refer to one more sacred text that echoes the *Corpus Hermeticum* and the radical mystical paradigm we are approaching: Gaudapada's *Mandukya Upanishad Karika*. In this lofty text, Gaudapada, pioneer of the Advaita Vedanta tradition, addresses many different philosophies and paradigms that attempt to reason out the existence of the world from God. He casually steps over the idea that God could have created the world as in Abrahamic religions. He casually steps over the idea that the world is a play of God as in aspects of Tantra or Shaivism. He doesn't rest until he arrives at his most radical claim: This world *is* the very nature of God, and that nature is nondual. Echoing this teaching, Shankara taught that the world was unreal, that Brahman alone exists, and that Brahman is the world. This can allude to three stages of spiritual progress. In the first stage, the seeker realizes they will not find the ultimate truth, or happiness, in the objects of their experiences (through money, love, accomplishment, et cetera). The second stage is realizing that the ultimate truth is consciousness. The third stage is realizing that this very consciousness *is* the world. Consciousness being the world is the main point here. It's the same being as YHVH. It's the same being as Hermetic literature propounds: The maker (consciousness) is recognized as the made (the world), and there is no difference. I believe this is one of the highest peaks of inquiry into truth, and I have found it in many traditions. In the system of Qabalistic tarot, this is how the knight, the yod, is made from the Fool, the divine 0. This is the logos, where the one of Plotinus emanates into the nous, the paradox of self-knowledge. From here, an infinite feedback loop is created to form the world as the Divine continues to objectify itself in its own awe. This feedback loop is expressed in our Tree of Life, the tetragrammaton just as it is the tetractys, the numbers, and other maps of reality. All of this is to point out that the Real, the universe, is the very nature of itself. "I am that I am."

THE KNIGHTS

Out of the nondual 0 comes the knight, the Hebrew yod, and the +1. One might connect this to the *primum mobile*, the "first mover." The knights are attributed to the sephirah Chokmah, "wisdom." Chokmah is attributed to the zodiac, and hints at the ever expansive and liberative nature of God and the universe. This is the divine masculine, the creative outpouring of possibility, and what Gaudapada might consider to be the very nature of the God. The knight represents the subtlest connection between the maker and made. The knights are on horseback. The horse is a symbol of the yod and the freedom, movement, and expansion of all these associations. The knights represent any moment you ever said, "What would happen if…" or "I wonder if…" or "Maybe I could…" These aren't definitive statements. They are more like questions that open possibilities. Phrases like these are what create our reality: Curiosity. Manifestation doesn't occur easily with attachment and desperation. Manifestation happens naturally when we choose with curiosity, openness, and excitement. Remember the exercise about you as a creative process? Remember that first inspiration? That's what the knights are all about. The knights embody the question that the universe/God is asking itself to become you.

In the tetractys, this is the first point reflecting on itself through one of the points in the second row. Macrocosmically, the knights and the yod are attributed to the first of the four Qabalistic worlds. Remember, the worlds, like the court cards, illustrate how something (the world) comes out of nothing (God). This first world is called *Atziluth*, the "archetypal world." Each court card is attributed to a part of the soul, the microcosm. Microcosmically, the knights are attributed to the *chiah* or "creative force," the will. The knights are attributed to the element of fire.

Characteristically, the knights initiate the process. They are impulsive, quick, and powerful but do not endure. Each of the knights approaches the element of their suit with extreme force, but unscrupulously. The Knight of Wands is daring but chaotic. The Knight of Cups is romantic but flaky. The Knight of Swords has the quickest mind but can be violent and discriminating. The Knight of Disks has great work ethic but not much else.

THE QUEENS

The equation of the absolute, 0, is always maintained. The moment the knight shows up on the scene as +1, the queen is there to receive him as -1. If the knights are the first mover, the queens are the relationship that mutually arises by the definition of movement. The queens are attributed to the primal heh and *Binah*, "understanding," on the Tree of Life. Binah is attributed to Saturn. Saturn is a planet of limitation and form that gives boundaries and borders (in the same way its rings border the planet or its distant orbit creates a border for the geocentric model of the universe) to make things what they are. In the same way, the queens give boundaries to the knights so that their dynamic energy does not run off and fizzle out into nothingness (from which they came). The queens are the divine feminine, who take the creative outpouring of the knights and harness it into form. The thrones of the queens symbolize the Hebrew letter heh and their forming power. If the knights start asking the question "what would happen if ... ," then the queens continue with "... Joe wrote a book on tarot mysticism?" My inspiration to create was the knight. When I decided to start writing a book, the queen came in. The prince and princess finished the process (more on them later). The queens represent the aspect of the universe/God to begin to reveal itself to itself following the knight's question.

The partnership of the queens to the knights allows for the first "I AM." This is the second row of the tetractys and can be attributed to the ouroboros devouring itself in infinite self-knowledge. It represents the subject-object relationship. The knight and the queen together, with their source of 0, make up the triad: Pure awareness dividing into the observer and the observed, the knower and the known. This can be compared to the *nous* of Plotinus. Macrocosmically, the queens represent the Qabalistic world of *Briah*, the creative world. Recall how the second row of the tetractys is the highest a creator god can reach, because by definition, a creator has something to create outside itself, and is dualistic. The queens represent this faculty of creation through all these attributions. Microcosmically, they are attributed to the *neshamah*, the intuition. The intuition works by seeing the whole picture. It brings in seemingly disparate information and sensations to come to an all-at-once realization or knowing. The disparate pieces of information are picked up below by the princess and the prince. The princess is sensation and the prince is thought. When both of these channels, with all of their data, flow into the queen, she can see the full picture and deliver it to the knight to take inspired action. The queens are attributed to water.

Characteristically, the queens are intuitive, nurturing, and steady, and they have the ability to hold a great deal of energy. They don't always start things, but they can definitely maintain them and implement them. The Queen of Wands harnesses her fiery nature to inspire others and lead. The Queen of Cups holds her watery intuition to heal and reflect others, often therapeutically. The Queen of Swords holds her airy sharp discernment to reveal the truth of people to themselves. The Queen of Disks harnesses her earthly prowess to maintain life and abundance in a balanced ecosystem.

THE PRINCES

When the +1 and the -1 combine, they can cancel each other out in mystical union, or create a third thing in manifestation. The latter brings us the prince. The prince is the first born from the union of the knight and the queen. If the queen is the relationship that mutually arises from the knight's movement, the princes represent the conceptualization of that relationship. They are the higher self, or holy guardian angel. They are attributed to Tiphareth on the Tree of Life. Tiphareth is attributed to the sun and all dying gods. The dance of the +1 and -1 allows for difference, which is experienced as change in time and space. At a very deep level, this is pure mind: The ability to project or interpret difference as a localization of consciousness. What's a localization of consciousness? It's the space between your ears, behind your eyes, doing all the differentiating. The ability of the mind's differentiation comes from a polarity instigated by the knight and queen. The princes are the intellectual image and vehicle of their parents, whose sacred marriage takes place in secret. The horses of the knights combine with the thrones of the queens to create the Chariots of the princes. They are the vav of tetragrammaton, the letter that symbolizes the link between the macrocosm and microcosm. The princes are the link between the big mind and the individual mind. If the knights symbolized my desire to create, and the queens symbolized that desire becoming a book, the princes symbolize the writing of that book and the completion of the manuscript. The princes take the divine impulse and curiosity of the knights, with the harnessing and shaping power of the queens, and, combining both, localize an intellectual image of their dance.

It can also be as existential as a soul. This is what creates individual selves. In the tetractys, this is the third row of three points reflecting the first two rows above, the moment when one can say "I am a self." Macrocosmically, the princes and the vav are attributed to the third Qabalistic world, *Yetzirah*, the world of formation. This is the blueprint of reality. Microcosmically, the princes are attributed to the *ruach*, "intellect." This should not be confused with the *nous* in Plotinus's system that is also frequently translated as "intellect." For our purposes here, I see the ruach as the rational mind with all its thoughts. One might connect the princes to what Plotinus calls the soul. The princes are attributed to air.

Characteristically, the princes represent an intellectual application of their element. Each one represents ego, mind, and individual consciousness operating through their element. The Prince of Wands gets an ego boost when fueled by fire. They are confident, entertaining, and cunning, but oftentimes boastful and arrogant. The Prince of Cups applies their mind to their feelings and emotions. This predisposes them to art, philosophy, and deep thinking. The Prince of Swords applies air to air, making them the smartest of all the court cards. However, with so much air, they can lose themselves in their own thoughts and have trouble bringing abstract ideas into practical application. The Prince of Disks, on the other hand, only applies their intelligence to practical matters. They are great at planning but often lack empathy or drive.

THE PRINCESSES

The newly combined princes (+1 and -1) find their fulfillment in matter through the princess. Just as the queen immediately follows the knight to keep balance in the universe, the princess follows the prince. The primordial marriage conceptualized by the prince directs the embodiment of the princess. In this way, matter follows mind. Can you really separate the two? The princesses are attributed to the final heh of the Holy Tetragrammaton, attributed to Malkuth on the Tree of Life. Malkuth is attributed to earth. This is where we are, in this moment, unless you're reading this in a dream. The princesses, and the heh final of tetragrammaton, represent matter. They symbolize this by standing on the earth (except the Princess of Wands, inspired by spirit). Unlike the rest of the family, they have no seat or vehicle besides the earth. This represents a sort of ignorance of their divine origin. It's us!

The princess is attributed to the last row of the tetractys, where the "self" of the prince finds itself enmeshed in circumstance through the princesses' reactive quality. This is the

Chapter 3

realm where difference is experienced and interpreted as a reality (hence the ignorance of the princesses). This can be compared to what Plotinus calls "nature." Qabalistically, this is Assiah, the world of action. To (crudely) paraphrase the entire Hermetic tradition, this is the below, where things are done, made, different, and changeable as opposed to above, which is eternal, singular, and unchanging. Cosmically, this is any type of embodiment. Crowley and the Golden Dawn specifically attribute the princesses (or pages/knaves in other decks) to four quarters of the earth and heavens in space as opposed to time like the other court cards.

Microcosmically, the princesses are attributed to the *nephesh*, the "animal soul." These are our less conscious desires and aversions, and may include aspects of our autonomic nervous system. They are not bad! They are useful. This includes things like hunger and sex drive. More subtly, it includes our somatic reactions to things, our feelings. All feelings can be found in the body and all feelings are useful. Some people bring consciousness (the prince) to their feelings (the princess) and process things to create more freedom. Other people ignore their feelings (do not follow their higher self) and are run by their lower natures. This is why Crowley references Éliphas Lévi to compare the princesses to elementals: They are divinely unconscious embodiments of their elements. Again, this doesn't make them bad. This makes them filled with elemental forces that direct their actions. If they turn to the prince, they can be elevated and become a queen, but they must choose awareness. This leads me to the most important point: Redintegration.

Redintegration is the moment where the climax of materialization signals a time of return to the source. It's the extreme bottom of the Tree of Life, and thus, the very top. In their divine unconsciousness, the princesses can choose to embrace their higher mind, the prince, in Tiphareth. In doing so, the prince sets them upon a throne in Binah, and they awaken the power of the knight in Chokmah, the logos, and realize the "purpose" of the universe.

In my opinion, the concept of redintegration is not just one of individual mystical ascent, but of collective ascent. It's happening right now, as you read this book. To explain this, I will have to continue the (quite meta) metaphor of writing this book. As you'll remember, the knight carried the creative inspiration (force) to the queen, who had the idea of writing a book (form). She delivered this order to the prince, who thought about it and then wrote a manuscript (intellectual image). The princess took that intellectual image and manifested it into the book you are physically reading now (material fulfillment). But, the process doesn't end there. You see, this book is doing things to you (hopefully good).

You are a participant. The information flowing into your mind will influence your creative processes, whether that's your tarot practice, or something else entirely. This book was my Malkuth, and it can be your Kether. You will (and probably already have) created a Malkuth to be someone else's Kether. This is because every creative process is the Tree of Life. Every creative process is YHVH. Creation is reality, the cause, result, and continuation, and there's not a spot where it is not. It is what it is. "I am that I am."

THE PERMUTATIONS AND PERSONALITIES OF GOD

The personalities of the court cards can be studied by their components. These include the element of their office, the element of their suit, their letter of the tetragrammaton, and their corresponding part of the soul. The combination of the office element and suit element will subdivide the four elements into sixteen natural manifestations, oftentimes weather patterns. These can be used to symbolize character traits. This is a great method if you have a good imagination or clairvoyance. These are expressed in the traditional Golden Dawn titles of the court cards that predated the Thoth deck. The Queen of Swords, for example, is the water aspect of air, conceptualized as lofty clouds which that also appear on the card.

The microcosmic attributions of the soul will also be important. We will go over them now. The knights and wands represent the *chiah*, "creative force," symbolized by the yod. The queens and cups represent the *neshamah*, or "intuition," represented by heh primal (the first heh). The princes and swords represent the *ruach*, the rational mind, symbolized by the vav. The princesses and disks represent the *nephesh*, the "animal soul," symbolized by the heh final (the last heh). In this way, the court cards show interactions of aspects of our soul.

The Queen of Swords, for example, holds the element of water as a queen (office), with the element of air from the suit of swords. One could say she is the "heh of vav." Considering the microcosm, she could be interpreted as the *neshamah* (intuition), acting upon the *ruach* (rational mind). This is very useful in understanding personalities, as most people push their awareness into specific layers of themselves and avoid others. In the case of the Queen of Swords, this is someone who values their intuition (water) and logic (air), but perhaps avoids physical action (earth) and may be uninspired (fire).

In this way, the components of the court cards make them permutations of the Holy Tetragrammaton and its correspondences. The court cards are thus ways that consciousness/God recombines itself to produce the many personalities of its divine play.

Chapter 3

ASTROLOGICAL, ALCHEMICAL, AND VEDIC ATTRIBUTIONS

In addition to the "tetragrammatic" correspondences in the previous section, court cards also have astrological, alchemical, and Vedic associations. To best understand this, we should begin with the three gunas of the Vedic tradition. In western mystery traditions, the four elements are used to understand the properties of nature, which stem from mystic philosophers as early as Parmenides. In eastern mystic traditions, we find three *gunas*, stemming from as far back as the Samkhya philosophy. They have been roughly translated to "properties" or "tendencies" to describe nature, or *prakrti*. To really understand the gunas, you will want to read the *Bhagavad Gita* (and use the Fortune card as a bookmark as it bears some relevant symbolism). The *Gita* states that "Material nature consists of three modes—goodness, passion, and ignorance. When the eternal living entity comes in contact with nature, O mighty-armed Arjuna, he becomes conditioned by these modes."[112] The gunas include *rajas*, *tamas*, and *sattvas*. I conceptualize them as stages of personal development. Tamasic characteristics are lazy or inactive. They relax the world. Rajasic characteristics are ambitious and filled with desire. They activate the world. Sattvic characteristics are spiritual and unattached. They pacify the world. These three gunas are attributed to three of the four offices of the tarot court.

It's first important to note the three alchemical elements, another analog to the guna: Sulfur, salt, and mercury. This system was introduced as early as 800 CE with the alchemist Jabir, and later popularized in the sixteenth century with Paracelsus.

For our purposes, we will study the Vedic and alchemical attributions together. Rajas and sulfur represent the active, passionate, expansive, and initiating qualities of the universe. They are attributed to the knights of the tarot. Tamas and salt represent the passive, still, contracting, and responsive qualities of the universe. They are attributed to the Queens. Sattva and mercury represent the mediating, airy, connected aspect of all things. These are attributed to the princes. The three gunas together make up prakrti, nature, attributed to the princesses. It's important to note that these associations do not perfectly mirror the original Samkhya philosophy, but were incorporated into the construction of the esoteric tarot with its synthesis with astrology.

Now that you understand the gunas, you will see why the astrological correspondences are the way they are. It's a little complicated but when paired with the gunas, the system is harmonious. To quickly review some astrology, the cosmos is divided into 360 degrees in thirty-six decans of ten degrees each. Each zodiac sign is given thirty degrees which includes

---
112. Prabhupada, *Bhagavad-Gita*, 534.

three decans. The knights, princes, and queens govern thirty degrees each of the zodiac. Unlike the zodiacal major arcana cards that are attributed to full signs of thirty degrees, the court cards (minus the princesses) are attributed to two decans of one sign and one decan of another, totaling in thirty degrees each, but overlaying two signs at once. They each begin at twenty degrees of one sign and end at nineteen degrees of another. Why can't the court cards just govern full signs like the major arcana? Why must it be complicated? Because people are complicated, and court cards represent people. They are not simple expressions of the elements like the aces or direct correlations to the signs like the majors. That would create blockier archetypes already covered. The court cards, and people, are complex combinations of multiple forces, multiple archetypes. Each person is a whirlpool of diverse influences and currents within the boundless ocean of consciousness. In the same way, each court card is a unique combination of zodiacal energy funneling into our solar system amidst boundless space. Remember, "when the eternal living entity comes in contact with nature, O mighty-armed Arjuna, he becomes conditioned by these modes."[113]

This complexity adds dynamism to the court cards personalities by adding in a very interesting ingredient: The shadow decan. The "shadow decan" is the first ten degrees associated with each of the court cards (minus the princesses). I first heard this term used by the amazing Mel Meleen and T. Susan Chang.[114] I see the "shadow decan" as an obstacle, shadow-side, or negative motivation for the card. I like to interpret them as aspects of the card's personality that they avoid, but secretly desire, or perhaps their biggest illusion of lack. This creates a more subtle dynamic between the signs they unite and a more cohesive understanding of the energy of the signs that create our experience. Furthermore, it follows the logic of Shankara that it is our ignorance that produces desire, which produces action (karma) and thus incarnation.

Now, let's explore how the court card's astrological correspondences balance their office and Vedic/alchemical correspondences. Remember that each sign of the zodiac has a mode: Cardinal, fixed, or mutable. In addition to the court cards, the modes of astrology are also attributed to these three Vedic/alchemical properties. The cardinal signs are rajasic/sulfuric. They stir things into action. The fixed signs are tamasic/salty. They fix the energy in one place. The mutable signs are sattvic/mercurial. They relax the energy and allow for change. To maintain a harmonious balance, each court card (minus the princesses) corresponds to two signs (two decans of one, one decan of another) with properties

---

113. Prabhupada, *Bhagavad-Gita*, 534.

114. Mel M. Meleen and T. Susan Chang, *Tarot Deciphered: Decoding Esoteric Symbolism* (Llewellyn Publications, 2021).

Chapter 3

different from the property attributed to their office. That way, each court card (again, minus the princesses) gets a dose of each of the three general qualities: Their first quality comes from their office and by extension their Vedic and alchemical attribution. The second quality comes from their first zodiacal attribution (twenty degrees of the zodiac). The third quality comes from their second zodiacal attribution (the other ten degrees of the zodiac, their shadow decan). This balances them. The Queen of Swords, for example, is considered tamasic/salty because she is a queen. To balance that, she rules the last decan of Virgo (a mutable and thus sattvic/mercurial sign) and the first two decans of Libra (a cardinal sign, thus rajasic/sulphuric). Through these correspondences, she has all three properties of the universe and is a balanced expression of nature (see the tables on page 186 and the wheel graphic on page 185 for a better understanding).

Now, let's discuss planetary rulerships. Each sign (thirty degrees of the whole 360) is ruled by a planet. Each decan of ten degrees is also ruled by its own planet. Thus, each court card except the princesses govern three decans, each ruled by a different planet. These decans are also attributed to the numbered minor arcana, minus the aces. In this way, the knights, queens, and princes each have three minor arcana cards to explain aspects of their personality.

To conclude, the zodiac is made of 360 degrees divided into twelve signs of thirty degrees each and thirty-six decans of ten degrees each. Each court card (minus the princess) governs three decans each: The last decan of one sign and the first two decans of another. Each decan is ruled by a different planet. The thirty-six decans each correspond to a small card (minus the four aces). Each court card thus corresponds to three small cards. The court cards' alchemical attribution is balanced by their zodiacal attributions.

What about the princesses? They are different; they are the prakrti. They govern space. Each princess is attributed to a quarter of the heavens surrounding the north celestial pole. Their quarter is centered on the fixed sign of their element, covering ninety degrees of the zodiac, totaling nine decans each. The princesses are known as the thrones of the aces because they embody their element. One could say they bring the conceptual world of Yetzirah and the invention of time into an experience of concrete matter in Assiah.

I strongly recommend studying the court cards in this way: Take each court card and lay them next two the minor arcana cards corresponding to their three decans. You can lay the princesses next to the three major arcana cards that correspond to their three corresponding signs.

The Court Cards

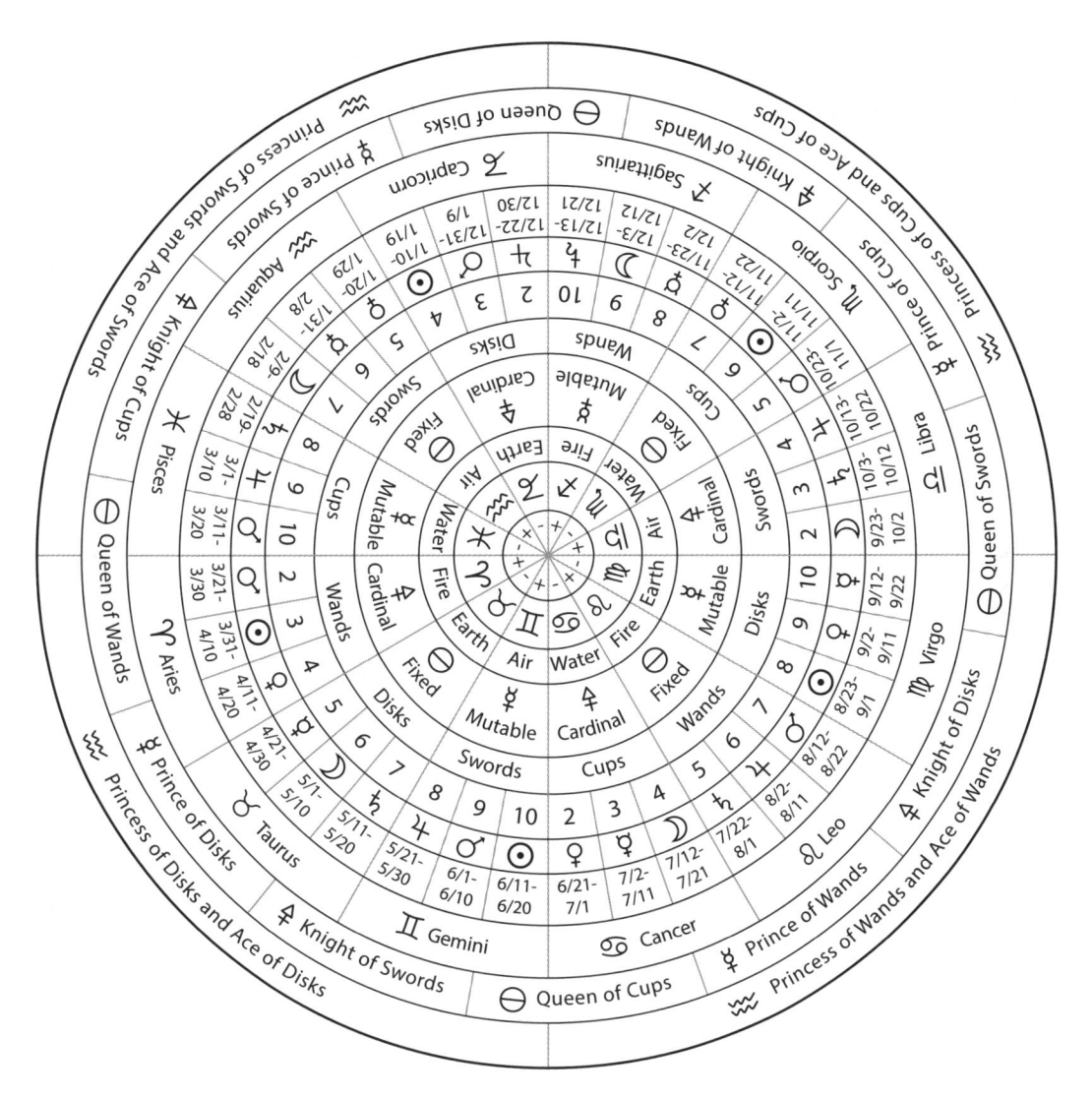

Zodiac Wheel with Full Tarot Deck Overlayed

In the tarot, the court cards tie the astrology together. They are associated with at least three minor arcana cards each, themselves combining the major arcana cards through their associations with planets and signs. Whereas mystical traditions such as Qabalah offer a map of our emanation as consciousness, astrology offers a map of life. Below is a graph detailing how the zodiac represents life, from entrance to exit, through the court cards and their associated major arcana and pip cards:

CHAPTER 3

ASTROLOGY GRAPH FOR COURT CARDS

COURT CARD	DECAN	SMALL CARD	MEANING	MAJOR ARCANUM	MEANING OF TRANSITION
Queen of Wands	Pisces 3	10 of Cups	Satiated from life, one returns to the formless	The Moon	
	Aries 1	2 of Wands	Destruction of the formless into form and incarnation	The Emperor	The individual self emerges into life from the threshold of death in the Moon
	Aries 2	3 of Wands	Development of character		
Prince of Disks	Aries 3	4 of Wands	Completion of the individual self		
	Taurus 1	5 of Disks	Learning to walk/finding stability	Hierophant	Learning and stabilizing in the new body/material matters that first emerged in the Emperor
	Taurus 2	6 of Disks	Success in stabilization/relationship with matter		
Knight of Swords	Taurus 3	7 of Disks	The fear of failure, wanting to progress		
	Gemini 1	8 of Swords	Interest in details and diversity of thought	The Lovers	The duality/multiplicity of the mind expanding after body is stabilized by the Hierophant

The Court Cards

COURT CARD	DECAN	SMALL CARD	MEANING	MAJOR ARCANUM	MEANING OF TRANSITION
	Gemini 2	9 of Swords	The mind overworking and unchecked		
Queen of Cups	Gemini 3	10 of Swords	The illusion of separation and the illusion of death		
	Cancer 1	2 of Cups	The reconciliation through love	The Chariot	Integration of parts introduced by the Lovers for holistic emanation of the Divine and personal integration
	Cancer 2	3 of Cups	The enjoyment of love and form		
Prince of Wands	Cancer 3	4 of Cups	The unease of luxury and too much comfort		
	Leo 1	5 of Wands	Disruption of comfort for more activity and self assertion	Strength	The joy of exercising the strength enabled through the previous integration in the Chariot
	Leo 2	6 of Wands	Victory and Popularity		

CHAPTER 3

COURT CARD	DECAN	SMALL CARD	MEANING	MAJOR ARCANUM	MEANING OF TRANSITION
Knight of Disks	Leo 3	7 of Wands	Adversity to self-assertion		
	Virgo 1	8 of Disks	Release of effort for natural growth	The Hermit	The life force of Leo is now focused through Virgo in a disciplined operation to create, a humble service in one's own work removed from opposition
	Virgo 2	9 of Disks	Gain from discipline and consistency		
Queen of Swords	Virgo 3	10 of Disks	Resulting wealth/ accumulation that now must be redistributed in balance		
	Libra 1	2 of Swords	Balance required to redistribute energy	Adjustment	The dynamic balance of universe through YHVH required to grow the seed of Virgo through karma
	Libra 2	3 of Swords	The loss following the gain to maintain balance		

The Court Cards

COURT CARD	DECAN	SMALL CARD	MEANING	MAJOR ARCANUM	MEANING OF TRANSITION
Prince of Cups	Libra 3	4 of Swords	The resulting compromise		
	Scorpio 1	5 of Cups	The experience of loss and the motivation for change	Death	Transformation resulting from Libra's dynamism
	Scorpio 2	6 of Cups	Letting go which allows one to receive, pleasure without attachment		
Knight of Wands	Scorpio 3	7 of Cups	Attachment to pleasure		
	Sagittarius 1	8 of Wands	The Logos in flight, accelerated movement free from attachment	Art	The transformation of Death becomes the alchemical journey of Art, free to recombine into a new substance
	Sagittarius 2	9 of Wands	Mastery and freedom through the balance, experience, and flexibility of the alchemical process		

CHAPTER 3

COURT CARD	DECAN	SMALL CARD	MEANING	MAJOR ARCANUM	MEANING OF TRANSITION
Queen of Disks	Sagittarius 3	10 of Wands	Oppression of prey in the natural world that results from the freedom of all species		
	Capricorn 1	2 of Disks	The circle of life and change which ensures stability	Devil	The sexual generative faculty of nature to continue life, enabled through Art's combination of the necessary ingredients
	Capricorn 2	3 of Disks	Nature's development of intelligent design		
Prince of Swords	Capricorn 3	4 of Disks	Attachment to familiar design/a structure that needs change		
	Aquarius 1	5 of Swords	Rebellion met with conflict, personal defeat from oneself (ego)	The Star	A glyph of the individual, born from the Devil's generative faculties on earth, yet no different than the pure space of consciousness/Nuit
	Aquarius 2	6 of Swords	Success of rebellion leading to progress		

COURT CARD	DECAN	SMALL CARD	MEANING	MAJOR ARCANUM	MEANING OF TRANSITION
Knight of Cups	Aquarius 3	7 of Swords	Progress weakening and effort waning		
	Pisces 1	8 of Cups	Lower motivation and letting go	The Moon	Anubis, the threshold between life and death
	Pisces 2	9 of Cups	The wish of this life granted, ready to return		

THE SIXTEEN COURT CARDS

The sixteen court cards are permutations of four aspects of absolute reality. These four creative stages help express the single creative act that alone transcends all, and is imminent in all. To understand this single act, it is divided into four general stages, or worlds in Qabalah. Each stage is further divided into four stages, the Holy Tetragrammaton. This analysis helps us look deeper into the creative process of the Divine and ourselves. After a thorough understanding of all sixteen sub-elements, they can be synthesized again back into the whole for mystical insight. These sixteen sub-elements are expressed through the court cards. To help learn these permutations, you can make correlations. The element of fire, the suit of wands, and the knights represents the first movement of a creative process. The element of water, the suit of cups, and the queens represent the relationship that arises by that movement. The element of air, the suit of swords, and the princes represent the concept, idea, or "self-hood" that arises from the relationship that was just established. Lastly, the element of earth, the suit of disks, and the princesses, represent the embodiment directed by and resulting from the sense of "self" that emerged previously.

You will learn each court card's macrocosmic and microcosmic meanings by way of analysis of its Qabalistic and elemental attributions as well as its connection to the Pythagorean tetractys. Following that, you will learn about its astrological attributions. Each section will integrate all the major ideas into divinatory meanings. This creates a typology where each unit (each court card) is a part exemplifying the dynamic balance of the whole in the same holographic nature as the Tree of Life and other mystical technologies introduced so far. Of course, one can use this information in divination, but the main purpose is to enjoy the whole in each part. What I mean by that is to see each court card as an expression of the eternal will driving the whole creative process of not just the tarot but all existence.

And all of this represents you. Of course, the court cards can represent other people in a divinatory sense, but we never meet anyone in life that doesn't reflect some aspect of ourselves. From a mystical perspective, there is nothing but you. Let's begin.

THE WANDS COURT

The first family is the suit of wands. They represent the Holy Tetragrammaton in the world of Atziluth, the archetypal world. This world is where everything in reality emanates from. It is the most subtle and difficult to grasp. It is the closest to ain soph, the primordial nothingness from which all arises. Nothingness is not nothing in the colloquial sense. It is a complete lack of a "thing." The four families ahead will illustrate for us the way all "things" come out of this one nothing. They illustrate how the universe is done, made, differentiated, changed, here and there, coming and going. They will express the movement of the absolute to create edges within the edgeless and measurement within the immeasurable to carve out our human experience. The process begins with the suit of wands and fire. Fire is transformative, creative, and destructive. It makes sense that fire is the closest element to the void, as it burns up form. As was described in the major arcana, the Thoth deck maintains a general philosophy that cosmic love is death. In true love, one sacrifices themselves by losing their sense of self in the vision of the beloved. In the same way, death allows the universe to keep moving in its cosmic lovemaking. According to Crowley, we have entered the new æon of Horus, one of fire. At the level of Atziluth, love and death are united in ecstasy.

To really understand this level, an aspirant must reach the third level of spiritual progress. The first level is the discovery that the physical world is, in some way, an illusion and not the ultimate truth. The second level is the discovery of that through which everything physical and mental is experienced. This is the higher reality (I use the word "consciousness" for convenience). The third level is discovering that the nature of this reality, or consciousness, is to reveal itself in what was first considered illusion in the first level. This three-level system is seen in the *Corpus Hermeticum*, Vedanta, and other traditions. There are methods to arrive at these states of consciousness I teach elsewhere, but further comment exceeds the scope of this present work. For now, it's important to understand that the nature of nothing is to become something, and our family of wands personifies this process. It starts with the Fool.

Knight of Wands

KNIGHT OF WANDS

Out of the Fool's divine folly issues the divinely unscrupulous Knight of Wands. This is the first death. He personifies the death of "no thing" (the Fool) into the earliest possible idea of "something." This "something" will be realized in the family of cups, mentally interpreted in the family of Swords, and embodied in the family of disks. The Knight of Wands is the yod of yod, fire of fire. Elementally, this could be interpreted as lightning. To understand the Knight of Wands, meditate on lightning's sudden but brief moment of elucidation. We might compare him to the lightning flash that comes out of ain soph on the Tree of Life.

Macrocosmically, he is the creative force, the chiah, of Atziluth, the archetypal world. As its pure force, he is almost purposeless, emanating into reality without the limitation of reason. He has barely any focus outside of pure becoming. He commits fully to the creation of everything, and in doing so, offers all his energy. After his moment, there is no energy left for a second chance. He is all in. In this way, he can be compared to the Sanskrit *purnam*, "fullness" of the Vedanta. Conversely, you could compare him to the *sunyam*, the doctrine of the void. In this sense, there is no part of him that is not fully involved, no piece of him separate from his one divine motion.

Microcosmically, he is the will of will itself, yod of yod. This is the subtle, almost invisible force that guides us all along. It's what continues reality. It is the ultimate characteristic of consciousness, what wakes us up in the morning, what continues us. Furthermore, it is that divine spark of creativity. This describes not just the creative process of the cosmos, but our individual selves. We constantly create our experiences, consciously or subconsciously. Whatever direction you are looking, there is an entire Tree of Life, made up of more trees, just as you are a Tree of Life in a larger tree.

On the tetractys, the Knight of Wands bridges the first row to the second row of points. This draws out the words "I am" from the primordial silence. The Knight of Wands is the primum mobile, the first step toward "something" coming out of "nothing." On the Tree of Life, he is Chokmah, the second sephirah, meaning "wisdom." This is the wisdom of the expanding universe, and the wisdom of your own consciousness expanding. It is the unbridled, supernal masculine force. The Chokmah has also been connected to the logos, the intelligence and subtle purpose or will behind reality.

The knight's explosive nature is echoed in his astrological attributions. He rules the last decan of Scorpio and the first two decans of Sagittarius. He draws the energy from the Death card to Art. This illustrates the death and reintegration of our recurring ontological question: How does some "thing" come out of no "thing"? This transition summarizes the main concern of tarot and mysticism that is appropriate for the first court card of such high rank. In the Knight of Wands lies the seed pattern of everything else to follow. We might say that the combination of the cards Art and Death yield the "art of death." In a way, this is what the tarot is. It calls into mind Plato's claim that philosophy is a practice of death. When you read Aleister Crowley, you soon become aware of how similar death is to love, and how both are movements of energy on the Tree of Life. When you truly love something, you offer yourself fully to it, and "die." The knight certainly gives himself fully. Conversely, all death and change in the universe is an expression of divine love, and the Knight of Wands is the first change arising out of the unchangeable, unitive monad of Kether.

The first two decans of Sagittarius represent the knight's free spirit. The first decan, ruled by Mercury, is the Eight of Wands, Swiftness. The second decan, ruled by the Moon, is the Nine of Wands, Strength. His main qualities of swiftness and strength make him a force to be reckoned with. They describe the swift strength of Chokmah in the suit of wands. His last decan of Scorpio is ruled by Venus. Scorpio, again, is the Death card, and Venus is the Empress, love. Here, there is another nod to the doctrine that love is death. The tarot card attributed to this decan is the Seven of Cups, Debauch, which represents a secret motivation. His greatest fear is realizing his pursuits were tied to lower cravings, and this is often possible. With the Seven of Cups representing his shadow decan, he loathes distraction. He wants to be all in. But one of the greatest mysteries of the Knight of Wands is that his entire pursuit of nothingness into something is one infinite ontological distraction. It's called the logos. Qabalistically, everything is downhill from here.

In a reading, the Knight of Wands represents someone totally free, kind, and genuine, but who leaves behind a path of chaos. They don't think before they act, which is both their blessing and their curse. They are often on the move, physically or internally, and value novelty and discovery. They are not always dependable, not because they are untrustworthy, but because they don't sit still. Like the unstoppable arrow of Sagittarius, they are fully in motion. Such is the glory of the yod, the apostrophe of God, the first letter of the sacred name that creates all. It is the sudden record scratch on the cosmic turntable (the Magus) that issues from the cosmic joke (the Fool). As chaotic and disorganized as they may be, they are generous and will give all they have.

QUEEN OF WANDS

The Knight of Wands does not get a second chance. He needs the Queen of Wands to ensure his Sagittarian arrow hits the target. This queen is the heh of yod, the water of fire. Elementally, this could be interpreted as the fire's fluidity, form, color, or light. To understand the Queen of Wands, meditate on fire's attractive and luminous nature.

Macrocosmically, she is the intuition of the archetypal world. She is the primordial shaping power of the universe. She is the ability of the universe to know where and how it needs to go to create, totally intuitively, without effort, but with great pleasure. When scientists talk about the mathematical improbability of the universe to create human life, she winks. She is the life of the universal party.

Microcosmically, she is the intuition of the creative force within us. She is the natural way that our will directs us, and the natural way that will is directed by a more subtle, cosmic volition. She harnesses the will of fire to maintain consistency in our life's progress. You can think of her steady flames as the energy body, constantly changing but maintaining a

Queen of Wands

general design through the tempering of her watery nature. Through fluidity and movement, the fire of life continues to burn.

On the tetractys, she is the second row of points. She gives the words "I am" to the voice of the Knight of Wands. She ensures his existence by taking his energy and putting it into form. The whole act is the glory of the universe which screams its existence in every vibration, in a friction of sexual and divine ecstasy. The Queen of Wands is the participation of everyone and everything, all possible forms expressing the formless. This is echoed in her home on the Tree of Life, Binah, the supernal mother, bringing the formless into form. For all these reasons, her functions are similar to that of Babalon in the Lust card.

Coming into form is a serious matter, and this weight is reflected in her astrological attributions. She governs the last decan of Pisces (the Moon) and the first two decans of Aries (the Emperor). This is the end and beginning of the zodiac, marking the birth of the soul taking form, the entrance to incarnation. This starts the whole process of time. The first decan of Aries is ruled by Mars, the Two of Wands, titled Dominion. The second decan is ruled by the Sun, the Three of Wands, Virtue. Dominion and Virtue describe her process: She receives the logos from the Knight of Wands and transmits it into the first form. Her action takes a lot of control, and the control she needs is supported by the Mars rulership of her first two decans. Mars's aggressive nature is used to direct this energy by creating friction and will. It is the friction and will that shape the attractions and aversions of incarnated beings. Compare this to the Vedic doctrine of karma and the Hermetic doctrine of incarnation and necessity, which involves daimons. The general idea is that all incarnation results from an illusion of lack that spurs attraction and aversion. The gear behind this process is Mars, the god of war who destroys nothingness to create something at the first decan, and does the reverse at the last decan. In doing all this, the Queen of Wands exemplifies the highest character, virtue, the second decan of Mars, the glory of birth. Virtue is good character, connected to the Sun in Aries. The life-giving Sun brings out the character of Aries, the Emperor, the arcanum of the established self.

Her shadow decan is the last decan of Pisces, ruled by Mars, the Ten of Cups. This represents both her fear and unconscious interest in the card's title, Satiety. She both desires and fears completeness and satisfaction. To adjust for this, she is constantly creating, starting, and maintaining a vibrant and active dance of energy. She represents sex—not just in the literal sense but the sex of existence, the orgasm of the universe. The symbols on the Thoth card all allude to the divine feminine and her sexual and magical prowess.

In a reading, she represents attraction, passion, creativity—and most importantly—the ability to harness it. She steadies her flames so they can be experienced. As the first forming agent of the universe, she is God's intrigue in itself, a quality we all share. She is an intuitive flow (neshamah) of creation (chiah), especially in a stabilized way that creates something out of nothing (Aries). Ill-dignified, she is the darker aspect of the diversity of form: Vanity and jealousy.

PRINCE OF WANDS

With the divine abandon of the knight and the subtlest forming power of the queen, the Prince of Wands has a lot to live up to. On a cosmic scale, the Knight of Wands might be compared to the big bang, and the Queen of Wands might have been the first mysterious form that followed (maybe hydrogen and helium?). But my ability to bring words together to conceptualize all of that, and your ability to read and interpret, is the Prince of Wands.

Prince of Wands

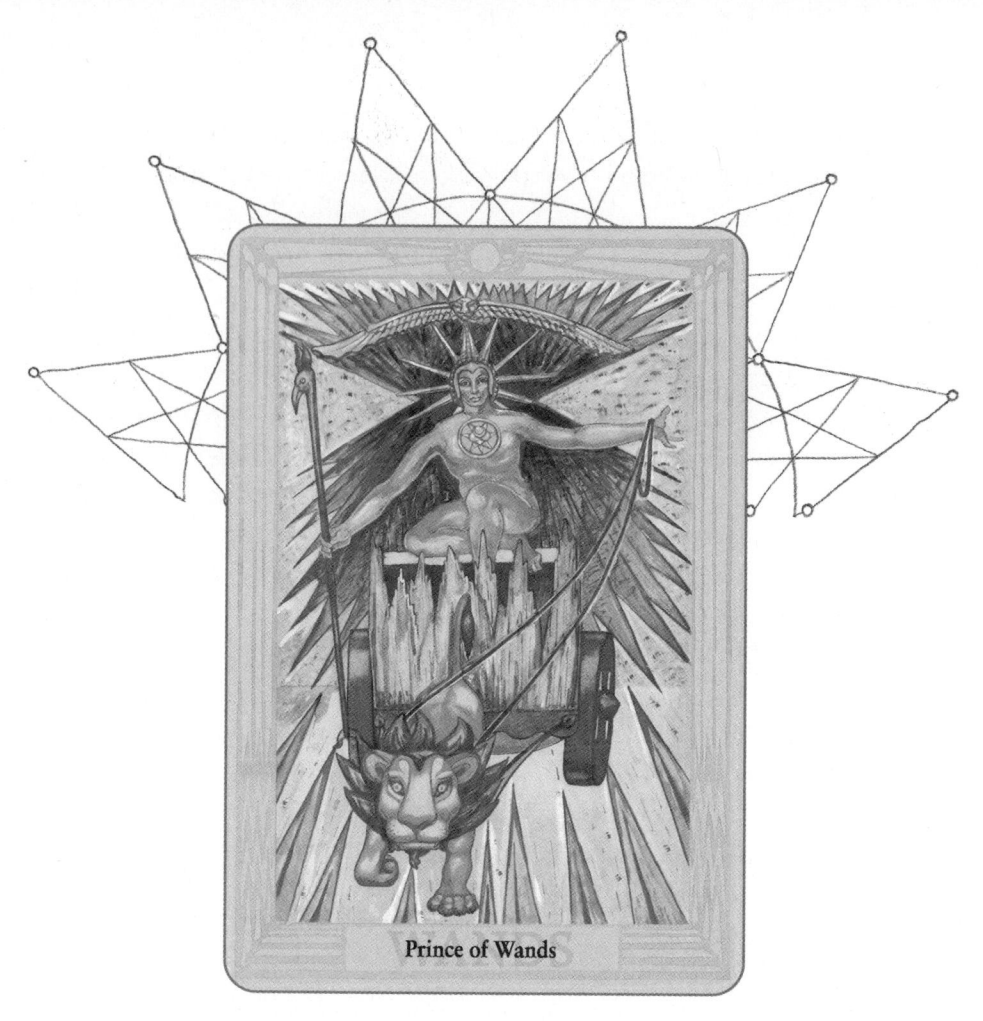

The Prince of Wands is the vav of yod, the air of fire, the intellectual application of creativity. When air and fire meet, there is expansion and volatilization.

Macrocosmically, the prince represents the intellect of the archetypal world: The way reality enacts many inspired designs and ideas of itself. As the vav, he links the ideal reality above the abyss with the actual reality below it. The yod and heh primal of the tetragrammaton are associated with Chokmah and Binah, both situated above the abyss. Vav is the first letter of the tetragrammaton below the abyss, corresponding with Tiphareth. Because of this, every prince expresses the formula of the dying god. Tiphareth, as you will recall, is the heart of the tree, the place where spirit meets matter. Here, the spirit dies to embody below and body dies to return to spirit above. A higher interpretation of this is consciousness enters into the realm of life and death below from the nonduality above (refer to the earlier section on astrology in chapter 1). The realm of "life and death," "here and there," "coming and going" is the realm of the mind. The Prince of Wands is the ruach of the world of fire. He receives the intuition of fire from the queen, and divides it into separate ideas...mostly for fun.

Microcosmically, he is the intellect of the creative force. When we are connected to our true will, this is how inspiration seamlessly flows into our minds and then passes into action. This is getting lost in creativity.

On the tetractys, the Prince of Wands hangs out in the third row. If the queen is the forming power, the prince is the conceptualizing power. The queen delivers the words "I am" to the prince, who answers "a self." The essential point is that the Prince of Wands represents the egoic gravitational center resulting in between the extremes of his parents. He becomes an organizing principle for the creative fervor of fire. He is the intellectual and abstract emanation of the unbridled creative force set out before him. He is an ego to be reckoned with, especially with his astrological attributions.

The division of the queen's intuitive fiery prowess in the prince's fiery "self" is done through two main processes: Creativity and pride. No better astrological sign expresses these two than Leo, which the Prince of Wands connects from Cancer. Leo is the proud and creative lion, attributed to the Lust card, a card of surrendering to the sexual-magickal-creative act. Cancer is the Chariot, which represents the vehicle that literally carries sexual-magickal-creative act (the holy grail or cup of Babalon). In the same way, our prince here carries his parents' creative act as a sort of avatar.

An avatar needs an audience to get his message out. It follows that he governs two decans of Leo. The first decan is ruled by Mars, the Five of Wands, Strife. This offers our prince the courage to differentiate himself, even if it means opposing his surroundings. Esoterically, this is his ability to differentiate himself from boundless consciousness to become an ego. The next decan of Leo is ruled by Jupiter, the Six of Wands, Victory. Mystically, this is the victory of a universe becoming a localized self in a profound (and literally hot) creative process. The prince is thus the strife and victory in the development of a human mind.

His shadow decan is the last decan of Cancer, ruled by the Moon. This corresponds to the Four of Cups, Luxury. This card represents mixed feelings of comfort, boredom, and uneasiness. The Prince of Wands is a showman. He will say or do anything to keep those bored feelings away and yet secretly may wish for them. A mystic might argue that the universe was comfortable, bored, and somewhat uneasy so it became *you*, localizing in your mind—this is the prince's pride.

CHAPTER 3

In a reading, the Prince of Wands represents someone with great courage and wit. They use their cleverness (air) in creative pursuits (fire). Oftentimes, they make great speakers, entertainers, actors, or performers. They are great communicators. They are unafraid to disrupt the status quo and make a scene (Five of Wands) but make great leaders (Six of Wands). Ill-dignified, they become mean, judgmental, bombastic, argumentative, and angry. They start trouble out of boredom.

PRINCESS OF WANDS

The initial force of the knight, the stunning shaping power of the queen, and the proud mind of the prince all find themselves embodied in our Princess of Wands. She is the energy running through your body right now. She is the heh final of yod, the earth of fire. To understand her elementally, meditate on the flammability of the earth's fuels. Notice that this combination suggests a *potential* fire. The Princess of Wands is the potential of the heh final to realize its source as and in the yod. She is literally floating into the yod in the Thoth deck. This all represents the divine urges (for many unconscious) of all humans to reconnect with their ultimate reality. This largely untapped inner thirst manifests in so many ways and is only ever truly quenched by realizing the absolute. Tarot is just another tool affirming the path ahead like all other mystical traditions.

Macrocosmically, she is the conclusion of the archetypal world. In Atziluth, all is united, all says yes. Here, the intention of the universe arises in the locus of its absence (ain soph, the void). This contradiction is expressed in the radical ontological affirmations expressed earlier, like "I will be what I will be." The key concept here is affirmation. This isn't personal affirmation like "I am strong" or "I am capable." It is a radical, ontological affirmation—"I exist." It is an ecstatic state of absolute certainty. It is a cosmic orgasm. No court card shouts this louder than the Princess of Wands, who takes on, and confirms, the unbridled eruption of becoming from her unstoppable family.

Microcosmically, she is the animal soul that the universe's creative force fuels. The animal soul includes your autonomic nervous system and somatic responses to stimuli, including your feelings! Put another way, feelings are simply subtle sensations in the body that motivate you to take action, the lower passions so often mentioned by philosophers. Through the Princess of Wands, we recognize this animal aspect in us that reacts unconsciously with striking feelings and knee-jerk reactions. What's more, we recognize that such reactions are fueled by the will-force of the knight (and thus the queen and prince). When we understand this, we learn that everything we do, consciously or unconsciously,

Princess of Wands

"good" or "bad," has a benefit and harmony with the entire cosmos. Every moment in our princess-reactive lives is under the intelligent direction of the prince (our higher self) to express the sacred marriage of the knight and the queen. In this way, the Princess of Wands is the embodiment (earth) of enthusiasm (fire). What is enthused in this sense? The love of the sacred marriage of knight and queen, subject and object, action and reaction, above and below. Unlike the prince, who uses his airy intelligence to fan the fire, her earth is the fuel for it. The Princess of Wands is us, the fuel for the fire of divine play.

On the tetractys, she occupies the last row of four points. She hears the words "I am a self" from the prince answering the queen. She interprets this through divine ignorance by incarnating, itself a conclusion that there *can* be difference and separation; remember that the tetrad exists because of difference and creates circumstance. The Princess of Wands is the limitless, self-luminous consciousness in an experience of limitation. This makes her a

CHAPTER 3

very excitable character, as there is now much to get excited about for her to experience, for better or worse. She is traditionally interpreted to be as quick to anger as she is to fall in love. On the Tree of Life, she is attributed to Malkuth, the kingdom, where it all happens.

Astrologically, the Princess of Wands governs the quarter of the heavens centering on Leo. This gives her many of the qualities of her prince: Courage, pride, creativity. Influenced by this fixed fire sign, she is fixated on keeping things exciting. Leo's tarot attribution is lust, emphasizing her lust for life. And by "her" I also mean the lust of the tetragrammaton becoming her from the standpoint of the absolute. She is the lust of the universe to become you.

The Princess of Wands also governs Cancer and Virgo. Cancer, the crab, is a sign of incubation and containment in the way that the crab's shell contains and protects. The Chariot card is a glyph of the containment of the absolute in one vehicle or another to direct its will. In the same way, the princess fuels the will-force of fire (and Atziluth) by providing it the apparatus of embodiment. She is the vehicle of the yod.

She also governs Virgo, the sign of self-perfection. As the embodiment of fire, she is in the process of the Divine perfecting the earth through its own manifestation. Virgo is also attributed to the yod, the letter of fire that so radically enthuses our princess.

In a reading, this represents the aspect of ourselves to get excited. She is our automatic, and sometimes childlike reactions to stimuli. She lets fiery enthusiasm possess her, making her loud, proud, uplifting, courageous, and a sight to see. She is quick to fall in love and quick to anger. As the host (heh final) of fire (Atziluth), she has a lot of high energy running through her. If ill-dignified, she is dangerous, vengeful, fickle, cruel, and irrational.

THE CUPS COURT

Our next family is the suit of cups and the element of water. You will notice it shares the same pattern as the wands but in a very different context. The wand court cards expressed the sacred name coming into being out of primordial nothingness, and now the cups court cards will teach us the same divine name but through a reflection of itself. In the suit of cups, we are in the world of Briah, the creative world. If Atziluth is the nearest to God, Briah is the throne. This is where God can be conceptualized as a creator, as it is the first moment where unity splits into duality. In the Vedantic tradition, this might be compared to *Saguna Brahman*, or "god with attributes," as opposed to *Nirguna Brahman*, "god without attributes."

Where do the attributes come from? In the tarot, this happens through emanation. Emanation can be thought of as creation through reflection, where some aspect of reality is issued forth from a more perfect source. In the macrocosm, the world of Briah gives form to the will-force of Atziluth. What is formed is the subtle idea what will manifest below. Theologically, this would be the idea of a creator that can be worshiped. This is the path of bhakti yoga, devotion. In devotional work, there is always a duality between the devotee and the object of their devotion. The family of cups will continue a theme of devotion and love.

They will also uphold the power of intuition. In the microcosm, the queens (and their thrones) give form to the life force of the knights below. The part of the soul that reflects the Briah below is the neshamah, the intuition. The neshamah largely serves the chiah, the creative force, the divine spark of our souls. I will share a brief and very relevant anecdote about this. When I was starting to focus on tarot more professionally, I had many doubts; my analytical mind got in the way. I asked many teachers the same questions: "How do you know your intuition is working? How do you grow your gifts?" In one year, I got the same answer from three different teachers from three very different traditions: "It feels like I'm making it up." How could they give such shockingly accurate messages and just feel like they were making it up? It was later, after much study and growth, that I realized how close the intuition was to the creative force within. In a way, they were making it up because they were operating from a mental place closer to the collective creative process of whoever or whatever they were reading for. The neshamah is literally the receiver of the chiah in the same way that the queens receive the knights and the cup receives the wand. Intuition is so close to creation because it has that instantaneous, all-at-once quality, the same one that is experienced by the biggest lightbulbs, inspired ideas, and creative explosions. In those moments, there is little to no separation between the experiencer and the world. Distance is collapsed in a creative idea or intuitive glimpse that arrests the mind or rather frees it from the normal machinations of rationalization (rationalization itself is for the next family). Simply put, creativity and intuition are very close in the hierarchy of the soul.

With intuition, the distance in time or space required by rationalization is lessened or collapsed. That is why the intuition, and by extension the suit of cups and the queens, are attributed to Binah on the Tree of Life. Binah is the threshold of time.

KNIGHT OF CUPS

With God's infinite name now established in the family of wands, it begins reflecting on itself with the Knight of Cups. Elementally, he is fire of water. To understand this knight, meditate on harsh, pouring rain or water's power of solution. Rain can be forceful but only because it is pulled by gravity. In the same way, the will of the Knight of Cups is at the

Knight of Cups

mercy of his attractions. This makes sense because the Knight of Cups, as you will see, is all about the power of giving, pouring oneself into another just as water pours into any container. This pouring into the other is the general function of the creative world and duality.

Macrocosmically, the Knight of Cups represents the pure will of the world of Briah, the creative world. Briah offers "something" to the "nothing" at the edges of Atziluth. This "something" is form, a container, something to be measured, experienced, enjoyed, and adored. It implies distance to engender desire and devotion. In the illustration, the Knight of Cups offers his crab, the container of life fluid (see chapter 2 on the Chariot); whereas the Knight of Wands came into being without an object of focus, the Knight of Cups certainly has an object of focus, even adoration. Remember that Briah is the creative world. Here, God can be conceptualized as a creator, and can be worshiped. The whole process of the suit of cups is the development of the adorer and the adored. The Knight of Cups does this in two ways. The commonly interpreted way is through love of another person, the knight who wears his heart on his sleeve. But more deeply, he is the adoration of God the creator. As fire of water, he is the passion of the forming power of the absolute. The knight, made passive in the suit of cups, surrenders himself to the divine creative will of the yod. This yields artistic and creative fervor, and makes for the attraction between all things in the universe. Compare this attraction to the Queen of Wands, who inverts the elemental attribution.

Microcosmically, he is the creative force orchestrating the intuition. This Knight represents the development of relationships. Intuition *synthesizes* relationships and data points to arrive at large amounts of information in an all-at-once moment of insight. The knight's will is motivated by the relationship opportunities he senses, and that will continues to direct their development—in other words, art. If the Knight of Wands is the divinely pointless becoming, the Knight of Cups is divine giving, pouring himself into the love of the other through intuitive relationship building.

In the tetractys, the Knight of Cups bridges the first point to the second two. He is the silence from which the queen utters "I am." But this silence is dualistic. For this knight, silence is the quiet gaze into otherness, precipitating the "I am" from the object of his own desire. When he hears this "I am" from the queen, it renders his own point of view. They play this game of Marco Polo to find each other out of silence. More accurately described, it is a mutually arising moment. In Briah, being is dualistic. The best way to understand these advanced concepts is to read Plotinus on the nous.[115] The apex of this will emerge in the queen. On the Tree of Life, he corresponds to Chokmah, wisdom, and the zodiac. This attribution emphasizes his expansive quality. We might say that the wisdom of Chokmah and the expanding universe happens through this knight's function of relationship building. How else do "things" come to be, except by their relationships to other things?

Like the Knight of Wands, the Knight of Cups does not endure. He represents swift but only momentary action. This is even less sustained in the suit of water, and we will also see his astrological correspondences. He rules the first decan of Pisces, ruled by Saturn, attributed to the Eight of Cups, titled Indolence in the tarot. The Knight of Cups does not self-generate his motivation like the Knight of Wands. He must be pulled by his attractions, like rain pulled by gravity. Luckily, he rules the second decan of Pisces as well, ruled by Jupiter, titled Happiness. This inspires his romantic advances with a dreamy desire. Saturn is the greater malefic and Jupiter is the greater benefic. This puts our knight

---
115. Plotinus, *Enneads*, trans. Stephen MacKenna (London: Penguin Books, 1991), 431.

in drastic emotional rhythms, up and down. However, this should be expected, as the suit of cups is the establishment of dualism. In any dualism there is difference, and difference opens up the invented realities of good and bad. The Knight of Cups is an artist, and art doesn't often come without a dark night of the soul. The dance between dark and light is a sort of alchemical process, symbolized in the Knight of Cups's crest, the peacock. This symbol hails the end of the alchemical *nigredo*, a process of transformation, the result of the absolute (YHVH) running itself through infinite vessels, themselves creators that work through an experience of duality as a result of being created. In this way, the Knight of Cups represents the fractalizing power of consciousness.

The Knight also rules the last decan of Aquarius, ruled by the Moon. This is the Seven of Swords, Futility. In this card, the Moon weakens or quiets Aquarius's will to assert and differentiate itself, or modifies the act of self-distinguishing into a passive process. In the same way, the Knight of Cups softens his individuality to serve the divine spark of his creativity (the yod). This occurs in his art-making, lovemaking, and all types of making. It establishes the passive state required to receive divine inspiration.

In a reading, the Knight of Cups represents the aspect of ourselves that is drawn forward. He might be considered the libido. He is attraction, romance, creative flow, adoration, and the invitation of the universe to participate in itself. All of these are possible through his attributions, making him the instigator of the world of duality. However, his romantic invitation is unanswered without the rest of the tetragrammaton. Crowley describes him as a dilettante. He romanticizes instead of actualizes and may be lost in his idealistic daydreams.

QUEEN OF CUPS

The Queen of Cups is the heh of heh, water of water that could elementally be interpreted as the deep, dark sea. To understand this queen, meditate on sitting at the bottom of the ocean, or watching a perfectly still pond reflect the sky. In fact, the sea is the symbol of Binah, and no queen is more intimate with the mysteries of Binah than the Queen of Cups. Both her suit and her office correspond to Binah and heh primal, the supernal mother.

Macrocosmically, she is the intuition of the creative world, the most receptive and reflective aspect of our tetragrammatic combinations. To know her is to know how much effort it takes the water to reflect our gaze. This is how the universe creates. It doesn't plan or desire. It is, and then it is, "I am that I am." As the deepest neshamah in the watery world of Briah, she is infinite subtlety. Mystically, she is the moment before life-forms become

Queen of Cups

what they are. This moment is hard to put into words, but can best be understood as a sort of hiccup, or glitch, where one specific part of the universe reflects on itself in relation to the rest of the universe. This self-reflection of consciousness is the first moment of localized awareness. It happens intuitively, quietly, and humbly, effortless as the salt in the sea.

Microcosmically, she is the deepest intuition, having her office and element both attributed to the neshamah. The intuition is a nucleus to the apparatus of thought below. It serves the will and creative force above. As the second Qabalistic layer of the soul, this queen is the most subtle illusion that attracts the Knight of Cups (the will) into a local experience. Simply put, she is your ability to reflect which allows your ego to exist. This is what I call a "localization of consciousness." It is the space between your ears and behind your eyes. But that space can only exist by relationship to what is beyond your ears and ahead of your eyes. The Queen of Cups, on a deep level, represents the arising of this relationship.

The ability of a unit of consciousness to reflect the cosmos's creative agency is the whisper of the Queen of Cups to the knight: "I am." On the tetractys, she draws down the entering monad into the dyad (second row). It is the germ of the knight's desire now fertilized as our literal intuition and ability to receive.

The Queen of Cups is the ability of every unit of consciousness to receive what is "outside" of it (being localized, there is now an inside and an outside). She is the ultimate antenna, receiving perfectly whatever signal passes by. We all have this ability (as we are all expressions of YHVH). However, many people choose to lower their awareness in so many ways. Such sensitivity is not always comfortable, and is often vulnerable. That said, higher awareness always allows for higher freedom. At this level, awareness pours into us from others in a nonlinear fashion. One might call this empathy.

The sensitivity of the queen to the "outer" is emphasized in her astrological attributions. She rules twenty degrees Gemini to twenty degrees Cancer. In the majors, this is the transition from the Lovers to the Chariot. This emphasizes her function: Reflection of "the other" to formulate the organized self. Cancer is the crab, the Chariot, the ability of consciousness to create containers for itself. The Queen of Cups is the ultimate container. Being the heh primal of heh primal, she is the intuitive container (neshamah) of the macrocosmic container (Briah). She contains the universe by reflecting it back out in love. "Love" is the title of the Two of Cups, attributed to her first decan, Venus in Cancer. Venus gives her the loving ability to relate with all things. Her next decan of Cancer is ruled by Mercury, connected to the Word. This hints at her ability to contain and reflect the logos of the knight to create the earliest forms of life by their own self-reflection. Mercury is also the shaping power of the universe. This is expressed in this decan's tarot card, the Three of Cups. It represents the descent of intelligence (Mercury) into matter (Cancer, the container) to shape it. The Thoth deck expresses this through the symbol of the pomegranate and myth of Persephone. This myth warns us of departing from the universal for the enjoyment of the particulars below.

This is emphasized in her shadow decan, the sun in Gemini, which corresponds to Ruin, the Ten of Swords. Like all things related to Binah, there is a cost. The ability of consciousness to localize and reflect the universe from its individual point of view allows for that unit to experience separateness. This is the real meaning of intuition. It is only through a vivid and intimate knowledge of the experience of separateness that the intuition can work, since the intuition works by synthesizing that which is separate and connecting that which is remote (in space, time, or any dimension). The intuition is the nucleus of the apparatus of diverse, disparate thought. It is the job of the intuition to connect (usually very quickly) all these data points. But, if those data points aren't separate, then there's nothing to connect, and the intuition would lose its job. In a way, this is the mystic's goal. But until we reach such spiritual heights, the intuition is useful, and runs by subconsciously connecting countless lived experiences (in this lifetime or another). The Ten of Swords represents all those experiences, other lifetimes, past challenges, even traumas, that have given rise to a tighter intuition. It represents all that was disconnected for the Queen of Cups to reconnect via her reflection and empathy.

All these attributions make our queen deeply intimate with the furthest reaches of the human experience. Having a general connection to the Moon (as a queen of water), she is connected to past lives, the evolutionary process of life, and the onward flow of consciousness. Being the most extreme aspect of the neshamah and having the sensitivity of Cancer, she is intuition at its highest state, quietly aware, and calmly connecting the dots. In a reading, this is someone who is very psychic, quiet, reflective, sensitive, healing, nurturing, mysterious, and beautiful. She will take on the characteristics of whoever is nearby, showing them themselves. She is a perfect mirror. Ill-dignified, she is too dreamy, inattentive, unrealistic, and needs grounding.

PRINCE OF CUPS

As you have probably seen by now, the family of water is all about the other. If the Knight of Cups represents the attraction of the universe and the Queen of Cups represents arising localized consciousness through reflection, the Prince of Cups expresses what accumulates around that self-reflection through the apparatus of thought. In the Prince of Cups emerges the full ego, causing a feedback loop with Briah's mode of relationship building (cosmically transpersonal, but socially interpersonal). The Prince of Cups is the vav of heh primal, the air of water. Crowley compares this combination to hydrostatic equilibrium. To understand the Prince of Cups, study and meditate on fluid dynamics. To illustrate, here's a brief anecdote. Following Crowley's instructions on yoga, I was meditating on the image of a red triangle. I would count how many times my mind would lose focus from the red triangle. Admittedly, it was a lot. As my awareness and concentration grew, what I discovered was deliciously scary: Thoughts don't come and go like concrete abstract ideas with definition—they are really just subtle sensations that flow like fluid. And not only do they flow like fluid, but the flow of fluidic thought affects itself in what I can only describe as complex weather

Prince of Cups

patterns or, rather, the visual effect of dropping colored dye in water and watching its form warp in all directions. Thoughts flow into feelings. Feelings flow into thoughts.

Microcosmically, the Prince of Cups represents the rich causality and fluid dynamics between thought, emotion, and feeling, being the intellectual image (air) of emotion, intuition, and relationships (water). Observe your body and mind, especially when in an emotional state. This is the playground of the Prince of Cups. In a way, he is constantly changing by plunging into his own complexity (the Scorpio attribution will emphasize this later).

This complexity is due to the prince's role. Macrocosmically, he serves as the intellect of the creative world. The world of Briah is all about the something that came out of the nothing. The Queen of Cups applies her silent intuition, but it's the Prince of Cups that handles the next phase with the machinations of his mind. This is one of the most complex things. His job is to conceptualize the prism of duality that first arose in the localization of consciousness in the Queen of Cups. This makes him a philosopher in all ways, in an unending hunt for his own self-knowledge. (If you've understood the first few chapters, you'll know this is a *fool's* errand, and that's what it's all about.)

This "self-knowledge" is found in the third row of the tetractys. The Queen of Cups whispers, "I am...," and the Prince of Cups responds with violent curiosity, "—a self." If the queen fertilized the seed of life in the dualistic world of Briah, the Prince of Cups was its first thought. On the Tree of Life, he corresponds to Tiphareth, the sphere of the dying god. He is constantly dying and being reborn under the dynamic complexity developing from Briah's infinite reflection. The dynamic fluid dynamics of his thoughts and emotions push him through continuous rebirth and transformation.

The complexity and transformative nature of the Prince of Wands's fluid dynamics finds its expression astrologically as well. He rules twenty degrees Libra to twenty degrees Scorpio. This is the transition from Adjustment to Death, describing a disruption of poise (and social law) in the confrontation of mortality, the real burden of philosophers. This transition can also be understood through fluid dynamics. The causal aspect of the science is introduced by balanced Libra, while the changeability is emphasized in Scorpio.

The first decan of Scorpio is ruled by Mars. Mars represents the aggression behind his changeability and the grossness of the alchemical putrefaction of Scorpio, letting the old rot away. It is the aggressive questioning of the airy prince to further know himself, an unquenchable teleological search for meaning. The second decan, the Sun in Scorpio, titled Pleasure, brings out Scorpio's best qualities. Having plunged the depths of his unconsciousness, he pulls out the treasure from the queen's ocean (Binah). From his introspection, he brings gold to the surface, the highest art, philosophy, intellectual and creative design. Here, he can enjoy extreme pleasure from life, at least before the next desperate plunge.

The Prince of Cups is intense but not on the surface. The last decan of Libra is his shadow. It is ruled by Jupiter and attributed to the Four of Swords, Truce. This card is all about compromise and social harmony. This represents the equanimous compromise he chooses with himself (and others) in between his desperate introspective searches. Such a compromise momentarily forces his ruling planet of war to a truce. This makes the prince socially calm, approachable, and even charming. But even this is one of his inventions that he pulled from the deep. As the air of water, he is a mad scientist of emotional engineering. He represents manipulation, a capacity in which we all share. The Prince of Cups flows through us in the largely unconscious flows of conversation. He is the subtext, flirtation, passive-aggression, body language, and all patterns that hint at the deeper recesses of shared experience. One might interpret him as the fluid dynamics of energy exchange between people.

In a reading, the Prince of Cups represents someone who is mysterious, deep, secretive, but pleasant. This person is probably going through a major transformation, for better or worse. When venturing past their charming facade, be careful but stay curious. You might find gold if they let you in deep enough.

PRINCESS OF CUPS

The Knight, Queen, and Prince of Cups express the development and consequence of a relationship arising in consciousness reflecting upon itself and folding it into duality. They personify the mysteries of the "something." The last stage of the process is embodiment. The knight and Queen of Cups's divine union is conceptualized by the Prince of Cups. This abstraction governs the materialization of life below, symbolized by the Princess of Cups. When the relationship development of the world of Briah reaches matter in the nephesh, life begins. This is a great mystery symbolized in the Thoth deck's Princess of Cups by the swan and tortoise. She is the heh final of heh primal, the earth of water. To understand her elementally, meditate on the ways water supports life. She rules the chemical combination that is the basis of all life. She is also crystallization, represented by the crystals at the edge of her gown.

Macrocosmically, she is the animal soul and embodiment of Briah, the creative world. She concludes the Briatic development of self-reflection into manifest life. She is the ability of a subconscious intelligence to emerge and direct material to support growth, metabolism, reproduction, adaptation, homeostasis, and responsiveness. All of these exist through more subtle relationships fractalizing and complicating into physical matter. This is the essence of the Princess of Cups. She is the automation of the formation of units of consciousness emerging from the element of water, the reflective, creative aspect of God.

Microcosmically, she is the intuition descending into the body's automatic processes and the relationship between intuition and instinct. This will be covered in the Queen of Disks. For now, you can understand the Princess of Cups to be the cybernetic feedback system that maintains a body's actions in line with the brain's thoughts. For many people, the creative process happens naturally. Whether words on a page, paint on a canvas, or even in running a business, it is common for the most successful creators to report some aspects of seamless flow. This is the dance of the Princess of Cups, who goes about her work silently, bringing her dreams and visions into materiality. This isn't the only part of a creative process, though, which is why we have fifteen other court cards.

Princess of Cups

    She corresponds to the last row of the tetractys. She listens to the Prince of Cups, "I am a self," and interprets this self-hood as a condition of difference which creates circumstance. In that difference, the diversity of life curiously coalesces at the edge of the waters, and cells start to form. This ability of differentiation in the princess (the effect of the prince's Briatic ego), allows for great creativity. In the suit of cups, this creativity is fluid, quiet, and interdependent, like a dream. The Princess of Cups represents the dream of life emerging from the subject-object relationship. But this dream is natural, and without effort, just as the princess's beautiful dance. There is not too much meaning in this world. The sharp coordination of meaning and abstraction will follow later in the family of swords.

    The effortless dance of creativity is further emphasized by her astrological correspondences. She governs the quarter of the heavens centered on Scorpio. Like her brother, she is highly changeable and transformative, all themes of the Death card. Part of the princess's dance is that of death to create new life, as she is the dance of cells dying and dividing, growing and copying DNA, all taking part in a collective great work of a larger ecosystem. What is death and destruction on one scale is harmony on another. And there are a lot of scales, maybe even infinite. To understand, we must turn to the turtle on the card. Father of modern psychology William James wrote an essay entitled "Rationality, Activity and Faith" that first introduced the idea of what might be called irreflexivity, where something cannot define itself without incorporating something else.[116] If one was to ask, "what is the ground of this reality?" one could answer "The world sits on a turtle, and underneath that, another turtle, and underneath that, yet another turtle … it's turtles all the way down." Though scientists have not found turtles to be the ground of reality, they have continued to look deeper (smaller) and have always found another layer, from atoms, to subatomic particles, quarks, forces, strings, quantum foam, and the unknown. Are there infinite forms as far as you go? Only the Princess of Cups knows, but she will never tell. She only continues to dance the forms into being, following the cosmic self-inquiry of the prince. The mode of the all-encompassing consciousness attributed to Scorpio is "imaginative intelligence," which imagines the world of life, and at the same time, that of death.

The way consciousness imagines life is through action and reaction fueled by curiosity. These two facets are ruled by the Princess of Cups's other two signs, Libra and Sagittarius. Libra governs action and karma. All actions create karma which creates birth which creates more action. This is expressed in Libra's corresponding card, Adjustment, symbolizing the action and reaction pattern of the tetragrammaton and the universe becoming self-aware (a process our court cards express in detail). Recall from the earlier chapter on the major arcana that Adjustment is the ox goad that guides the ineffable creative power of the ox (the Fool).

The other sign is Sagittarius, the sign of journeys, higher knowledge, and limitless possibility. It is the intense transformations of Scorpio that yield and quantify the long, deep journeys of Sagittarius. These journeys and explorations are expressed in the Art card, a spiritual journey of alchemy. In this card, the appropriate modifications are made to propel the aspirant forward into a higher and more expansive integration of their true selves. It is through the action and reaction of Libra that these journeys of Sagittarius are made. All of these together maintain the life, death, changeability, and evolution of Scorpio. These transformations are all based on relationships between the aspirant and the goal, which is the mode of Briah, duality. This is not just a spiritual quest of the individual, but a collec-

---

116. William James, "Rationality, Activity and Faith" in *The Princeton Review* vol. 2 (1882): 82.

tive quest of evolution. This transformation is led by the ego of the Prince of Cups and embodied in the life processes of the princess.

In a reading, the Princess of Cups represents our inner dreamer. She seamlessly dances life into existence but does so quietly. This is the part of ourselves with big imaginations. One might consider this our inner child who stays curious and allows their creative spirit to flow through them, untethered by shackles of judgment often accompanying future conditioning (the next family). If safety and trust can be maintained, creative genius may arise. The Princess of Cups is very passive, being made up of the two passive elements. She does not necessarily generate her creativity alone, but is rather a sensitive conduit of all influencing forces, and synthesizes them into new forms, in the same way that life itself is a result of an immeasurable (and improbable) combination of the perfect cosmic conditions.

Spiritually, she represents the end of the world of Briah and the beginning of Yetzirah. She is the end of the relationship aspect of the universe and helps introduce the universe's mental conceptualization of itself by virtue of those relationships. This leads to our next family.

THE SWORDS COURT

Individual self-awareness really takes shape with our next family, the suit of swords, in the world of Yetzirah, the formative world. Briah is associated with creation. It offers Atziluth, the archetypal world, an idea of itself to be created. The idea is not localized in a mind. It's much more subtle. The idea exists out of what it is *not*. Briah creates through the this-or-that relationship. Yetzirah, for its part, is the conceptual apparatus that shapes Briah's core idea into an intelligent design. We might say that Briah establishes life's potential but has no parameters until it is measured, mapped, and made through Yetzirah. This will be the job of our family of Swords, the formative world, air, and the vav of the tetragrammaton. Microcosmically, Yetzirah is reflected in the ruach, our intellect.

KNIGHT OF SWORDS

The process begins, like it always does, with a flash of inspiration. In the suit of swords, that flash is a mental curiosity, the Knight of Swords. He is the yod of vav, fire of air, the will and creative force of the formative world. Elementally, this could be interpreted as winds, or a whirlwind. These stormy winds illustrate the violence and passion of a racing mind. But it can also be a nice breeze, a breath of fresh air. In the same way, the mind can bring innovation and freshness, but also destruction and catastrophe, just like weather.

Knight of Swords

    Macrocosmically, the Knight of Swords is the will of the formative world to localize itself in duality and ultimately increase its detail. By consciousness "increasing its detail" it folds within itself to create (or become) greater levels of limitation. With more limitation, there is a higher level of experience, and one might argue, more total information in the universe. This is very much in line with the Knight of Swords and all his associations. As the first court card of the suit of swords, he introduces dual thinking, which is what renders the ego. The more egos, the more dual thinking. This fractalizes the universe into more and more experience and more and more information.

    The Knight of Wands is the paradoxical terrestrial event of an organism becoming self-aware. There are three major themes the seeker must get comfortable with to understand this: Duality, illusion, and disruption. The duality is clearly expressed in the formative world, the suit of swords—which literally cut things in two. To understand the second piece, the illusion, we must first understand the ego.

The ego is not really a "thing." It is rather an organizing center that arises out of an interpretation of countless experiences. To use a metaphor appropriate to the Knight of Swords, the ego is like the eye of a hurricane. The hurricane, with its rushing winds, is our sum total of thought and experience (doing, making, changing, differentiating, projecting, judging, inferring, concluding). The focal point of all of that experience is the eye of the storm, which is really still, where nothing is happening. It's just space. Everything we experience points to this "thing" called "I," and yet all mystical traditions, in one way or another, show that the "I" doesn't exist. And yet, we experience the "I" without a second thought. That is because the knight continues to ravage the world with his storm of inspired thought and abstraction. The space at the center of the rushing wind is maintained, even though there is nothing there. This eye ("I") of the storm will be more intimately understood in our queen.

There's one more meteorological metaphor that explains the ego and also further elucidates the sacred marriage and the tetragrammaton. To really understand the Knight of Wands, the ego, and the marriage of fire and water into air, study the Coriolis force. This is a force that has to be measured in objects with a rotating reference frame. If a ball rolls across a spinning disk, the spin of the disk will have to be calculated to accurately predict the ball's movement. The spinning disk is not the movement of the ball but must be considered when tracking its trajectory. Meteorologists measure this in wind currents. What's interesting is that the Coriolis force is not a real force. It is a force that only *appears* to exist but is really the result of the earth rotating. Since the earth rotates, an object moving over its surface appears to be deflected from its straight-line path. The ego is a similar appearance. It's an illusion that arises between the movement of one thing and the stillness of the other. In our case, this is the movement of our experiences (thoughts, feelings, sensations, and so on) against the absolute stillness of our awareness. In the tarot, the awareness that sheds light on everything is like fire (yod and chiah and also the yechidah, the highest part of the soul). The experiences passing through us would be the element of water and the objective world (heh and neshamaha). The ego is the fictitious force we measure that arises in between the two (vav and ruach). The Knight of Swords is the first swirlings of that ego.

Now that we have covered duality and illusion, what about disruption? This force can be understood as the surprise of consciousness to localize in an individual point of view and ultimately get in its own way. This is the curse that follows the blessing of incarnation and our prefrontal cortexes. It is when the gift of discernment becomes the curse of judgment and discrimination.

Microcosmically, the Knight of Swords is the intellect willed forward. This is the mind's passion and curiosity. This knight describes the human nature to move forward toward an object of focus and then move even closer to the objects making it up. It is the mental capacity to break things down, and explore details. It is the ability to split things apart to know them.

On the tetractys, the Knight of Swords bridges the monad to the second row. This tetractys is one of air, so a relationship had already been established in the tetractys of water. Here, we are watching the birth and development of an individual self. Like the other knights, this one expresses the silence of the monad. However, in the world of formation, this silence is more of an "a-ha!" A lightbulb goes off. This is the birth of the individual, localized mind. There is such excitement and novelty in this evolutionary step that no words can follow… until the Queen of Swords answers sternly: "I am."

These three themes of duality, illusion, and disruption are perfectly expressed in this knight's astrological correspondences. He governs the first two decans of Gemini and the last decan of Taurus. Gemini is the sign of the twins, governing thoughts, curiosity, communication, multiplicity, and *duality*. In duality, there is choice and detail through multiplicity. This is both the boon and curse of the Knight of Swords. Gemini governs the third house in astrology, where we learn to use our minds to communicate. The first decan of Gemini is ruled by Jupiter, and is associated with the Eight of Swords, Interference. This card is all about how we get in our own way, and how the mind can deter progress with its overthinking and attachment to details. The second decan is ruled by Mars and is associated with the Nine of Swords, Cruelty. Here is the result of an unchecked mind that leads the ego to disruption and unconsciously into disarray, fear, and harm against others. The knight has darker aspects that give him negative discrimination and bullying qualities. They express the cost of ego and identifying with illusion, separated from reality.

The Knight of Swords is also attributed to the last decan of Taurus, ruled by Saturn, associated with the Seven of Disks, Failure. In this decan, the fixity and weight of Taurus increases with the heaviness of Saturn, anathema to the knight's airy and agitated character. Yet it may be what he secretly wishes for in all his mental squirming. The passage of the Hierophant (Taurus) to the Lovers card (Gemini) is very important. The Hierophant represents consciousness descending into matter, and the Lovers card represents the method of that process, which is separation and localization.

The Knight of Swords's associated minors are not very fun: Failure, Interference, and Cruelty. Why is that? It is the cost of incarnation in general and mind specifically. The best way to understand this is through the metaphor of a videogame. A videogame without challenges and limitations would not be fun. A good game requires rules, organizing principles, and effort. In the same way, consciousness requires its limiting adjuncts within the mind that allow it to play. The Knight of Swords is the first major stage of consciousness pouring itself into its avatars through their self-conceptualization. The way we get in our own way is by imposing limits by self-conceptualizing. When we identify with smaller aspects of our Self, we fail. We interfere with the natural process. We are cruel. When we identify with the more holistic reality of our Self, we find peace and things get easy. In a way, the Knight of Swords enjoys the suffering. In a way, consciousness enjoys the limitation.

The deeper doctrine here, which is explained elsewhere, is that limitation is what renders consciousness to be. What "thing" could consciousness be aware of if there was "no thing"? All these "things" provide more detail, the major theme of the Knight of Swords. Within his self-imposed limitation, he enjoys all this high-definition detail in the formative world, Yetzirah. Within his self-imposed limitation, he enjoys a world of detail, rendered in the ultimate high-definition experience of the formative world, Yetzirah. But wherever there is detail, there is stark difference—and whenever there is difference, there is fear. The Princess of Cups represented the quiet, blissful arising of life forms at the end of the Briatic world. The Knight of Swords is the difference interpreted and projected on life-fluid, pumping through dualistic Gemini. The cosmic motivation here is curiosity. What will be next to "become"? This cosmic curiosity is much more than a mystical philosophy. It is a state of consciousness that can be arrived at through direct knowledge, requiring a synthesis of all the ideas of this present work.

In a reading, the Knight of Swords represents the aspect of ourselves that races toward an abstract idea, intellectual pursuit, or solution. The Knight of Swords loves solving problems, but when he doesn't have a problem to solve, he will make one. He is discerning, discriminating, detail-oriented, intensely smart, innovative, curious, distracted, and unpredictable. His two weapons symbolize his dual thinking and his race to dissect, analyze, and discern. He speaks fast and harshly but with great passion. His egoic nature keeps him moving. He is idea in motion, for better or worse.

Queen of Swords

QUEEN OF SWORDS

If the Knight of Swords is the hurricane, the Queen of Swords is the eye of the storm. She is the fully formed "I" in the egoic sense and thus the widowed matriarch of suffering that comes with the "I." What makes her a widow? The death that mutually arises with the birth of "I." If an "I" is formed, an "I" will be unformed. She is the intuitive understanding of such formation and dispersion of the "I" and intellect. Remember that this formation is the very capacity of the Yetziratic world, reflected in her Qabalistic attribution: She is the heh primal of vav.

Elementally, she is the water of air. To understand her, meditate on the freedom, height, and form of the clouds. Clouds are a unique balance between form and formlessness, being the condensation of water vapor (gas, airy) into water droplets (liquid, watery). In the same way, one could conceptualize the formation and dispersion of the ego. Like the clouds, she reaches an impressive height with her spiritual awareness. She decapitates the head of the ego at the neck of knowledge (Da'at on the Tree of Life) and draws us upward. From here, she sees all and reigns over all units of localized consciousness.

She knows where every piece of the cosmos begins and ends, including you. She knows the edges of every "thing"—her suffering and joy. As the intuition of the mind, she outlives the mind. Connected to Binah, she is the supernal mother, but in the suit of swords, this manifests as the dark mother, who mourns death instead of celebrating life. On the tetractys, she would sit on the second row. She receives the inspired mental curiosity of the knight and reflects it back to him. This is our own ability to observe our own abstraction, how we conceptualize the world into being. She whispers "I am" and the formative world gets to work on an identity.

Microcosmically, she is the intuition (neshamah) approaching the intellect (ruach). This happens in two steps. First, the intuition has an insight that connects disparate elements. Then, the intellect applies thought to expresses them sequentially, one item at a time. When we explain an experience or describe an image, this is what we are doing. Language is always linear and dualistic, even when describing a single moment. The relationship of the intuition to the intellect can be thought of as a printer. The printer prints an image (intuition) but only one thin line of ink at a time (intellect).

These ideas are expressed in her astrological attributions. She governs the first two decans of Libra and the last decan of Virgo. Libra is the sign of balance, poise, relationships, and social harmony. Libra is attributed to Adjustment, mythologically associated with Ma-at and the harlequin, both rulers over justice on the human scale and causality on the universal scale. Both causality on the cosmic scale and justice on the human scale require an event to be a cause or effect. Otherwise, what would the Libra's scales balance? An event is always interpreted or projected amidst the total unity of reality/consciousness, the monad. When about eight billion people, and countless organisms, have beginnings and endings in time and space, and project and interpret events, we get a world. This queen governs the quiet diversity of these countless perspectives perceiving events and thus separating out one unitive consciousness into many, *many* things. Recall the Knight of Swords and his lust for detail and information. The queen gives birth to the countless units that refract consciousness through their own self-reflection. It's as if she folds the paper of consciousness infinitely so it can continue to rub against itself. This folding of consciousness is what makes the origami of time and space. For each fold, an event must take place. There must be a change. Something must come out of something else.

CHAPTER 3

On the human scale, this includes the experience of birth and death, related to Ma-at. On the universal scale, this is pure causality expressed through the harlequin on the Adjustment card. The Queen of Swords shares this power of causality with the universe. She sees all the pains and joys of karma. Outwardly, she expresses the pains as the widow. This sorrow is expressed in the second decan of Libra, ruled by Saturn, attributed to the Three of Swords. This is ruled by Saturn and also attributed to Saturn through Binah (number three). Saturn is the greater malefic, and brings limitations and endings. This makes our queen the queen of ending, the queen of edges.

But she has a secret. Inwardly, she is not the mourning widow—she experiences great peace. Her other Libra decan is ruled by the Moon. The Moon offers perfect flexibility and rhythm Libra needs to enforce perfect balance, attributed to the Two of Swords, titled Peace. The Saturnian decan represents life and death since Saturn always brings limitation. The lunar decan represents the fulcrum point of the scale which arises through the lunar rhythm. Amidst the intensity of life and death, the Queen of Swords maintains perfect equanimity and poise through dynamic balance. She is the perfect stillness of the truth in all its motion.

Her shadow decan is the last decan of Virgo, ruled by Mercury. Virgo is a sign of constant improvement and perfection. In a very subtle way, this is antagonistic to our queen. Remember that she governs exact balance to maintain the equilibrium of all things. Virgo, in its efforts to perfect itself, continues to cause events and change that the queen has to balance in the perfect zero equation of the universe. One might consider her Virgo decan at odds with her Libra decans. On the other hand, it is this Virgoan effort to constantly improve that makes the balancing act of Libra so dynamic.

The card attributed to Mercury in Virgo is the Ten of Disks, named Wealth. Wealth is both the fear and secret desire of our Queen of Swords. Situated so high in the clouds of Yetzirah, it would appear that she doesn't concern herself with such earthly matters. Yet, her governance of balance must also reach every exchange of every unit of currency. Wealth *is* the result of a dynamic balance of exchange!

In a Qabalistic order, wealth would be the last card of the deck, occupying the last sephirah (Malkuth) in the last world (Assiah). In the Thoth deck, this signals what Crowley calls a "redintegration." This means that materialization has reached its climax and must return to spirit, back to its origin. In the same way, the Queen of Swords governs life, death, and causality. She is the Queen of ego death, the wise widow governing the borders that mark every individual life.

In a reading, the Queen of Swords shows someone who is honest, poised, incredibly discerning, perceptive, balanced, equanimous, direct, intelligent, and generally to the point. Her throne flies high up into the clouds. She brings with her a severed head (the ego). She is sometimes cold. Well-dignified, she will help the querent deal with something and will do it fast. She is the type to rip off the bandage. Ill-dignified, she may intimidate the querent or make them doubt themselves.

PRINCE OF SWORDS

The Prince of Swords takes the established ego and develops it into further complexity: A self-*concept*, in all its horrors and glory. This is different from self-awareness. In the creative world (Briah), consciousness becomes of itself through its own reflection. This requires a subtle separation of itself. In the formative world, that self-reflection elaborates and fractures itself into the countless pieces needed to make the design of the universe. This can be interpreted as the self-reflected consciousness becoming individual localizations of consciousness that through their experience renders the world below (in Assiah). This process is very complex. The Princess of Swords fills a vital role. He maintains a feedback loop between the Knight of Swords and the Queen of Swords. The Knight of Swords is always asking a question fueled by the curiosity at the top of the formative world (yod of vav) to explore multiplicity. The Queen of Swords satisfies that curiosity by offering the birth of form through idea and ego. In the formative world, this is the birth of individual self-hood (which, as described earlier, always has a beginning and ending). This dance between Knight and Queen of Swords *is* the individual self. The knight is the impulse and movement, while the queen is the reflection of that movement, which engenders the knight's movement again. When this pattern happens fast enough, it appears as a static thing, the self-concept. One way to understand this is with a firebrand. If you take a fire brand and spin it in a circle fast enough, it will eventually look like one static circle of fire. The movement is the knight. The circular path is the queen. The illusion of a static circle is the prince. The Prince of Swords is divinely full of all sorts of illusion and is called "concept."

The Prince of Swords is the vav of vav, air of air. As air of air he is the extreme of air. To understand the Prince of Swords, meditate on air's elusive, tenuous, and—in particular—invisible quality. Like air, the ego is invisible because it doesn't really exist. That means its concept of itself also shares in its unreality. It is an interpretation of a center that appears only because of the relationships between sensations and thought. The Prince of Swords is about to elaborate on the illusion of the eye of the storm.

Prince of Swords

Macrocosmically, the Prince of Swords is the intellect of the formative world. The intuitive forming power of the Queen of Swords has made an "I." The moment that "I" conceptualizes anything, it is in the realm of the Prince of Swords.

Microcosmically, the Prince of Swords is the apex of the intellectual part of the soul. His entire reality is abstraction. This makes things easy to create and formulate but also easy to destroy. This contradiction pulls him in opposite directions, just like the undines/humanoid figures on the Thoth card. Spiritually, air is the space that appears between fire and water, the microcosm that appears between the sacred masculine and sacred feminine of the macrocosm.

In his futile abstraction, there is great profundity. And to understand it, we must return to the Fool. The Fool is the spiritual element of air, aleph, the mother letter of air. Crowley interprets this as a vacuum. When this vacuum folds itself into masculine (fire) and feminine (water), the space remaining becomes what we might consider "terrestrial air," the element of swords. When that folds in on itself, we arrive at the Prince of Swords, which is the mind's concept of its own workings. The Prince of Swords is thus the ability to think about thinking. He is the ultimate meta. He is a brain in its own thought bubble. In an inescapable loop, he can't get much done.

On the tetractys, he is the third row, which brings the points to a total of six, the number of the Hebrew letter vav. Having taken form from his mother, he can now experience a point of view of his own self. He says "I am a self" only to recognize that he himself thought that.

This realization is the problem with the Prince of Swords. He is constantly searching for himself through abstraction, idea, symbol, meaning, and language. He is the semiotic masturbation of the mind, trapped in a prison of duality. He constantly creates meaning, but every meaning leads to another meaning that destroys the old one. As the dying god, he is the constant rebirth of thought. He is the beauty (Tiphareth) of our mental apparatus, constantly breaking apart through analysis and rebuilding through synthesis and association. However, he will never be ultimately satisfied—not until he surrenders his efforts and returns his power to his parents in mystical ascent. Sounds like humanity right? For this reason, he is astrologically associated with the first two decans of Aquarius (the Star) and the last decan of Capricorn (the Devil). Aquarius is the sign of humanity, which is fitting due to its fixed air nature. Most people are fixated on their minds, truly at the expense of their real being (a problem mysticism solves). The Prince of Swords marks the transition from material, concrete Capricorn into abstract, idea-driven Aquarius. The first decan of Aquarius is ruled by Venus and is attributed to the Five of Swords, titled Defeat. Venus is all about values, beauty, and pleasure but doesn't often initiate. The passivity of Venus with the idealistic nature of Aquarius makes for empty optimism. This is the part of the Prince of Swords (and many people of the world) who have everything to say about how things should be but no real means to get there.

The solutions they seek exist in the Prince of Swords's second decan of Aquarius, ruled by Mercury, the Six of Swords, what Crowley entitled Science. This title includes conventional science as well as the spiritual science of the great work. This card is essentially problem solving. Here, Mercury, the logos, communicates the right path for the navigating Aquarius, humanity. When the Prince of Swords's hyper-conceptualizing capacity is used as a tool for a higher intelligence, it leads to spiritual and social progress.

CHAPTER 3

The shadow decan of the Prince of Swords is the last decan of Capricorn, ruled by the sun. The card attributed is the Four of Disks, Power. This card signifies material power and the establishment of a physical structure or reputation. This is anathema to the Prince of Swords, who is constantly destroying and recreating abstract ideas of himself. Having an established reputation or concrete structure would limit his intellectual freedom, yet at the same time, it may be *just* what he wants. Perhaps all of his theoretical inventions seem like they will be the final masterpiece, the powerful structure he's always wanted, until he destroys them.

In a reading, the Prince of Swords shows someone who is totally in their head. They may have the qualities of a genius (Aquarius) but lack practicality (Capricorn). They constantly find new solutions for things but don't always follow through with action. Well-dignified, they are unique innovators and pioneers of their field. Ill-dignified, they are their own worst enemy, plagued with self-doubt. Spiritually, the Prince of Swords is the distraction and glory of incarnation through Self-interpretation and invention. He is the sum total of all self-concepts that form a personal identity. The personal identity, filled with attractions and aversions (first introduced by the karma of the Queen of Swords's attribution to Ma-at), finds its embodiment in the princess.

PRINCESS OF SWORDS

The feedback between thought (Knight of Swords) and thinker (Queen of Swords) renders the personal identity (Prince of Swords). This personal identity finds its embodiment in the Princess of Swords. At the bottom of the formative world, this princess starts the transition from mind to matter. She is the heh final of vav. Elementally, this is the earth of air, the materialization of idea, or alchemically, the "fixation of the volatile."[117] In alchemy, fixation is a process by which a previously volatile substance is transformed into a form (often solid) that is not affected by fire. It separates the substance or object and puts it back in the same or different shape at a subatomic level. This is symbolized by her crest, medusa, who turns people (mind) into stone (matter). To understand this princess, meditate on smoke or dust in the air.

Macrocosmically, she is the conclusion of the formative world. Remember that this world creates the blueprint of our physical reality. She helps finalize that blueprint, and begin its departure from the abstract into the material world of action below. She does this by pouring the identity of the Prince of Swords into the physical body.

---

117. Crowley, *Book of Thoth*, 163.

Princess of Swords

    Microcosmically, she is the ruach reaching into the nephesh. This is the rational mind directing the autonomic nervous system. Recall that the Knight and Queen of Swords have a feedback loop. The Knight of Swords represents the impulsive intellectual movement while the Queen of Swords is its reflection in ego. This dance creates the Prince of Swords's identity and self-conceptualization. In a similar way, the Prince of Swords's identity has a feedback loop with the Princess of Swords. This makes the embodiment into the "animal soul" or lower nature in a cybernetic relationship, as cybernetics is a field concerned with feedback loops and constant adjustment. The Prince of Swords says "this is who I am now." The Princess of Swords follows that instruction with physical action. The dark secret is this is largely unconscious. This is why words have power. This is what is colloquially called the "law of attraction." When we say "I am smart, rich, and capable," the conscious mind puts that carrot ahead of the donkey. The donkey follows the carrot, in the same way as the

CHAPTER 3

physical body follows the thought. The embodiment of the Princess of Swords follows the ideas of the Prince of Swords. This is the method of magick and manifestation. It's simply the body automatically behaving in accordance with the mental input.

For many people, creating the world they want—whether through manifestation or magick—isn't easy. That's because while they create what they want, they subconsciously create what they don't. Many people will chant mantras such as "I am wealthy" and see no financial improvement. This is because for ninety percent of the day, they are unconsciously worrying about their financial security. When we worry, the universe gives us something to worry about. Most of what the body is doing is unconscious. It's a record of all our years, and maybe other lifetimes too. The body is always following programs. The donkey has so many carrots it is chasing from the past. We can't add a new carrot without removing the old ones. How do you change the carrot? One might call it feeling—manifestation occurs from the feelings that outweigh other feelings. Remember earlier on, you learned how the feeling sense is what links the mechanical/body level to the subtle/causal level. This is the glue that brings mind into matter, our prince to our princess. It can take time to clean out old residual feelings from the past (or past lives), but the rewards are worth it. But sometimes the body resists. Sometimes the body is listening to older orders. And so, the princess on the Thoth card stabs downward defending an altar as the sun rises across from her. This is the union and friction of the body and mind, coming together, and also revolting, characteristic of her Aquarian nature.

The Princess of Swords is situated in the last row of the tetractys. She hears the prince's words "I am a self." This, she interprets into difference and circumstance. An ideal is not the actual. The distance between the actual embodiment and the mental ideal create the difference which makes the circumstance of the Princess of Swords. The very embodiment of mind delineates its location and its source. This can be understood by where the princess is and where she wants to be. It is her urge to move and act toward the ideal and identity established by the prince, which she also resists.

The unconscious factor that brings mind (prince) into matter (princess) is further emphasized by this princess's astrological attributions. She governs the quarter of the heavens centering on Aquarius. She shares the very human element with her prince. The ideal mentioned above is emphasized by Aquarius. However, instead of relishing in the pleasures of mere abstraction, she takes action. This is symbolized by her other two attributed signs, Capricorn and Pisces. Pisces is attributed to the Moon card and the Hebrew letter qoph. Qoph is the back of the head, referring to the unconscious factor of life we share with lower species. This is her mechanism, the animal soul fulfilling the desires of the prince, the donkey following the carrot. The action she takes is represented in Capricorn, attributed to the Devil card, further emphasizing the generation of the body as well as its ambition to happen to the world and take action. This is all led by the ideals of Aquarius.

In a reading, this card denotes someone who is fully invested in a cause. They are unafraid of confrontation, especially if it supports their ideals. They apply their ideals to practical pursuits (as their body follows the instructions of their mind). When dignified, they are assertive, graceful, brave, clever, strategic, actionable, unique, and unafraid to assert their beliefs. When ill-dignified, they are violent, defensive, incoherent, argumentative, and rebellious without a cause.

THE DISKS COURT

With the Princess of Swords having started the shift from mind to matter, the fourth and last world can begin its work. Assiah is the world of action. This world is attributed to the heh final of tetragrammaton, the element of earth, and microcosmically, the nephesh or animal soul. It's the material plane where things bump into each other to create sensation. Just as in the other three worlds, the tetragrammaton expresses its dance, but now, through matter. In the world of action, things slow down and get heavy, but also the most detailed. The movement from the above (Atziluth) to the below (Assiah) is a journey from the elusive and the abstract, to the concrete and defined. One way to think of it is in terms of pixelation. The more pixels on a screen, the more detail. The more detail, the more information. One view is that the universe is on an unending quest to create more and more information (see the Lovers and the Knight of Swords). At the apex of information, one would expect profundity and genius, but what we will find is the mundane. The family of disks represent the glory of the mundane, the natural, and the "normal" day-to-day in all its divine detail. Upon deeper consideration, one may find that it is genius after all. What makes it genius? The fact that it is created by us!

The generally accepted idea of tarot and its influences (Qabalah, Neoplatonism, Hermeticism, and so on) is one of emanation. The divine issues from high to low, and in so doing, creates denser forms of itself. However, these denser forms include us, and we are co-creators. When the abstract formative world meets the material world, it involves our own minds. Matter is simply the measurement of experience. Matter is nothing but meter. When people think of the "world," what they are referring to is a large, complex, collectively agreed-upon mass of measurements. Matter is a detailed interpretation of countless so-called things, and remember that each thing is something made, done, different, or changeable, here or there, coming or going, with a beginning or ending in time, space, or other dimensions. They are rendered by the family of swords in the formative world and embodied and sensed directly by the family of disks in Assiah, the world of action.

KNIGHT OF DISKS

The world of action begins with the Knight of Disks, the yod of heh final. Elementally, he is the fire of earth. This can be conceptualized as the might of a mountain, a sprouting plant, or the power of gravity. In one direction, the Knight of Disks is the reaching upward of the earth into its spiritual origin in the manner of the mountain or sprout. In reverse, he is the gravity that pulls the lust of the germ of life into the fertile soil to create organisms.

This germ of life symbolizes his macrocosmic function. The germ itself is the yod of tetragrammaton and the yod of Virgo (more on that astrological attribution below). This germ in this context represents a physical beginning of a living "thing" (something done, made, different, or changeable, here or there, coming or going, with a beginning in time, space, or other dimension). It is the will and force of the world of action, the seed going into manifestation. It is the mysterious spontaneous impulse for anything to live, move, grow, act, and become itself on the earth. This all occurs in the humble silence of the fertile earth.

Microcosmically, the knight is the will-force manipulating the animal soul. There are some levels to this. First, this is our subconscious and nervous system serving our will. When we want to walk somewhere, our will to go there engages the subconscious walking program in the body. We don't have to will each muscle separately. Not only does this knight govern the service of the body to the will, but he also governs service of other bodies to the will. In the human scale, he represents husbandry and agriculture, the ability of our will to manipulate animals and plants to create the lifestyle we want.

On the tetractys, he is the first point that, by existing, reflects on itself to become the dyad. This dyad, in the world of action, is the first movement of embodied life, unobstructed by the complex cultivation ahead.

He is the tendency of nature to slowly grow, complicate, and perfect itself. No other sign better describes these characteristics than Virgo. The Knight of Disks rules the first two decans of Virgo, attributed to the Hermit. The Hermit in the Thoth deck represents the silent and humble process of birth (notice the sperm cell in the bottom left corner) that, like death, is always a passage one must go through alone. He also represents the logos, the intelligent shaping power, heading toward the fertile earth, fueled by the power of the sun.

Knight of Disks

As mutable earth, the Hermit-Virgo energy is the flexibility of earth to receive the seed and shape itself into the life form of its secret design. The first decan is ruled by the Sun, attributed to the Eight of Disks, titled Prudence. This rulership and card both point to the process of the sun's energy entering into terrestrial life through photosynthesis. The next decan is ruled by Venus, the planet of beauty, values, and love. This decan is attributed to the Nine of Disks, Gain. After the sun's energy enters the fertile earth of Virgo, it is transfigured into the beauty of diverse life forms. The world gains its character from the solar system, and we incarnate. Recall that the Hebrew letter of Virgo is *yod*, "hand." This yod is considered the source pattern of the Hebrew alphabet, the seed of creation, and the hand of God. This summarizes the method and result of the logos in matter. The Knight of Disks personifies the humble beginning of this process. But all is not so humble.

His shadow decan is the last decan of Leo, ruled by Mars (the Tower). Leo is attributed to the Lust card and Mars the Tower to form a pretty significant combination of cards. Lust is the card of magick and sexual energy that fittingly follows the previously mentioned symbolism. Remember that the function attributed to yod is sex. Our Knight of Disks draws that sexual energy from Leo/Lust and the yod into the fertility phase of Virgo, the virgin. However, the transition makes a sharp contrast. In Leo and the Lust card is an orgiastic, unbridled fanfare of power. In Virgo and the Hermit, the energy is directed with careful reverence and delicate detail into the earth. Though the Knight of Disks might not admit it, his process of procreation and cultivation cannot begin without a dramatic level of Leo's fiery courage and excitement. Through the Mars rulership, the Tower card allows the Knight of Disks to break down nutrients into the organism that will result from careful work.

In a reading, the Knight of Disks represents the part of the self who is not afraid of work. In the story of the three little pigs, this is the pig who built the brick house. This knight is the only knight whose horse has all four hooves on the ground. Unlike the other knights who are racing, loving, or fighting, this knight is working tirelessly. He is confined to the production of life. This represents someone who is hardworking, detail-oriented, patient, dependable, and enduring. Ill-dignified, the person may seem unintelligent, boring, unapproachable, or stubborn. Spiritually, he can be summarized to represent the action of the material world toward life.

QUEEN OF DISKS

If the first movement of the world of action is toward life, the second step is that initial life spreading and growing into a diverse ecosystem. This process is governed by the Queen of Disks. She is the reaction of the first action and all the relationships that mutually arise from the first movement of life. She is a cell splitting in two and the complication of life into multicellular life-forms and beyond. Elementally, she is water of earth, heh of heh final. This can be conceptualized as the oases beginning on the card in the Thoth deck. Or, we can understand this as the quality of nature to spill over. To understand her, meditate on images of nature taking over deserted lands. Reflect on the words of nature to say "if it is possible, it will happen." This flexibility and passivity to the potential seed of the Knight of Disks is similar to the Empress, Lust, and even the Tower. These three major arcana bridge the right and left pillars of the Tree of Life. Like the Queen of Disks, each of them is an expression of love.

Queen of Disks

Macrocosmically, she is the intuition of the world of action. We can understand this to mean the ability of the material world to continue itself. It is the passivity of the physical world to become what it will become when the corresponding conditions are set. She is the world appearing passively as a result of all of the particles, waves, and forces being where they are. This queen says yes to every seed the dedicated knight offers—from acorns, to sperm cells, to quarks. She is the effortlessness of organisms to grow, heal, and multiply. Like nature, she doesn't try or conceptualize. She allows.

Her radical allowance brings us to her microcosmic scale. She is seated so high in the neshamah, the intuition. From this perspective, she views the whole ecosystem of the world, in all its diversity. She is the intuition guiding the "animal soul" or autonomic nervous system. This is a very unique pair that sheds light on the relationship between intuition and instinct. There have been many tools in recent therapeutic practice, energy work, and personal growth movements that deal with healing through the body and somatic experience. By connecting to the body, one can connect to their intuition. This may seem contradictory to the traditional Qabalistic system, where the body is lower and the intuition is higher, but it is one of the major secrets between the relationship of Malkuth to Binah, princess and queen. Remember, the princess becomes the queen. The body becomes the intuition. This helps the seeker get out of their mind which is oftentimes the overly used part of the soul. You'll see this in other parts of the tarot as well. For example, the Moon card and Pisces are related to the body and animal instinct, and yet Pisces is the most spiritual sign, ruling the last house. The Princess of Disks will exemplify this too. These correspondences connect the highest highs with the lowest lows, which is the aim of the great work and mystical quest. The intuition and instinct still have a big difference at the human level. The intuition is a sudden, all-at-once grasp of complexity, while the instinct is an automatic response pattern. Yet at the level of the Queen of Disks, they are not so separate. Recall that the Queen of Disks is the response to the initial action of the Knight of Disks. She causes the seed to sprout in response to the proper conditions. The physical world's automatic responses can be interpreted as intuitive intelligence.

The seed sprouting is a change. On the tetractys, this is the change of the seed's silence into movement, the second row, where the queen says "I am." It is always through change that she accomplishes her work. On the Tree of Life, she corresponds to Binah, representing the change from unity into duality in the manifest world and the diversification of matter. But this can only happen through change.

Change is the title of the Two of Disks, one of her astrological attributions. This card corresponds to the first decan of Capricorn ruled by Jupiter. Capricorn is the Devil card, the ambition of matter and lust of life (you can actually see the cells dividing on the Devil card in the Thoth deck). Jupiter is the fortune card. Fortune brings in an expansion of possibility for our queen to work with in producing all of her life forms. The actual form of life is produced by the next decan of Capricorn, ruled by Mars. This is attributed to the Three of Disks, Work, a card about the production of energy into material form. This is her work, and it is supported by Mars, a planet that gives us the will to live, corresponding with the Tower card. The will to live represented by the Queen of Disks is obvious, but there is a further connection. The Tower and Mars destroy. Remember how the family of wands introduced the doctrine that love and destruction were the same? The results of that secret doctrine are experienced in the family of disks. Through destruction and reconstruction, she leverages the power of Capricorn to generate the material world. She reconstructs all nature into new life forms, all the time.

But this all happens intuitively, without effort or force—usually. Her shadow decan is the last decan of Sagittarius, ruled by Saturn. Sagittarius is a sign of freedom, curiosity, and limitless potential, very much in alignment with the queen's freedom to make any organism she wishes. And yet the last decan she corresponds to is ruled by Saturn, the greater malefic, corresponding to the Ten of Wands, Oppression. This energy is anathema to the queen's intuitive freedom, but it is also in her power to oppress. In the name of freedom, all forms of life are allowed to be born and *are* born. But because of such diversity, not everyone's form is equal: Organisms feed on each other. The freedom that begets the predator also begets the death of the prey. Life forms are oppressed below in certain circumstances to allow for the freedom of the whole. This is both the sorrow and joy of our Queen of Disks, who hides her face in awe of the material show.

In a reading, the Queen of Disks shows us the aspect of ourselves to nurture life, especially physically. She is intuitive, instinctive, and in a way, ambitious, but not loudly, who applies herself mostly to practical matters. She is not so inspired or intellectual, and follows her instinct instead of logic. She is incredibly grounded and hospitable, and makes a great caretaker, cooks, and cultivator of life. If ill-dignified, she may seem mechanical, devoid of spirit, and even ignorant. Spiritually, she is matter's ambition to take part in the great work.

PRINCE OF DISKS

As we have seen, the knights introduce action, and it is no different for the Knight of Disks. Next, reaction and development come from the Queen of Disks. The feedback loop between the two brings us to the Prince of Disks and the third phase of Assiah. He is the natural agency of the intelligence of fructification. He is the vav of heh final, the air of earth. One way to understand him is to meditate on how formless space is designated through the form of intelligent life's design. Life takes form based on certain processes happening in certain designs and patterns, from molecules, to cells, to tissues, to organs, to organisms, and so on. The patterns of sacred geometry evident in life forms are under his domain. It is in this manner that air, the element of intelligence, governs earth, matter, to create intelligent design and advance evolution.

Macrocosmically, this prince is the intellect of the world of action. It is the ability of the material world to organize itself to complicate itself, which directly reflects the development of the formative world to do the same with abstraction. In Assiah, this creates more and more physical, tangible forms, from organisms to cities. In fact, one way you understand this is by watching time-lapse footage of cities. Countless motivations in countless

Prince of Disks

human bodies direct countless vehicles and energy currents in specific directions to busy the streets, power the buildings, and pollute the sky with light, noise, and chemicals. And yet, amidst the chaos, there is a fine intelligence directing everything and everyone. A more natural example would be detailed patterning in cellular division and fertilization. In the Prince of Disks, you see what might look like eggs in the background, signifying intelligent design and the multiplication of life.

Microcosmically, the Prince of Disks represents the animal soul and autonomic nervous system (nephesh) in service to the mind, (ruach). This is similar to the Princess of Swords, who shares the combination of elements and thus soul-parts. However, in the Princess of Swords is emphasis on the mind as the organizing principle of automatic processes. In the Prince of Disks, there is an emphasis on the automatic processes and their physical results, the result of a more distant organizing mental principle. We see the eggs on the card but not what laid them. The general idea of the card is maintenance and continuation of patterns already set out. He is the intelligence that guides the continued materialization and development of his parents' introduction of matter.

On the tetractys, he sits on the third row of points. He states "I am a self." The self he is talking about is the body and its actions that answer to his intelligence. On the Tree of Life, he is situated in Tiphareth, the sephirah of the dying god. The dying god formula in this context represents the constant change of matter to ensure its stability, reflected in his astrological correspondences.

Taurus represents this stability and corresponds to the Hierophant, a glyph of the logos realized in matter. The method of this realization will be explained: The Prince of Disks rules the first two decans of Taurus. The first decan is ruled by the planet Mercury and corresponds to the Five of Disks, titled Worry in the Thoth deck and Lord of Material Trouble by MacGregor Mathers. Although airy, flighty Mercury does not like being in still, grounded Taurus, he plays a very important function here. We know that Mercury is the logos, the will and shaping power of the universe. He is also communication and mind. In this decan, the mind worries about the material world. But why would such a stable Prince of Disks need to worry? It has to do with the illusion of lack. From a Vedic perspective, the very reason we incarnate into material bodies is because we have previously taken action for a desired result of something we lacked. Whenever we take such action for a result, we surrender to the illusion of lack. What result could we ever need if we recognized our completeness? As consciousness, we lack nothing. As incarnated humans, we lack everything we are not, and so we enter the chase of samsara. The stability of the material world exists through its constant chase. This constant change is ensured by action (karma) of its units (such as humans). The harmony of this action and karma are expressed by Binah and the queens giving birth to actualized duality below the abyss (as opposed to ideal duality above the abyss) on the Tree of Life. The prince continues the development of this duality by continuing the illusion of lack that inspires a continued effort. The "worry" of the first decan of Taurus is the worry of the mind being embodied into an experience of limitation and lack, which motivates effort. At higher levels of meditation, you may find that all efforts are a subtle manifestation of the illusion of lack and the ignorance to completeness.

In the second decan of Taurus, the inspired effort pays off. It is ruled by the Moon and corresponds to the Six of Disks, Success. The flexibility of the watery Moon ensures the stability of material Taurus. Flexibility, by definition, demands that a thing is able to move, and all movement must have a here or there, coming or going. These are the qualities of things, anything made, done, different, or changeable. All things are limited and under the illusion of lack. In all we do, we search for completion. From the countless searches of countless organisms and countless cosmic bodies, a complete universe reigns.

That completion is seen in the Prince of Disks's shadow decan, the last decan of Aries ruled by Venus, corresponding to the Four of Wands, titled Completion (or Lord of Perfected Work by the Golden Dawn). This card takes the initial creative force of Aries and tempers it with Venus's gentleness and tact to complete the sign. Like the other shadow decans, contained within it are both a fear and secret goal. If the prince completes his work, there would be nothing left to do, yet everything he does *is* to complete his work. This is the inescapable paradox of spirit becoming matter. When someone asks what the meaning of life is, any intellectual answer can only be offered as a temporary comfort. The real answer is not intellectual—the real answer cancels itself out and can only be arrived at by the highest self-inquiry, which I can only call mysticism.

In a reading, the Prince of Disks represents the aspect of us to stabilize and maintain. He is smart, focusing mostly on practical affairs. He uses patterns and logic to optimize the cultivation that was intuitively brought about by his mother. This makes him a great businessman, manager, financial advisor, or accountant. He is great strength applied to material matters but lacks emotion. He is reliable, steady, and trustworthy if well-dignified, but sometimes unapproachable and lacking in empathy. If ill-dignified, his qualities are degraded. He is stubborn, less intelligent, and materialistic.

PRINCESS OF DISKS

We learned that the Prince of Disks hides his illusion of lack through an impressive veil of material stability. The Princess of Disks represents the moment before that veil is removed and the illusion dispelled. She is one of the most profound tarot cards, the last of the court card system. However, it is important to understand that the end begets the beginning. There are certain techniques I teach my students directly that can't be explained here, but their general philosophy is summarized here in the context of Qabalistic tarot.

Our Princess of Disks is the heh final of heh final, the earth of earth. To understand her, meditate on the center of the center of the center of the smallest possible unit of measurement, and then do the same with the largest of the large. Remember that all matter is just measurement. The Princess of Disks, as the earth of earth, is not just the measurements which render the material universe we perceive, but the capacity of that measurement. She is the measurement of the measurer. And in this role as infinite, ubiquitous

Princess of Disks

measurer, she takes note of and thus makes all things, *but* she doesn't know that she is the one doing all the measuring. You might compare her with something like the standard model of physics. The model does not exist in some epic cosmic manual—it is an abstract invention of the human mind to explore reality, an interpretation by our own brains' gray matter. If the very building blocks of reality are only an interpretation, can we ever find the truth? Yes and no. No, because the truth will not be found as an object. Yes, because the truth can be found by the subject observing the object. The Princess of Disks represents the slippery epistemological problem and the pinnacle of nonduality. She shows that matter, which is measurement, cannot exist without the measurer. This principle is symbolized in the silent, perfectly innocent child dipping the diamond of Kether into the farthest reaches of the earth. She is the observer that pervades everything. The yin-yang disk she holds is the duality she transmutes into the unity. This unity merges measurer with measurement, mind with matter, observer with observed. It is the same unity from which the Knight of Wands rushes out. She is the vehicle for its return.

The same concept of "redintegration" introduced in the Universe card and the Ten of Disks is applied here. In the context of the court cards, the Princess of Disks is the last card of the system, providing the same function to the court cards as the Ten of Disks does for the pips and the Universe card does for the majors. These three cards represent the climax of materialization: The Princess of Disks is the last card of the court card system in the same way as the universe card ends the majors and the Ten of Disks ends the small cards. These three cards represent the climax of materialization, which signal its return to spirit. This return can be interpreted as the mystical quest, the great work, the spiritual journey that brings us to our ultimate reality. There are countless paths. I have found that the Prince of Disks hints at two. The first is the commonly understood path of high magick, which climbs the Tree of Life through ritual. This path is detailed in other works. The other path she hints at is a direct path that I have and continue to refer to in this book. The direct path is an immediate apprehension of the real that the tarot expresses holographically. In every symbol on every card is a reference back to the whole, what I call consciousness. And it is this whole that our princess is about to become aware of, symbolized by her pregnant belly. She will give birth to the Fool, pure consciousness itself, the same fool who is the "no thing" from whence issued the Knight of Wands. The no thing is "no thing" because it is not a measurement—it is the measurer. It has no form because it is that which experiences all form. It is the same formless nature that is observing these words now. The words have form. The observer does not. Fullness meets emptiness. The end begets the beginning.

Macrocosmically, she is the last phase of the last world, Assiah. She is action as we experience it every day. She takes the intelligence of her prince and manifests it fully into our direct, inarguably *real* experiences. She is not the experience of the real but the reality of the experience in all the glory and horror of the phantom-show of time, space, and incarnation. She is the mundane as a perfect expression of the transcendent. She is the physical within the metaphysical, the result, completion, and method of the Knight of Wands's purposeless movement. She will return to him under the same divine conditions: Purified of purpose.

Microcosmically, she is the animal soul and all its automatic processes. She is what drives us unconsciously to do what we do. She is your resilient body which works from an impressive storehouse of memories: Ancestral, evolutionary, planetary, cosmic. She is every feeling and sensation you have as a perfect result of countless forces interacting. She is the gamble of the universe to become a saint or a murderer, and the ultimate truth of her is never affected. To really understand the Princess of Disks is to understand that there is no right or wrong, good or bad. Whatever happens is a perfect result of innumerable forces at play, countless particles and forces and interference patterns rendering the current experience. All experiences simply are. When we conclude that an experience is "good" or "bad" we just layer another mental experience on top of it.

The Princess of Disks is the infinite limitations of the one limitless truth. When the prince says "I am a self," she arises naturally with all the experiences and embodiments a self can have through folding the mental identity into embodied conditions and circumstance. She is situated on the last row of the tetractys, where the full detail of so-called things can be done, made, different, or changed, here or there, coming or going in all its stark clarity and contrast. On the Tree of Life, she sits in Malkuth. It is said by Kabbalists that Malkuth is in Kether. She is the last of the last, and thus the first.

The paradox of this redintegration process brings to mind the paradox introduced in the Prince of Disks. Recall that matter's stability is ensured by action and change, which are insured by the illusion of lack and incompleteness (limitation exists through measurement). The princess shares this paradox, having an overlapping attribution of Taurus. She rules the quarter of the heavens centered on this stable sign. A very profound doctrine arises with her attribution to Taurus. She reveals that the stability of Taurus is not ensured just through the instability of change (like the Prince of Disks) but rather, is ontologically promised by another sort of instability. In the Princess of Disks is the instability of knowing herself. What she is about to become aware of is the single most frightening and amazing discovery any conscious being can make: There is no teleology. There is no purpose or reason for being. Even the logos cannot know who or what sent it. This is not philosophy—it is a mystical experience. However, its truth cannot be transmitted through words. The method to reach that experience can be symbolized through the sacred marriage, which her other astrological attributions suggest.

This princess governs Aries and Gemini. The paradox she resolves is known as the sacred marriage. It expresses the canceling out of opposites. Whether in yoga, alchemy, high magick, or otherwise, there comes a point where all particulars are resolved in one ineffable universal. The zodiacal attributions of our princess express different aspects of this marriage. Aries is attributed to the Emperor, who represents the masculine force of the marriage, wedded to the Empress. Aries is also the first sign, hinting at the princess's return to the beginning. Gemini corresponds to the Lovers card, an obvious connection to the sacred marriage, though do note that the Lovers card is not just the union of opposites for mystical return; it is the division of opposites for manifestation. And finally, Taurus corresponds to the Hierophant, the officiator of the marriage, a card that expresses the materialization of the word.

In a reading, this card is not easy to understand. It usually takes on the characteristics of surrounding cards. Oftentimes, it represents an innocent aspect of ourselves about to become aware of something. It can represent youth or a youthful temperament. The characteristics themselves are paradoxical: Someone who is peaceful and grounded yet unpredictable and bewildered. Usually this is someone pure of heart who surrenders themselves fully in their reactions to their circumstances. But in that surrender is its own glory in a manner almost charming.

Spiritually, the best way to understand the Princess of Disks is through the "Measuring Me" exercise on page 24. Notice how anything made, done, different, or changeable in your experience has edges in time or spaces. Notice how awareness has no edges in time or space. This contradiction between awareness and its objects is the primary concern of the sacred marriage, the great work, and the tarot, all summarized in the Princess of Disks.

INFINITE REGRESS AND THE INTRANSITIVE VERB: YHVH

The Princess of Disks brings about an ontological paradox proposed by Madhyamika Buddhists. They teach a doctrine of emptiness by refuting any claim about the absolute substance of reality. When looking for the smallest, most subtle thing that makes up reality, there are two outcomes. If it does indeed exist, then it must have some measurement (remember, a "thing" that exists has edges). If it has some measurement, it can be divided further. If it can be divided further, it's not the smallest, subtlest thing. But if everything can be constantly subdivided infinitely, that leads to infinite regress.

Infinite regress is a sequence of causes or justifications that never end. Physics has discovered molecules to be made of atoms, which are made out of subatomic particles, and so on. If this continues infinitely, it would be considered infinite regress. A foundational cause would never be reached. This type of thing is anathema to logicians, but fun for the mystic. The important thing is that there is no ultimate ground or beginning (to the Buddhist), at least not as an object of our awareness (to the Vedantan).

There are four court cards I would like to explore as symbols of infinite regress: The Knight of Wands, Queen of Cups, Prince of Swords, and Princess of Disks. These all share the same element of their office with the element of their suit. This is not a traditional tarot attribution but another way to contemplate the far-reaching nature of the sacred name.

The Knight of Wands is fire of fire, the yod of the yod. As such, he represents the source of the source of YHVH. But why is he not the source of *that*, the source of the source of the source? I like this idea because in the mode of infinite regress, we never reach the ground of the knight's existence ... that is, unless we go to the Fool. But the Fool is 0. the Fool is "no thing." And nothing is ever so simple! Because the Fool is nothing, it's really nothing we can consider and there is nothing to say about it.

The Queen of Cups is water of water, the heh primal of heh primal. She is the reflection of reflection itself, the ability of the universe to even know it exists. She is the infinite reflections between two mirrors. Because the reflections are infinite, there is no origin. She matches the beginningless quality of the Knight of Wands. In this way, the infinite regress of heh primal matches the infinite regress of yod.

The Prince of Swords is air of air, vav of vav. He is the son and vehicle of the sacred marriage of his parents. He matches their infinite regress with self-conceptualization. He represents the ability of consciousness to conceptualize itself infinitely. Think of yourself. Now notice the one doing the thinking. You will either find another concept of yourself that will lead to infinite regress, or you will find a vast nothingness, the Fool.

The Princess of Disks is earth of earth, heh final of heh final. She represents the paradox of the earlier mentioned Madhyamika Buddhist. She is both all the "things" of the universe and the notion that none of those "things" have inherent reality apart from what makes them up (a realization that can continue in an infinitely smaller direction). She represents how nothing is what it is when you zoom in far enough, and so she pushes the diamond of Kether into the center of the earth.

What I like about this system is that it makes the court cards, as a representation of YHVH and being, an intransitive verb. First, let's talk about verbs. YHVH, and us, as creative processes, are verbs. We aren't static people, places, and things like nouns. We are movements of energy, space, or consciousness. We are processes of energy moving around in a repeating pattern. We are happening! But more specifically, the ultimate reality of things and YHVH are not only the same verb but that verb is an intransitive one—it has no object. There are of course objects in our experience, but when we look deeper at every object (whether it be the car you drive, the thoughts you have, the people in your life, or even this book you are reading), we find that each object exists only to the subject of our awareness. It is the action and intransitive *verbiage* of our consciousness that is more real than the objects born from it. The infinite regress of the four court cards leads to this higher reality.

Chapter 3

In this way, YHVH becomes… the source of the source of the source… (ad infinitum, symbolized by the Knight of Wands)

Which is:

The reflection of its reflection of its reflection… (ad infinitum, symbolized by the Queen of Cups)

Which is:

The conceptualization of its conceptualization of its conceptualization… (ad infinitum, symbolized by the Prince of Swords)

Which is:

The infinite process of zooming into the universe to find more and more subtly, forever… (ad infinitum, symbolized by the Princess of Disks)

At this level, maybe the very idea of measurement is meaningless. If there are no meaningful measurements, there are no edges, no beginnings and endings, and no "things." When there are no things, there is "no thing." Here we might just peek at the Fool, where nothing matters. I'll never forget the sparkle in my student's eyes when it hit her. She looked at me and said, "Ah! Nothing *matters*." In those two words, she summed up the entire tarot and Tree of Life and quite literally, everything.

CHAPTER 4
THE SMALL CARDS

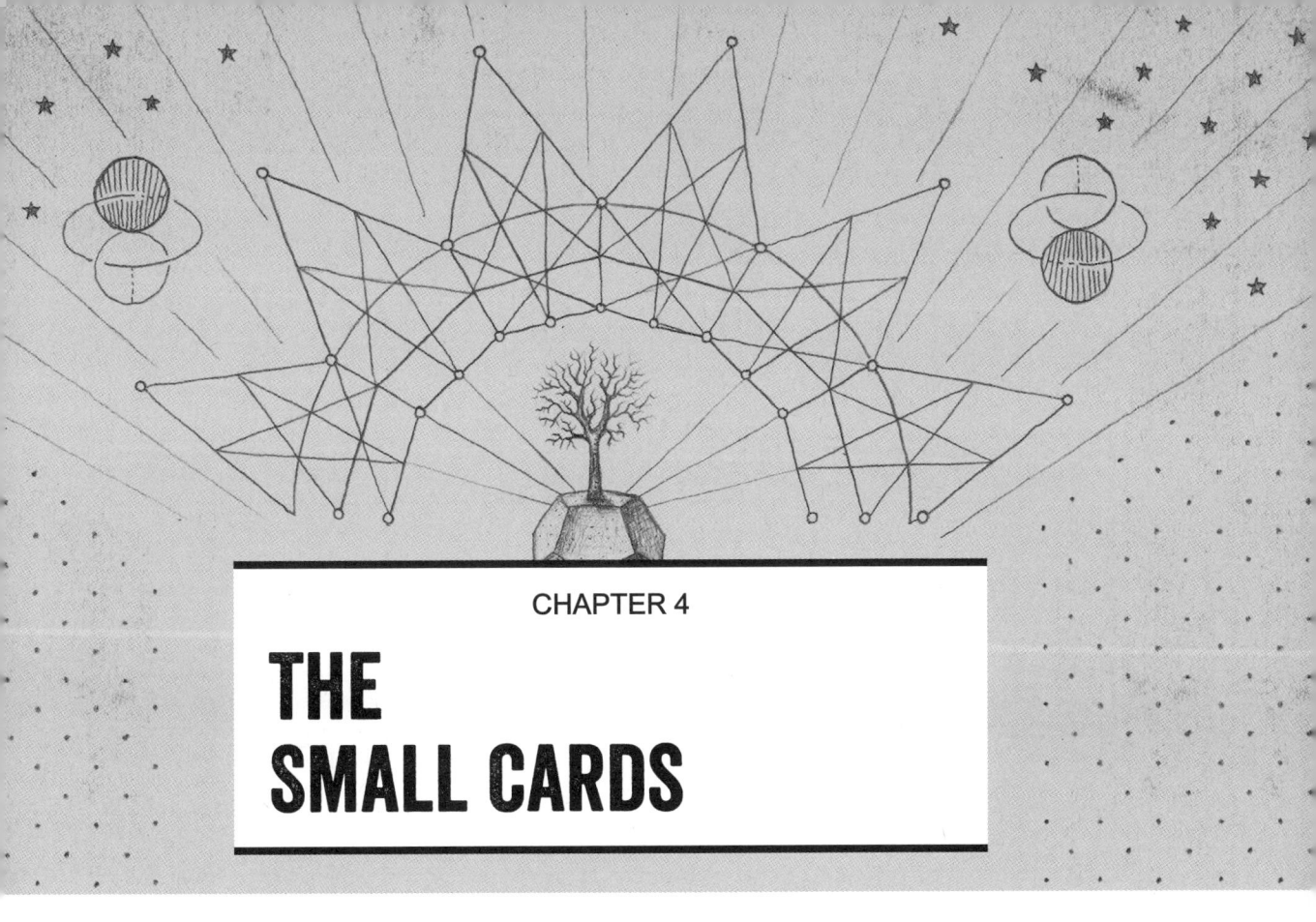

Now that we understand the permutations of the Holy Tetragrammaton, we will study the Tree of Life in depth. The tree can be thought of as an elaboration of the sacred name that we just explored four times. The Tree of Life takes the four letters and expands their functions into ten spheres of emanation in the same way as the Pythagorean tetractys represents four rows of ten points. We are taking four big ideas introduced through the court cards and elaborating on them by expanding them into ten still very big ideas. These ten big ideas coincide with the same four worlds symbolized by tarot's four suits. The minor arcana cards show a more detailed look at consciousness, creation, the universe—and thus you.

THE FOUR BIG IDEAS

First, let's review and establish the four big ideas introduced so far. These will be used to help understand the four suits as they express the four worlds. The specific words I use for

CHAPTER 4

these four big ideas are for teaching purposes, though you will find parallels in multiple traditions below. These four big ideas describe the four elements, four court cards, the Holy Tetragrammaton, the four worlds, and the tetractys. Having gone through the four families of the four court cards, they may be familiar to you: Movement, relationship, concept, and embodiment. They all come out of nothingness:

4 BIG IDEAS CHART

BIG IDEA	NUMBER	SEPHIROTH	WORLD	SUIT	SOUL	OFFICE
Nothingness	0	Three Veils of Nothingness	Ain soph	(None)	Yechidah	(None)
Movement	1 and 2	Kether and Chokmah	Atziluth	Wands	Chiah	Knights
Relationship	3	Binah	Briah	Cups	Neshamah	Queens
Concept	4 through 9	Chesed through Yesod	Yetzirah	Swords	Ruach	Princes
Embodiment	10	Malkuth	Assiah	Disks	Nephesh	Princesses

These four ideas express how something comes out of nothing in the youniverse. They literally show how some "thing" comes out of "no thing" in the process of being. "No thing" moves and creates a relationship with itself by its movement. The relationship is conceptualized through dualistic ideation and complex embodiment is carved into reality, making a "thing." A "thing" is anything made, done, different, or changeable, here or there, coming or going, with edges (a beginning or ending) in time, space, or any dimension. Remember that YHVH expresses reality's nature "to be." More so, YHVH is the "to be" that bridges "no thing" to some "thing":

"No thing" → YHVH (TO BE) → Some "Thing"

If you understand these four basic but big ideas, the esoteric tarot will get much simpler and much deeper. It's all about how reality does, makes, differentiates, and changes itself. Imagine consciousness like paper. Before any manifestation, it has no folds; it is a perfectly flat plane. The paper reaches in all directions. It is the primordial absolute and thus contains all; nothing exists apart from it. Thus, this is our "no thing" or Qabalistic ain soph.

Because this "no thing" encompasses all, there is nothing outside of itself. To create something out of nothing, it must do so within itself. To do this, it *moves* within itself. This is the first big idea, "movement." This is also called the *primum mobile*.

The movement of the paper of consciousness causes it to fold and eventually touch itself. This creates "relationship," our second big idea. All relationships are consciousness rubbing up against itself, subject and the object. Have you ever had an experience of something that wasn't in your consciousness? This is the secret joy of the mystic. Suffering is the illusion of a relationship with anything else but one's real nature (consciousness).

Now, this doesn't mean we will all melt into one single soup of consciousness. Luckily, the third big idea, "concept," will hold and elaborate on an experience of form. Concept comes in and says, "Ah, this is paper." The concept is the blueprint of reality, including our relationship with it. It is the ability of the mind to measure "things" into "being." In the relationship stage, there was only paper touching paper because of movement. In the concept stage, the fold itself is interpreted and measured. The dimensions are conceptualized. It achieves a certain quality and form, and even a name. All conceptualization is a measurement of the mind.

Lastly, we have embodiment. What the mind measures, nature can materialize. To riff on Alan Watts, what has meter has matter. We could compare matter and meter to the Vedic *maya*, the layer of name, form, and function that comprise the world of illusion we are so familiar with. In our metaphor, the paper of consciousness gets so folded within its concepts of itself, it becomes the origami of our daily life in a process that mutually arises.

A relationship between the paper and itself is automatically defined once the paper is folded. It goes from a clean 180-degree flat page to a clear angle. And once the fold has degrees, it's in the realm of concept. The concept dependently originates with the relationship which dependently originates from the movement. So how does embodiment arise? That happens in the direct experience of the whole process.

Many traditions reflect this pattern; the ones briefly summarized here belong to mystic philosopher Plotinus, Hermeticism, and Advaita Vedanta. Plotinus taught four hypostases, four emanations that made a sort of ladder—what he calls the chain of being—to the absolute reality. In descending order, we have the one, the intellect, the soul, and nature. First is the one, which can be compared to nothingness. The one is singular and there is no second to it, so it cannot be quantified as a thing since there is no other thing to quantify it and define its edges. For this reason, it is nameless. The Hermeticists also call it "the one," and in Advaita Vedanta, it is called *Nirguna Brahaman* ("God without attributes").

CHAPTER 4

The next hypostasis is the intellect (Plotinus uses the word *nous* which is untranslatable). This word merges the meanings of "being" and "knowledge." For something to exist, it must exist in the knowledge of something. This is the folded paper of consciousness touching itself. Mystically, nous is the paradox of a knower knowing itself through itself. It is the ability of a relative point of view or localization of consciousness to recognize the absolute—its real nature—especially through recognizing that that real nature is the one doing the recognizing. In my nomenclature, this is the mutually arising moment of movement and relationship. The words "movement" and "relationship" allow for the one reality to move and experience itself as dual through its relationship to itself without admitting duality. In the Hermetic tradition, it correlates to the *ennead*. In Advaita Vedanta, it could correlate to *Iśvara* or *Saguna Brahman* ("God with attributes"). The attributes can only come about when there is a perception of *something* that always happens through relationship.

The next hypostasis of Plotinus is the soul, which I would stretch to correlate to concept. It's the soul's ideals that attract it (or not) to virtue and can draw it out of the identification with the body and toward the intellect, the real self. It is through concept and differentiation that the soul leaves the immeasurable and is embodied in the measured. In the Hermetic tradition, this might correlate to the ogdoad. In Advaita Vedanta, this could correlate to *Hiranyagarba*, "the cosmic mind."

Plotinus's last hypostasis is nature, which I would correlate to embodiment. It is important to note that Plotinus did not see nature as bad or evil but as totally natural. Nature had a quiet and humble quality in its creation. In the Hermetic tradition, this includes the seven governors (planets) and the earth below. In Advaita, it might correlate with *Virat*, the entirety of the physical universe. There are many other systems and traditions that reflect this four-fold nature. Mine are not strict correspondences, just comparisons.

The court cards were introduced previously to train you in working with these four big ideas. We learned how the four court cards not only express each of these individually but how the four families express each of these as a whole. The family of wands expresses the movement from nothing into something in the macrocosm. The knights express this specifically in the microcosm. The family of cups expresses the macrocosmic relationship that forms between the something created and that which it is not. The queens express this microcosmically. The family of swords expresses the conceptualization of that relationship to create more things in the macrocosm. The princes express this microcosmically. Finally, the family of disks expresses the embodiment of all these things in the macrocosm. The princesses express this microcosmically.

This creative process hints at the fractal nature of reality expressed in the popular axiom of the Emerald Tablet, "As above, so below." It also suggests a holographic nature of emanation, the method, as we have discussed, through which the Divine/consciousness/the ground of being overflows itself into its own reflection to arrive at our current experiences. The same patterns of our daily lives are nothing more than the complicated details of subtler, divine patterns. And these patterns are the subject of the minor arcana.

But how does four become ten? To understand, I use the tetractys and the tetragrammaton. The tetractys is, among other things, a visual expression of the theosophic extension of 10 (1 + 2 + 3 + 4 = 10). We can break this simple formula into four stages:

$1 = 1$

$1 + 2 = 3$

$1 + 2 + 3 = 6$

$1 + 2 + 3 + 4 = 10$

The four stages result in the sums one, three, six, and ten. On the Tree of Life, one is Kether, the crown. Three is Binah, understanding. Six is Tiphareth, beauty. Ten is Malkuth, kingdom. When you remember that the tip of the yod starts in Kether, this aligns perfectly with the Holy Tetragrammaton and Crowley's attributions of the four worlds. The four worlds are attributed like so: Atziluth includes Kether and Chokmah. Briah includes Binah. Yetzirah includes Chesed, Geburah, Tiphareth, Netzach, Hod, and Yesod. Assiah includes Malkuth. What's given here is not the only way to attribute the four worlds to the Tree of Life, but it is the most cognate for our system and aligns best for the Thoth deck. When combining this with the other correspondences detailed above, we get a beautiful system.

Recall that each suit of the four court cards represented the sacred name in each of the four Qabalistic worlds. In the same way, each suit of the small cards represents the Tree of Life in one of the four worlds. There are actually four trees (a development from the great sixteenth-century Kabbalist Isaac Luria), fitting perfectly with tarot's forty pip cards. The small cards express the sephiroth of the four-tree system. Notice in the chart above how each suit can correspond to one of the four big ideas—movement, relationship, concept, embodiment.

It is important to note that the small cards are *not* the sephiroth but simply expressions of them. Tarot is a Yetziratic tool that exists primarily in the mind. To go beyond the Yetziratic tarot, one must synthesize all the knowledge in this book with a regular spiritual practice to begin rising above the planes. This is not some esoteric secret. You can do it sitting, with your

Chapter 4

eyes closed. But it's not something that can be taught through words. This is something I teach students in long-term training.

It is at this time I recommend reviewing the sephiroth detailed in chapter 1. It is a good idea to draw up your own Tree of Life with notes and images of the various correspondences, especially now, after having run through four families that express four big ideas. These four big ideas are now going to extend to ten.

NUMBER MNEMONICS FOR THE SMALL CARDS

What follows is a series of number mnemonics to help the reader memorize and become comfortable with small cards and how they express the sephiroth in away especially helpful to those new to tarot or the Tree of Life. Additionally, this will help you draw the abstract and wide ranging meanings of each sephirah into concise, portable ideas for the small cards, ace through ten. It's best to study this section alongside chapter 1. Each number represents a phase in the creative process:

First, the aces are number one. One is simply the beginning. All the aces show a potential beginning to the subject of their element. The aces are not the elements but the roots of the elements. They express Kether, the crown. The crown is put over the head, in the same way as Kether is higher than the mind and is suprarational. They are pure potential, being unity (the paper before its movement and fold). Because it's simply potential, the one is self-explanatory and doesn't need a mnemonic.

Next are the twos. The mnemonic for two is "to." The twos in the tarot represent going "to" something. In the same way, Chokmah represents the universe expanding, going "to" somewhere. One and two both represent the first big idea: Movement. This is how some "thing" first comes out of "no thing." This is *not* duality. In this case, the movement itself is all that exists. Because it is unity in motion, the twos in the tarot represent the pure element, unalloyed and unmixed, until the next number. It is only through movement that something can arrive. Without movement, there can be no experience. Because this is the purest, earliest possible experience of unity, the twos of the tarot represent the purest state of the elements themselves. You will notice each of the twos represent the purest force of their suit. But the movement does go "to" something: The three.

Three is what receives what is moving toward it, and so the mnemonic for three is "receive." In the metaphor of the paper, this is the first fold. The paper touches itself and receives itself, leading to our second big idea, relationship. There is a relationship now between what the two gives and what the three receives, a relationship mutually arises in the movement of the unity. Binah represents three as the forming power of the universe.

All the threes of the tarot express the reception of something allowing for form. The threes of the tarot represent the fertilized idea of the element, instead of the pure element of the twos. But who is having the idea? Three is duality, not two, because this entire process takes place in the first person by definition of the number one. One is not one *other than* itself, so there is no "one" that is really visible in Kether. One is pure awareness. Two is the direction of that pure awareness. In two, there is really one: The trajectory. In three, there is the first choice between one trajectory and another.

Four's word is "floor." The floor is what stabilizes us. The fours of the tarot stabilize us through their element, just like merciful Chesed. A floor designates space in the same way as Chesed designates three dimensions. Here marks the entrance into the third "big idea," concept. A concept can begin to congeal around the subtle forms in the duality of three. A concept exists through the physical or semantic edges of what it is not. It is an extension of the subtle idea formed in the three. The sephirah of mercy allows for all concepts, which is really where maya, the world of illusion, starts to shine. Maya is all the names, forms, and functions that make up the world. All the fours of the tarot represent a stabilization, solidification, and materialization of their element.

The mnemonic for the number five is "survive." The names, forms, and functions that were conceptualized in the stable mind space of the four now have to compete to survive. None of these names, forms, and functions will exist forever. Five represents Geburah, severity, the sephirah of struggle, friction, and challenges. All the fives in the tarot express the same. The fives of the tarot offer motion to the fixed state established in the fours

The mnemonic for six is "fix." Six is the heart of the third big idea, concept. All solutions that have ever come about by human design were born out of a concept. The word "fix" summarizes the nature of Tiphareth, the center of the Tree of Life. It is the solution for the manifestations below to become the spirit above. More deeply, it is the solution of the spirit above to become matter below. Gods and humans are jealous of each other. The six mediates them. Each of the sixes in the tarot has to do with harmony and oftentimes "fix" the problem introduced in the five. They show the elements' practical best.

The mnemonic for seven is "engine." This is what keeps one going after the "fix" of the six. The solution inspires continued work. The sevens in the tarot represent Netzach. Netzach is the nature of desire, including one's values and ambitions, one's "engine." All the sevens in the tarot show the motivation, ambition, and efforts of their elements. The word "engine" in the seven is especially used to describe the relationship of an individual moving in contrast to their surroundings. This is very important to understand Netzach.

Crowley is hard on the sevens, describing them as a frantic struggle because they are low on the tree and off of the middle pillar. The sevens represent a degeneration of their elements.

The mnemonic for eight is "fate." To remedy the selfish ambition of seven's "engine," eight gives up all effort to "fate." It's a radical letting go. Instead of effort, there is flow. Hod expresses both intelligence and submission. The harmony of the two ideas is explained in chapter 1. I would argue that eight is the "fate" of the youniverse to organize itself in name, form, and function. This self-conceptualization is a natural flow and echoes the self-becoming nature of the logos (remember that the logos is attributed to Mercury, itself attributed to the number eight). All the eights in the tarot express some level of submission to natural design. They alleviate and remedy the sevens' descent into illusion.

The mnemonic for nine is "finish line." This is the end of the race, the last stage of the creative process. It is the shift between our third big idea, concept, into our fourth and last big idea, embodiment. The ninth sephirah is Yesod, the foundation of the Tree and final blueprint of reality. This is where the energy crystalizes. All the nines in the tarot show a culmination of the suit's energy, representing its fullest impact.

Lastly, the mnemonic for ten is "again." This is where the end begets the beginning and the creative process starts again. All the tens in the tarot show an overflow of their element's energy. This is our last of the four big ideas, embodiment. We could say that the embodiment of something as a finished product is the inspiration and thus beginning of someone else's journey, starting with a new ace. All the tens represent an excess of their element and are thus a warning.

ASTROLOGY AND THE SMALL CARDS

In this chapter is a quick review of astrology for the small cards. The aces represent the force of spirit acting upon the elements. They are not the elements, but the roots of the elements, and are said to occupy the north pole of the universe. Imagine standing on top of a geocentric universe, right at the center. That is where the aces would be. If you drew a cross there that extended in all four directions, this would divide a spherical universe into four quarters. Each of those quarters would be governed by a princess. Dividing those quarters further, based on the ecliptic, would give you the zodiac, which is connected via the other court cards in the dimension of time.

The zodiac is further divided by the small cards, minus the aces. They each represent ten degrees of the zodiac. Recall that each ten-degree segment is called a "decan." There are three decans in each of the twelve zodiacal signs, resulting in thirty-six total decans.

These correspond to the small cards, two through ten. Each decan also has a ruling planet. The seven ruling planets loop around the zodiac. The first decan of the zodiac is ruled by Mars. The next is ruled by the Sun, then Venus, followed by Mercury, the Moon, Saturn, then Jupiter. The eighth decan is ruled again by Mars, and the pattern continues. Each ruling planet adds its energy to that sign's decan. On the Thoth cards, you will see the glyph for both the planet and sign. When you add these two energies to that of the sephiroth/number and world/element, you get the card's meaning.

I strongly recommend studying the cards in the following way. For each of the small cards, take the two major arcana cards corresponding to its decan and ruling planet and lay them together. For example, to best study the Two of Wands, lay it out in between the Tower and the Emperor. The aces can be studied next to their corresponding princesses.

THE SUIT OF WANDS

The first wheel of the tarot was the majors, started by the Fool. The second wheel was the court cards, started by the Knight of Wands. The last wheel of the tarot will be the small cards, the numbered minor arcana cards, starting with the Ace of Wands. The same infinite self-becoming nature of the last two wheels will be explored again in the small cards.

We begin as we did with the court card system, with the suit of wands. They represent the element fire, the world of Atziluth, and the part of the soul called the chia. As Atziluth, they are nearest to the absolute (nothingness). As the Chiah, they represent the creative principle within us, the divine spark that moves is into being. For more practical purposes, the suit of wands represents creativity, work, business, purpose, passions, spirituality, sexuality, and life-calling. They show what motivates us through life, especially unpremeditated inspirations and impulses that are evidence of our true will. It is important to remember that the numbered small cards represent the sephiroth of the Tree of Life, and the sephiroth are emanations of the Divine. Each one emanates farther from the Divine, losing its purity. In the same way, the suit of wands will lose its purity card by card, beginning in perfect potentiality in the ace. The pure fiery energy is found in the two, Dominion. Its idea of itself arises in the three, Virtue. It solidifies in the four, Completion, which is then destroyed in the five, Strife. It is balanced again by the six, Victory, only for more frenetic opposition to arise in the seven, Valor. The effort eases and accelerates in the eight, Swiftness, only to culminate again in the nine, Strength. It has its final desperate issue in the ten, Oppression.

ACE OF WANDS

The Ace of Wands introduces the suit of fire. The big idea of fire is movement, and the Ace of Wands, being one, is the source and possibility of that movement. To understand this card is to understand the mystical heights of Gaudapada and nonduality. In a way, the Ace of Wands suggests the very "nature of the Effulgent Being," especially in the context of ontological movement from nothing to something.[118] In Crowley's nomenclature, this might be called the "true will."

In the Thoth deck, we see a huge wand of ten yods. Crowley sees this as the phallus and the sun. The yod is the first letter of the tetragrammaton, the letter of fire. I see the yod as the record scratch of the universe remixing itself. It's the apostrophe of God/conscious-

---

118. Gambhirananda, *Eight Upanishads*, 197.

ness. The yods are in the design of the Tree of Life, since they contain all. Lightning issues from the wand, which may allude to the lightning flash of creation that made the tree. This lightning flash is how things in reality are done, made, differentiated, changed, creating the possibility of here or there, coming and going, and all beginnings and endings.

In a reading, the Ace of Wands signifies a burst of inspiration. This is not a planned movement, but a spontaneous one, usually in a direction that will benefit the questioner. It's an explosion of possibility. This card is spiritual vigor, creative fervor, and divinely purposeless passion. A mundane interpretation could be any creative or professional opportunity, especially concerning one's calling or life's purpose. Ill-dignified, this is wasted or uncontrolled energy.

TWO OF WANDS

Crowley calls this card Dominion. It represents Chokmah in the world of Atziluth. Chokmah is the wisdom of expansion. It is the dominion of God/consciousness in all reality becoming itself. In the world of Atziluth, this action is taken to the highest extreme, on the largest scale. This "becoming" nature will be revealed in all its associations.

Here, the mnemonic "to" (from the number two) is applied to the big idea of "movement" (from the suit of wands). They combine to emphasize the highest idea of a directed force. Crowley says that this card "the will in its most exalted form. It is an ideal will independent of any given object."[119] To crudely summarize Crowley's philosophy, the only real freedom any one conscious being has is to do their true will, their higher purpose: A bee will buzz and should buzz. A fish will swim and should swim. The sun will shine and it should shine. Every single body in the cosmos has a perfect trajectory and divine influence on the whole. Doing one's will without the "lust of result" purifies the will. Compare this to the Indian concept of karma. All karma is born from action with a desired result. When the action is totally selfless and without attachment, one is doing karma yoga.

The will of the Two of Wands is a specific trajectory compared to the pure potential in the ace, or pure nothingness of ain soph. When consciousness/the universe becomes something, it develops the unique and specific attributes to carry that thing's will. Here lies the cost of incarnation and the secret of the Mars attribution of this card. The general idea is that the Two of Wands takes the infinite potential of the Ace of Wands and directs it, through the force of Chokmah, into a specific direction or "will" (remember the two can correspond with the line). As Chokmah of Atziluth, it shows us how the dominion of the

---

119. Crowley, *Book of Thoth*, 189.

absolute/consciousness can direct itself into a "thing" out of the potential "no thing" that Kether emanates from ain soph. The cost of a "thing" is always the blank "no thing" that precedes it. When a thing is, "no thing" cannot be. This is called "opportunity cost." When one choice is made, all others are not. The Two of Wands is the opportunity cost of all creation, choice, incarnation, and manifestation.

This cost is represented by Mars. Mars is destruction, corresponding to the Tower card. It is the destruction of "no thing" that allows for Chokmah's expansion into "things." This is how you incarnated. Consciousness chose to be you out of every other possibility, a notion expressed astrologically in the first decan of Aries. Aries rules the first house, the house of personality. It is in this house we look for the ascendent sign; in natal astrology, this house describes the face the client shows the world. This is the face consciousness is choosing to express itself to the world through you. This is the face of the Emperor, the localization of a "self," attributed to Aries. He represents the sovereignty of individual existence imprinted upon boundless consciousness.

There is a parallel to this idea of imprinting in the *Sepher Yetzirah* that describes how God creates the universe through numbers and letters. However, the universe is not technically created but rather engraved.[120] As Aryeh Kaplan brilliantly points out, engraving suggests a sort of removing. We can think of consciousness removing its infinitude to create the finite dimensions of the experience of your incarnation. Compare this to the Indian concept of maya and the tantric idea of lila and the powers of shakti.

We come next to a deep mystery, how infinite freedom and potential becomes and *is* infinite limitation. If God/consciousness is everything that is and can possibly be, it is the infinite of all outcomes. This includes the infinite of all possible limitations. This is the secret of Chokmah.

Let's return for a moment to the God name YH, transliterated as "Jah." Not only does Jah engrave to create the thirty-two paths of the Tree of Life. Jah is also the God name attributed to Chokmah. The Hebrew word YHShVH, transliterated as Joshua (the original name of Jesus) uses the same root, YH. *Joshua*, in Hebrew, can be interpreted to mean "Jah liberates." In this name, the liberative, salvific, and infinite nature of the Divine is expressed. This nature is one of freedom. Compare these ideas to the explanation of Chokmah in chapter 1. You'll find that the nature of consciousness is expansive, symbolized by the expanding universe. Western esoteric traditions were influenced by the Ptolemaic model of the universe, a geocentric model with spheres expanding outward toward the firmament. The spiritual path was an ascent up these spheres into greater levels of expansion.

In a reading, the Two of Wands is a card of freedom, opportunity cost, choice, and powerful motion in a specific direction. Whenever you choose one "thing," you deny the infinite possibilities you could have chosen. This is a card of action, impulse, power, passion, charge, and great force exerted in a particular specific way. If ill-dignified, it could suggest anger, aggression, or the force may be softened.

THREE OF WANDS

The Three of Wands is titled Virtue. It represents Binah in the world of Atziluth through the suit of fire. Binah is the forming power to Chokmah's force. Though still forceful, the destructive, masculine powers of fire are tempered by feminine Binah. Binah harnesses the

---
120. Kaplan, *Sefer Yetzirah*, 13.

energy of fire and puts it into a sustainable pattern, giving it the seeds of structure to continue fire's creative process in the same way as the Queen of Wands did for the Knight of Wands. The mother receives the will and gives birth to manifestation. Without the three, the Two of Wands would fizzle out like the knight. The sustainability of the three creates life.

The number mnemonic of three is the word "receive," and the big idea of the element of fire is movement. The Three of Wands is the ability to receive movement in general. It's the ability of anything to receive the primum mobile, the movement of consciousness, and participate in creation. It is fitting then that the card is called Virtue. Terrestrially, the "movement" being received in the Three of Wands is from the sun to animate life. In doing so, life on earth is a manifestation of the light of the sun, itself a manifestation of even higher intelligences. Related ideas to this include budding, germinating, shaping, unfurling, quickening, development, and progress. It is a card of spring.

Astrologically, this is the second decan of Aries, ruled by the life-giving sun. This emphasizes the idea of light becoming life. Virtue can be thought of as a living human characteristic that resembles golden characteristics. We see this in the Emperor card, which is associated with Aries. Having incarnated through the Two of Wands, Aries now passes through the three. The Sun sheds light on our life and brings out the best qualities of Aries. The associated major of the sun is the Sun. In the Thoth deck, this card depicts radical liberation. Recall the doctrine in the last card of radical freedom becoming all possible limitations. The Sun card is the radical freedom of consciousness and the Emperor is the localization of that consciousness which manifests through cosmic limitless limitation.

In the Thoth deck, the lotus wands allude to Binah and Isis. The six straight rays refer to the number of the sun. It has a calmer texture than the two.

In a reading, this is a card about being in the right path. It signifies good character and being in alignment with your purpose. Honor, dignity, and purpose help establish auspicious opportunities and a clear direction, but not without some pride. If ill-dignified, there is conceit and arrogance.

FOUR OF WANDS

The Four of Wands is called Completion. It represents Chesed in the world of Atziluth. This is the mercy of the archetypal world to stabilize its primordial energy into structure.

Four's mnemonic word is "floor," suggesting a common ground for things to happen and be experienced. The big idea of the suit of wands is movement. In the Four of Wands, we get a dance floor. There is freedom, passion, expression, in addition to cultural agreement and organization. The pattern-setting of the Three of Wands has now materialized into a safe structure for fire to continue its movement. The activity of fire is manifested into a solid system. There is order.

The balance required for the order of fire's chaos is expressed in the astrological attributions: Aries and Venus. Aries's loud entrance into incarnation is now tempered by the gentle qualities of Venus in his last decan. In the Thoth card, the ram symbolizes Aries and the will while the dove symbolizes Venus and love. Their appearance together alludes to the law of Thelema, "love is the law, love under will." Aries is the Emperor and Venus is the Empress. In this card, they come together to complete and perfect their work.

In a reading, this is a major completion, usually of a labor of life. It is a moment to celebrate and rest from hard work. This card can bring together disparate characters in collaborative efforts and for major accomplishments. The job is done, for now. If ill-dignified, this is feeling rushed or a project incomplete. It could also be about something finished one might regret.

FIVE OF WANDS

The Five of Wands is entitled Strife. It represents Geburah in the world of Atziluth. This is the severity of the archetypal world, the tensions and pressures behind something coming out of nothing. Atziluth is already the world of fire. With the fiery sephirah Geburah, the heat is turned up even higher.

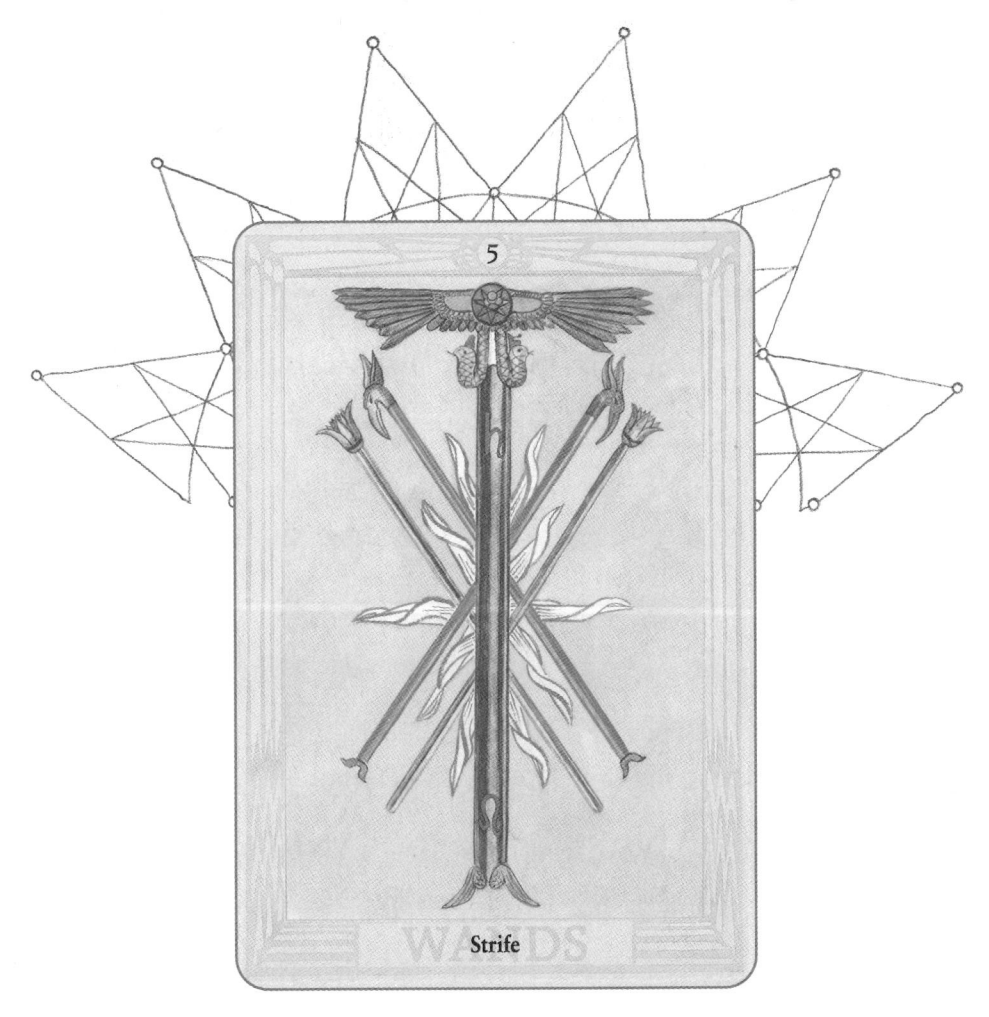

The mnemonic for five is "survive." The big idea of the suit of wands is "movement." Can we survive all of this primeval movement? To understand this, stand still in a busy city. Notice the movement of energies from all directions. Thoughts, feelings, sensations, and locomotion are happening in every direction. It's a divine mess. And yet, it is this very chaos that the order of Chesed now allows. The shaping power of Binah has shaped the initial will-force of Chokmah into separate life vessels, given structure and room to move in the four. In the Five of Wands, these life vessels now have their own agency, and unlike the Four of Wands, they don't always agree. Here we find the beauty of conflict and opposition. Difference and contrast render diversity. Compare this to the five shaktis in Tantra.

The ideas of differentiation and opposition are expressed in the first decan of Leo, ruled by Saturn. As stated before, the Five of Wands shows us separated life vessels now divided, moving in opposition to each other. The life-energy ingredient to this is Leo. Leo is the sign of creativity, expression, fanfare, play. Its card is Lust, Babalon. Saturn is the greater malefic that enforces limitations and endings. Just like its sephirah, Binah, these limitations create the edges of things in the world and ensure diversity. When Saturn imposes limitations on the self-focused, creative pursuits of Leo, we get a war.

In the Thoth deck, this conflict is expressed by ceremonial wands of the adeptus minor ritual of the Golden Dawn. According to Michael Osiris Snuffin, their colors and setup are mismatched.[121] This expresses a certain dissonance. We also notice Crowley's seal of the beast on the chief adept wand. This decan is Crowley's ascendent. Crowley was not afraid of conflict. The phoenix wands symbolize the change occurring from the pressure of Geburah. The ten flames foreshadow the Ten of Wands, also ruled by Saturn.

In a reading, this card signifies conflict of any type but especially ones involving strong opposing forces, such as quarrels, arguments, or disagreements. The card can also be related to creative differences or competition. If ill-dignified, the forces are weakened and the conflict is more of an annoyance.

SIX OF WANDS

The Six of Wands is titled Victory. It represents Tiphareth in the world of Atziluth, the beauty of the archetypal world. Here is a completely balanced manifestation of the subtle workings of our first world. Tiphareth brings its beautiful mediating quality to bring out the best practical use of the element of fire. Notice on the Tree of Life how Tiphareth draws the perfect energy of Kether and balances it into manifestation through Chokmah, Binah, Chesed, and Geburah.

This perfect balancing act is why the mnemonic for six is "fix." In the suit of movement, this is how reality fixes movement to go exactly where it needs to go for exactly what needs to happen. The tension and opposition of the Five of Wands will resolve one way or another, and the six is that resolution. Consciousness and reality will continue. All forces involved will get to one destination or another (though not always the destination intended). This is how the universe "fixes" you to be the contribution that you are for the people who need it. Every conscious being is a contribution somehow, as we each have a higher self in Tiphareth.

---

121. Michael Osiris Snuffin, *The Thoth Companion: The Key to the True Symbolic Meaning of the Thoth Tarot*, (Llewellyn Publications, 2007), 113.

Victory

The harmony of this six is expressed in the second decan of Leo, ruled by Jupiter. Leo wants to express himself. He wants to draw in an audience and share his creative passion. Expansive Jupiter allows him to do just that. Jupiter says yes to every sign he is placed in. The associated major arcana cards are Fortune and Lust. Fortune accelerates and expands the domain of play for the Lust card to enact her joy.

In a reading, this is a significant victory, especially one following labor. The meaning extends to ideas of inspiration, gain, creative success, and being at the right place at the right time to make your contribution. It can also show a position of power or influence which can manifest as a leadership role and responsibility. If ill-dignified, it can suggest pride, attachment to riches or success, or the energy can be muddled.

SEVEN OF WANDS

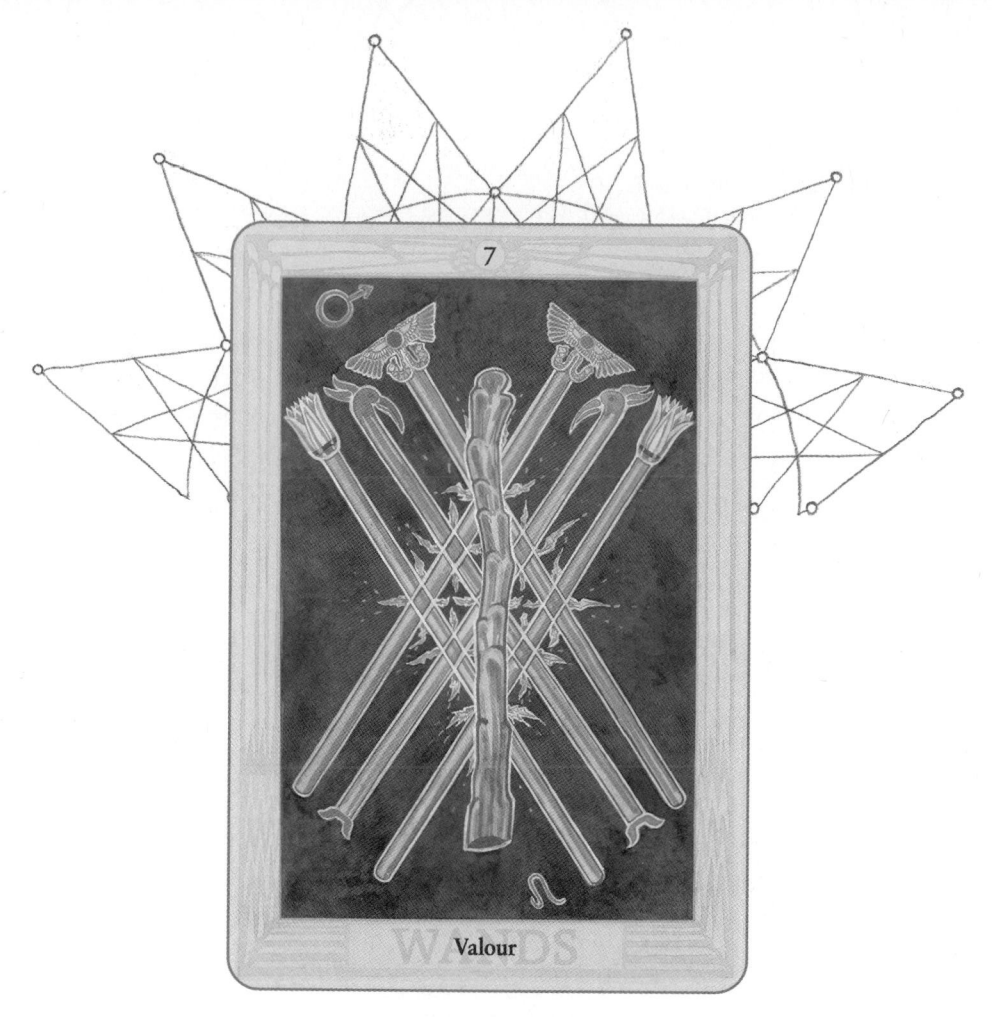

The Seven of Wands is titled Valour. It represents Netzach in the world of Atziluth. This is the victory or ambition of the archetypal world, the desire of consciousness to continue becoming something out of nothing. Note that Netzach is already a fiery sephirah like Geburah, so the heat of fiery Atziluth turns it up even further.

The mnemonic for seven is "engine," and the big idea of the suit of wands is "movement." The seven usually emphasizes the engine of the individual moving against the environment. That is because Netzach introduces the illusion of opposition between "me" and "the world." It is connected to individual sovereignty and motility. Here, attractions and aversions seep into localized consciousness and that localization begins to forget its connection to unity. Crowley stresses how Netzach is both low on the tree and unbalanced, being off the middle pillar.

Like the other sevens in the Thoth deck, the Seven of Wands is a frantic struggle. In the suit of fire, this is one of intense energy and force. This is the last decan Leo has to express himself. It's his last attempt to hold the audience before they walk out. Leo is the Lust card, the joy of creativity and strength exercised. But that exercise is disrupted by the crumbling tower of Mars, the ruling planet of this card.

In the Thoth card, the many adorned ceremonial wands find themselves challenged by the one crude club. The sparks flying off their place of impact emphasize the desperate and violent struggle of Netzach in the suit of fire. This hints at individual valor, especially against opposition, in the same way as Netzach, though brave, opposes the balance of the middle pillar (in the same way as Chokmah secretly opposes Kether, and Kether opposes ain soph).

Luckily, the club will probably win, but at what cost? This card indicates a struggle and strained effort against the status quo. It will likely be a victory, but it may not be worth it. The valor of the individual is admirable, but they should pick and choose their battles. If ill-dignified, the opposition is less significant, but the questioner may still need to prove a point.

EIGHT OF WANDS

The Eight of Wands is called Swiftness. It represents Hod in the world of Atziluth. Hod is the sephirah of intelligence and submission and is attributed to the planet Mercury. In this card, consciousness submits itself to its own natural intelligence. This remedies the individual effort and ambition of the seven. When the effort is released, things find their path of least resistance, and the process accelerates.

It is this theme of surrender that brings us to the mnemonic for the number eight, "fate." All the eights suggest a surrender to the divine fate of their element's trajectory which helps continue a process. For the Eight of Wands, that's the fate of movement. And so, in the Thoth card we see electricity and geometry moving in perfect intelligent design. All the energy is surrendered to the movement of intelligent design. In life, this is when we stop trying so hard and just be the intelligent vessel of awareness we are. This gets us out of our own way.

When you're out of your own way, you can move on. Movement is not just expressed through the suit of wands here, but also the first decan of Sagittarius. Sagittarius is the sign of travel and journeys (physical or intellectual). It is probably the sign most commonly attributed to freedom and movement. The first decan is ruled by Mercury, the planet of communication and technology, the traveling messenger Hermes (note the double Mercury of the card). All these attributions make this card speedy, efficient, and free.

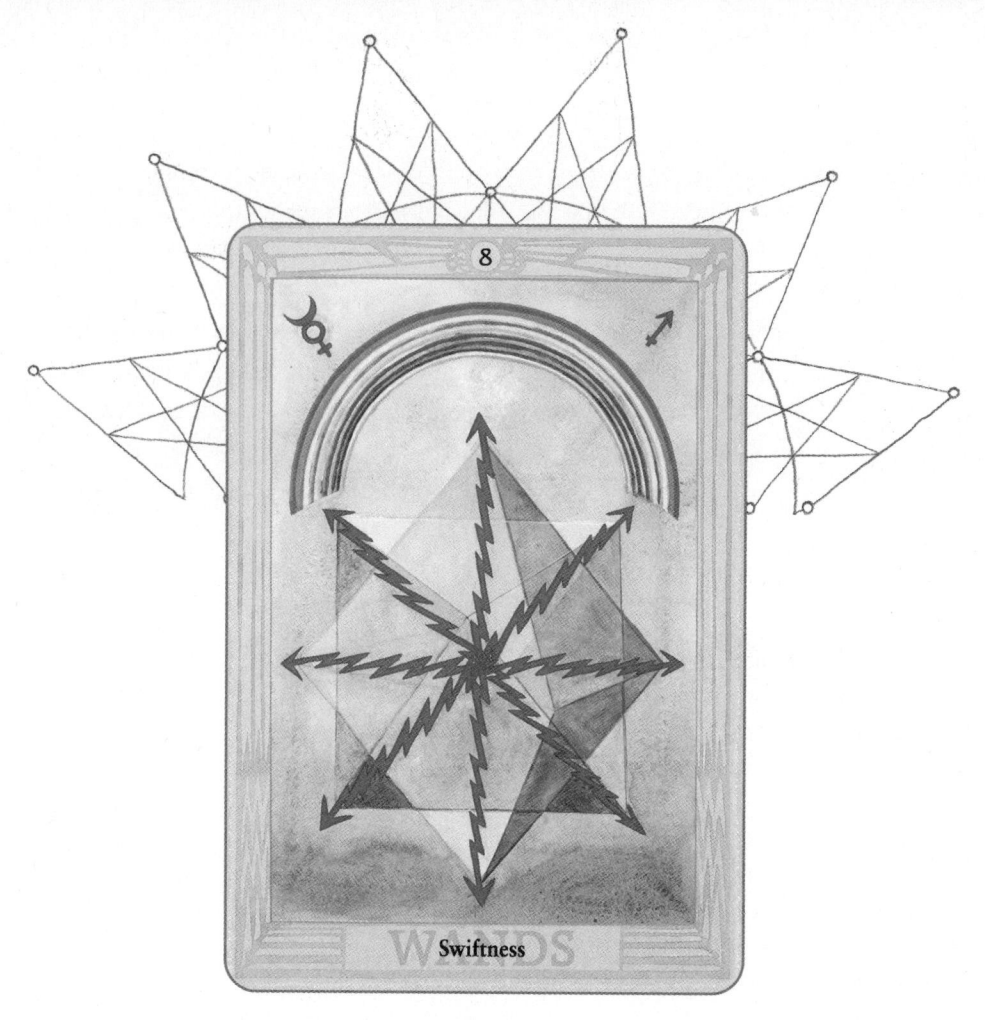

The majors associated with this card are the Magus and Art. Art is the mixing of opposites in perfect balance to expand possibility. The Magus is the logos and intelligence of the universe that connects everything. Both of these are about drawing connections for things to move and flow. Both work together to create freedom and the unbridled movement of consciousness to continue its self-uncovering.

In a reading, this card is about a major acceleration, especially one through release. There is a quickening process and efficiency, and the questioner is approaching their goal. If ill-dignified, it could signify feeling rushed, anxious, jittery, or over-caffeinated.

NINE OF WANDS

The Nine of Wands is entitled Strength. It represents Yesod in the world of Atziluth. Yesod brings with it the doctrine of "change equals stability." With all the sephiroth piled on top of it, Yesod must bring together so many opposing energies. In doing so, it serves as a dynamic vessel of constant flow and change that ensures the continuation and stability of the universe. How does change ensure stability? Consider how the movement of a bike's wheels keep it from falling over. Yesod does the same for the Tree of Life, and nowhere is this more obvious than in Atziluth.

The mnemonic for nine is "finish line." This is the finish line of the race of the archetypal world toward "something" from "nothing." And it was a race. The big idea connected to the suit of wands is "movement." This is the movement of consciousness passing the finish line into the astral blueprint of our material experience. That takes a lot of energy. The

CHAPTER 4

nines do a similar job as the sixes but a step below. The six and Tiphareth will "fix" the pure light of Kether into thoughts, feelings, and emotions below. The nines take all of that and run it through the finish line of the astral world, our own subconscious, bringing the physical world into manifestation in the tens.

Astrologically, this card is the second decan of Sagittarius. In the Thoth deck, the wands are now arrows with crescent moons on them. Sagittarius, by the way, governs the legs, which further supports our metaphor of the race. Sagittarius is the mutability of fire, its ability to change. The Art card (attributed to Sagittarius) expresses this change through alchemical mixing of materials to reach subtler states. In the Nine of Wands, the fiery forces of the preceding cards are continuously mixed to ensure the continuation of the creative process. This decan of Sagittarius is ruled by the Moon, itself associated with the Priestess. The Priestess provides her own sort of change but through her lunar style: Subtle, amorphous, and fluid alteration and flux. She is the original, subtle cosmic mind stuff above. Her path leads directly to the path of Art, signifying that this mind stuff precipitates into denser energies to be alchemically exchanged. This allows for the Art card to continue to mix and remix, continuing the flow of astral *idea* into physical *matter*, literally pouring mind stuff into what we experience in our more mundane world. There is vertical emanation from the Priestess, and horizontal exchange from Art. In the same way, the wheels of the bike spin and gravity stabilizes it on the pavement. This is the strength of the Nine of Wands.

For this reason, the Nine of Wands represents great ability and strength backed by support, past experience, and other great influences (vertically/spiritually or horizontally/dynamically). Whatever context the questioner is asking about, this represents reaching an impressive level of mastery where one's experiences have imprinted into subconscious reflexes (Yesod). We might call the Nine of Wands a symbol of unconscious competence. This card especially employs such faculties in creativity, professional work, or one's higher calling (all related to fire and movement). Stakes are high, but the questioner is ready. The card stands for alacrity, readiness, and flexibility. If ill-dignified, this could be a waste of energy or using too much force.

TEN OF WANDS

The Ten of Wands is called Oppression. This card represents Malkuth in the world of Atziluth. Malkuth is the fully realized material world, matter carved out with meter. It is the sum total of all the "things" consciousness does, makes, changes, and differentiates through

10

Oppression

name, form, and function. But the suit of fire does not want to stop. In the suit of fire, there is a relentless drive to continue. This continued activity starkly contrasts the passive and receptive nature of the last sephirah, Malkuth, and creates the potential for tyranny.

The mnemonic for ten is "again," and the big idea of wands is "movement." When the same movements happen again and again, it brings a dark, authoritarian nightmare. The element of fire does not want to stop, even at the very end. However, to ensure the perfect balance of the universe, it must proceed to the next suit. The "again" must repeat but only in the next world Briah. The movement must finally cease in order to be rendered by the suit of cups, which will engender all the relationships in the universe.

The oppressive nature of the Ten of Wands is emphasized by the last decan of Sagittarius, ruled by Saturn. Sagittarius wants freedom to travel wherever it pleases, but heavy Saturn imposes its usual limitations. The Art card is one of alchemical spiritualization, but

CHAPTER 4

the Universe card erases its hopes of mystical ascent by grounding it into Malkuth. It is interesting that the major arcana associations of the Nine and Ten of Wands make up the middle pillar of the Tree of Life.

In the Thoth deck, these themes of tyranny and force are emphasized by the claw-like design of the wands. The two main Wands resemble prison bars. Atop the bars are dorjes resembling the wands of the Two of Wands. This hints at the potential imbalance result of the Two of Wands goes unchecked.

In a reading, this card signifies forced energy. What was once a passion or calling has now degraded into a chore. Here there is cruelty, malice, false purpose, tyranny, and oppression. If ill-dignified, the intensity can be lessened but may even be invited by the kindness of the questioner.

THE SUIT OF CUPS

We continue with the suit of cups. They represent the element water, the world of Briah, and the part of the soul called the neshamah. As Briah, they are the creative world, where the seeds of ideas are born through the development of duality. As the neshamah, they represent the intuitive principle within us. Considering these themes of duality and intuition, it follows that the practical meanings of this suit include relationships, love, emotions, family. More specific to the Thoth deck, we find themes of desire, pleasure, and attachment to form. This is because the element of water and the suit of cups are connected to the feminine and the moon, which correspond to form as opposed to the masculine sun (force and will).

Each card of the suit of cups will show another step down the path of desire and enjoyment constantly hinting at a Buddhistic theme of transience. The ace is the pure potential of desire. The element of water finds its purity in the two, Love. Emanating further, it becomes Abundance in the three. In the four, the energy gets too comfortable and bored and is titled Luxury. It needs the disturbance of the Five, Disappointment, to continue. Balance is found in the six, Pleasure, which innocently reflects the purity of the ace above it on the tree. The descent into the seven yields Debauch, and the pleasure loses its innocence as it plunges into gratification and attachment. This is remedied by the eight, Indolence, for a period of sad and sobering inaction. A balance is found in the nine, Happiness, only to yet again get too comfortable in the ten, Satiety.

ACE OF CUPS

The Ace of Cups introduces the suit of water. The big idea of water is relationship. Ultimately, the Ace of Cups is the ability to receive. This is the relationship that consciousness has with itself. The suit of cups is the domain of all forms of worship, reverence, and love. These are best exemplified in the mystical heights of bhakti yoga. These traditions often speak of an ecstatic pleasure. All pleasure comes from some sense of duality. How else would pleasure be experienced without an experiencer? The suit of cups will show us a journey into the horrors and glory of pleasure and desire.

While the Ace of Wands was a phallic representation of the sun, the Ace of Wands is a vessel that represents the Moon. In the Thoth deck, we see the light of Kether or the holy spirit descending into a cup causing a scallop-like refraction. This cup is the cosmic yoni, the holy grail, and the cup of Babalon (see the Lust card). All these symbolize the vessel of life.

Chapter 4

On the Tree of Life, the Ace of Wands is associated with Chokmah while the Ace of Cups is associated with Binah. Binah takes the force of Chokmah and puts it into form, just as the Ace of Cups does to the Ace of Wands, and the world of Briah does to the world of Atziluth. The three circles on the cup can allude to the supernal sephiroth on the Tree of Life, or possibly the three æons discussed in the Æon card. The water is quite fittingly called the "sea of Binah." Beyond water, the red liquid is blood or wine, more symbols of life, depending on the use.

In a reading, the Ace of Cups represents fertility, beauty, productiveness, great pleasure, and happiness. In a way, it is pure life itself being poured into a vessel to create experience. It is the ability of consciousness to receive itself in parts. This suggests the idea of enjoyment. Ill-dignified, it can be passivity or meekness, or a wasted opportunity to enjoy something.

TWO OF CUPS

The Two of Cups is titled Love and represents Chokmah in the world of Briah. This is the wisdom of the creative world. Chokmah is the supernal father, the masculine sephirah that expands and moves creation along. The world of Briah is about creation through relation. The wisdom and expansion of Chokmah puts Briah's creation through relation enterprise in motion. We call it love. Put another way, the force (Chokmah) of all possible relationships (Briah) is love.

The mnemonic for two is "to." Chokmah brings creation forward in a direction. The big idea of the suit of cups is relationship, so combined, the Two of Cups symbolizes anything going "to" or toward a relationship and can refer to both our interpersonal and cosmic relationships.

Astrologically, this energy is expressed by the first decan of Cancer ruled by Venus. As the cardinal water sign, Cancer begins the suit of water and is the perfect sign to do so. Remember how the Ace of Cups symbolized the creation of life with a vessel? Cancer is that vessel. Cancer is the crab. The crab has a hard shell but a soft inner body. The hard shell represents protection and the container that allows for life. The Chariot card symbolizes this as a vehicle for a more subtle, higher intelligence. The body is the chariot of the mind. The mind is the chariot of the intellect. The intellect is a chariot of something even more amorphous. The general idea of Cancer is embodiment of a higher intelligence into a lower, more materialized plane. This is what allows for love. When you love someone, you look into their eyes and recognize that both bodies and minds are different chariots of the same charioteer—consciousness. And so, the first decan of Cancer is ruled by Venus, the planet of love, associated with the Empress. The Empress is the diversity of the universe through allowance, the condition for all possible relationships.

In the Thoth deck, the green sea is the color of Venus. We see two fish, creatures sacred to Venus. The eye of one fish is gold and the other silver, a symbol of the love affair of the Sun and moon. It should also be noted that fish are sacred to Mercury. Mercury, like Chokmah, both correspond to the logos. In this card, we see the logos, the will of the universe, reaching through Briah as love.

When this card shows up in a reading, it signifies any kind of relationship, especially one of love. It can be a platonic or business relationship, and definitely a romantic one. It is a balance of masculine and feminine forces. This can manifest as pleasant company, harmony of a situation, marriage, and connections. If ill-dignified, it is foolish love, puppy love, or the illusion of sympathy.

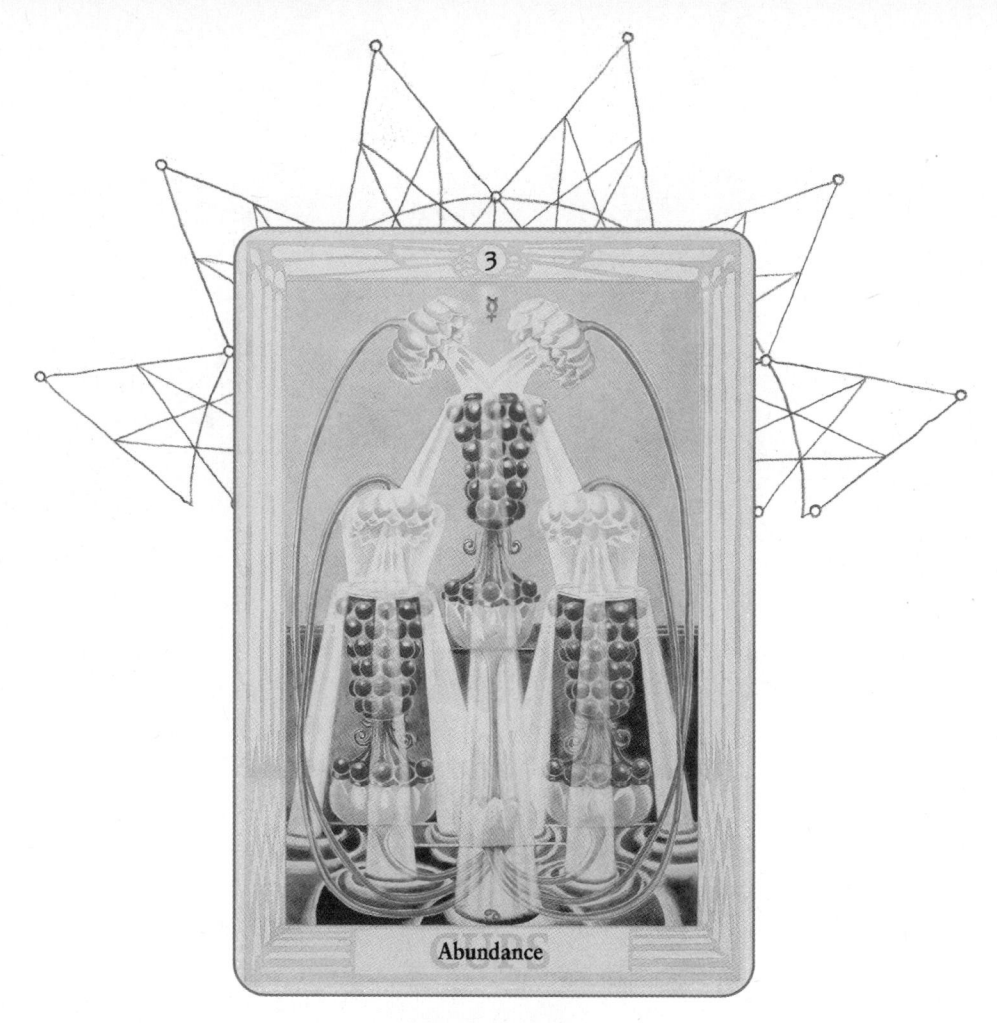

THREE OF CUPS

The Three of Cups, entitled Abundance, represents Binah in the world of Briah. This is understanding in the creative world. This is one of the most energetically and archetypically feminine cards. It is *all* about form. Both Briah and Binah create through duality and form. They both express, on different planes, how consciousness creates by reflecting and dividing itself into the "other."

Three is "receive," and the big idea of the suit of cups is relationship, making this card about receiving relationships. But, as mentioned earlier, three is really the duality. It is the observer observing the difference between one object of awareness and another. If you enjoy a pomegranate, for example, the enjoyment can only exist because the consciousness that you really are is aware of your body *and* the pomegranate happening to each other.

THE SMALL CARDS

These are the fundamentals of all pleasure. It always requires a separation, which is why all pleasures can be enjoyed but not fully trusted.

The pomegranate is specific to this card. To understand, we will first look at its astrology. This card is associated with the second decan of Cancer, ruled by Mercury. Cancer is the embodiment of life-force into a vessel. It's what allows for consciousness to be aware of the enjoyer and the enjoyed. Mercury is the messenger, a planet of communication and connection and also the logos, the intelligence of the universe. Together, Mercury and Cancer create the universe's intelligent design. This is the way consciousness is poured into so many vehicles to populate the cosmos—from planets, to plants, to people, and more. Mercury is like the subtle forces of the universe connecting all things (one might compare it to the strong force, weak force, electromagnetism, and gravity). Cancer represents all the forms that arise from those complex relationships (relationship being key in this suit). This gives us all the many things to experience. In the Rider-Waite-Smith deck, this is symbolized by the cornucopia. In the Thoth deck, this is symbolized by the pomegranate cups.

The pomegranate symbol takes the abstract ideas of duality and enjoyment above and summarizes them in a more linear fashion through the myth of Persephone. Persephone was the daughter of Demeter, goddess of fertility and harvest. Hades, god of the underworld, fell in love with Persephone. While she was picking flowers, the earth opened and he captured her, bringing her to the underworld and making her his wife. This sent Demeter into grief, and all the crops stopped growing on earth. Life on earth was at risk. Zeus finally sent Hermes into the underworld to retrieve Persephone. Unfortunately, she could not be totally freed from the underworld. Hades has cleverly fed her a few seeds of a pomegranate, which partially trapped her there. A deal was made for her to spend half of the year in the underworld and the other half in Olympus with Demeter. This alteration's effect on Demeter is what created the seasons.

The story of Persephone elaborates on the relationship between Mercury and Cancer, especially in the context of pleasure and incarnation. Mercury represents Hermes, the logos, and knowledge. In this case, Cancer represents the underworld, which symbolizes matter, incarnation, and life and consciousness being poured into bodies. The pomegranate seeds represent the enjoyment of the diversity below, which can only be surrendered through knowledge. But for many people, the spiritual knowledge of the logos can only bring them out of the underworld's temptation for a period of time before they return.

This dance between the logos, knowledge, the underworld, and matter point to the meaning of the card: Abundance to be enjoyed but not fully trusted. This card shows our rhythms between the physical world of form, with all its diversity, and the moments of unitive clarity in spirit. It is the temptations and glory of matter. If it appears in a reading, it's time to enjoy what you have, whether that's the people in your life, food, your home, your plans, or even aspects of yourself in this current body with this current mind. If ill-dignified, the things to enjoy may be a distraction, or may be simply a passing appeasement to one's appetite.

FOUR OF CUPS

The Four of Cups is called Luxury, which might seem an odd choice at first. It represents Chesed in the world of Briah, the mercy of the creative world. It is the business of Chesed to materialize the supernal sephiroth through complete mercy and allowance. The suit of cups expresses the desire of an object. When the object of your desire is given to you through the mercy of Chesed, it could be called "luxury," but it's a little more complex than that. Chesed is also a sephirah of fixing things into manifestation. When the pleasure of water is fixed for too long, there is no longer a desire, since the pleasure becomes the new constant. What was once considered rich abundance becomes a simple indulgence with enough time. Additionally, Chesed is a watery sephirah. In the suit of cups, that's a lot of water. This card reaches an extreme of passivity where too much comfort leads to apathy and then discomfort from too much comfort.

The mnemonic for four is "floor" to express the idea of stability and fixity below the abyss. The stability Chesed provides is oftentimes compared to loving kindness. The big idea of the suit of cups and Briah is relationship. When that loving kindness meets with relationship, things get a little bit *too* comfortable, and that is the essence of the Four of Cups. When a relationship between any two things is maintained and fixed under the same conditions for too long, what happens? Nothing. Things are simply maintained. According to Newton's first law, an object at rest will stay at rest unless acted upon by another object or force. If it stays at rest for long enough, it gets bored. Unlike the fire in the Four of Wands (which has self-generated movement), there is no self-generated movement in the Four of Cups's water.

The uncomfortable levels of comfort are expressed in Cancer's last decan ruled by the Moon. The Moon rules Cancer and is very comfortable there. Remember that we already have a double dose of water (the cups and Chesed): The Moon adds even more water. A passive planet in a passive sign in a passive sephirah yields no action. With no activity, all this water can become a swamp through Chesed's mercy.

In the Thoth deck, we see four large cups. Two are overflowing with water, but the water below is trembling as if anxiously anticipating the coming change. The sky above is darkening.

This card represents the weakest aspect of water. In a reading, it signifies pleasure mixed with anxiety. It is attempting to enjoy something one no longer enjoys or the forcing of a relationship. It's not all negative. It can be the enjoyment of desires that are maintained through a structure. Thus, it can literally signify luxury. But most of these pleasures are temporary. If ill-dignified, it can signify boredom and apathy.

FIVE OF CUPS

The Five of Cups, titled Disappointment, represents Geburah in the world of Briah. This is the change that the Four of Cups is secretly awaiting, the severity of the creative world.

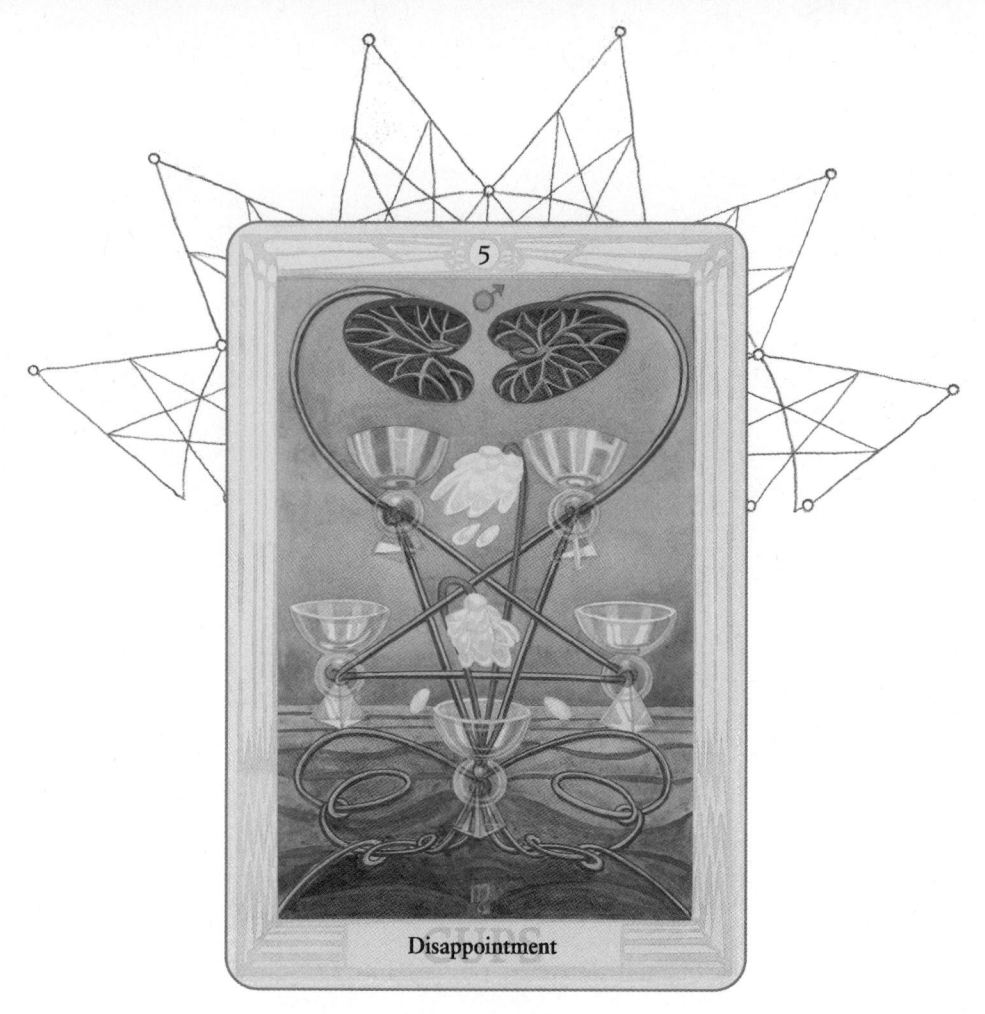

Remember that Briah takes the "something" that first arose out of "nothing" from Atziluth and develops it through relationships. Part of all relationships is the coming and going. Fiery Geburah brings with it the going and dries up the stagnant waters of Chesed.

The mnemonic for the number five is "survive." When anything is enjoyed when it is present, one must survive the suffering of its absence. Here lies the cost of pleasure.

This is astrologically expressed by the first decan of Scorpio. The coming and going of relationships (again, both interpersonal and cosmically) is the constant change that is so characteristic of Scorpio, the fixed (and thus most intense) water sign. Scorpio is attributed to the Death card, whose themes aptly apply to the Five of Cups. This first decan is ruled by Mars, the Tower card. Together we have death and destruction, but the suit of water does not put up a fight like the suit of fire. Its passivity renders the energy simply "disappointment." Scorpio is the most intense of signs. You will notice how the next two cards, like this one, have the same planetary ruler as the sephirotic planet. Each one of Scorpio's minor arcana cards has a double dose of a specific planet.

In the Thoth deck, we see a reddish sky, the color of Mars. Below it, the water is dried up into a desert. The cups are arranged in an upside pentagram, suggesting the rule of matter over spirit.

In a reading, this card signifies the end of pleasure. The object of your desire is no longer present. A major loss must occur (commonly involving another person), but it is one that was probably needed. This isn't a card of death, but it is a card of the death of *something*, such as a relationship. More accurately, it can be about realizing that what you thought would be at the end of a journey is not there, requiring you to redirect your trajectory. If ill-dignified, the misfortune is less severe but the questioner may not be learning from it or take proper action in response.

SIX OF CUPS

The Six of Cups is titled Pleasure. It represents Tiphareth in the world of Briah. This is the beauty of the creative world. Tiphareth always finds the practical best of the energy of the suit. In this card, we see the beauty of relationships, which is pleasure.

Six's mnemonic keyword is "fix." The Six of Cups here fixes the relationship problems we have seen in the past two cards. In the Four of Cups, there was too much. In the Five of Cups, there was none at all. In the Six of Cups, there is a balanced dance of presence and absence. This dance is what makes all relationships worth having. All sensations come in waves, the crests of presence and the troughs of absence. Or, put triadically, there is the absence of the object of desire and then the onrush of the experience of that object, following its recession. Compare this to the three modes of astrology. This is the formula of all balanced enjoyment, including the sexual act.

This relationship is further emphasized by this card's astrology: The Sun in Scorpio. Scorpio is a sign of radical change, intensity, and sex. Like the three-phase wave-form, Scorpio has three phases (explained in chapter 2 on the Death card) where it continues to die to become better. Through reaching extremes, Scorpio continues to transform itself further and further. The Sun brings out the best wherever it lands. In Scorpio's case, it brings out its transformative and sexual characteristics in a balanced way. Thus, the Six of Cups shows the pleasure of any relationship being enjoyed mutually and with balance.

This balanced pleasure is symbolized in the Thoth deck by the flowers pouring water into cups that don't overflow. Instead, the waters swirl around flirtatiously. The cups are also arranged in a hexagram, suggesting Tiphareth and the Sun. The image is the harmony of the sun on the water, a perfect balance of fire and water, a relationship of extremes.

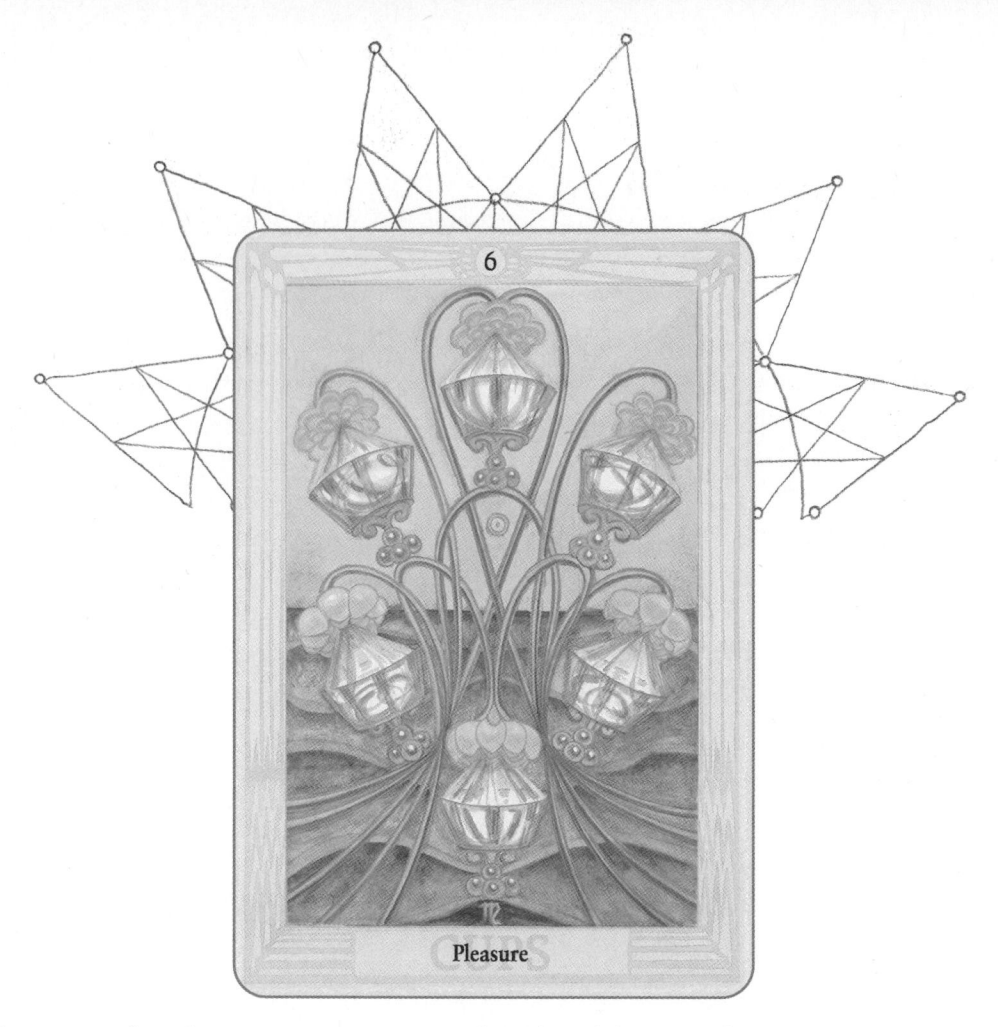

In a reading, this card signifies pleasure, especially through harmonized forces. The important thing to note is that it is *not* gratification. There is a curiosity and openness with the card that allows for play, flirtation, and rhythm; there is no attachment or expectation. For that reason, we might conceptualize it as the very beginning of a wish. If ill-dignified, it could refer to a passing or insignificant pleasure. It could also show pleasure disturbed or ruined by the surrounding cards.

SEVEN OF CUPS

The Seven of Cups descends from balanced Tiphareth into the temptations of the element of water and is thus called Debauch. It represents Netzach in the world of Briah, the victory of the creative world. The victory of creation is to have a created object for the creator to enjoy. Netzach is the effort toward that object. Remember, the suit of cups is about desire. Here, in Netzach of Briah, the ambition of consciousness pushes forward to achieve that which, under its own self-imposed illusion, it believes not to have. In the suit of cups, the effort is for love of the other. Unlike the Six of Cups, which brought beauty and balance to the desire-nature of the suit, the Seven of Cups brings attachment and effort which yields imbalance, indulgence, addiction, and illusion.

The seven keyword is "engine," and the big idea of the suit of cups is relationship, making the Seven of Cups is the engine behind all relationships. This is the motivation for and behind not only romantic relationships but any relationship, even that of Persephone and the pomegranate. However, unlike the Two of Cups and the Four of Cups, the Seven of Cups is low on the Tree of Life, so the merciful nature of the pillar yields more waste than productiveness.

The indulgent nature of this seven is mirrored in its associated last decan of Scorpio ruled by Mars. Scorpio loves pleasure, sex, and intensity, and isn't afraid to go to the very edge, and this is *his* very edge. His last decan is ruled by Venus. Venus is the planet of love, value, and relationships. Netzach is also attributed to Venus. This double loving Venus combined with the already aroused Scorpio yields debauchery.

In the Thoth deck, the cups are arranged in two descending triangles suggesting the pouring of their contents into the lower nature. But instead of water, we see green (color of Venus) and yellowish poisonous slime oozing out.

In a reading, this is a card of illusion and attachment. It takes the purity of the six and vulgarizes it into all that draws out the lower passions. In this place, pleasure does not happen spontaneously; it is forced. This card can show up for any forms of addiction or illusions of grandeur. If ill-dignified, it is less severe and more a passing distraction.

EIGHT OF CUPS

The Eight of Cups is entitled Indolence and represents Hod in Briah. Here we find the glory of the creative world. But how does the glory of the creative world yield indolence? We must understand the nature of Hod. Recall that Hod is both intelligence and submission. It is the ability of the units of the universal to submit to that universal. In that submission, the units form an intelligent design (the seeds of which lie in Binah, the forming power of the tree). This is the real meaning of omniscience. The universe knows itself through intelligent design. In all of the eights there is a submission to this design. In the context of the suit of cups, this is even more passive than the other suits. Both Hod and the suit of cups are attributed to water, making it especially passive, almost lazy. When you add a negative connotation to laziness, you get indolence. The negative connotation comes at this stage of impurity. After Tiphareth, the energy of the element is thoroughly polluted by the attachment to the material world below.

The submission of eight is expressed in the mnemonic "fate." Here, we are forced to surrender to fate. The big idea of the suit of cups is relationships, so this card is about the fate of our relationship with our object of desire. The ultimate fate of all objects to the subject of consciousness is annihilation because all objects are things. All things have edges in time or space; they begin and end. For an object to be experienced, it must have form, and if it has form, it has an end. The Eight of Cups is the card of letting go of the object of

Indolence

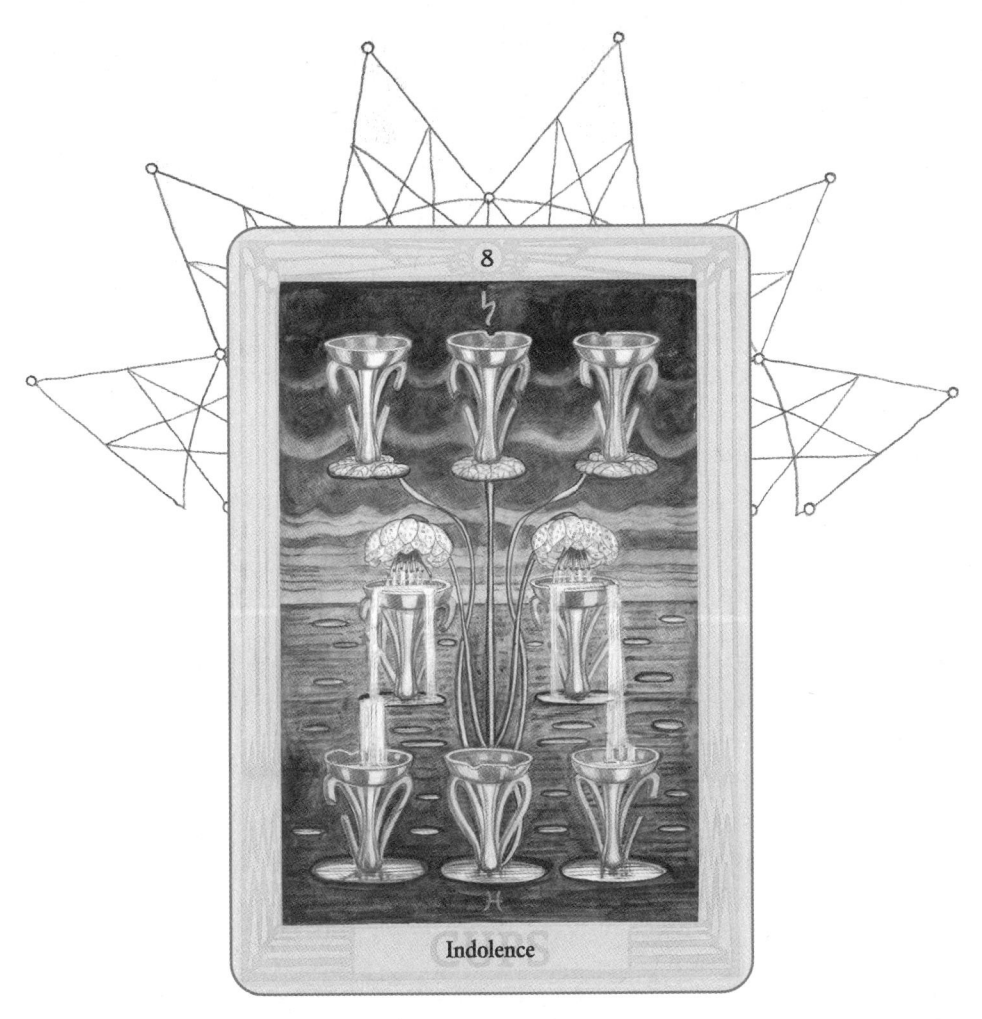

desire and in doing so, surrendering to the intelligence of the universe (Mercury, attributed to Hod). It is the opposite of the Seven of Cups, which is forced effort toward the object of desire.

The first decan of Pisces declares this card's need to let go. Pisces is the last sign, governing the twelfth house, the house of sorrows, the representation of the last chapter of life. It is often looked to for spiritual and transcendental matters. What is transcendent is expressed in Pisces's tarot card, the Moon. The Moon illustrates the pouring of the collective unconscious into all life forms and evolution itself. Connect that with the doctrine above of, that submission is intelligent design. Pisces exemplifies this mystery: In some ways, mutable water yields the most passive and sensitive of signs. Their first decan is ruled by Saturn. Saturn is all about limitation. Saturn comes in and stops the enjoyment of the

CHAPTER 4

pleasure that has precipitated up to this point in the suit. This, in combination with Hod, provides a much needed remedy for the compounding indulgence.

In the Thoth deck, we see dark black clouds of Saturn and chipped cups. The water is reduced to mere puddles. Crowley describes this as the "morning after" but without having had the night before.

In a reading, this card is major unpleasantness oftentimes accompanied by lack of motivation, laziness, and sometimes depression. It indicates the abandonment of success, a decline of interest, stagnation, lack of creativity, and decreased motivation. The good news is that one can change their direction. The most important thing the questioner must do is change their target and redefine their goals to get moving again. When your target is in the right place for you, in alignment with your true will, you will have the support of the universe.

NINE OF CUPS

The Nine of Cups is titled Happiness. It represents Yesod in Briah, the foundation of the creative world. Remember how the questioner that receives the Eight of Cups needs to change their target? Here is the new target. Actually, this is the target of the whole Tree of Life. The very foundation of the creative world is happiness. The whole reason and method of consciousness splitting itself into the duality of Briah was happiness. In the Eight of Cups, we surrender our attachments, and in the Nine of Cups, that natural happiness that is what we really are is revealed.

Nine in our mnemonic system is the "finish line," and the big idea of the cups is relationship. The foundation of any true relationship should be that which precipitated it in the first place: Happiness. In the love of the other, whether human love or cosmic, there is a recognition of the self. That shared experience in its purity is happiness. In this card, the wish that was made in the six is now granted but not yet received (that will be the work of the Ten of Cups). This is consciousness about to give itself to itself, and all the enjoyment wrapped up in the anticipation.

We find the same general ideas with Jupiter, who rules the second sign of Pisces. Jupiter (like Chesed) wants to give everyone what they want, letting Pisces's dreams come true. Here, the Wheel of Fortune (Jupiter) accelerates the process of the Moon (Pisces) to pour its unconscious intelligence into more and more life forms so all the dreams of unitive consciousness can exist.

In the Thoth deck, we are met with "Victorian clutter" as Crowley calls it. The stability of Yesod and Jupiter is expressed with the neat arrangement of the Cups in a square. In a way, this is the fullest enjoyment of water.

Happiness

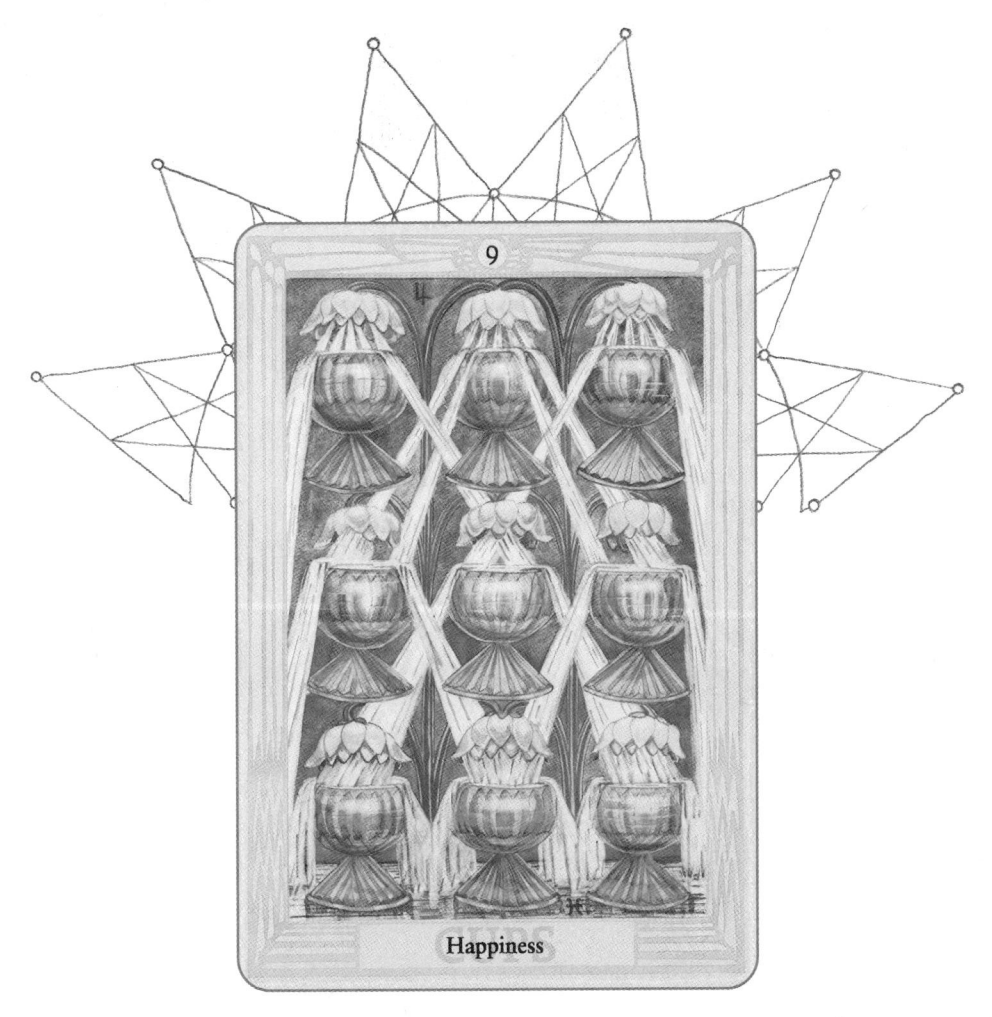

In a reading, this card suggests getting what you wanted. However, it's not so much the process of enjoying it but rather the moment of receiving it, which is oftentimes more pleasurable. It's like the moment before you bite into the piece of cake. The first bite is always the best; the subsequent bites offer diminishing returns: They never compare to the first. What follows is satiety.

TEN OF CUPS

The Ten of Cups is entitled Satiety. We've received the cake, eaten it, and now we're full. This is the kingdom of the creative world, the overflow of the water of the suit of cups. Whereas the Ten of Wands became tyrannical in its excess, the Ten of Cups becomes satiated in its excess. This is the ability of the physical world below to fully enjoy, and be completely submerged, in consciousness above, metaphysically speaking. However, there is a dark side to this card that repeats and summarizes the general theme of the desire of water: When you get exactly what you want, you will realize you want something else or still won't feel fulfilled. This is both the curse and blessing of the suit of cups and Briah. The reason why a subject will never feel whole through an object of its desire is because the subject-object relationship is itself a split within the whole. This is the policy of the Briatic world: Separate to enjoy.

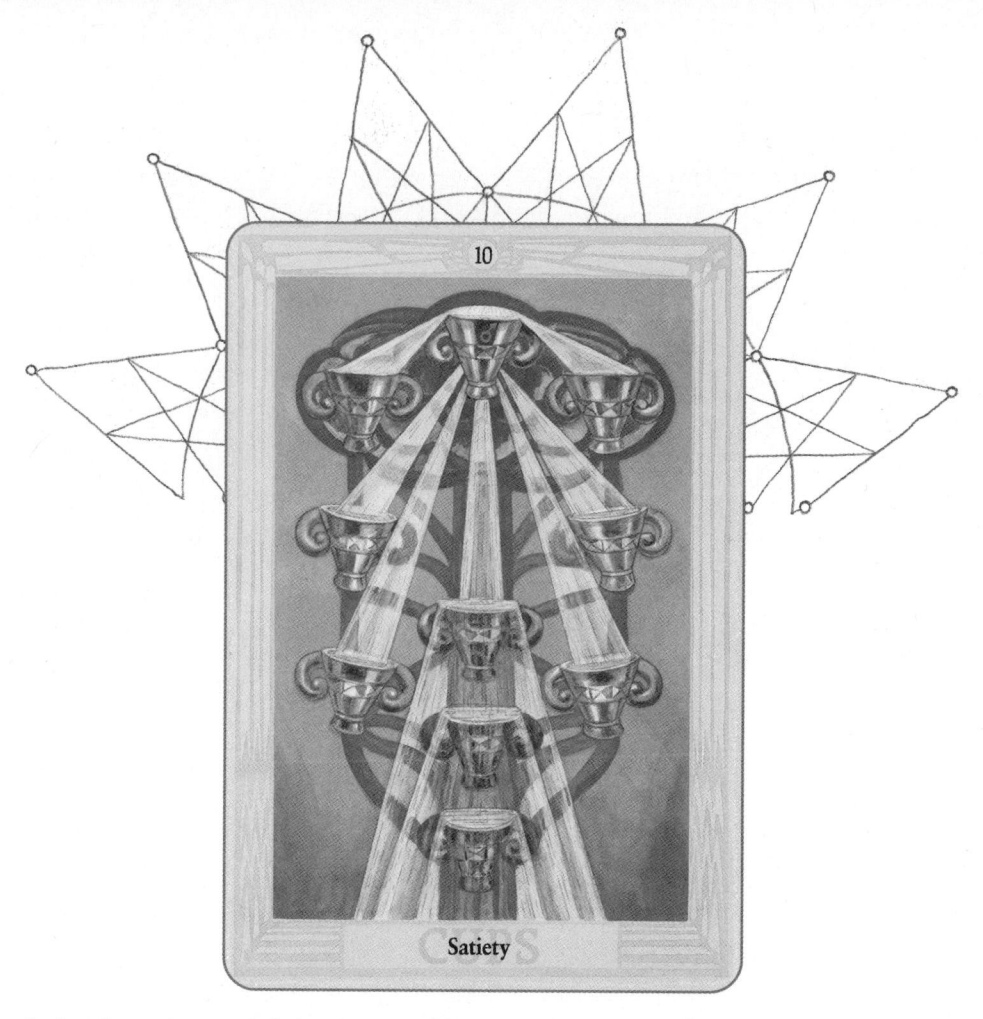

Ten's mnemonic keyword is "again." When we are met with everything we ever wanted, we start again with a new desire. This is the creative process that never stops. The big idea of the suit of cups is relationship, so in the Ten of Cups, our relationship with the object of desire has reached its maximum capacity. No more activity can be done. The waters overflow, and the energy will be poured into the next big idea, concept, in the suit of swords.

Mars rules the last decan of Pisces. It is about inevitable disturbance (in the same way as the Four of Cups and Seven of Cups had to be disturbed to continue flowing). Mars is the Tower card, about breaking down what has materialized. The last decan of Pisces is also the last decan of the zodiac.

In the Thoth deck, we see the cups arranged in the Tree of Life. The first three stand nobly in a cloud—these are the supernals. Below them, the cups are either tilted or overflowing, suggesting the excess of water in the material world. The color red here represents Mars, a planet of gross matter.

In a reading, this card is about is getting more than what you want—more than you asked for. It can be a card of lasting success, fulfillment, and peacemaking. It can also be a card of waste, wantonness, and debauchery, depending on its dignity.

THE SUIT OF SWORDS

The marriage of fire and water allows for the honeymoon of air. On the macrocosmic scale, the suit of swords represents the world of Yetzirah, the formative world. This is the blueprint of our physical reality. The blueprint itself establishes the dimensions of time and space that populate reality with all its diverse "things." Space and time allow for an individual experience: The very point of view that exists within a specific space and time. I call this the localization of consciousness. On the microcosmic scale, the part of the soul associated with the suit of swords is the Ruach, the intellect. This is that sense of "I," that gravitational center of your experience that organizes said experience into proper conclusions. Notice how that sense of "I" is usually at the center of your experience, always at the center of space and at the center of time. Without space and time (and the elaborate formations that come with it) there would be no central point of view called "I." The best way to understand the Tree of Life in Yetzirah is like this: Imagine that you are at the center of infinite space. Imagine that very thin lines start to appear going in different directions. More thin lines start to appear and run in more directions. Eventually, enough lines start to appear to suggest three-dimensional shapes. The many lines start to form mountains, rivers, trees, buildings, skyscrapers, and so on. The sum total amount of information rises and the more detailed of an environment you can see. This is the blueprint of the world.

Practically, the suit of swords shows us our mind and our relationship with ourselves. The cards have a destructive quality derived both from the suit symbol and what it represents, the mind. A sword is a weapon: It can kill and destroy. But a blade can also be a tool: It can be a life-saving surgical scalpel. Similarly, the mind can hurt through hateful discrimination but also heal and mature through wise discernment. In both cases is a categorizing faculty, and the small cards in this suit will show us the best and worst. More specific to the Thoth deck, the sword represents will. It is not so much the spontaneous will and solar power of the wands but rather an invoked and more personal will for us as individuals.

Each card of the suit of swords shows another step down the path of intellect until its utter destruction. Remember that the energy of the sephiroth lose their purity as they travel down. The ace represents the pure potential of the element, the unseen individual will. The two represent the initial movement of mind which, at this level of purity, is simply meditation. The three represents the ego forming and thus the grief that comes with its birth and death. The four represents a collection of egos: Society itself. The five represents conflict within that society. The six represents the collective progress resulting from the dynamic swing between societal harmony and conflict. The seven degenerates the energy into the individual effort apart from society. The eight represents a surrender to the mind, and overthinking. The nine represents the ego's descent into the body as pain and the animal instinct. Finally, the ten represents the death of the ego.

ACE OF SWORDS

There are two types of knowledge: Knowledge that separates, and knowledge that joins. The knowledge that joins has been called *gnosis* by various Greek mystery schools and *jñana* by Indian mystics. This knowledge is comparable to the *nous* of Plotinus and the *ennead* of the Hermetic tradition. This is the knowledge a unit of consciousness has of the universal through which it exists, the knowledge of the mystic. In this context, "to know" suggests direct experience and intimacy with the Real. We might call this the knowledge of one's true nature.

The other type of knowledge is divisive, about knowing facts, figures, data. In Greek, this is *epistome*. It is not the intimate knowledge of the Real but the ability to conceptualize its parts. All so-called things are parts of the whole. Remember that every thing is made, done, different, or changeable, here or there, coming or going, with edges in time or space. The apophatic theological argument is that God is no thing. We might say that gnosis is the knowledge of nothing and epistome is the knowledge of things.

The suit of swords illustrates for us the process of knowledge descending from knowledge of nothing to the knowledge of all things, a process that always happens through the experience of edges in time or space (and perhaps other dimensions). Literally and figuratively, the swords cut reality into pieces—into things. This process is the development of the subject-object relationship established through the desirous nature of the suit of cups,

Ace of Swords

which sprang out of the creativity of "no thing" from the suit of wands. This is what makes the blueprint of reality, Yetzirah, the formative world.

With the possibility of a relationship now established, the suit of swords can differentiate. The suit of swords in general, and the Ace of Swords specifically, is about invoked force. It is invoked because it represents a specific thing drawn into the life of the querent that is "not" the querent (or was not). The suit of swords can now play with what is the "self" and what is the "other." This is one reason why the suit of swords can be difficult. Its extrapolation on the "other" engenders unfamiliarity and even suspicion. This is the work of the ego and all mental or abstract identification. This propagates the "things" and "thinks" of the universe macrocosmically, and society microcosmically.

One of the most profound ways we can work with the suit of swords and its associations is through confronting mortality. The suit of swords is the ego. The ego is the "I" we think exists as a separate entity. Its edges in time are marked by what we have named birth and death. Its edges in space are marked by skin. To that "I," death is a reality. To the reality of consciousness, there is no death. Consciousness is not mind. Mind might be said to be a container or form within formless consciousness.

Mind can be further understood through the other attributions of the suit of swords. The Ace of Swords is generally attributed to Tiphareth, the son, and the sun. In the Thoth deck, we see the sun on water. This is the relationship between fire and water. Together, this sacred marriage produces the element of air and the suit of swords. The air is the space that is created between this sacred marriage, between the supernals Chokmah and Binah. This is the essence of the vav of tetragrammaton, and thus to Tiphareth, which draws the balancing forces from all preceding sephiroth. This is the microcosm, the place of the mind, humankind, and the intellect (ruach). Like the mind, the element of air is invisible but always blowing. Its currents are deeply connected with the earth's weather.

In the Thoth deck, we see a crown with twenty-two rays. This is eleven, the number of magick, multiplied by two, the number of Chokmah and will in a suggestion of the manifestation of the word. This manifestation of the word is the twenty-two letters of the Hebrew alphabet and twenty-two paths. *Thelema*, Greek for "will," is engraved on the blade, the word of the law according to Crowley.

In a reading, this is a new awareness or goal. As mentioned, this is an invoked force (as opposed to the Ace of Wands which is a sudden inspiration). Here there is direction, trajectory, and focus. It can represent a great idea, a powerful insight, and the whole capacity of mind. Ill-dignified, it may suggest a resistance to the mind or a great idea.

TWO OF SWORDS

The Two of Swords is titled Peace, similar to its original Golden Dawn title, "Lord of peace restored." The suggestion in the theme of this card is in the opposite sequence, as if it were following the Three of Swords and going up the tree. The theme of this suit is duality, separation, ego, mortality, and thus suffering. However, this card is so high up on the tree that its purity is untouched by the machinations of mind below. Remember that the twos are the element in their pure, unmixed state. This is pure mind, and the purity of mind is peace. Peace is your natural state. It is consciousness that always remains undisturbed by its contents. Even in the most tragic of human experiences, the awareness of suffering is not affected *by* the suffering. This is the wisdom of the formative world. This is the ability of the "knower" or "observer" to expand outward and become the universe. It is the force of mind itself.

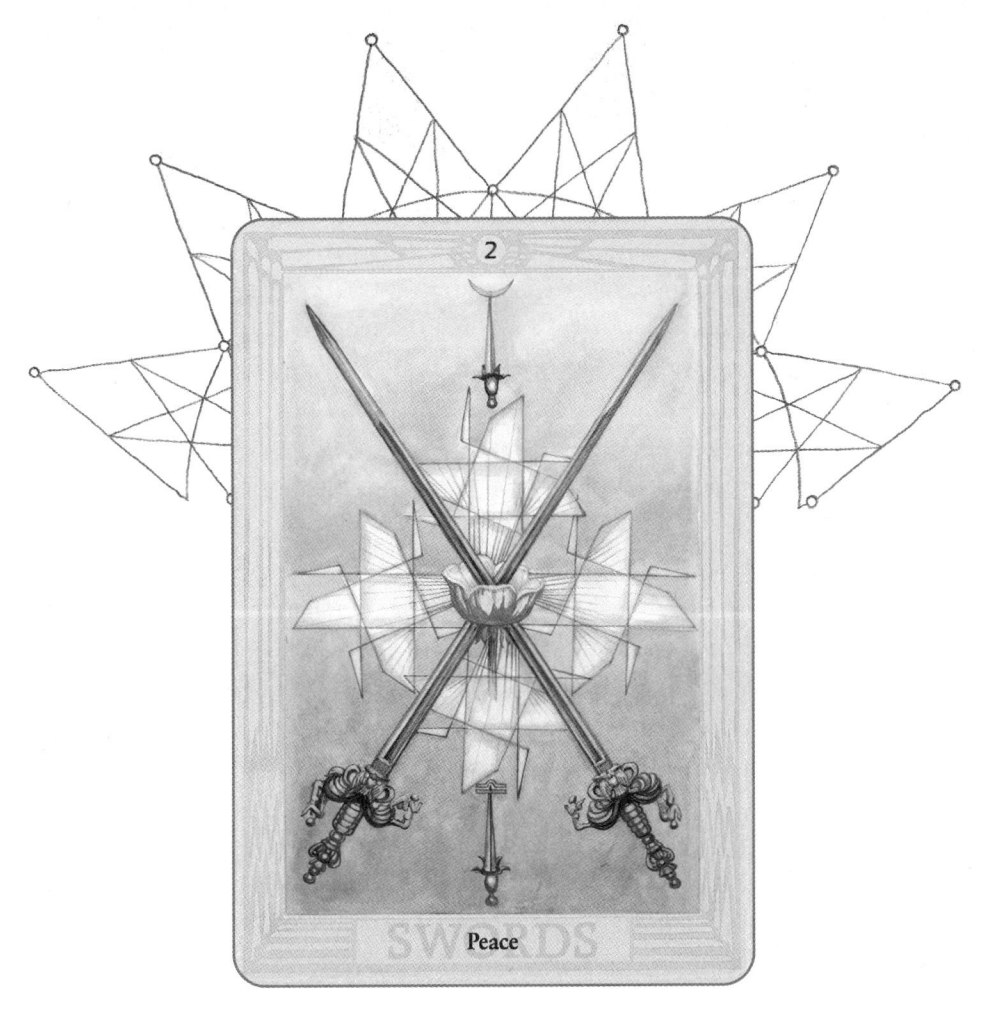

The number two's mnemonic keyword is "to," and the suit of swords has to do with concept. This is therefore a card about the mind going "to" a "concept," the knower approaching the known. The most fundamental manifestation of this is meditation, contemplation, or prayer, and that is what this card is about. Western prayer is a misunderstanding of what was originally more like meditation. There are many forms of meditation. Probably the highest form is consciousness simply becoming aware of itself. In the Two of Swords, this is possible. Here, we are met with the paradox of thinking about the thinker. The paradox eventually enforces a radical surrender, where one realizes there is no possible grip you can get on reality. This method is common in many traditions, the result of which is a profound peace.

This peace is expressed in the corresponding decan, the first decan of Libra. Libra, cardinal air, introduces the suit. She is symbolized by the scales, a sign of balance, a hint at the

CHAPTER 4

balance between the previous elements, fire and water, and previous sephiroth, Chokmah and Binah. The perfect balance of both produces the human mind, the microcosmic child of macrocosmic duality. Libra is attributed to Adjustment, a card which illustrates, through the goddess Ma-at, the perfectly balanced formula of the tetragrammaton, the creative act of God (recall YHVH as the "being" of the universe). Libra is also balanced in temperament and is a sign of poise. Her first decan, the Two of Swords, is ruled by the Moon. The Moon's phases bring rhythmic dynamism to the balancing act of Libra. If we look at it through the majors, we see the Priestess, the primordial light of the universe, brought into manifestation through Adjustment, what Crowley calls the "phantom show of time and space," whose function (according to the *Sepher Yetzirah*) is action, the very nature of YHVH.[122]

In the Thoth deck, we see two crossed swords that meet in a blue flower. The background is the green of Venus. Angels pray in the hilts of the swords. We also see an abstract aleph in motion. Remember that aleph is the mother letter of air. In the suit of swords, that air is put into motion to create the human mind, which is thought. Thought is to consciousness as air is to space. These abstract alephs will suggest the themes of the pips throughout the suit of swords in the same way the quality of the water did for the suit of cups.

In a reading, this is a card of peace, mental equanimity, and resolution of division. It's a moment to relax, where things are balanced. It can also signify speaking the truth, honest conversations, meditation, reflection, and inaction. Ill-dignified, it can be inaction when action is necessary, or a brief pause.

THREE OF SWORDS

The Three of Swords is titled Sorrow. It represents the third sephirah, Binah, in the world of Yetzirah. Here we find understanding in the formative world. The deep understanding of form contains sorrow. This will be made clear by the overlapping influences: First, remember that Binah is duality and the forming force. It takes the expansive nature of Chokmah and separates it into form. In the formative world, that form is being applied to formation itself. The suit of swords is already dualistic, being the weapon of division. Binah brings that to the extreme. In the Three of Swords, we are faced with the dark side of duality: Mortality. This is the ama, the dark sterile aspect of the supernal mother. Here we find the beauty and tragedy of universal sorrow. This is a card of grief.

---

122. Crowley, *Book of Thoth*, 87.

Sorrow

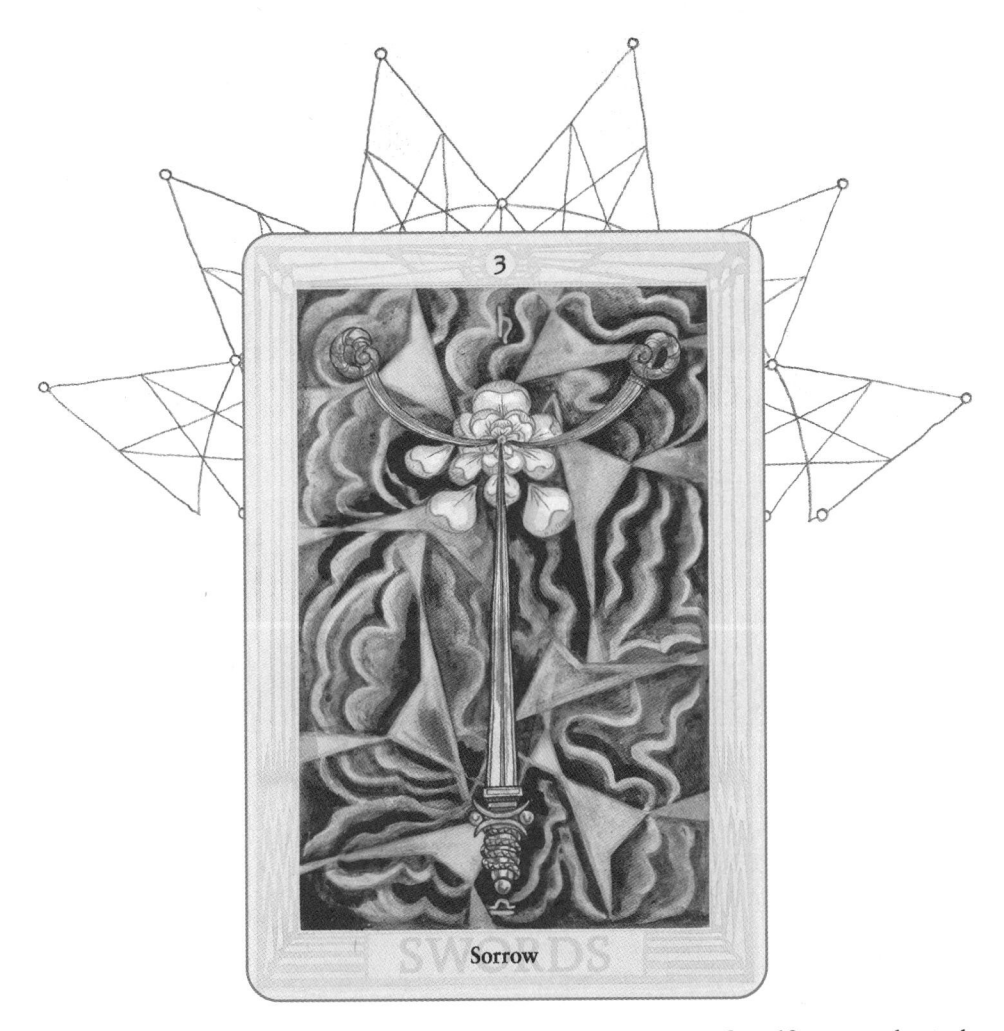

    In the three, air begins to lose its purity in its own concept of itself. Personal mind and ego begin to emerge within consciousness. The mnemonic for three is "receive" and this suit's big idea is concept. If there is something to receive, there must be a receiver apart from the thing. Here, we find the duality of the ego. The ego is the illusion of the "I" that begins at birth and ends at death. To receive that "I" fully is to come under the illusion of life and death, both in ourselves and others. It can also be understood in reverse: The illusion of the ego brings about the fantastic experience that we are "receiving" a world outside of us when in reality, there is no outside apart from us.

    Astrologically, this is expressed by Libra's second decan, ruled by Saturn. This decan answers the question, "How does Libra balance the universe?" Through life and death. Libra is associated with Ma-at, who measures the soul's heart on a scale in the afterlife. The very ceremony marks the liminal space between life and death. Through these edges of beginning and ending, things in the cosmos exist, manifested by the formula of YHVH, anthropomorphized in the Adjustment card and symbolized by Libra. Saturn rules its second decan and its main theme is limitation, symbolized in the planet's rings, further emphasizing the ending side of any length of life or existence. Saturn is also exalted in Libra, giving it extra strength. Remember that Saturn is attributed to Chronos, god of time. For any object of consciousness, time will eventually bring its end. Death is the phenomenological condition of time. This is the sorrow of the human (mind) experience.

In the Thoth card, the black clouds suggest Saturn's presence. The white rose is brought to an end, ripped apart by three swords.

In a reading, this is a card of sorrow, grief, separation, disruption, melancholy, unhappiness, and tears. The card is about the pain of these things just as much as it is about their beauty. Whatever suffering is signified, it is due to the loss of something other than the self, making it a testament to the beauty of the thing (or person) that was lost in the questioner's life. If ill-dignified, it is less severe but one may be in denial.

FOUR OF SWORDS

The Four of Swords is titled Truce, originally Rest from Strife. The truce and rest could refer to the recovery from the preceding Three of Swords, or, if going up the tree, a recovery from the defeat of the Five of Swords. This card represents Chesed in Yetzirah, the mercy of the formative world. Chesed is a sephirah of rule and law. Applied to the mind, here it is related to the ideas of social and human law. In this card, we find the manifestation of the subtle principles introduced in the first three cards. In this card, ego is manifested and complicated into society itself. You can think of the Ace through the Three of Swords as the development of the personal ego, including mortality. Chesed always expands the form of Binah. In the suit of swords, Chesed expands this ego into civilization.

Civilization is the abstract "floor" (the mnemonic keyword for the number four) that we live on and in the suit of swords is about concepts. We might say that social harmony stands on a common ground, or "floor" of shared concepts that include law, culture, and even architecture. To live in a society, one must surrender some aspect of themselves. If everyone did exactly what they wanted all the time, there would be chaos. This is the "truce" of the Four of Swords but also its restriction.

These ideas are further established with our last decan of Libra. Here, Libra enacts not just the more subtle balance of the universe and mind (as she did previously) but manifests that balance outwardly through justice and law. That outward manifestation is further established by this decan's ruler, Jupiter. Chesed is also attributed to Jupiter, doubling its strength. As Jupiter is the largest planet, it represents kings and ruling deities as well as optimism and possibility. Through enacting its law and rule, it ensures the balance (Libra) required for more to happen.

In the Thoth deck, we see four swords with elemental symbols engraved on their guards. They each point toward a flower in the center of the card. The flower has forty-nine petals, the mystic number of Venus. Venus may allude to the general rulership of Libra and the passivity required for the truce to be maintained. The swords are contained in what might be St. Andrew's cross, a configuration that may suggest rigidity. In addition to the color green of Venus, the background is Jupiter's blue/violet color.

In a reading, this card often represents a compromise. It's a deal between two or more people to ensure some agreed-upon policy or structure. It can mean conventionality. It

CHAPTER 4

can also represent rest from strife, recovery, a vacation, or ease of mind, as well as any sort of formatting, government, or publication. If ill-dignified, there may be a misalignment between a social ideal or policy and actual circumstances.

FIVE OF SWORDS

The Five of Swords is titled Defeat. As it is with all fours, the rest will not last too long. Disruption is due. This card represents Geburah in Yetzirah, severity in the formative word. This is the challenge of the mental world and the dark side of ego. In the Two of Swords, the mind was in harmony with itself in meditation. In the Three of Swords, that harmony is destroyed under the illusion of mortality. In the Four of Swords, the pattern of mind is manifested outwardly into the harmony of civilization. In the Five of Swords, that civilization breaks out into conflict.

Five's keyword is "survive." The suit of swords is "concept." In the suit of swords, we must survive our own concepts of each other. This is the battle of any group of people with any other group. It's the clash of ideals, lifestyles, symbols. More specifically, this card expresses the defeat of one group by another, which is really the outward manifestation of self-defeat. We can never war with anyone but ourselves. Everything we interpret through another person or group is just a *concept* we love or hate within us. Literally, it is impossible to interpret any so-called thing without the mind. The mind does the interpreting. When the mind interprets, it produces an idea or thought. Being a product of the mind, all interpretation always contains a trace of itself.

It has been said that "hurt people hurt people." Those who have been abused may seek to abuse others. One of this card's major themes is abuse; we see the domination of a weaker entity by a stronger one due to the latter's own fears and insecurities. This is best detailed in David Hawkins's book *Power vs. Force*.[123]

This card marks a major pivot point in the swords suit. When incarnating into the microcosm and the personal mind, we have a choice. We can either be or prove. When we are simply being, our mind is a natural overlap of multiple divine and material forces becoming us every moment. We literally are an expression of the universe. However, if we forget that—and it can happen often—we stop being and start proving. We prove we exist through all sorts of elaborate identifications (religion, class, profession, ethnicity, culture, age, sexuality, political views, and so on). Proving is trying to persuade others that you exist

---

[123]. David Hawkins, *Power vs. Force: The Hidden Determinants of Human Behavior, Author's Official Authoritative Edition* (Hay House, 2012).

and you exist as value. The Five of Swords takes this notion a step further—it is about the attempt to prove one's existence through the oppression of another.

Astrologically, this is expressed through the first decan of Aquarius. Aquarius is the sign of the individual. Its nature is to differentiate itself from others, to be or *prove* what they truly are. In the Five of Swords, Aquarius uses the violent friction of the five to differentiate itself from everything else. With the severity of the five, and the ego focused suit of swords, we get major conflict. You might find this odd, since the ruling planet is Venus, planet of love. Crowley's rationalization is that Venus and Aquarius are too passive against the aggressive Geburah in Yetzirah. He calls this "intellect enfeeble my sentiment."[124] I interpret this as Aquarius taking advantage of the peaceful, loving rulership of Venus. Aquarians do not love as easily as the other signs; they prefer abstraction, thought,

---
124. Crowley, *Book of Thoth*, 205.

and data. Their abstract ideas of themselves and the world become a strict compass that helps them maintain their specific unwavering trajectory, regardless of who accompanies them. This is the commitment of the individual to themself.

There is one more interpretation for this card's astrology that's a bit more advanced. Venus and Aquarius together can form a very specific kind of weakness that is its own strength. Together, they represent the strategy of certain people to play the victim. One thing I learned from my mentor is that you are always either a creator or a victim—you can't be both. The benefit of being a creator is you can create the reality you'd like to have, but it costs the taking of responsibility. The benefit of being a victim is that you can give up your power and free yourself from responsibility by blaming others, but the cost is you won't get the life you would like to have. Neither position is right nor wrong. Remember that the victim will always create elaborate fantasies based on what is right and wrong. In one interpretation, Aquarius is the bully of Venus, but maybe that's exactly what Venus wants. The "creator versus victim" concept is not a philosophy or political commentary at any level. It's the distinction between two different states of mind for personal development. It is *not* meant to minimize the lived experiences of any victim—only to empower them.

In a reading, this is a nasty card. It is one of conflict, jealousy, judgment, manipulation, ego, abuse, and taking advantage. If it shows up, you should ask yourself "who is taking advantage of whom?" If ill-dignified, the severity is lessened but there is still subtext that may be draining the energy from a situation, and not everyone should be trusted. It's time to stop playing the victim.

SIX OF SWORDS

Crowley named this card Science, and MacGregor Mathers called it Earned Success. It represents Tiphareth in Yetzirah, the beauty of the formative world. Meditate on the beauty of the blueprint of the universe. One might consider the harmony of the standard model. At the very heart of the tree, spirit meets matter. Here, the omniscience of the universe, its knowability, becomes reflected in the microcosm. This is the human mind's ability to see the patterns of the universe and play with them. This is science. In practical application, this is success that is earned through the effort of inquiry and problem solving.

Six's keyword is "fix." In the suit of swords, our big idea is concept. We use concepts to fix things, that's science: A systematic approach to problem solving involving observation, hypothesis, experimentation, data collection, and analysis to learn. And most of it deals with concepts of reality. But the fixing extends beyond scientific inquiry. It shows us all rational solutions. Here, the six balances the social harmony of the four with the disharmony of the five and refines both through the divine influence of the supernals. The six represents the dynamic balance of agreement (four) and disagreement (five) for scientific advancement and "earned success."

This collective advancement is exemplified in the second decan of Aquarius. Aquarius is all about progress; they are the navigators, pioneers, and inventors, especially with regard to the intellect and the abstract. Their very symbol is a human (or angel). They are in some ways the most humanistic. Their second decan is ruled by Mercury, which brings even more intelligence, communication, and speed to their progress. Mercury is not only the mind but the logos. Here, the humanity of Aquarius combines with the apex of their mind (Mercury) to achieve major progress. This combination itself is just one more phase of the logos.

In the Thoth deck, this is symbolized by the rose cross at the center of the card. The rose cross symbolizes the microcosm and humanity as a blossoming rose within the macrocosm of the unfolding cube. This is an index of the tarot itself and a symbol of the great work.

In a reading, this card represents the highest practical application of the human mind. It can signify major problem solving, innovation, systematization, organization, truth, and even genius. For a moment, quarreling forces harmonize to maximize moral and mental faculties. Success is ahead. The mind is working in harmony with the rest of the soul. This is a card of self-esteem and success after labor, and it can also suggest travel by water or air. If ill-dignified, it may show delays or resistance to progress.

SEVEN OF SWORDS

The Seven of Swords is called Futility by Crowley and Unstable Effort by MacGregor Mathers. It represents Netzach in the world of Yetzirah, the victory of the formative world. To understand how futility could be a victory, we need to revisit the very important pattern of energy downward from the pillar of neutrality into the pillar of mercy, a process that happens three times. The first is Kether descending into Chokmah. This one emanation is really the whole pattern of reality and the Tree of Life, being connected to the Fool, knights, aces, and twos. The second is when the energy of the supernals cross the abyss and manifest as Chesed. The last is when Tiphareth sacrifices its balanced state to descend into Netzach. In each descent, there is a slight loss of unity for an elaboration into selfhood. Each sephirah on the pillar of mercy takes the *ehieh*, "I am" nature of Kether and manifests it lower in a more detailed and composite form. Chokmah does this through the logos and expansion. Chesed does this through materialization, space, and the demiurge. Netzach does this through personal volition.

In the Seven of Swords, we are met with the third descent into individual sovereignty in the formative world. The formative world offers enough detail for Netzach's desire nature to really form. To have desire, there must be some lack, resistance, or distance from the desired thing. The mental framework and blueprint of the universe offered by the formative world and the suit of swords provides the perfect conceptual landscape for that lack. This landscape of lack ensures a world of resistance and distance to offer more and more paradigms for desire to arise. In a way, all desire and all effort are futile and unstable at this level because so much multiplicity has taken place through the sword's fracturing of unity. The more multiplicity, the more things with edges in the universe. The more things with edges, the more we must navigate (Aquarius is the navigator) to get our desire.

Futility

There's one major difference that should be noted between the suit of swords and the suit of cups. In the cups, the main idea is of relationship, which involves two. Briah represents the love affair of the creator and the created. The suit of swords, by contrast, reveals the conceptual virtual realities that arise between the primordial relationship of the other. In this suit, there is not just a love affair, but an entire fantasy or nightmare of ideas emerging within it. There is not just the pain and pleasure of gain and loss like in the suit of cups, but an elaborate phantom show of meaning. At this level, various things can be gained and various things can be lost, all depending on the individual and where they are in space and time. That individual, and the effort behind what they want to gain and avoid losing, is best expressed in the Seven of Swords.

Seven's keyword is "engine," a symbol of effort. The unstable quality is due to the individual working against the environment, something that arose through the formative blueprint of Yetzirah. There is now quite a place to go! The big idea of "concept" makes the ambition of seven one of abstract identity, symbol, or ideal. This is a card of fighting for what you believe is right amidst adversity.

The individual's effort against the environment is very characteristic of Aquarius, who always strives to set themselves apart and fully embody their unique truths. But it is actually the resistance of the status quo that renders the Aquarius unique. Their last decan is ruled by the Moon. Crowley notes that the Moon and Aquarius are both passive, making the intellectual effort weak. The changing Moon brings vacillation to the stark, bold choices and ideals of Aquarius. We could imagine this card to be one great and powerful idea that is not well received by the masses because of their own weakness and dullness. Whoever had the idea did not assert it enough, and the genius was lost.

This loss is symbolized by the six smaller swords ganging up on one larger sword. The larger sword features the glyph of the Sun on its hilt, representing the ruach. The other six classical planets are seen on the hilts of the other six swords representing the other aspects of our psyche/other influences resisting the intellect and the powerful idea.

In a reading, this could signify several things. The most obvious is that of resistance to the questioners point of view, especially if their contribution is smart or valuable. It's having the right idea but at the wrong place and in the wrong time. It can signify fantastical dreamwork that is not followed through with action because of self-doubt, procrastination, and sensitivity to other influences that are not aligned. With the Moon in Aquarius, this is also a card of risk, secrets, strategy, tactics and mischief. If ill-dignified, the value of the intellectual work is even more strongly resisted or possibly ignored.

EIGHT OF SWORDS

The Eight of Swords begins our descent into madness, titled Interference (Crowley) and Shortened Force (MacGregor Mathers). As Yetzirah continues to expand reality with its own intellectual fascination with itself, the machinations of mind become more and more elaborate. The eight is the apex of this semiotic indulgence. As Hod in Yetzirah, it is thought in its own world. The glory of the formative world is getting lost in thought, and that's exactly what this card is about.

Eight's keyword is "fate," calling to mind ideas of surrender and submission in the suit of swords, of concept. This is the surrender to concept, being too much in your head. In a fun way, this is the omniscience of reality, where every *thing* is really a *think*. All edges of things are really conceptual edges in our mind's interpretation. But practically, the Eight of

8

Interference

Swords is the extreme of the thought world, creating a conceptual prison, getting lost in a labyrinth of meaning and overthinking.

This is expressed astrologically with the introduction of Gemini. Gemini's symbol is the twins. This mutable air sign is all about dialogue, thought, detail, chatter, and meaning. It is associated with the Lovers card, a glyph of the universe coming into being through the engine of division. Both these cards' Qabalistic and astrological attributions reflect the ongoing fractal division of the universe to create more and more parts, and thus more and more information between "things" within the whole. This first decan of Gemini is ruled by Jupiter, where it wants to see things from the whole. It wants to expand through generalization, summarization, and seeing the whole picture. Gemini is the opposite, preferring instead to indulge in the details of the parts. Indeed, Jupiter is in its fall here. Another interpretation of this pairing is that Jupiter accelerates the particularization and information exchange of

Chapter 4

Gemini to the extreme, causing confusion and overwhelm. However you interpret it, progress is impeded by distraction and arbitrary details.

In the Thoth deck, this impediment is symbolized by two vertical long swords crossed by six shorter swords of varying designs.

This is one of the most relatable cards in the deck for many querents. It is a card of overthinking and getting in your own way. It signifies too much attention to detail at the expense of the whole project. There is little persistence in the face of arbitrary obstacles in the querent's path. If ill-dignified, the distractions are minor and may be easier to overcome, but grounding is still necessary.

NINE OF SWORDS

The Nine of Swords is titled Cruelty, and it represents Yesod in Yetzirah. This is the foundation of the formative world. Why would cruelty be the foundation of the blueprint of the universe? This is one place in which the tarot represents a manifestation of the energy but is *not* the energy of the sephiroth. To understand this, we need to understand the various meanings of Yesod. Yesod is the foundation because it is the astral and subconscious world that frames our physical experience. This includes the realm of thought, archetype, symbol, and dream, but also the autonomic nervous system that runs our bodies without our conscious attention. The majority of the work that happens here goes unnoticed. In the suit of swords, this manifests as all sorts of neuroses, subconscious reactions, and reflexes for our survival. It's not so pretty. It's a descent into our animal nature. This is the lowest we've gotten with the small cards. Duality has run its course, and the experience of the separate self is no longer just a conscious experience, but a subconscious assumption and false reality. At this level, the false reality of the ego is not just strong, but fully embedded in our system. This is the realm of fear. In relative reality, fear can be helpful—it can save us from a tiger. However, whenever there is fear there is separation between the self and the other. In relative reality, I would not want to be eaten by a tiger. But in absolute reality, there is no me and there is no tiger. The mystic will ask you to look deeper and deeper. There are no clear edges of where prey ends and predator begins.

Unfortunately, this low on the tree, we *are* in relative reality. There is a real experience of the differentiation between prey and predator. And that differentiation is so integrated into our survival. Nine's keyword is "finish line," and in the suit of concepts, this is the finish line of all concepts. We have bought the concepts of our individual identities so much they are no longer concepts but automations. They are the unconscious apparatus of our activity.

Cruelty

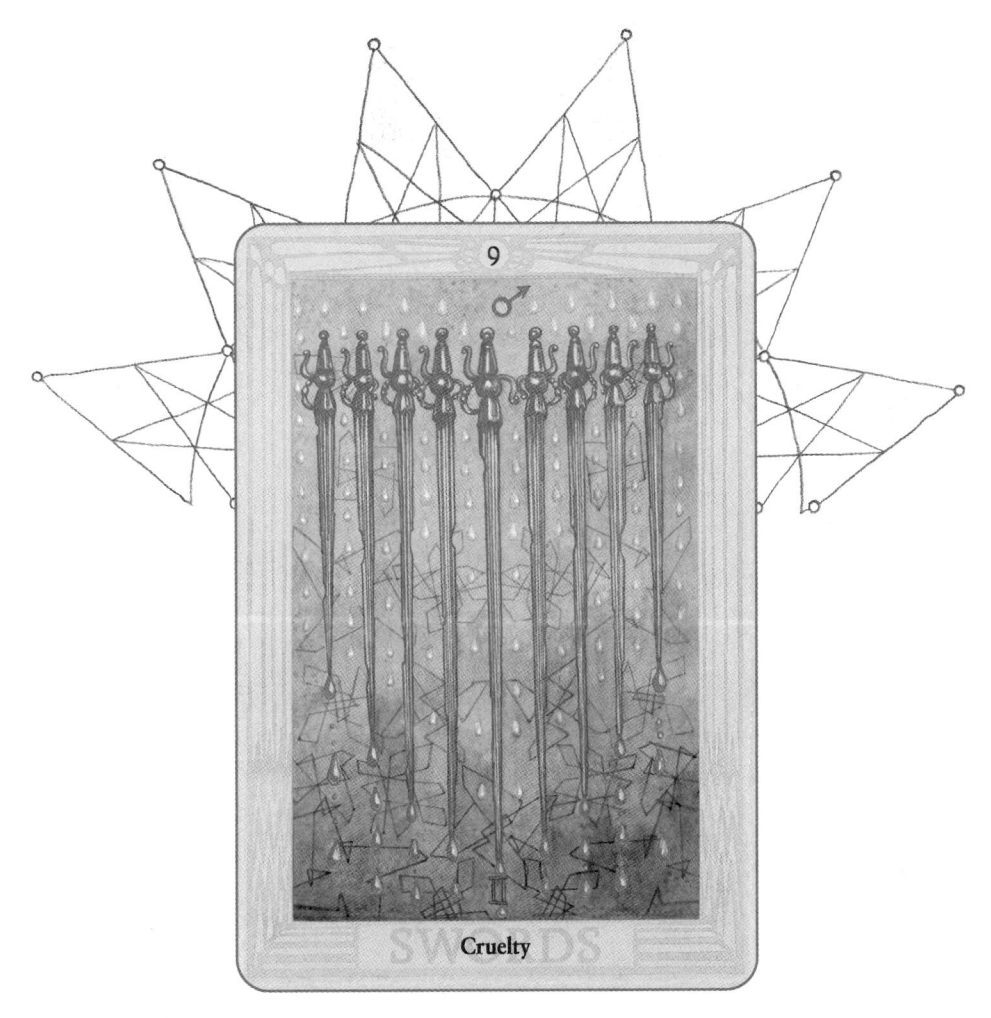

It is now the autonomic nervous system. This is trauma, what Eckhart Tolle calls the pain body, our wounds and somatic reactions to triggers.[125] Here, circumstances occur through our reactions instead of conscious responses. But there is a beauty to this. The conceptual blueprint of reality (Yetzirah) has elaborated itself so much that there are entire conceptual worlds running in each of its units. The units are us! This is the automata of life and the way omniscience is poured into the microcosm. This populates the world with minds.

Astrologically, this is expressed by Gemini's second decan, ruled by Mars. As previously discussed, the complication and elaboration of the conceptual suit of swords finds its apex in the multiplicity of Gemini. However, the rulership of Mars brings violence and the survival instinct to this multiplicity. The twins go from chatting with each other to war. We might summarize this pairing as the war of the mind. More deeply, Mars drives things into

---

125. Eckhart Tolle, *The Power of Now: A Guide to Spiritual Enlightenment* (New World Library, 1999).

CHAPTER 4

gross matter. Mars is the Tower, the gross material universe in perpetual destruction and change. There is a profound doctrine here. Remember that the Tower is just a lower manifestation of love expressed higher up on the tree by Lust and the Empress. In the same way, the innumerable energies, reflexes, subconscious and somatic reactions in the body are a confluence of many forces but are all ultimately love. They can manifest as fear, jealousy, anger, hate, and murder, and all of these stem from the illusion of separation and the fixation of difference. However, all of these are also a desperate cry for love. It has been said that all actions are either acts of love or cries for love. In the separated world of the swords, we see more of the latter.

In the Thoth deck, we see nine red swords, the color of Mars. Poison rains on them and blood drips from their blades. The poison is a symbol of the consequences of the illusion of division and fixation of difference (mainly fear but also jealousy, anger, hate, and so on). The blood is the manifestation of those errors: Murder, slander, lies, and destruction.

In a reading, this card brings our attention to the fear in us or someone else. This is a card of anger, hate, violence, pain, all things that come from the illusion of lack and separation. It can signify arguments, altercations, repressed or suppressed feelings about someone or a situation, contempt, grudges, mistrust, anxieties, and all forms of suffering. When it shows up, it's time to take a different direction. If ill-dignified, these forces are less significant, but be careful not to ignore them.

TEN OF SWORDS

The Ten of Swords is titled Ruin. It represents Malkuth in Yetzirah, the kingdom of the formative world. The venom of the Nine of Swords has run its course. Fear has taken over. In the ten, we reach the final destruction. Here, the intellect breaks. At this level, so low in the conceptual blueprint of reality, the concepts have reached such detail and lucidity that they are taken as real. The concepts are no longer enjoyed as the elaborate expression of the primordial relationship developed in Briah between creator and created. They are now a prison of meaning. The many beginnings and endings of "things" are emphasized and mortality is faced.

Ten's mnemonic keyword is "again," the swords is our suit of concepts. For something to happen "again" it's happening must first stop. Here we are faced with the sharp edges of concepts that make up all "things" in our reality, including our selves and our egos, the edges of which are birth and death. Because concepts are now interpreted as real "things," death is now a reality. Here, reason is separated from reality. Without this deeper insight, the physical world, in all its illusion, can be enjoyed through the following suit of disks.

Ruin

The last card of the suit of swords corresponds to the last decan of the last air sign. Here we find the Sun in Gemini. Gemini disperses the Sun's rays, something Crowley views negatively. However, I see it as another expression of unity reaching duality. Wholeness is surrendered for divided form in the same ways as sunlight lands between the shadows of a tree's leaves. Gemini's dualism fractures the Sun's light into the blueprint of our physical landscape. Another interpretation is that the Sun illuminates a choice. The Lovers card (Gemini) often represents a choice between two paths. The Sun may help us choose by shedding light on the paths ahead. In a larger scale, this could be the choice to incarnate or not. To be born is to eventually die. In this way, the Ten of Swords represents a crossroads between the madness of the illusion of self in incarnation, and the truth of ourselves as one boundless, formless consciousness. Both perspectives will surely seem insane to the other. The mystic may seem mad to the ordinary person, and the ordinary person seems mad to the mystic.

This brings us back to the beginning of the suit of swords. Remember that there are two types of knowledge: Mystical knowledge of the Divine (the whole) and informational knowledge of matter (the parts). It may be argued that a full intimate knowledge of one is the destruction of the knowledge of the other. This symbolism appears in the card as the broken center sword, an allusion to the destruction of the intellect. Traditionally, this is the destruction of the self as it descends into madness. However, considering the larger makeup of our Qabalistic framework, the meaning could be linked with the mysterious sephirah Da'at, where knowledge of the particulars shifts to knowledge of the whole and vice versa.

In a reading, the Ten of Swords is an ending—something is totaled. However, that ending is important. The questioner must let go of old ways or attachment. Sometimes, the Ten of Swords can be a card of crisis. I have found that most people will manifest a crisis in order to make a change they are afraid to make without being forced. Everything has a benefit and is for our growth. If ill-dignified, the ending is not as significant or may be delayed, ignored, or slowed down.

THE SUIT OF DISKS

In the world, a blueprint developed to detail the many manifest forms. And now in the suit of disks, those forms will materialize. On the macrocosmic scale, the suit of disks represents the world of Assiah, action. This is where it all happens. This is the world as we know it, in its strikingly beautiful and terrible high-definition detail. The sense of "I" previously established now allows for a sense of "this," "that," and "the other thing." The "I" can experience a tactile "here" versus "there." It can see, hear, smell, taste, and touch everything that has been loading on the computer screen of consciousness since its download from Atziluth. Assiah is connected to Malkuth (if using one single tree), and thus the four elements. On the microcosmic scale, the part of the soul associated with the suit of disks is the nephesh, the animal soul. This includes our instincts, our bodies, our nervous system, and our reflexes. It's all of the unconscious reactions we have, symbolized by the princesses who are so possessed by their elements (they are considered to be the thrones of the aces). The best way to understand the Assiah and the suit of disks is to go for a walk, feel your feet on the ground, and be grateful for every sensation that passes into your awareness. The mystery of Assiah is that every sensation you experience is a *testament* to your own awareness. It is this awareness that the princesses will become aware of through their marriage with the prince, which ascends them to the role of queens, awakening the Knights and the logos.

Practically, the suit of disks shows us our bodies, money, health, and physical stuff. It has a generally slow and heavy quality, being the element of earth. The general concern of the suit of earth is "bodies." This isn't just the human body—it is any body. The bodies can be planets, atoms, galaxies, quarks, and more. The suit symbol of the disk can be applied to all of these bodies more universally than the pentacles of the Rider-Waite-Smith or coins of older decks. These bodies were first established in the matrix of space, time, distance, and difference in Yetzirah. Now, here, they finally emanate into matter.

Each card of the suit of disks represents a sephirah of Assiah in the Tree of Life. Each one shows a degeneration and further manifestation of energy. The ace represents the seed idea, the sexual merging of the sun and the earth and also Chaos and Babalon (reflecting the higher union of Hadit and Nuit). The two represents the force of earth; any force at this material level can only be carried out through Change, the card's title. This change allows for the emergent of forms, introduced in the three, titled Work. The forms develop further and establish a more evolved structure in the four, titled Power. This structure breaks down in the five, Worry. The building and breaking down balance each other out in the six, allowing for material Success. The seven degenerates the process further, causing Failure. The eight remedies said failure through Prudence. This results in the Gain of the nine and the accumulated Wealth in the ten.

ACE OF DISKS

In the previous suit of swords, we were met with a sort of death. The edges of all the concepts of things emerged throughout the skeletal blueprint of Yetzirah. Countless things fractured into being through ego, birth, and death in a semiotic landscape of name, form, and function. This emphasized beginnings and endings. In the suit of disks, these beginnings and endings become so embedded in the content of consciousness and *being* (YHVH) that they appear as the physical world. This rhythm of beginning and ending becomes the sex of the universe.

As a product of Aleister Crowley, the Thoth deck is very interested in sex. The sexual symbolism has many layers, from practical sex magick, to patterns of the universe, and even mystical experiences. The Ace of Disks brings us to the teleology of tarot, creation itself. To recall the general formula: Nothing becomes something through a splitting into opposition that is eventually resolved. The opposition has been mentioned already but includes all pairs within the general dual principle of the sacred marriage: Above and below, Shiva and Shakti, purusha and prakrti, subject and object, ain soph and the sephiroth, Yahweh and the shekinah, and so on. The very tetragrammaton represents this dance of opposites and has its

Ace of Disks

conclusion in heh final, represented by the suit of disks and the Ace of Disks specifically, which specifically represents the result of the sexually ecstatic process of duality.

The "big idea" of the suit of disks is embodiment. The Ace of Disks is the source code and sexual component to embodying in incarnation. This is symbolized by Crowley's seal. We first notice the words *"To Mega Therion,"* Greek for "the great beast," a reference to the beast of Revelation. Crowley's mother called him "the beast" at a young age, a title he reinstated around 1915 after becoming a magus, a specific level of initiation corresponding to Chokmah on the Tree of Life. At the center of the card are two overlapping pentagons totaling in ten points, a reference to Malkuth, which itself corresponds to heh final and the world of Assiah. All of these are attributed to the suit of disks. The heptagon with its seven points refers to Babalon (refer to the Lust card). Babalon is the feminine counterpart who sits atop the beast in chapter 17 of Revelation. Crowley reinterprets this to be what I consider (at least in one context) another expression of the sacred marriage, creation through opposition. This marriage could also by symbolized by the two central ovals, alluding to the lingam and yoni. At the very center of the card is the mark of the beast: Three circles, a crescent moon, and the numbers 666. This configuration refers to the conjunction of the sun and moon, similar to the sexual union of Babalon and the beast. The number six refers to the Sun. If you've read this far, "666" shouldn't scare you. When Crowley was questioned about his identification with this number, he said "it means sunshine."

The Sun is one of the most important cosmic bodies and symbols in the Thoth deck and Crowley's system, being a symbol of the phallus. In the Ace of Disks, we are met with the energy of the Sun beating upon land and becoming life. In this way, we see the terrestrial love-making of Sun and earth becoming the literal life that we are, a more ecological appreciation of the sacred marriage.

In the suit of disks, mind becomes matter. How does this happen? Measurement. Remember that "things" are anything made, done, different, or changeable, here or there, coming or going, in time or space. "Things" are the very edges rendered by names, forms, and functions. All of the things in the world create the Vedic idea of *maya*, the world of illusion. In the suit of disks, abstract "things" become concrete things. Remember the dynamic balancing act introduced in Libra (Two through Four of Swords) and elaborated upon in Gemini (Eight through Ten of Swords)? The end of the suit of swords embedded the illusion of separation into unconscious embodiment and instinct. In the suit of disks, this becomes both human bodies and celestial bodies.

In a reading, the Ace of Disks can signify materiality in every sense, whether for the better or worse. It can often mean gain, labor, power, or wealth, especially as an opportunity or beginning of material undertakings. If ill-dignified, the opportunity is less obvious or easily missed, especially because of distraction, confusion, or inaction.

TWO OF DISKS

The Two of Disks is titled Change; specifically Harmonious Change by the Golden Dawn. It represents Chokmah in the world of Assiah. Here we find the wisdom of the world of action. All action is change, and we might say that the constant change of the material world is its wisdom. Remember also that Chokmah is the ability of the universe to expand as well as the will and the force of consciousness. However, when applied to the fixed suit of earth, such expansion only exists as change. Consciousness has already folded itself through the world of Yetzirah into the origami of countless virtual realities. It has surrendered itself to a blueprint of diverse abstractions and many borders making up many "things." At the low level of materialized Assiah, the expansive energy of Chokmah can only be experienced as one "thing" knocking into another "thing" since so many "things" are now made (remember the imagery of space filling up with lines becoming everything). But this isn't a tragedy or limitation of Chokmah's freedom. Rather, it is a limitation of our own localized minds to perceive the profundity of Chokmah. In the material world, we can only perceive Chokmah's expansion and wisdom *as* change. Still, this is an insight of something higher hiding in our daily lives. In the Two of Disks, we find the logos in our very physical experience of constant change. All your sensations are change. Without a change, nothing would be sensed. A change needs a coming or going. All change serves that one, undefinable consciousness. All the "things" that come and go in your life *are* your own perception of Chokmah.

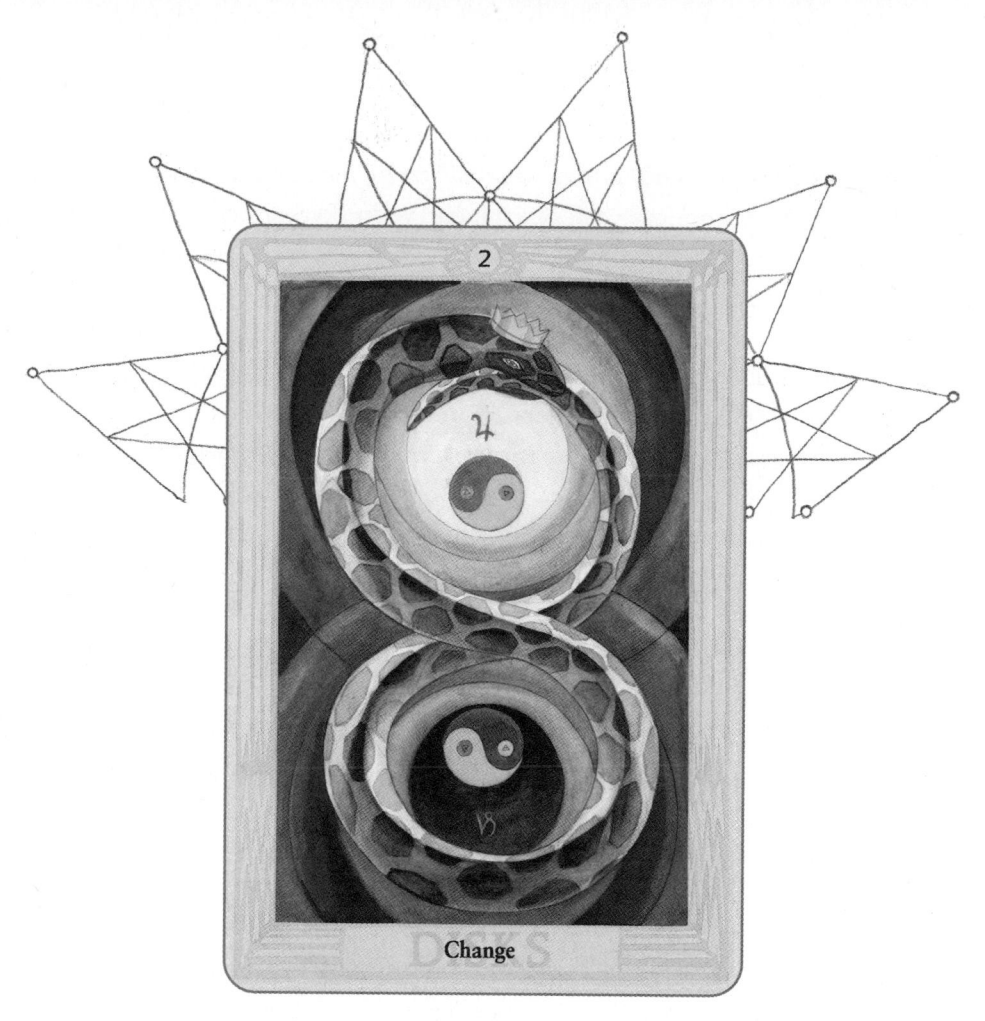

The mnemonic for this number is "to." In the suit of disks, the big idea is embodiment. This card shows how the logos moves *to* embodiment. This simple idea is that movement to (two) anywhere requires change if it is done in an embodied state.

Astrologically, this card introduces Capricorn. Capricorn is the cardinal earth sign, and thus represents the onrush of materialization. Corresponding to the Devil card, this sign represents the lust of consciousness to happen as matter, the ambition of the sea goat to climb the mountain. The first decan of Capricorn, attributed to the Two of Disks, is ruled by Jupiter, Fortune. There are a couple ways to interpret this. First, Jupiter brings general expansion and optimism. In the earthy sign of Capricorn, this expansive nature is the very change of the physical universe, its very lust to become, to be realized. In this way, Jovian benevolence grants the mountain-climbing Capricorn all its capabilities to reach the summit. Jupiter, the Fortune card, literally allows for the change required for manifestation to occur. Another interpretation is less friendly. Jupiter is in its fall in Capricorn. Ruled by Saturn, Capricorn is disciplined, patient, and focused on the present task, whereas Jupiter wants to see the whole picture. Capricorn's focus on the work at hand may contradict Jupiter's desire for the whole picture, and the energies go back and forth, expressed in the Thoth card as the serpent eating its own tail. This serpent is known as the ouroboros and, in this context, represents the logos. Its octagonal spots represent Mercury (the planet oftentimes connected with the logos) and its seven-pointed crown may symbolize Venus and Babalon. The two symbols together may hint at Crowley's famous words "love under will." The serpent may also represent the dance of life and death, the measure of "things" that was previously established in the suit of words. We see two yin-yang symbols that contain the glyphs of the four elements rotating in opposite directions.

The symbols together show the universe as constant change. Crowley emphasizes the doctrine that change is stability which has been covered in the Nine of Wands and elsewhere. The most precise meaning of this card is the movement of subatomic particles and subtler forces that maintain the illusion of fixity in the world.

In a reading, this card signifies generally pleasant change and harmony. There may be a rhythm of gain and loss, but it is usually for the benefit of the questioner. It is a card of opportunity, alteration, movement, and exchange. Ill-dignified, it could veer more toward indecision, wandering, and lack of confidence or commitment. It could signify a difficult choice.

THREE OF DISKS

The Three of Disks is titled Work, or specifically Material Works according to the Golden Dawn. This card represents Binah in the world of Assiah. The simple idea is form (Binah) in manifestation (Assiah). With the stability of the material universe now established through its own constant change (Two of Disks), the forms of matter can fully emerge. This card represents any form you can sense. All the threes express the *idea* of their element. All ideas exist by what they are not, which renders form. In the Three of Disks, this is the earth's idea of itself. This card shows us the process of how material forms come about in physical reality through knowledge. There are two ways to interpret this: Mundanely and spiritual/phenomenologically. On a mundane level, this is how knowledge produces form. A contractor can build houses through the knowledge of the relevant trades, and through the knowledge of subcontractors. In the Rider-Waite-Smith card, we are met with three experts commissioned to construct some architecture. In this way, their knowledge is combined to build form. However, the spiritual level draws this idea deeper: This is how "things" materialize in a phenomenological sense. It's only through the knowledge of the "thing" that the "thing" exists to a subject. This brings us back into our big question—"how does something come out of nothing?"—the main thesis of the Tree of Life and the general concern of tarot. This is how the material universe *works*, by having knowledge of itself that creates its form—the meaning of omniscience. Compare this to the similar ideas introduced in the Ace of Disks. The Three of Disks takes the measuring agent of the ace and puts it to practice.

The mnemonic for three is receive. In the suit of disks, this is the reception of embodiment. In this card, we (and/as the universe) receive its physical forms. Remember how Binah is all about duality. In the world of Assiah, this duality is the diversity of physical forms and the very constructed mechanisms of our daily life, from our bodies, to architecture, to technology, and all sensation.

Astrologically, this duality is expressed in Capricorn's second decan, ruled by Mars. Mars is exalted in Capricorn, which sort of inverts the typical destructive tendency Mars brings. In this decan, it's actually *constructive*. In Crowley's view, Mars represents grossness. It is attributed to the Tower card, representing the constant destruction and change of the material world. These ideas are very appropriate for the Three of Disks and Capricorn. Capricorn is the Devil card, the desire to incarnate. Similarly, Mars is the will to live (remember that all will is both love and destruction). The will to live of Mars employs the ambitious and materially focused Capricorn to build through the power of Binah in Assiah. This is an intense desire to create physical things. More deeply, the corresponding majors, the Tower and the Devil, both express the following: To beget is to die. Study all these cards together.

In the Thoth deck, this desire to create is expressed by a pyramid in a desert. The desert is an expression of Binah. Normally, Binah is expressed as a great sea, but in the element of earth, the sea is crystalized into a desert. The three grounded points of the pyramid overlap three wheels with the three alchemical glyphs representing mercury, sulfur, and salt. This connects to all models of three (see chapter 1). Like the Vedic rajas, tamas, and sattva, these are the three agents of matter.

In a reading, this is any sort of material creation or construction. It can oftentimes signify collaboration, hard work, an exchange of service, passion projects, commissions, planning, and commerce. If ill-dignified, the project may be shorter or less significant, or possibly derailed by a contradiction between idea and action.

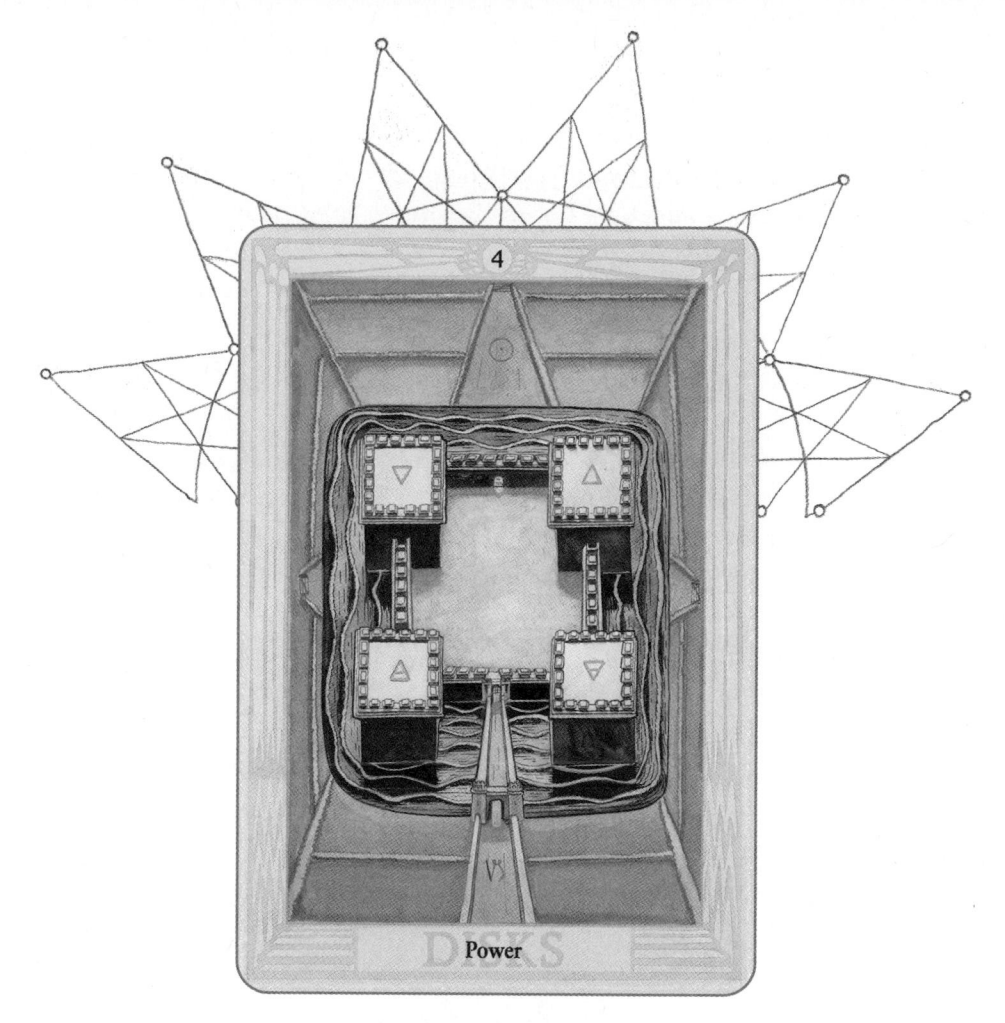

FOUR OF DISKS

The Four of Disks is titled Power, specifically Earthly Power by the Golden Dawn. It represents Chesed in the world of Assiah. This is the mercy of matter. Chesed already has a materializing quality. This combined with the materialization of the element of earth makes for extra stability, but also extra rigidity. The four builds complex structures from the forms that emerged in the three, which themselves could only exist due to the stability of the constant change of the two (a result of the ace's measuring). Chesed establishes three dimensions for matter to play. The Four of Disks is matter as we experience it daily.

The mnemonic for four is "floor." This card is the symbolic floor, the very ground of our embodiment. Here we find the stability of our material existence. The measuring that becomes matter (maya) introduced in the suit of disks has now reached the level of mundane physical experience. These are the structures that pass by our daily awareness, from our homes, to phones, to clothes, to dishes, and so on. On a wider scale, it is the structure of different cultures and our identifications within them.

Astrologically, this card corresponds to the last decan of Capricorn ruled by the Sun. Remember that Capricorn, the Devil card, desired to happen to the world, to come into matter. Graced by the light and energy of the sun, he achieves this. The Sun (connected to the twin deity of Horus) brings about life, liberation, and the achievement of will, bringing out the best of whatever sign it finds itself in. Capricorn's desire to happen to the world doesn't just manifest physically but also culturally and societally. Capricorn is the sign of public image. This card represents both the physical and cultural structures of worldly success and reputation. This is why it has been superficially interpreted as a miserly card in some tarot decks.

The material and cultural success is symbolized in the Thoth deck by a castle. Similar to the Three of Disks, we are offered a bird's-eye view. We see four towers with the glyphs of the four elements. Each side of each tower has six crenellations, representing the sun. This castle is just as physical as it is symbolic of material power and influence. Crowley hints that this structure, though fixed, also moves, and that its revolution allows for its fixity (change equals stability).

In a reading, this card simply means material success and earthly power. It brings ideas of law, security, and order, but more so in the context of material affairs. It can signify a good reputation and great influence. If ill-dignified, the fortress can become a prison, and it may manifest as greed and reluctance to change, grow, or give.

FIVE OF DISKS

The Five of Disks is titled Worry (or Material Trouble by the Golden Dawn). It represents Geburah in the world of Assiah, severity of the world of action. Geburah applies its typical pressure and struggle to the comfort of Chesed to continue the creative process. In the world of manifestation, this becomes particularly tense. The tension is not so much destruction as it is a pause of anxious inactivity, hence its title. The stability of the Four of Disks was ensured by its secret revolution. Its disruption is due to a freeze. In a way, such a pause is anathema to the element of earth since it was literally built on change (see the Two of Disks). As you may have noticed, the suit of earth is much more patient in its creation than the suit of air and contains many delays for incarnation beings to fully appreciate and experience embodiment. This is one of them.

The mnemonic for five is "survive." In this suit, we are asked to survive our embodiment—the very cost of living an embodied life. The body needs enough calories, enough sleep, and enough heat to survive. This manifests as the need for food and shelter and thus money. Those things can cause us much worry. In the Five of Disks, our normal way of securing these needs is disrupted. In many tarot decks, this is expressed through the image of poverty and sickness. It is so important to remember how low we are in our creative process on the Tree of Life. At this level, we experience all material suffering, but through a radical self-inquiry (which would involve reading this chapter in reverse) we will find that there never is any lack.

Astrologically, the material struggle is expressed in the first decan of Taurus, ruled by Mercury. Taurus is a sign of stability, security, peace, and groundedness. It corresponds to the Hierophant, which manifests physically the elusive logos, symbolized by the planet Mercury. This first decan of Taurus is the very problem that will be solved: Lack of stability, expressed via the Mercury rulership. Flighty Mercury is hard to ground in material Taurus;

this dissonance creates anxiety. It is similar to how one may grapple with their spiritual faith under harsh material conditions.

In the Thoth deck, this tension is symbolized by the grotesque gears of a clock jammed in place. We find the typical upside-down pentagram, however, this time, its points lie under the five tattvas. Tattvas are aspects of the universe and human experience seen in the Indian Shaivite and Samkhya traditions. In the Five of Disks, we see the lowest five tattvas: Air, fire, water, earth, and akasha (space). Crowley asserts that these are all required to keep the human organism together, lest it be completely dispersed.

In a reading, this card often shows material difficulty and challenges. In the Thoth deck specifically, these challenges entail intense strain, inaction, pause, anxiety, stress, and worry, especially about money, health, or material concerns. It could also be a race against time. If ill-dignified, the card could represent a momentary dip in finances, or confusion and disconnect about material matters. There is a block in manifestation and a disagreement between mind and matter, or overthinking may be delaying actionable steps.

SIX OF DISKS

The Six of Disks is called Success and specifically Material Success. It represents Tiphareth in the world of Assiah, making it the beauty of the world of action. This is the beauty of exchange that can be as fundamental as the movement of sensations between bodies or as cultural as the exchange of goods. It is the harmony of materialized units within consciousness to have diverse, embodied experience.

Six's keyword is "fix." And here, it brings out the suit's practical best. What is being fixed is our big idea, embodiment. We are fixing things (made, done, different, or changeable) into existence from the material development of the past five cards. It is through the merciful establishing agent of the four and the derailment of the five that we have the opportunity to fix a new design into matter. You might say that the six fixes the broken clock of the five. The ability to fix, improve, and update brings us back to the stable nature of change and adaptability. Because of this, we find a card of manifestation and fecundity.

Change and adaptability are huge in the astrological correspondences of the card. This second decan of Taurus is ruled by the Moon, the plane of alteration, change, and rhythm. You might think that stable, fixed Taurus and the watery flux of the Moon have opposing energy, but the Moon is actually exalted here, providing the movement for Taurus to stabilize in the same way that tides and weather patterns maintain so much life on earth (remember, change equals stability). The corresponding major arcana cards are the Priestess and the Hierophant. The Priestess represents the inner spiritual function of initiation, which is elusive and mysterious. The Hierophant represents the outer spiritual function of initiation that is ritualistic and materialized. The former defies form like the moon in its phases, while the latter is experienced in form like grounded Taurus. Mystically, there is no difference between the formless and form. The experience of material form within the constantly changing formlessness is the heart of the manifest world, Tiphareth in Assiah.

This doctrine is further expressed in the Thoth deck by the rose cross at the center of the card. It represents the union of the microcosm with the macrocosm. The cross's red color represents Geburah while the blue of the rose represents Chesed. United, they represent Tiphareth and the Sun, here surrounded by a hexagram of the other six classical planets. This design will be revisited in a lower sephirah, the Nine of Disks.

In a reading, this card represents success in material things, prosperity in business, power, influence, nobility, and fortunate events. Mundanely, this can be a raise or promotion or new successful job. This card usually denotes a blend of preparedness with flexibility and openness to create opportunity. If ill-dignified, the questioner may be distracted from the opportunity, or the success may be minimized or underrecognized. It cautions one not to let fixed ideals or points of view detract from the gift of the present moment.

SEVEN OF DISKS

The Seven of Disks is titled Failure, or Success Unfulfilled by the Golden Dawn. It represents Netzach in Assiah, victory in the world of action. As we have found with the other sevens, this may first appear like a contradiction. Why would victory of the manifest world be failure? But it's not so much failure as it is the lack of success. Because the sevens all have an enfeebling effect, they are weakened by their imbalance and low level on the Tree of Life. As expressions of Netzach, the sevens bring about an individualizing force. They show a descent from a harmoniously localized consciousness (Tiphareth) into some sort of personal ambition (Netzach). Personal ambition requires a desired result, something that an individual perceives to be lacking. The lack of something brings the unfulfillment that motivates the desire of Netzach, and *this* is what fuels the seven's mnemonic engine! From the perspective of pure consciousness, this is character development. All characters need an arc, a motivation. The victory of Netzach in Assiah is a certain failure that precipitates the motivation for a journey. It might sound like a stretch at first, but how many times do unpleasant situations inspire us to change our world?

Related to the mnemonic keyword, it is here we find the engine behind our efforts in matter. On a lighter note, a lack of fulfillment—called curiosity—is our motivation to continue. Think of a baby learning to walk.

It's important to note that in the realm of earth and embodiment, things are much slower than in previous realms. For this reason, it can take more time to progress. When we manifest the reality we want, there is always a delay. The delay is the test that helps us refine our vision. If we manifested everything we thought instantly, it would be very dangerous, and many would quickly be caught in a nightmare that only gets worse, as many don't have control over their minds.

My teacher once taught me a Buddhist parable: A man was wandering. Everything he thought immediately came to be his reality. Upon discovering this, he created a life of luxury. Eventually, he became complacent. A negative thought slipped in, and the paradise

Failure

started to unravel into a hell. Every negative thought he had came to be. With each passing ordeal, his mind reacted more negatively and thus produced an even greater ordeal until he was tortured and finally killed. The victory of Netzach in Assiah is the delay between our thoughts and our physical realities. In the Seven of Disks, there's a moment to restart the engine and set it in a new trajectory, a moment to slow down.

    This slowdown is emphasized in the last decan of Taurus, ruled by Saturn. We already know Taurus is a fixed and heavy sign. Saturn is the heaviest planet, always bringing with it endings (the Universe card) and limitations. The combined heaviness brings about the idea of failure. But Saturn is also the planet of time, which, like its associated Universe card, brings with it the gift of delay to test our trajectories. It's interesting to note that in the Thoth deck, both the corresponding majors of Taurus and Saturn share the four kerubic beasts, themselves representations of the Holy Tetragrammaton in manifestation. This link further emphasizes the idea of a manifest universe emerging from eternity into time. One could argue that the manifest universe is the school of time before graduation into eternity, especially if we take the Buddhist parable seriously.

In the Thoth deck, we find leaden disks engraved with the sign of Taurus and glyphs of Saturn. Surrounding them are failed crops, emphasized by the card's dark colors. The Disks are arranged in the geomantic figure Rubeus, the most difficult outcome in geomancy.

In a reading, this card represents little gain after much labor, a low return on investment. It can show up for loss, abandoned work, unprofitable enterprises, and disappointment. It can also represent anything slowing down, from finances to the body. It's a time to reflect and redirect one's time and energy. If ill-dignified, it represents cutting losses and finally considering other possibilities.

EIGHT OF DISKS

The Eight of Disks is titled Prudence. It represents Hod in the world of Assiah, the glory of the world of action. Like all other eights, this card offers a remedy to the seven, and we are met with almost the opposite quality. Remember that Hod is both the intellect and submission. The Eight of Disks expresses the manifestation of consciousness in both these contexts. On the intellectual side, prudence represents intellect applied to matter. Philosophically speaking, this is the efficient cause of the material universe, the intelligent design of all growing life (symbolized by the Thoth card). Practically speaking, this is the intelligence of something like agriculture. Additionally, Hod brings a submissive quality to the creative process. In this context, the Eight of Disks shows the surrender of effort which allows for the natural growth of the material world. This would be the progress of a tree's growth without our intervention.

The mnemonic for the number eight is "fate." Applied to our big idea of embodiment, this card is about the fate of the embodiment process, the natural way in which life happens on earth as a result of the sun's energy. In the Seven of Disks there was a desperate effort accompanying (and perhaps causing) the failure. In the eight, that effort is relinquished for trust in the natural process. The release of effort allows the organism, project, or business to grow. This do-nothing approach draws energy from the Five of Disks's pause while also being influenced by the harmonizing Six of Disks to keep things moving.

The astrological pairing of this card perfectly expresses the natural and intelligent process of life growing on earth from the energy of the sun. This is the first decan of Virgo.

Virgo, the virgin, is fertile, mutable earth. Its mutability allows its readiness and flexibility to take part in life-giving, which always requires allowance and flow. Virgo corresponds to the Hermit card, a glyph of the logos descending into the earth to take form through sexual union in a process fueled by the Sun. The first decan of Virgo is ruled by the Sun, which Crowley emphatically connects to the phallus. Thus, we have the masculine Sun entering the feminine earth to create the intelligent design for life.

This relationship is expressed on the Thoth card by a beautiful tree bearing eight fruits and flowers. Its roots are deep into the earth and we clearly see the yellow-orange light of the Sun behind it. The fruit/flowers are arranged in the geomantic populus.

In a reading, this card can represent inaction that allows for growth. It's the strength of doing nothing, releasing your effort, and letting nature do its job. It can also represent applying the intellect to matter, such as in agriculture or engineering. Further, it represents skill, prudence, long-term plans, and smart investments. If ill-dignified, it may represent impatience or overthinking a natural process.

NINE OF DISKS

The Nine of Disks is titled Gain, or specifically Material Gain by MacGregor Mathers. It represents Yesod in the world of Assiah, the foundation of the world of action. We are now nearing the end of the last tree in the last world. Yesod combines all the energies of the previous sephirah and funnels it into the complete manifestation in Malkuth. This card is so close to our daily, mundane experience. It shows how physical things literally come into our life, thus the title. Specifically, Yesod represents our subconscious and autonomic nervous system. In the world of action, this is how automatic processes run the body and get us to take necessary action. This card may represent the argument of a neuroscientist against free will, a subject that would be compared with the Eight of Disks as well as the Art card.

Probably the deepest meaning of the card is how personal management—whether of money, culture, or life in general—reflects cosmic management. The suit of disks as a whole shows the gradual degradation of the logos into matter that then becomes nature, culture, and finally money. As Yesod in Assiah, this card funnels that whole creative process and manifests it as low as currency. In the same way as the sun's gravity creates a solar system, the gravity of our egos creates our lifestyle and financial circumstances, the literal gain of the Nine of Disks. Energy has become interpreted, at least on a cultural level, as money.

The mnemonic for nine is "finish line." In the suit of disks, this is the finish line of embodiment. It is the result of our patience through the past two cards in any material endeavor. More deeply, this card represents the threshold of personal awareness as opposed to universal consciousness. There is a limit to the content of personal awareness. We can be aware of our homes, families, bodies, money, and stuff, for example, but not all at the same time. We have a limited capacity of focus, like a flashlight in the darkness of the universe that reveals to us only so much at any given time. The gain of the Nine of Disks is the border of that flashlight's beam; it's the things coming into the visibility of our localized minds as we move through the darkness of reality. What comes into our flashlight of awareness results from where we put the flashlight, metaphorically, our actions (Assiah). What we do and where we go determines what is revealed... and what is revealed is to be enjoyed! Remember, the Nine of Disks is bringing together the progress of almost four trees that have been manifesting experiences into your life right now. It's a lot to be grateful for.

Enjoying the results of this long creative process (this whole chapter) is expressed through this card's astrological attribution, Venus in Virgo. Virgo is the reception of divine will into life. It's the perfect sign to end the minor arcana. Her second decan is ruled by Venus, the Empress, who brings with her love, relationship, and more precisely, the diversity of form.

In the Thoth deck, we see coins. Remember how matter is all about measurement? In that same way, consciousness has degraded and thus complicated itself so much that energy has become money, a simple measurement of energy to be exchanged. This emanation from energy into money through measurement is symbolized in the central three circles that beam outward and emanate into the six coins above and below. Each of the coins represent one of the planets in the form of a face, while the central three circles represent the sun. This arrangement is seen in several other cards, such as the Six of Disks, from which this card descends on the Tree of Life. Both the Nine and Six of Disks echo the Ace of Disks above them, showing how the energy of the sun is transmuted into life on Earth.

In a reading, this card simply represents material gain: Income, the beginning or growth of wealth, inheritance, independence, and resourcefulness. The Venusian influence brings tact, culture, beauty, luck, sophistication. Combined with Virgo, it is related to good management of material affairs. If ill-dignified, it can indicate a lack of appreciation, the presence of pride, or a disconnect from or the waste of valuable resources.

TEN OF DISKS

The Ten of Disks is titled Wealth, and it represents Malkuth in Assiah, the kingdom in the world of action. This is the last sephirah of the last world, and thus the last possible manifestation. The Ten of Disks shares this hypostatic real estate with the Princess of Disks and the universe card. All these cards represent what Crowley calls redintegration, both the climax of the descent into matter and the signal for the return—once you reach the bottom, you arrive at the top again. If you look at the Tree of Life as a fountain, this last sephirah in this last world contains all the divine energy that has been overflowing throughout this whole chapter *and* this whole book. The idea of redintegration allows this energy to overflow back to the top.

This cycle is why I use "again" as the mnemonic for the number ten. Concerning embodiment, one might think of reincarnation. However, a more accurate application of the idea would be creative processes begetting further creative processes, especially on smaller and smaller scales. For example, procreation is a creative process between two people. Energy overflows between two people in the sexual act. That energy overflows into fertilization and zygote formation, to embryo development, fetus growth, and birth. From there, a creative process happens again but on the scale of a new life. The child will grow up and have their own creative processes as they shape their world. Perhaps they will start a successful nonprofit that brings education to children all over the world. All those children receive the output of that creative process and, in turn, start their *own* creative processes from education. The cycle continues.

A more cosmic example might be that of the sun. The sun is in a constant creative process. Its gravity causes inward pressure causing nuclear fusion that causes outward pressure only to be balanced by its gravity. The gravity also brought about the other planets, including the earth. In this way, we might conceptualize the creative process of the sun causing the creative process of the earth and everything living on it.

Wealth

    This idea of divine overflow is very important. It's like the universe saying, with joyful laughter, "Again! Again! Again!" A student once asked me, "Is the overflow from one sephirah to another the same as from ten going back to one?" I was immediately brought to my favorite theological and ontological thesis that I can't really put into words, aside from a quote of a certain radical nondualist, Gaudapada. He argues that the very nature of the world *is* Brahman (or "God" or "consciousness" or whatever you want to call it). It is this existential "is"-ness that is as high as language can reach. Another name for this "is"-ness is "to be," the essence of YHVH. To answer my student's question about the divine overflow, I said that the overflowing from one sephirah to another *is* that "is"-ness. The redintegration from Malkuth back to Kether is also that same "is"-ness. Not only that, there is nothing that *isn't* that "is"-ness. This quality is what makes the Tree of Life a truly holographic and infinite model of the universe. It expresses this "is"-ness at every level both in manifestation and in ascent. It's the ontological "is"-ness. In the Abrahamic paradigm, this is a creator. In the pantheistic paradigm (such as Tantra) this is what becomes the world. In the nondual paradigm, this is simply what *is*. I like to just call it the logos.

So that logos (the quality of the universe to create, become, or more accurately, be) is represented here by Mercury, which rules this last decan of Virgo. No sign better expresses the end of the creative emanation of the divine than Virgo, mutable earth. Her fecundity and mutability allow for the transmission of the divine will, Mercury, into infinite material forms. This creates wealth both in a spiritual and material sense. Remember that in addition to the traditional association with Hod, Mercury is also correlated with the logos and Chokmah. In the Ten of Disks, it is as if the mysterious logos, the ouroboros, the very nerve of the universe and consciousness called "to be" takes a sneak peek at the final result, only to return the energy back into itself and start again.

In the Thoth deck, the overflow of divine energy guided by Mercury is represented by ten large coins that form the shape of the Tree of Life. Each coin has a glyph related to Mercury and its correspondences. The bottom-most disk offers us the caduceus of Hermes made of the three mother letters in Hebrew.

In a reading, this card can indicate wealth and riches. More accurately, this card is about reinvestment. It's the point when accumulation is no longer the goal. Money, time, energy, or focus must be redistributed to something greater than oneself, whether in business, philanthropy, or any kind of new enterprise or mission. The questioner has more than enough resources. If ill-dignified, there may be stagnation, fear of change, and passive accumulation without action.

CHAPTER 5
PRACTICAL APPLICATION

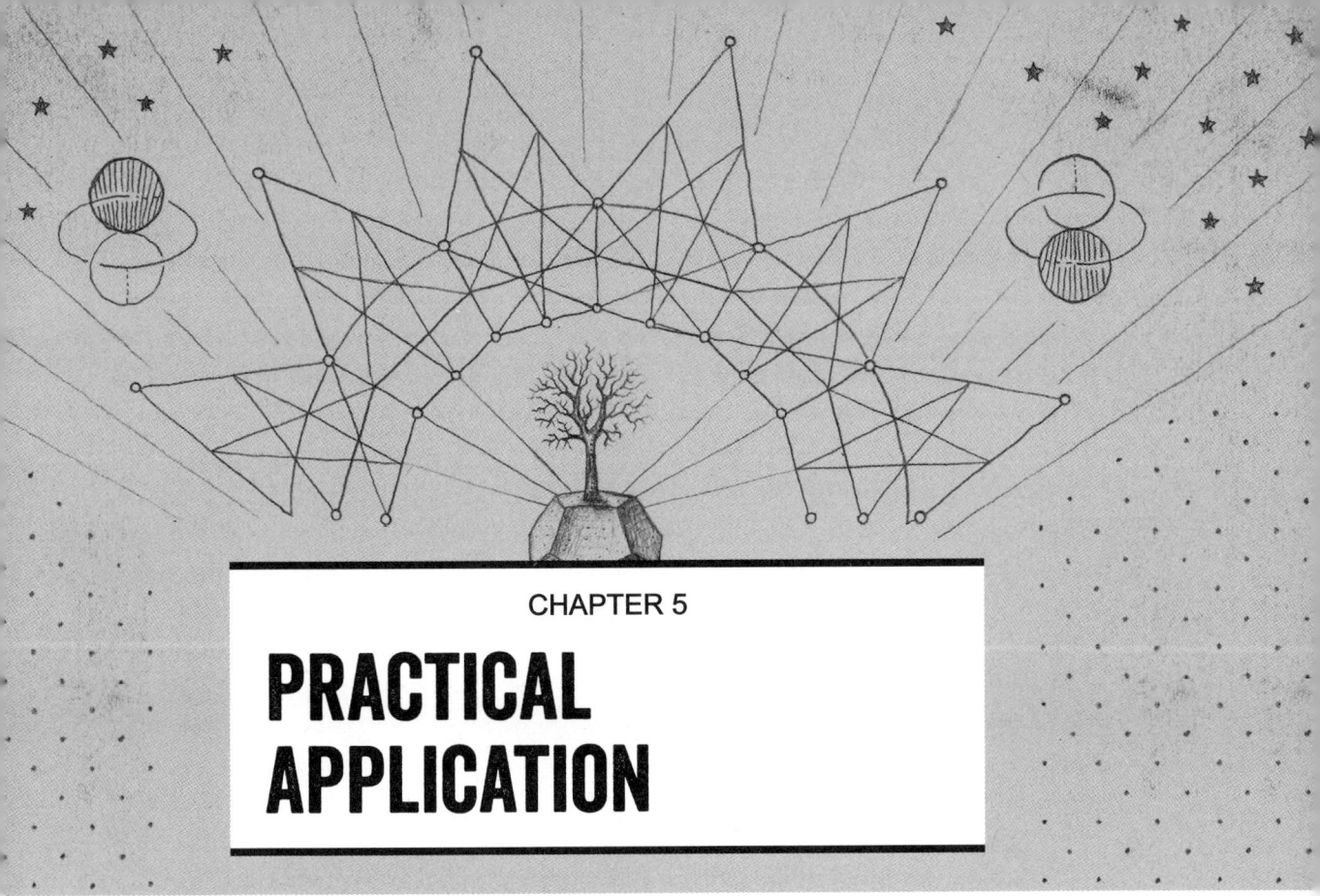

In the initial "Measuring Me" exercise in chapter 1, you could find the edges of your body but there were no edges to your awareness. That exercise compresses so many mystical traditions, including tarot. The tarot is an expression of the infinite self-beholding of reality appearing as finite. Through so much symbolism, association, and many ideas, it expresses the way something comes out of nothing to extend to the scale of the cosmos, human life, or just a moment. What is important to note is how universal this "something coming out of nothing" really is. Whether the Vedic Brahman, the One of Plotinus, the Buddhist sunyata, or the Qabalistic ain soph, there is an absolute "non-thing" that transcends all "things." And yet, things are experienced. Things, as we know them, are made, done, different, and changeable. They come and they go, they are here or there, and they all have beginnings and endings in time, space, and all dimensions. All things exist in an infinite "non-thing," an incommunicable substratum of being, an ontological "is"-ness that was titled and formulated in chapter 1 with YHVH. All things are soaked in this non-thing of "is"-ness. And it is the very nature of this non-thing to be all things.

Up to this point, this book focused on tarot as an illustration of our true nature, the naked, simple, eternal, infinite being. I have taught so many courses, given so many lectures on this topic, and from experience, I understand that as existentially interesting and mystically revolutionary I may find these insights, many people want to lay down the cards and use them. Taking the knowledge of what we have covered, you will be able to do so in a new way. Instead of reading the tarot superstitiously and superfluously, you will get to incorporate its deeper mysteries. What does this mean in practical application? It means that the cards don't just show you what can happen or give you spiritual insight—they reflect your nature directly. We have established that tarot and the Tree of Life are both holographic systems that express the logos on every level. When reading tarot in this way, you can see yourself as nothing but the Divine. Just like every experience life throws at you, every card is an emanation from divinity. The Six of Cups is not just a fun date. It's the beauty of the creative world, the heart of the paradigm of duality that allows for the universe to flirt with itself. The Death card is not just a transition but the Divine casting itself from the beauty of Tiphareth and the dying god myth into the illusion of desire in Netzach. The Queen of Swords is not just a cold widow but a personification of the intuition guiding the ego to its own death and ultimate freedom. These are just some examples. Life is full of these divine emanations.

When we use tarot in this contemplative manner, I call it tarot mysticism. This concerns the third level of tarot, the mystical level. However, most tarot students are focused on the first and second level (the mechanical and subtle/causal). In this chapter, you're going to learn how to bring the wisdom of the mystical layer of tarot and this book into the subtle-causal and mechanical layer for practical application. When you use tarot for the subtle/causal level, or the mechanical level, you are exploring the "things" of your experience instead of the ineffable "non-thing" of the mystic. But remember the most important thing: Every "thing" in your experience is the nature of the "non-thing" creating, becoming, or being. There is no part of you separate from the Divine.

TAROT READING

Mysticism and divination are two very different, but related things. They occupy two levels of spiritual awareness. It is important to understand the difference as the methods and goals vary. When reading tarot, we are working with divination and operating from local awareness. When engaging in mysticism, we are connecting to the Divine, and operating from nonlocal consciousness. I will explain the difference.

All our experiences are like paint on a blank canvas of consciousness. Our egos are like whirlpools in an ocean of edgeless, boundless awareness. The paint on the canvas or the currents of the whirlpools are the patterns and experiences in our life. Tarot mysticism helps us go from the paint to the canvas or the whirlpool to the boundless sea. However, sometimes we don't want to go that far—sometimes we want to enjoy the diversity of color and form in the paint. Sometimes we want to ride the rapids of our own thoughts and experiences. Sometimes we just want to know what's going to happen! Tarot can help us. You can take all the information you learned in this book, plug it into the cards, and use it for deep insight into your life and the lives of others. If tarot mysticism is the use of tarot to become aware of the absolute Self, tarot reading is the use of tarot to become aware of the individual self.

And before we go into the self, we must remember that the self exists within the Self. By Self, I mean the incommunicable "non-thing" I call consciousness. The Self can be compared to Kether, or perhaps ain soph. The localized self particularizes as you go down the tree. Eventually, everything—which is Malkuth—comes out of nothing, ain soph. In the nondual view, there is *only* that non-thing. The non-thing is consciousness alone, and everything that can be said to exist exists within that consciousness.

When reading the tarot, consciousness is symbolized by the back of the card. This consciousness is the very cardstock on which everything appears. This is the same consciousness everyone is experiencing. No thing ever appears without consciousness in the same way as no symbol in the tarot is of the cardstock. Regardless of what information we are getting in a reading, whether it be through time, space, or other dimensions, it is experienced in consciousness in the present moment.

This is why presence is so important. Tarot reading is an opportunity for presence. The present moment holds the imprints from the so-called past, the seeds of the so-called future, and the patterns of karma/causality running the show. It is from this present moment that we interpret meaning through time, space, or whatever other dimension you work with. It all happens now. There's never been anything but!

Tarot reading is about choosing to be aware. You might ask, "Joe, I thought we were awareness? Now there's a choice to be aware?" Sort of. In the same way as there are multiple levels of reality (consider Plotinus's hypostases and the Tree of Life) there are multiple scales of awareness.

From the nondual perspective, awareness/consciousness is the ultimate (and only) reality. All things only ever exist in the "non-thing" of awareness. This is represented by the

Fool and the Sanskrit *chit*, understood as Kether. However, individual awareness as *mind* is different. The individual mind can choose to be aware of things and unaware of things. This individual mind/local awareness is represented by the suit of swords and the Sanskrit *chitta*, understood as Tiphareth. Local awareness is the mind explored through tarot reading. Non-local awareness is pure consciousness, explored through tarot mysticism. Local awareness is the space between your ears, behind your eyes. Non-local consciousness is what everything exists in.

When we choose to be aware in the local context, we can experience more and know more about what is happening to our individual selves. Being in awareness is simply a choice. When reading tarot, you are choosing awareness. You are allowing yourself to be aware of the things of your life: What you make, do, differentiate, or change here or there, coming or going.

Many people choose to shut down their local awareness for many reasons. I've met countless psychics, intuitives, and sensitive people who shut off their awareness at a young age because of the judgment of others. Awareness isn't always comfortable, but it is always freeing.

Briefly, to review "things" one more time: When you know about things, you know about everything. Divination is about becoming aware of things (in our nomenclature, include people and places). The so-called things of divination include any name, form, or function experienced in the conscious or unconscious of the questioner. These things are made, done, different, or changeable, here or there, coming or going, and always arise in consciousness. Everything is a thing. The reason I teach so much about things is to make a clear distinction between the relative world of things and the absolute mystical experience of no thing. Consciousness, in this context, is not a thing—it is no thing. It has no edges, no beginning or ending. It is infinite. You may have discovered this in chapter 1. Consciousness is not made, done, different from anything, or changeable. It is both here and there and neither coming nor going—it simply is. It is the very "is"-ness of reality. Tarot reading is about things. Tarot mysticism is about the consciousness through which they appear.

The things of divination can oftentimes be grouped into one of two levels. These two levels were first introduced in chapter 2: The mechanical plane contains physical things. The subtle/causal plane contains nonphysical things.

The first level, the mechanical level, is where things are physical with clear edges in space or time. By having edges in space, they have clear physical form. By having edges in time, they come and go, begin and end. They can include physical objects such as new homes or money. They can also include the people in our lives.

The second level is what I call the subtle/causal level. Here, things are not physical. They exist in our minds or potentially somewhere else, but they still have edges and are still made, done, differentiated, and changeable from other things. This level is about the inner world. Things on this level can include thoughts, thought patterns/complexes, feelings, energies, identifications, personality traits, traumas, desires, fears, memories, abstract ideas, archetypes, symbols, dreams, creative visions, and so on. All these have edges in time because they come and go in our awareness. Sadness, for example, rises and passes away. Thoughts come and go (about 40,000 to 70,000 each day). Memories also come and go. And in addition to temporal edges, any thing in the mind also has semantic edges. You might say that the edge of fear is where love begins. The edges are not as clear as in the physical world. They are much softer. The point is that the "things" of the subtle world begin and end.

The most asked questions to tarot readers concern love, money/work, then health (though it varies based on demographic). These are usually things in the mechanical plane. All these have definable edges in time or space. Let's explore some of these examples: A lover is a thing in this context, someone who was made by their parents. Their body has edges in space and time. And they come and they go. Money is a thing. It has the edge of its quantity and it comes and goes. Health concerns things in the body or mind. A health question can point to a virus, for example, which is made yet also different from the cells it is battling, and it comes and goes. All divination concerns things with edges that come and go in some way.

Oftentimes, readings will bring up things that are not physical, revealing things on the subtle/causal plane. For example, the Death card may point not to illness but a fear of change. Although that fear isn't something physical, the feeling exists in the body. That feeling of fear has its own subtle edges. Just like every thing else, it rises and passes away. It localizes in the body in a specific space for a specific time until the fear is overcome. Another example, the Princess of Cups, may point a querent to their inner child, some thing within themselves. The inner child is a memory, archetype, or pattern of the nervous system and energy body. It has clear characteristics and is different from the adult. In this way, it has a semantic edge. It has a temporal edge as well: It occupies a specific timeline in someone's history. The point of all this talk of things and edges is to recognize that in the same way the tarot cards are shuffled, our experiences come and go.

When you read for yourself, you are becoming aware of things with edges in your life, and the cards represent these things. You might not know why some thing is showing up. That's okay. Stay curious about the things appearing in the cards. The things of a tarot reading don't have to give detailed predictions. They can be things that come into your awareness for insight into the present moment or a new point of view.

When you read for someone else, you are becoming aware of things within someone else's life. The querent will receive the things showing up however they choose. You as the reader facilitate their experience with those things.

The important thing about both these scenarios is that things are showing up in the awareness of both the reader and the querent. The key ingredient is presence. When you are present with what is showing up, it can be useful no matter what it is. Presence leads to peace. Presence allows thought, feeling, emotion, sensation, and any other experience to process and run its course. Presence is the natural mode of consciousness, which is whole and lacking nothing. Presence is the natural occurrence of consciousness toward its objects. Presence is the marriage of non-thing with thing. A great tarot reader can be nothing and look at everything.

The Tetragrammatic Method

All things show up in "is"-ness by the definition of their being. As elaborated in chapter 1, "is"-ness is the formula of YHVH, the creation of and by the absolute. The tetragrammatic method uses the same formula to explore that same creative process on a human scale. As famously quoted in the Emerald Tablet (and echoed in many of the traditions previously discussed), "that which is above is like that which is below."[126]

In this method, we are working with the four big ideas from chapter 3 and their lower manifestations as the four elements. The four big ideas themselves are an expression of the four layers of reality corresponding to YHVH. Since we are all a reflection of the absolute, of YHVH, we manifest these four big ideas of the macrocosm in the microcosm. To review, the four big ideas are movement, relationship, concept, and embodiment.

In the tetragrammatic method, we make four piles. Each pile represents a manifestation of one of the four big ideas. To make the four piles, shuffle the cards and cut the deck to the left with your nondominant hand. These two piles represent the sacred marriage, the initial bifurcation of consciousness into duality. Next, cut each of those piles to the left,

---

[126]. Hermes Trismegistus, *The Emerald Tablet of Hermes* (Merchant Books, 2013).

starting with the pile on the right. Now you should have four piles total. Flip each pile and read the bottom card, which is now face up.

There are two ways to read this spread: On the subtle/causal level or the mechanical level. As mentioned previously, these two approaches show us two different categories of things. When reading on the subtle/causal level, we use the cards to explore the inner patterns and subtle things causing life to show up the way it does. When reading on the mechanical level, we are getting more insight on the details of the specific things showing up in life. The subtle/causal level helps answer the question "Who am I?" The mechanical level helps answer "What will happen to me?" We will explore both.

On the subtle causal level, the four big ideas map out how we are creating our lives. They manifest as the inner causes of what shows up externally.

The first pile represents the big idea of "movement." This is our personal inspirations, motivations, drives, and will. It's our creativity and what gets us up in the morning. It can figuratively and literally be what moves us, the manner and direction we move in the world. It's important to note that the direction we are moving in isn't always good. Sometimes people create a crisis subconsciously to enforce a needed change. The universe is neutral on everything. Energy flows where it will. The card on this pile will show the general direction the questioner is moving in and what they are creating for themselves. This pile is associated with the element of fire and the yod of tetragrammaton. Whenever we move, things pass us by. Those things have a relationship to us.

And so, the next big idea is "relationship," represented by the second pile (second to the right). This is what the universe gives us in response to our movement. It's the people, places, and things that reflect, in some way, our trajectory. The Five of Swords, for example, could represent a jealous person reflecting our inner jealousy. The Queen of Cups can represent nurturing souls that match our empathy. This pile can also represent the relationship formed between us and our desire. It's the ability to look at our goals as something separate from ourselves so that we can move toward them. It is how we advance toward objects of desire and avoid what we don't want. This pile is associated with the element of water, which reflects, and corresponds to heh primal of the tetragrammaton.

The third pile from the right corresponds to the big idea of "concept." This represents our thoughts and identifications that come about from the previous relationships established in the second pile. It's our points of view, belief systems, values, and thoughts that oftentimes overpopulate the present moment. It's also the blueprint of any physical result, the abstract plan that directs action in the direction of a goal. This card shows us our thought patterns mutually arise through all our relationships (with people, places, and things that are in turn created from our movement from pile one). This third pile corresponds to the element of air and the vav of tetragrammaton.

The last pile corresponds to the big idea of "embodiment." In the subtle/causal level, this is our ability to act and get results. The thoughts and planning of the previous pile finally become actionable steps that in some way enforce the will that originated in the first pile. Here we are shown what we are doing and what we can do. The last pile corresponds to earth and heh final of tetragrammaton.

This approach is more introspective than traditional tarot, and not every questioner will want to explore their inner world in this generic way. Luckily, you can approach the tetragrammatic method from the mechanical level. In this way, the four big ideas represent the most asked questions of the tarot: Purpose/work, love, the questioner themselves, money, and health.

The first pile, movement, represents career, work, passion, and/or life purpose because our drive and will often manifest as our contribution to the world. The second pile, relationship, represents all our relationships, including romantic relationships, family, and friends. The third pile, concept, represents how we think about ourselves and our environment. This is not a matter people often ask about consciously. However, building a better relationship with yourself is oftentimes one of the most important steps of healing and personal growth. The third pile can also simply represent the questioner themselves—and people always want to hear about themselves. The last pile, embodiment, represents money, health, and wellness.

You might wonder if you can use both approaches in one tetragrammatic reading—you can! However, I would do so with caution. I recommend using only one approach per reading. The two approaches work on two different scales, and I would be cautious about forcing connections between one scale and another. The structure is of course the same—based on YHVH—but not every pile on the subtle-causal level correlates perfectly with what is on the mechanical level. For example, the Knight of Disks in the subtle/causal first pile can represent the desire for patience and productivity. However, in the same pile on the mechanical level, it can predict a career in agriculture. Being too strict with correlations is the downfall of the New Age and pseudoscience. This work isn't about strict correlation, but brave self-reflection involving experiences that are subtle and not always clearly defined. It's not classical music. It's jazz.

PRACTICAL APPLICATION

TETRAGRAMMATIC SPREAD CHART

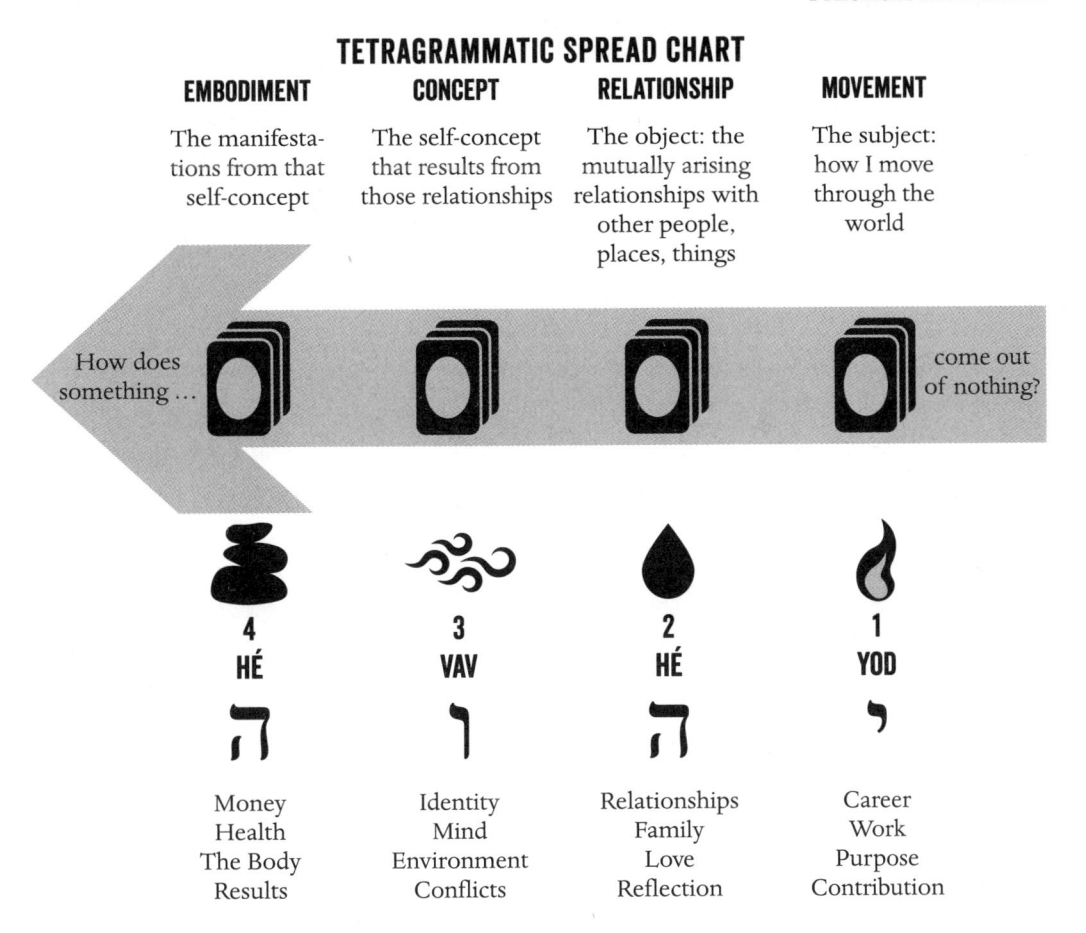

EMBODIMENT	CONCEPT	RELATIONSHIP	MOVEMENT
The manifestations from that self-concept	The self-concept that results from those relationships	The object: the mutually arising relationships with other people, places, things	The subject: how I move through the world

How does something … come out of nothing?

4	3	2	1
HÉ	VAV	HÉ	YOD
Money Health The Body Results	Identity Mind Environment Conflicts	Relationships Family Love Reflection	Career Work Purpose Contribution

The Tarot Mysticism Process

As described in chapter 1, there are three levels of tarot. The previous section taught you how to use the first level, mechanical, and the second level, subtle/causal. Next is the mystical level. Remember that when reading tarot traditionally, you are working on either the mechanical or subtle/causal. When you read for yourself, for example, you are the subject becoming aware of objects, things (the divination), within yourself (the reader) through the symbolic medium (cards).

Tarot mysticism is different. In tarot mysticism, you as the subject (reader) become aware of your Self through the symbolic medium (cards) instead of the things within you. The major contradiction of tarot reading is that you can only look at an aspect of yourself, never the entirety of you because you are also the one looking. How does one really

CHAPTER 5

know themselves if to know their full self requires knowledge of the one doing the knowing? To quote Plotinus, "at that, the object known must be identical with the knowing act (or agent), the Intellectual-Principle, therefore, identical with the Intellectual Realm. And in fact, if this identity does not exist, neither does truth."[127] In tarot mysticism, the knower and known begin to fuse. In yoga, the collapse of the barrier between subject and object leads to samadhi. This is enlightenment, the destruction of all separation and the full immersion into unity.

Tarot's mystical layer illustrates the smallest possible step below that unity. It creates an infinite loop of the universe beholding itself in the most subtle differentiation between knower and known. We see this symbolized in the ouroboros, the serpent eating its own tail. Specifically, this is the Magician (notice his belt in the Rider-Waite-Smith deck) that descends ever so slightly from the Fool (which is unitive consciousness).

The tarot shows the creative infinite loops in three cycles. The first cycle is the Fool to the World. The World is the Fool realized that, in its revelation, returns to complete nothingness/ignorance, back to the Fool, where it projects itself outward into the Magician and the process starts again (detailed in chapter 2). The second cycle is the court cards. They illustrate the recurring creative loop of the tetragrammaton (detailed in chapter 3). Lastly are the pip cards, which detail the creative loop of the sephirah (detailed in chapter 4). These three chapters offer an analysis of the infinite self-becoming and self-apprehending of consciousness, itself an elaboration of the splitting of consciousness into knower and known.

Further, the tarot illustrates Hermetic philosophy, which is holographic. The same process of creation illustrated by the whole tarot deck is illustrated in each card and potentially every symbol. After integrating all the knowledge of this book, you can approach each card as a compression of the whole. Each card becomes an infinite assertion of being.

Now—the big technique: You can take this same technique and apply it to every thought, feeling, emotion, sensation, or experience. Every "thing" that passes into your awareness is an assertion of "I am." When you can translate every possible experience into an assertion of pure being, you are a mystic.

---

127. Plotinus, *Enneads*, trans. Stephen MacKenna (Penguin Books, 1991), 369.

CHAPTER 6
WHAT'S THE POINT?

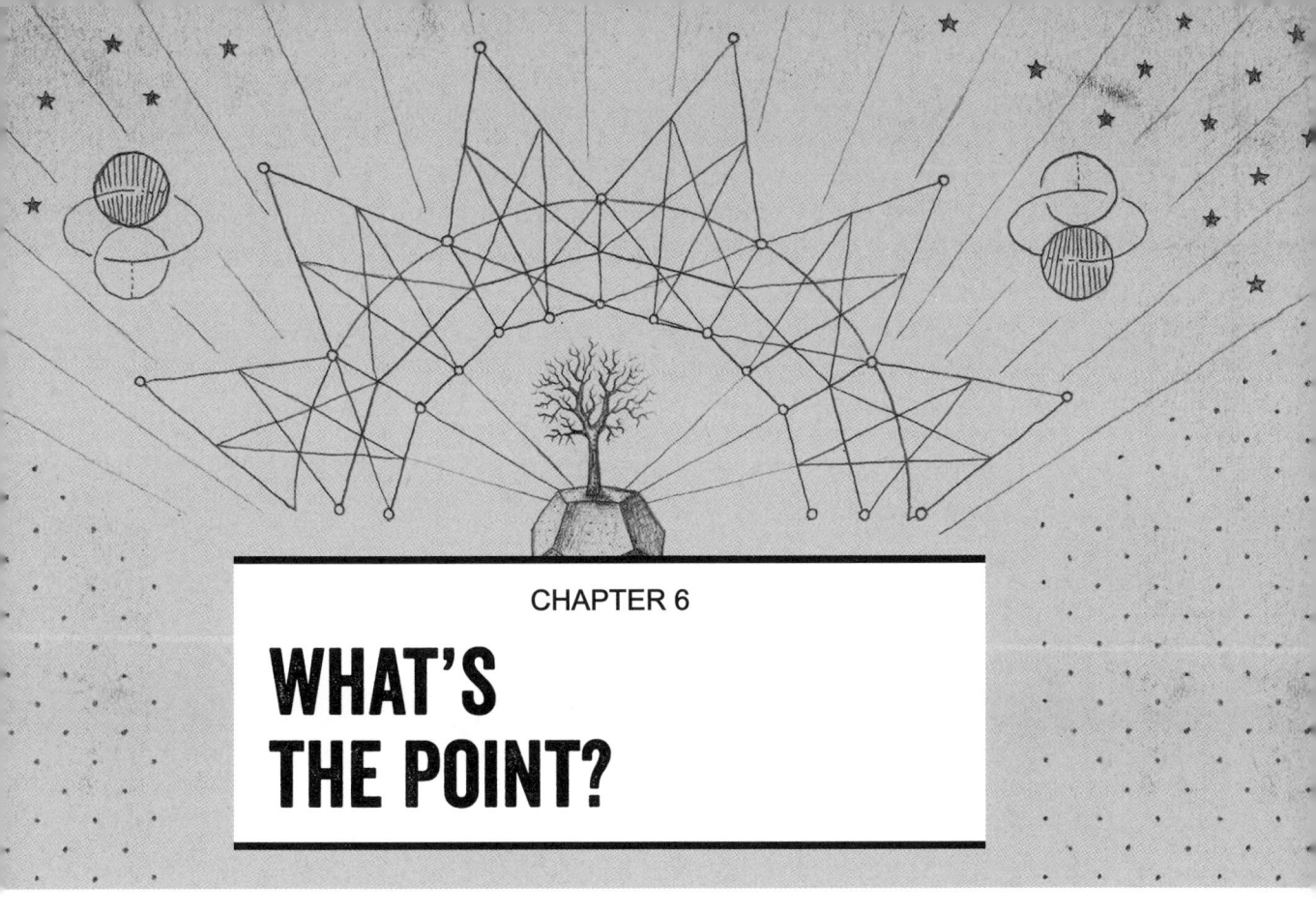

The great work is drawing oneself up to one's ultimate divinity. Whether through mysticism, magick, or any other method, the results are the same. There are glimpses of truth that act as singularities, certain recognitions of one's true nature which stays with the seeker forever. As one advances, teachings become less intellectual and more intuitive. They become less studied and more experienced. They require fewer words and more wisdom. Informational knowledge becomes mystical gnosis. Eventually, at the highest point, the teaching is simply silence. This is because nothing can be said of the ultimate truth. Truth contains and transcends all words and all dualistic language. Furthermore, silence metaphorically *describes* the all-encompassing truth. In the same way as all sounds appear against the backdrop of vast silence, all "things" appear to the vast backdrop of the divine nothing. Though a concession, silence is almost a quality of the simple and powerful recognition of "I am." The result of abiding in that absolute awareness is simply silence. So, what could be said of it? What's the point in all this?

The point is Kether. The monad. Kether is both the literal point and figurative point to this whole work: The singularity from which everything from nothing, from which the Tree of Life springs forth. Colloquially, the point of it all is consciousness. Specifically, that's you. The perennial tradition of truth is a mirror that reflects you, your real nature.

To conclude this treatise on the esoteric tarot, I'd like to refer again to some of the greatest sayings ever written, the radical ontological affirmations and mystical mic-drops introduced in chapter 1.

> Thou art that[128]
>
> I am that I am[129]
>
> It is, and that it is impossible for it not to be[130]
>
> Nothing real can be threatened. Nothing unreal exists.[131]

All these teachings say one thing: There is no part of reality separate from reality. Everything—if it is a thing, if it has existence—has the quality of "is," including you and everything within you. That is, by definition, *being*. This quality of being cannot be lost, and because of that, there is nothing to fear. This is the ultimate truth: Being, and *you* radically b*e*. That quality of being is your true nature, unchanging, infinite, and radically inclusive of all your finite experiences.

Most people walk around pretending that there is a private space in between their ears, behind their eyes. They believe that what goes on in that space is separate from the world. They may judge what goes on there and hate themselves. They may admire what goes on there and love themselves. Either way, they believe on some level that they are cut off from the perfection of reality. They are afraid because they believe the world is happening to them and they are being knocked around without control or connection, without being understood, without relation, like a struck billiard ball. They see the world as a Newtonian nightmare where life knocks into them from all directions. And yet the reality is there is nowhere where their true nature is not. We, as consciousness, are the table on which all billiard balls roll. Your true nature is not knocked around, because all the knocking is contained *within* that true nature which is your pure awareness.

---

128. Radhakrishnan, *Principal Upanishads*, 458.

129. Exod. 3:7–8, 13–14.

130. Poem taken from John Burnet's *Early Greek Philosophy*, 3rd ed. (A & C Black, 1908).

131. Foundation for Inner Peace, *A Course in Miracles*, 1.

What's the Point?

The teachings above point to truth directly. They each point to your consciousness, the very nature to which these words appear, your true self. Notice right now the awareness to which these words are read and known and to which they have their existence. That—*that* awareness right there! It is no different from the one I am writing from. Absolutely, perfectly, wholly the same. Nothing else has ever existed besides this silent awareness, underlying all the noise of all of life's finite experiences.

So what about the tarot? The tarot is the key that unlocks the doors between the silent witness and the noise of experience. It is a map that details the creative process or ontological waypoints between the observer and the observed. The primary map of this process is the Tree of Life. The tarot and the Tree of Life it expresses show the process of creation, becoming, or being, depending on interpretation. In a reading, it shows how the querent creates, becomes, or is their experience. On a macrocosmic scale, it shows how God creates, becomes, or is the world.

Let's start with the microcosmic scale by looking at a tarot reading. Using the knowledge in this book, you can go much deeper with your readings, far beyond divination. I pulled a card at random to use as an example for this conclusion and pulled the Universe card. It is appropriate since we are nearing the end of this book. The Universe card represents completion, synthesis, conclusion. Superficially, it may represent the completion of our journey together. But going further, you will remember that the universe represents the shekinah and the princess returning to their divine origin. It represents the climax of manifestation and the signal to return. It thus represents your integration of this knowledge. It represents not just the literal end of this book, but the very possibility of "endings" that we project onto eternity. It represents the path from Yesod to Malkuth, the astral world pouring itself into the physical. But even more so, it represents the culmination of this entire journey, and every possible journey, where the arrival mirrors the departure. It represents the moment when consciousness realizes itself as nothing but itself through all its experiences. It represents "thou art that." With the path of the Universe ending in Malkuth, it represents Kether, "I am." Ultimately, every card and every symbol represent "I am."

The Tower, for example, may in a reading represent a car accident. But that car accident manifested from subtler destructive energies influencing matter symbolized by Mars. And that archetype itself, the god of war, is really a movement of consciousness from Netzach to Hod. This movement of energy is a reflection of the Lust card and the Empress card, themselves reflecting the higher movement of consciousness from ain soph into Kether,

Chapter 6

which is just another way to express "I am." The accident doesn't become something to stress over; it is another expression of "I am."

In another reading, the Nine of Swords may represent depression, anxiety, and worry. But those experiences are simply the manifestations of Mars in Gemini. It is the ability of consciousness to fracture and war against itself. It is the thrill of consciousness to assume the various roles to create this horrifying but gripping experience we call cruelty. But Gemini is simply an aspect of our minds, and Mars is simply the animalistic urge to survive through hardship, and both exist within the vast peaceful state of the firmament, our real nature. Qabalistically, the Nine of Swords is Yesod, the autonomic nervous system that can turn against us. But even this nervous system is a reflection of Tiphareth above it and Kether above that. The cruelty of the Nine of Swords is another emanation of none other than the immeasurable "I am."

In another reading, the Queen of Swords may represent a widow. But a widow is an emanation of something deeper. The Queen of Swords represents the intuition descending upon and liberating the egoic mind (as she symbolically carries the ego into the sky). The widow, the mourner, is but another manifestation of the ego freeing itself. The ego freeing itself is the relationship between water and air, the heh primal and vav of tetragrammaton. With the loss of her beloved, the widow is faced with the destruction of the ego, another illusion superimposed upon the "I am" of Kether.

All these are real experiences but *not* experiences of the Real. In the context of mysticism, the tarot shows that every experience is an emanation of the Divine. Every experience is a dance of Shakti observed by Shiva. Every experience below can be appreciated from a certain height above. As a tarot reader, you allow yourself to observe; you give permission for presence.

This esoteric understanding does not even need the tarot cards. You can see everything as a divine expression of "I am" without consultation. In this moment, for example, you are reading these words. Your physical eyes and these words are Malkuth. Your subconscious is making sense of all the information and allowing you to read without too much conscious strain. This is Yesod. The thoughts passing your awareness are Hod and your feelings and intent to continue are Netzach. The space between your ears organizing all this experience is Tiphareth. The differences between one line and another line are made possible by Geburah. The space that the words, ideas, and experience take up is Chesed. The pure quality that all of the above shares is the "is"-ness, which is formulated through the supernals, the dance of Chokmah and Binah. Beyond that, nothing can be said, only to abide in the blissful, infinite brilliance of pure being… "I am."

CONCLUSION

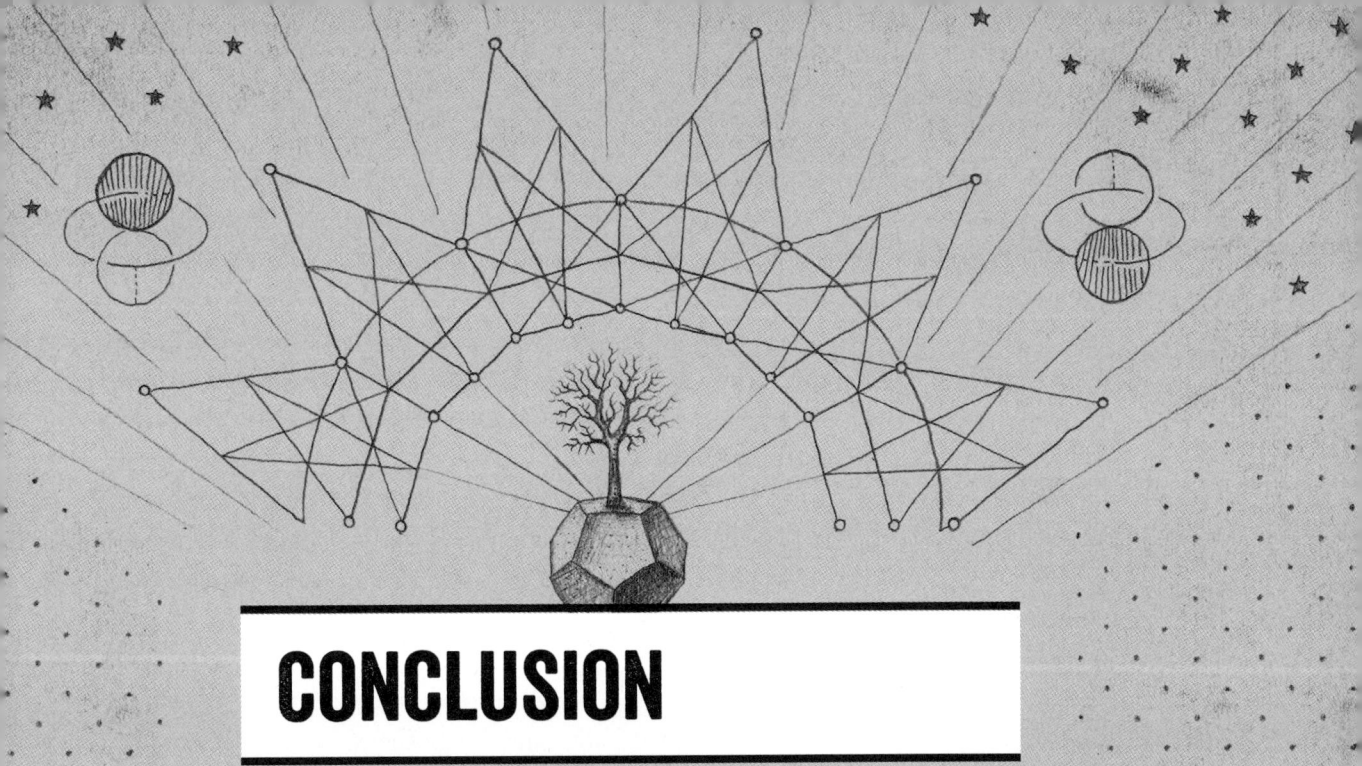

So, what's next? Remember that the end begets the beginning. Malkuth is in Kether. The path begins! It is my greatest hope that the culmination of my research and journey will be the Kether to your own journey.

You now have with you a psycho-spiritual tool to know, express, and revel in your true nature. No spiritual tool has drawn from so many bodies of knowledge to chart such a sophisticated map of our experience. You can now use the tarot for personal, transpersonal, or mystical realization. You can consult this book for deeper insights into your personal tarot readings, or for reading for others. More than that, you can integrate this knowledge as an archetypal and symbolic map of the human experience and its connection to the Divine. For example, sitting on a chair with four legs changes it from a chair into a manifestation of the four kerubic beasts, the Universe card, and the Holy Tetragrammaton. The sun over the water is no longer just a pretty sight to see but the Six of Cups, the middle decan of Scorpio, a symbol of the apex of pleasure. The next time you feel the futility of your efforts or are doubting yourself, remember the Seven of Swords is only one Death card away from the solution in the Six of Swords.

Most of all, tarot can offer a profound reverie for reality. Though it can offer many positive insights and experiences for us on the personal and transpersonal level, its highest use does not concern itself with experiences at all. Rather, it is an expression of radical surrender to that which is having the experience—you!

No matter what is done, made, differentiated, changed, be it here or there, coming or going, in time, space, or any dimension, there will always be you. This realization has helped me and so many of my students start to jailbreak our realities. I hope it will do the same for you.

For more information, visit www.tarotmysticismacademy.com.

RECOMMENDED RESOURCES

TAROT

Rachel Pollack, *Tarot Wisdom: Spiritual Teachings and Deeper Meanings*
   A great introduction to tarot's deeper mysteries for intermediate students.
Robert Michael Place, *The Tarot, Magic, Alchemy, Hermeticism, and Neoplatonism*
   A perfect introduction to tarot's rich history.

QABALAH

Alan Moore, *Promethea* (1999–2005, comic book series)
   The best way to learn Hermetic Qabalah and western esotericism for visual learners. This comic book covers tarot, Qabalah, Hermeticism, aspects of sex magick, and more in total visual splendor.
Paul Foster Case, *The Tarot: A Key to the Wisdom of the Ages*
   This is the best book to learn the Qabalistic attributions of the major arcana. Case's deck is similar enough to the Rider-Waite-Smith tradition to apply most of the knowledge.
Isabel Radow Kliegman, *Tarot and the Tree of Life: Finding Everyday Wisdom in the Minor Arcana*

RECOMMENDED RESOURCES

If you are coming from a tarot background, this is the best introduction to Kabbalah and the Tree of Life. It will organize the tarot for you in a whole new way. This is the best introductory book to learn the Qabalistic attributions of the minor arcana.

Lon Milo DuQuette, *The Chicken Qabalah of Rabbi Lamed Ben Clifford*

A perfect introduction to Hermetic Qabalah: Funny, deep, and easy to understand.

Aleister Crowley, *777 and Other Qabalistic Writings of Aleister Crowley*

A great reference guide for esoteric correspondences with Crowley's interesting commentary.

Aryeh Kaplan, *Sefer Yetzirah: The Book of Creation in Theory and Practice, Revised Edition*

An authoritative translation of the *Sepher Yetzirah*, a prekabbalistic text that greatly influenced western esoteric traditions and tarot.

Israel Regardie, *A Garden of Pomegranates: Skrying on the Tree of Life*

A thorough and technical exploration of the Tree of Life and its correspondences. It offers a lot of detail and important symbols to carry with you into your tarot practice.

Robert Wang, *The Qabalistic Tarot: A Textbook of Mystical Philosophy*

A great run-through of tarot and Qabalah following the three major tarot traditions (Rider-Waite-Smith, Thoth, and Marseilles) and also the Golden Dawn tarot.

ASTROLOGY

Corrine Kenner, *Tarot and Astrology: Enhance Your Readings With the Wisdom of the Zodiac*

This is a great book if you have familiarity with either tarot or astrology and want to learn about the other.

Steven Forrest, *The Inner Sky*

Steven teaches evolutionary astrology. This book offers so much depth and sophistication and freshly steers clear of superstition. I enjoy the more contemporary approach. It's the perfect way to meet the cosmic bodies.

THE THOTH DECK

Aleister Crowley, *The Book of Thoth (Egyptian Tarot)*

The authoritative work on the Thoth deck. This is not an easy read, especially if you are not yet versed in Qabalah, astrology, some mythology, tarot, and some of Crowley's work.

Lon Milo DuQuette, *Understanding Aleister Crowley's Thoth Tarot*

This is the perfect supplement to the Book of Thoth. It teaches the Thoth deck true to the context of Aleister Crowley, Thelema, and the western esoteric tradition.

Michael Osiris Snuffin, *The Thoth Companion: The Key to the True Symbolic Meaning of the Thoth Tarot*

This book will teach you almost every symbol on every card of the Thoth deck.

HERMETICISM

Hermes Trismegistus, *The Divine Pymander*, edited by Paschal Beverly Randolph, translated by John Everard

This is my favorite translation of the *Corpus Hermeticum*. It might not be the most academically rigorous, but that is a good thing. What it lacks in scholarship, it makes up for in mystical insight.

Three Initiates. *The Kybalion: A Study of The Hermetic Philosophy of Ancient Egypt and Greece* (Rough Draft Printing, 2012)

This might not be a historically Hermetic text in the strictest sense, but the ideas do carry Hermetic philosophy and the work has been very influential.

NONDUALITY AND EASTERN MYSTICISM

Swami Ahbayananda, *History of Mysticism: The Unchanging Testament*

One of my favorite books of all time. It will show readers the perennial philosophy underlying all religions, mysticism, and philosophy through the duality of gender.

Swami Gambhirananda, translator, *Eight Upanishads With Commentary of Sankaracarya Volumes One and Two*

Includes eight of the ten major upanishads and includes Shankara's commentary. It's more extensive than other translations.

NEOPLATONISM

Plotinus, *The Enneads*, translated by Stephen MacKenna (New York, NY: Penguin Books, 1991)

Plotinus was the father of Neoplatonism, a mystical adaption of Platonic philosophy. The truth was, he was a mystic. Neoplatonism helped shape the western esoteric tradition and tarot.

BIBLIOGRAPHY

Ahbayananda, Swami. *History of Mysticism: The Unchanging Testament*. Atma Books, 1996.

Bentov, Itzhak. *Stalking The Wild Pendulum: On the Metrics of Consciousness*. Destiny Books, 1988.

Brennan, Barbara Ann. *Hands of Light: A Guide to Healing Through the Human Energy Field*. Bantam Books, 1988.

Burnet, John. *Early Greek Philosophy*. A & C Black, 1908.

Campbell, Joseph. *The Hero with A Thousand Faces*. New World Library, 2008. Originally published 1949 by Pantheon Books.

Case, Paul Foster. *The Tarot: A Key to the Wisdom of the Ages*. Builders of the Adytum, 1990. Originally published 1947 by Macoy Publishing.

Chang, T. Susan. *Tarot Correspondences: Ancient Secrets for Everyday Readers*. Llewellyn Publications, 2018.

Copenhaver, Brian P. *Hermetica: The Greek Corpus Hermeticum and the Latin Asclepius in a New English Translation with Notes and Introduction*. Cambridge University Press, 2000.

Crowley, Aleister. *The Book of Lies*. Samuel Weiser, 1993. Originally published 1913 by Wieland and Co.

Bibliography

Crowley, Aleister. *The Book of Thoth (Egyptian Tarot)*. Samuel Weiser, 1991. Originally published 1944 by Chiswick Press.

———. *Magick Book 4: Liber ABA, Parts I–IV*. Samuel Weiser, 2008. Originally published 1913 by Wieland and Co.

———. *777 and Other Qabalistic Writings of Aleister Crowley*. Weiser, 1993. Originally published 1909 by Walter Scott Publishing.

Crowley, Aleister, and Israel Regardie. *Gems from the Equinox: Instructions by Aleister Crowley for His Own Magical Order*. Red Wheel/Weiser, 2007. Originally published 1974 by Llewellyn Publications.

Decker, Ronald. *The Esoteric Tarot: Ancient Sources Rediscovered in Hermeticism and Cabala*. Quest Books, 2013.

Douglas, Gary, and Dain Heer. *The Ten Keys to Total Freedom*. Access Consciousness Publishing, 2012.

DuQuette, Lon Milo. *The Chicken Qabalah of Rabbi Lamed Ben Clifford*. Weiser Books, 2001.

———. *Understanding Aleister Crowley's Thoth Tarot*. Red Wheel/Weiser, 2003.

Easwaran, Eknath, translator. *The Upanishads*. Blue Mountain Center of Meditation/Nilgiri Press, 2007.

Forrest, Steven. *The Inner Sky*. Seven Paws Press, 2012.

Foundation for Inner Peace. *A Course in Miracles*. Foundation for Inner Peace, 1992.

Gambhirananda, Swami, translator. *Eight Upanishads with Commentary of Sankaracarya Volume One*. Advaita Ashrama, 2020.

———. *Eight Upanishads with Commentary of Sankaracarya Volume Two*. Advaita Ashrama, 2019.

Hadot, Pierre. *Plotinus or the Simplicity of Vision*. Translated by Michael Chase. University of Chicago Press, 1993.

Halevi, Z'ev ben Shimon. *Adam and the Kabbalistic Tree*. Samuel Weiser, 1990.

———. *The Work of the Kabbalist*. Samuel Weiser, 1993.

Hall, Manly P. *The Secret Teachings of All Ages*. Jeremy P. Tarcher/Penguin, 2003. Originally published 1928 by H. S. Crocker.

Hawkins, David. *Letting Go: The Pathway of Surrender*. Hay House, 2012.

———. *Power vs. Force: The Hidden Determinants of Human Behavior Author's Official Authoritative Edition*. Hay House, 2012.

Hermes Trismegistus. *The Divine Pymander*. Edited by Paschal Beverly Randolph, translated by John Everard. Yogi Publication Society, 1972.

Bibliography

Hermes Trismegistus. *The Emerald Tablet of Hermes*. Merchant Books, 2013.

The Holy Bible, New International Version. Zondervan, 2011.

Huxley, Aldous. *The Perennial Philosophy*. Harper Perennial Modern Classics, 2009. Originally published 1945 by Harper & Row.

James, William. "Rationality, Activity and Faith." *The Princeton Review* vol. 2. Princeton, NJ: 1882. Accessed online: https://quod.lib.umich.edu/m/moajrnl/acf4325.3-01.010/86:6?page=root;size=100;view=image.

Kaplan, Aryeh. *Sefer Yetzirah The Book of Creation in Theory and Practice, Revised Edition*. Red Wheel/Weiser, 1997.

Kelley, Daniel. *Predicting the Present: Twenty-Two Fingers Point at the Moon*. Self-published, 2018.

Kenner, Corrine. *Tarot and Astrology: Enhance Your Readings with the Wisdom of the Zodiac*. Llewellyn Publications, 2011.

Kliegman, Isabel Radow. *Tarot and the Tree of Life: Finding Everyday Wisdom in the Minor Arcana*. Quest Books, 1997.

Knight, Mark Dean. *Trinity of Wisdom: Truth, Philosophy, & Hermetic Alchemical Qabbalah*. Cacti-Knights Publishing, 2010.

Kurtz, Ron. *Body-Centered Psychotherapy: The Hakomi Method, Updated Edition*. LifeRhythm, 2015.

Litwa, M. David. *Hermetica II: The Excerpts of Stobaeus, Papyrus Fragments, and Ancient Testimonies in an English Translation with Notes and Introductions*. Cambridge University Press, 2022.

Louis, Anthony. *Tarot Beyond the Basics: Gain a Deeper Understanding of the Meanings Behind the Cards*. Llewellyn Publications, 2014.

MacGregor Mathers, Samuel Liddell. *The Kabbalah Unveiled Volume One: The Book of Concealed Mystery*. Pacific Publishing Studio, 2011. Originally published 1912 by Theosophical Society.

Meleen, M. M. *Book M: Liber Mundi*. Atu House, 2015.

Meleen, Mel, and T. Susan Chang. *Tarot Deciphered: Decoding Esoteric Symbolism*. Llewellyn Publications, 2021.

Meyer, Marvin, editor. *The Nag Hammadi Scriptures: The Revised and Updated Translation of Sacred Gnostic Texts*. HarperOne, 2008.

Moore, Alan. *Promethea* (1999–2005). Comic book series. America's Best Comics.

Bibliography

Nagarjuna. *The Fundamental Wisdom of the Middle Way: Nagarjuna's Mulamadhyamakakarika*. Translated by Jay L. Garfield. Wisdom Publications, 1995.

Nikhilananda, Swami, translator. *The Gospel of Sri Ramakrishna: Abridged Edition*. Ramakrishna-Vivekananda Center, 2015.

Noa, Anthony. *The Book of Yirah: Ascension: Sepher Yirah (5)*. Self-published, 2022.

Ozaniec, Naomi. *The Watkins Tarot Handbook: The Practical System of Self-Discovery*. Watkins Publishing, 2005.

Place, Robert Michael. *The Tarot: History, Symbolism, and Divination*. Jeremy P. Tarcher/Penguin, 2005.

———. *The Tarot, Magic, Alchemy, Hermeticism, and Neoplatonism*. Hermes Publications, 2017.

Plotinus. *The Enneads*. Translated by Stephen MacKenna. Penguin Books, 1991.

Pollack, Rachel. *Tarot Wisdom: Spiritual Teachings and Deeper Meanings*. Llewellyn Publications, 2009.

Prabhupada A. C. Bhaktivedanta. *Bhagavad-Gita As It Is*. Macmillan, 1972.

Radhakrishnan, translator. *The Principal Upanishads*. HarperCollins Publishers, 1953.

Regardie, Israel. *A Garden of Pomegranates: Skrying on the Tree of Life*. Llewellyn Publications, 2015. Originally published 1932 by Rider & Co.

———. *The Golden Dawn, Sixth Edition*. Llewellyn Publications, 2006. Originally published 1937 by Aries Press.

Rinpoche, Khenpo Tsultrim Gyamtso. *Progressive Stages of Meditation on Emptiness*. Translated and arranged by Lama Shenpen Hookham. Shrimala Trust, 2016.

Satchidananda. *The Yoga Sutras of Patanjali*. Integral Yoga Publications, 2012.

Snuffin, Michael Osiris. *The Thoth Companion: The Key to the True Symbolic Meaning of the Thoth Tarot*. Llewellyn Publications, 2015.

Three Initiates. *The Kybalion: A Study of The Hermetic Philosophy of Ancient Egypt and Greece*. Rough Draft Printing, 2012. Originally published 1912 by the Yogi Publication Society Masonic Temple.

Tolle, Eckhart. *The Power of Now: A Guide to Spiritual Enlightenment*. New World Library, 1999.

Tzu, Lao. *Tao Te Ching*, translated by Charles Muller. Barnes and Noble Books, 2005.

Vedanta Society of New York. "Introduction to Vedanta." YouTube. January 19, 2017, https://www.youtube.com/watch?v=8mCkWGlO2x8&list=PL2imXor63HtRJbtP4mMt-Q2ke8XOkL7pX.

Vivekananda, Swami. *Raja Yoga*. Publication House of Ramakrishna Math, 2020.

Waite, Arthur Edward. *The Pictorial Key to the Tarot*. U. S. Games Systems, 1971. Originally published 1911 by William Rider.

Wang, Robert. *The Qabalistic Tarot: A Textbook of Mystical Philosophy*. U. S. Games Systems, 2016.

Watts, Alan. *The Way of Zen*. Vintage Books/Random House, Inc., 1989. Originally published 1959 by Vintage Books.

Wilson, Robert Anton. *Quantum Psychology*. Hilaritas Press, 2016.

INDEX

Adjustment, 14, 33, 70, 76, 107–110, 129, 133, 147, 171, 187, 188, 211, 214, 221, 222, 227, 292, 294

Æon, 14, 93, 95, 127, 144, 156–159, 172, 192, 272

Ain (*Also* ain soph, ain soph aur), 20, 27, 33, 56–58, 69–70, 82, 86, 109, 117, 147, 148, 158, 159, 168, 171, 192, 193, 200, 246, 255–256, 265, 309, 331, 333, 343

Air, 9, 14, 37, 48, 55, 63, 76, 77, 83, 90, 100, 107, 109, 116, 117, 123–125, 143, 146, 163, 179, 181, 191, 198, 200, 209–211, 215, 217, 218, 220, 223–226, 235, 243, 287, 290–293, 300, 303, 307, 317, 319, 338, 344

Aleister Crowley, 6, 12–16, 29, 32, 33, 36, 37, 64, 68, 69, 72, 74, 76–79, 82, 85, 86, 88–94, 96–100, 106, 107, 113, 117, 119–121, 125–127, 129–132, 135, 138, 139, 144, 145, 147–149, 152, 155–157, 159, 161–163, 170–175, 180, 192, 194, 206, 209, 222, 224–226, 249, 252, 254, 255, 262, 264, 284, 290, 292, 297, 298, 300, 302, 307, 309–311, 313, 315, 317, 319, 324, 327, 348

Aleph, 76–79, 109, 117, 142, 161, 162, 175, 224, 292

Alchemy, 19, 44, 87, 136, 142, 147, 214, 226, 241, 347

Anandamaya Kosha, 10, 46

Aquarius, 23, 146, 147, 149, 190, 191, 206, 225, 226, 228, 229, 297–300, 302

Index

Archangels, 135

Archetypes, 8, 54, 64, 81, 104, 183, 304, 335, 343

Aries, 93, 94, 96, 143, 155, 158, 186, 196, 197, 238, 241, 256, 257, 259

Assiah, 7, 168, 170, 180, 184, 222, 223, 229, 230, 235, 240, 246, 249, 308–312, 314–317, 319–323, 325, 327

Astrology, 6, 20, 26, 37, 39, 44, 47, 48, 51, 104, 146, 150, 182, 183, 185, 186, 198, 218, 252, 256, 275, 279, 298, 348

Atman, 20, 27, 30

Atziluth, 57, 168, 170, 176, 192, 193, 200, 202–204, 215, 229, 246, 249, 253, 255, 257, 259, 260, 262, 264, 265, 267, 268, 272, 278, 308

Aura, 105

Ayin, 77, 136–140

Azoth, 70

Bet, 81–84, 89, 133

Bhagavad Gita, The, 77, 116, 143, 158, 182

Binah, 37, 56, 58, 60–66, 70–72, 74, 81, 83, 87, 89, 90, 99, 105, 106, 116, 119, 122, 124, 138, 139, 147, 162, 164, 173, 174, 177, 180, 196, 198, 203, 206, 208, 211, 221, 222, 234, 237, 246, 249, 250, 257, 259, 261, 262, 272, 274, 282, 290, 292, 294, 314, 315, 344

Book of the Law (*Liber AL vel Legis*), 14, 15, 74, 91, 97, 100, 113, 119–121, 138, 142, 147–149, 155, 159

Brahman, 20, 32, 35, 57, 58, 61, 67, 72, 138, 161, 163, 171, 175, 202, 248, 328, 331

Briah, 61, 168, 170, 177, 202–206, 208–212, 214, 215, 223, 246, 249, 269, 270, 272–274, 276–282, 284, 286, 301, 306

Cancer, 103–105, 107, 116, 126, 133, 186, 187, 199, 202, 208, 209, 272, 275, 276

Capricorn, 139, 140, 143, 189, 190, 225, 226, 228, 229, 234, 313, 315, 317

Ceremonial magic, 4, 25, 51, 106, 161

Chakras, 70, 135, 138, 147, 153

Chariot, The, 44, 50, 94, 102–107, 116, 125, 126, 132, 133, 136, 152, 186, 187, 199, 202, 204, 208, 272

Chesed, 56, 61–64, 66, 67, 69, 71, 89, 96, 97, 109, 116, 117, 120, 138, 139, 144, 246, 249, 251, 259, 261, 262, 276, 278, 284, 294, 295, 300, 316, 317, 320, 344

Chet, 105–106, 107

Chiah, 10, 177, 181, 193, 197, 203, 217, 246, 253

Chokmah, 37, 55–62, 64, 66, 70–72, 74, 78, 87, 90, 94, 96, 97, 106, 112, 119, 124, 129, 139, 162, 163, 173–176, 180, 194, 195, 198, 205, 246, 249, 250, 255–257, 261, 262, 265, 272, 273, 290, 292, 300, 310–312, 329, 344

Clairvoyance, 181

Collective unconscious, 10, 86, 151, 152, 283

Consciousness, 4–7, 9–11, 16–18, 20, 21, 23–28, 30, 32, 34–44, 46–48, 50, 54–67, 69, 71–73, 76, 77, 79, 81–83, 86, 87, 89, 92–96, 99, 102, 104, 105, 107–112, 115, 119, 122, 125–127, 129, 131–134, 136, 137, 139, 142, 143, 145, 146, 148–155, 158, 161, 162, 164, 176, 178–181, 183, 185, 190, 192, 194, 198, 199, 201, 206–209, 211, 212, 214, 216–219, 221, 223, 237, 240, 243, 245–249, 255–259, 262, 264–268, 271, 272, 274, 275, 281, 282, 284, 285, 287, 288, 290–294, 307–309, 311–313, 319, 321, 323, 325, 326, 328, 329, 332–334, 336, 340, 342–344

Court cards, 13, 44, 45, 51, 57, 78, 99, 162, 165, 167, 168, 170, 171, 173–177, 179–186, 191, 192, 194, 200, 202, 212, 214, 216, 238, 240, 242, 243, 245, 246, 248, 249, 252, 253, 340

Cups, 12, 34, 135, 148, 177–179, 181, 186–191, 193, 195, 197, 199, 202–215, 219, 242–244, 246, 248, 269–272, 274–288, 292, 301, 332, 335, 337, 346

Da'at, 58, 62, 70, 221, 308

Dalet, 89, 125, 130

Death, 19, 40, 48, 71, 83, 84, 89, 92, 106, 107, 111, 117, 119, 120, 123, 126, 128–132, 134–136, 142–146, 150, 158, 161, 164, 186–195, 198, 211, 213, 214, 220–222, 230, 235, 278, 279, 288, 290, 293, 294, 306, 309, 313, 332, 335, 346

Decans, 48, 49, 143, 164, 182–184, 186, 194–197, 199, 205, 206, 208, 211, 218, 221, 222, 225, 226, 230–232, 234, 235, 237, 238, 252, 253, 256, 259, 261–263, 265, 268, 269, 272, 275, 276, 278, 282, 283, 287, 291–295, 297, 299, 302, 303, 305, 307, 313, 315, 317–319, 322–324, 326, 329, 346

Devil, The, 77, 129, 135, 136, 139, 140, 142, 145, 189, 190, 225, 229, 234, 313, 315, 317

Disks, 14, 34, 177–179, 181, 186–191, 193, 212, 218, 222, 226, 229–232, 234–244, 246, 248, 306, 308–323, 325–327, 329, 338

Divination, 2, 4, 5, 7, 9, 13, 14, 16, 84, 87, 90, 94, 97, 101, 107, 110, 113, 117, 122, 131, 136, 149, 153, 156, 159, 165, 175, 192, 332, 334, 335, 339, 343

Earth, 7, 14, 48, 55, 81, 83, 86, 89, 90, 92, 96, 107, 112, 113, 119, 121–124, 127, 133, 134, 136, 138–140, 147, 155, 162, 163, 172, 179–181, 190, 191, 200–202, 212, 217, 226, 229–232, 235, 238, 239, 243, 248, 258, 275, 290, 309, 311, 313–317, 319, 321, 323, 324, 327, 329, 338

INDEX

Elementals, 180

Elements, 28, 37, 39, 44, 45, 48, 55, 76, 90, 106, 116, 123–125, 155–157, 161, 163, 180–183, 215, 221, 236, 246, 250–252, 292, 308, 313, 317, 336

Emerald Tablet, The, 43, 54, 249, 336

Emperor, The, 14, 81, 88, 90, 92–94, 102, 116, 125, 147, 158, 186, 196, 197, 241, 253, 257, 259

Empress, The, 81, 87–90, 93, 96, 117, 122, 125, 129–131, 142, 164, 195, 232, 241, 259, 273, 306, 326, 343

Enochian magic, 51

Esoteric, 3, 4, 6, 12, 13, 15–21, 28, 50–52, 68, 69, 77, 93, 100, 102, 105, 106, 116, 117, 119, 120, 126–128, 139, 143, 154, 162, 175, 182, 183, 246, 249, 257, 342, 344, 348, 349

Fire, 10, 37, 48, 51, 55, 63, 77, 83, 90, 93, 107, 116, 121, 123–125, 127, 134, 141–143, 157–159, 163, 177, 179, 181, 191–193, 195, 196, 198–203, 205, 215, 217, 223–226, 230, 243, 253, 254, 257–260, 262, 265, 268, 269, 276, 278, 280, 287, 290, 292, 319, 337

Firmament, 122, 144, 148, 257, 344

Fool, The, 11, 17, 19, 32, 34, 57, 75–79, 87, 90, 93, 94, 107, 108, 110, 111, 129, 151, 152, 161, 162, 164, 171, 173–176, 192, 193, 195, 211, 214, 224, 240, 243, 244, 253, 300, 334, 340

Fortune, 26, 83, 93, 113–117, 131, 134, 142, 143, 150, 153, 158, 182, 234, 263, 284, 313

Four, 6, 13, 28, 34, 39, 44, 45, 47, 48, 51, 55, 57, 63, 72, 76, 78, 117, 124, 125, 148, 161, 164, 167, 169, 170, 176, 180–182, 184, 191, 192, 199, 201, 211, 226, 232, 238, 242, 243, 245–253, 259, 261, 270, 276, 277, 279, 281, 287, 288, 294–296, 299, 308, 309, 311, 313, 316, 317, 319, 322, 325, 336–338, 345

Gaudapada, 35, 36, 59, 60, 175, 176, 254, 328

Geburah, 57, 63–66, 71, 105, 106, 109, 120, 126, 127, 130, 249, 251, 260, 262, 264, 277, 278, 296, 297, 317, 320, 344

Gimel, 9, 86, 135

Golden Dawn, 13, 43, 51, 123, 126, 145, 155, 180, 181, 238, 262, 290, 311, 314, 316, 317, 321, 348

Hanged Man, The, 43, 123, 125–127, 131, 150, 152, 158, 164

Harris, Lady Frieda, 12, 159

Index

Heh, 60, 64, 66, 68, 71, 91, 93, 94, 99, 147–149, 162, 167, 168, 170, 173, 177, 179, 181, 195, 198, 200, 202, 206, 208, 209, 212, 217, 220, 226, 229, 230, 232, 235, 238, 243, 310, 337, 338, 344

Hermes Trismegistus, 6, 50, 51, 54, 59, 82, 124, 336, 349

Hermetic principles, 33, 83

Hermeticism, 6, 16, 33, 50, 51, 229, 247, 347, 349

Hierophant, The, 94–97, 99, 102, 105, 186, 218, 237, 242, 318, 320

High Priestess, The, 69, 84, 90, 151

Hod, 57, 64–66, 72, 126, 127, 139, 142–144, 153, 157–159, 249, 252, 265, 282–284, 302, 323, 329, 343, 344

Initiation, 4, 86, 123, 126, 310, 320,

Jupiter, 48, 63, 104, 116, 117, 134, 150, 199, 205, 211, 218, 234, 253, 263, 284, 295, 303, 313

Justice, 14, 90, 91, 108, 110, 221, 294

Kabbalah, 6, 7, 33, 36, 37, 50, 51, 54, 67, 68, 154, 164, 168, 348

Kether, 9, 37, 54–57, 59–62, 64–66, 69–72, 74, 75, 78, 81, 85–87, 124, 129, 154–156, 159, 160, 163, 171, 174, 175, 181, 194, 239, 241, 243, 246, 249–251, 256, 262, 265, 268, 271, 300, 328, 333, 334, 342–345

Kybalion, The, 20, 33, 82, 83, 86, 349

Kundalini, 36, 97, 107, 117–119, 138, 147, 155, 156, 158

Lamed, 76, 108, 109, 348

Leo, 91, 121, 122, 155, 158, 187, 188, 199, 202, 232, 261–263, 265

Lovers, The, 28, 93, 97, 99–102, 105, 109, 119, 121, 124, 132, 134–136, 186, 187, 208, 218, 229, 241, 303, 307

Magician, The, 18, 28, 32, 54, 81, 83, 85, 106, 340

Major arcana, 18, 51, 67, 73, 74, 77, 90, 91, 121, 135, 142, 149, 155, 162, 163, 165, 168, 170, 183–185, 192, 214, 232, 253, 263, 270, 319, 347

Malkuth, 54–57, 63, 66, 67, 71, 72, 147, 151, 157, 158, 160–162, 173, 174, 179, 181, 202, 222, 234, 241, 246, 249, 268–270, 306, 308, 310, 325, 327, 328, 333, 343–345

Manifestation, 19, 33, 37, 38, 62, 76, 78, 80, 83, 84, 89, 90, 97, 100, 102, 108, 109, 111, 114, 116, 119, 120, 125, 135, 136, 139, 144, 145, 147, 161, 163, 170, 171, 173–176, 178, 202,

INDEX

228, 230, 237, 241, 246, 256, 258, 262, 268, 276, 290–292, 294, 296, 304, 306, 309, 313, 314, 317, 319, 323, 325, 327, 328, 336, 343–345

Manomaya kosha, 9

Mars, 11, 48, 63, 93, 94, 130, 139, 140, 143, 144, 197, 199, 211, 218, 232, 234, 253, 255, 256, 265, 278, 279, 282, 287, 305, 306, 315, 343, 344

Mechanical plane, 7, 74, 104, 334, 335

Mem, 123, 124, 126, 127

Mercury, 37, 48, 65, 81, 84, 88, 93, 100, 112, 113, 117, 121, 136, 139, 142, 182, 194, 208, 222, 225, 237, 252, 253, 265, 266, 273, 275, 283, 299, 313, 315, 318, 329

Meta, 16, 79, 168, 180, 225

Minor arcana, 125, 184, 185, 245, 249, 253, 279, 326, 347, 348

Moon, The, 9, 36, 48, 58, 66, 85–87, 90, 93, 95, 96, 104–106, 122, 126, 135, 136, 146, 149–153, 186, 190, 191, 194, 196, 199, 206, 209, 222, 228, 234, 237, 253, 268, 270, 271, 273, 276, 283, 284, 292, 302, 311, 319, 320

Mystical plane, 11, 74, 104

Mysticism, 4, 6, 7, 9–12, 15–22, 25, 29, 31, 33, 34, 36, 45, 47, 50, 51, 56, 62, 77, 102, 112, 114, 115, 117, 119, 120, 127, 133, 136, 143, 147, 155, 160, 161, 164, 167, 168, 171, 173–175, 177, 194, 225, 238, 332–334, 339–341, 344, 349

Neoplatonism, 6, 7, 16, 33, 229, 347, 349

Nephesh, 7, 180, 181, 212, 227, 229, 236, 246, 308

Neshamah, 10, 178, 181, 197, 203, 206–209, 221, 233, 246, 270

Netzach, 57, 64–67, 72, 93, 116, 117, 129, 130, 139, 142–144, 146, 151, 249, 251, 264, 265, 280–282, 300, 321, 322, 332, 343, 344

Nonduality, 10, 16, 22, 27, 35, 50, 57, 58, 59, 69, 72, 74, 171, 175, 176, 198, 239, 254, 328–329, 333, 349

Nun, 92, 128–131, 133, 145, 146

Numerology, 31, 153

Parmenides, 21, 76, 182

Pentacles, 14, 309

Peh, 140–142, 158

Pisces, 116, 126, 129, 146, 150, 151, 186, 191, 196, 197, 205, 228, 234, 283, 284, 287

Plato, 47, 51, 104, 194

Plotinus, 6, 7, 9, 10, 15, 27, 34–36, 44, 51, 55, 57, 58, 62, 70, 176, 177, 179, 180, 205, 247, 248, 288, 331, 333, 340, 349

Pranamaya kosha, 9

Presence, 4, 5, 22, 23, 30, 279, 294, 327, 333, 336, 344

Qabalah, 7, 9, 13, 16, 17, 19, 20, 32, 33, 37, 39, 40, 50–53, 117, 143, 171, 173, 185, 191, 229, 347, 348

Qoph, 134, 149, 151–153, 228

Querent, 94, 223, 289, 304, 335, 336, 343

Ramakrishna, 15, 172, 173

Resh, 149, 153–155

Rider-Waite-Smith (RWS), 12–15, 43, 69, 71, 83, 104, 122, 135, 138, 151, 275, 309, 314, 340

Ruach, 9, 76, 85, 100, 144, 157, 179, 181, 199, 215, 217, 221, 227, 236, 246, 287, 290, 302

Sagittarius, 116, 134, 135, 158, 189, 190, 194, 195, 214, 235, 265, 268, 269

Samsara, 22, 25–27, 42, 43, 115, 119, 158, 171, 237

Saturn, 40, 48, 60, 109, 110, 139, 140, 146, 147, 162, 163, 165, 177, 205, 218, 222, 235, 253, 261, 262, 269, 283, 284, 293, 294, 313, 322, 323

Scorpio, 126, 130, 131, 143, 188, 189, 194, 195, 210, 211, 213, 214, 278, 279, 282, 346

Sephirah, 40, 42, 44, 55–58, 60–67, 70, 71, 74, 78, 81, 84, 93, 109, 122, 126, 130, 133, 141, 142, 144, 151, 152, 174, 176, 194, 222, 237, 250–252, 260, 262, 264, 265, 269, 272, 276, 292, 294, 300, 308, 309, 320, 325, 327, 328, 340

Sephiroth, 27, 35, 37, 38, 51, 54–57, 60–63, 66, 67, 70, 72–74, 89, 95, 116, 120, 246, 249, 250, 253, 267, 272, 276, 288, 290, 292, 304, 309

Seven, 38, 39, 44, 48, 61, 107, 116, 121, 125, 136, 147, 155, 163, 195, 206, 218, 248, 251–253, 264, 265, 270, 280–283, 287, 288, 300–302, 309, 310, 321–323, 346

Shin, 134, 157–159

Six, 43, 106, 125, 170, 199, 200, 225, 237, 249, 251, 253, 259, 262, 263, 268, 270, 279, 281, 282, 284, 288, 298, 299, 302, 304, 309, 311, 317, 319, 320, 323, 326, 327, 332, 346

Smith, Pamela Colman, 12, 91

Solar system, 64, 83, 123, 146, 154, 155, 183, 231, 325

Star, The, 22, 91, 107, 144–147, 149, 159, 190, 225

Strength, 14, 63, 90, 91, 96, 97, 105, 117, 120, 127, 187, 195, 238, 253, 265, 267, 268, 294, 295, 298, 324

INDEX

Subtle body, 39, 200, 228, 272

Subtle/Causal plane, 8–12, 34, 39, 40, 45, 66, 74, 94, 104, 112, 130, 183, 192, 194, 195, 200, 203, 207, 209, 211, 212, 215, 222, 223, 228, 237, 242, 251, 262, 268, 272, 275, 294, 332, 334, 335, 337–340

Sun, 36, 39, 48, 64, 86, 93, 112, 113, 116, 121–124, 136, 152–156, 159, 163, 172, 178, 197, 208, 211, 226, 228, 230, 231, 253–255, 258, 259, 270, 271, 273, 279, 280, 290, 302, 307, 309, 311, 317, 320, 323–327, 345

Sunyata, 20, 331

Symbolism, 9–11, 14, 18, 20–22, 27, 46, 78, 83, 86, 93, 97, 106, 112, 117, 120, 122, 133, 158, 163, 165, 182, 183, 232, 308, 309, 331

Synchronicity, 133

Tantra, 6, 20, 51, 175, 261, 329

Tarot reading, 2, 7, 10, 11, 21, 79, 332–334, 336, 339, 343, 345, 348

Tattvas, 319

Taurus, 95–97, 186, 218, 237, 241, 318–320, 322, 323

Temperance, 134

Tetragrammaton, 38, 45, 55, 60, 61, 64, 66, 70, 71, 78, 99, 112, 147, 161, 162, 164, 167, 169, 170, 173, 175, 176, 178, 179, 181, 191, 192, 198, 202, 206, 214, 215, 217, 229, 230, 245, 246, 249, 254, 290, 292, 309, 323, 337, 338, 340, 344, 345

Thoth deck, 4, 9, 12–16, 53, 54, 71, 78, 93, 95, 100, 104, 106, 107, 110, 111, 115–118, 127, 131, 135, 142, 143, 147, 149, 152, 155, 159, 162, 171, 172, 174, 175, 181, 192, 200, 208, 212, 222, 230, 232, 234, 237, 249, 254, 259, 262, 265, 268, 270, 271, 273, 275, 277, 279, 282, 284, 287, 288, 290, 292, 295, 300, 304, 306, 309, 311, 315, 317, 319, 320, 322, 323, 326, 329, 348, 349

Three, 5, 7, 26, 32, 34–41, 43–45, 48, 51, 55–57, 61–63, 66, 69–71, 74, 75, 81–83, 86, 88, 93, 95, 101, 104, 113, 116, 117, 123, 125, 126, 129, 130, 133, 134, 142, 144, 159, 163, 164, 170–172, 175, 179, 182–185, 197, 203, 208, 216, 218, 222, 229, 232, 234, 240, 246, 249–253, 257–259, 270, 272, 274, 279, 287, 288, 290, 292–294, 296, 300, 309, 311, 314–317, 326, 329, 339, 340, 348, 349

Tiphareth, 9, 40, 57, 63, 64, 69, 85–87, 94, 99, 109, 120, 122, 129, 130, 133, 135, 139, 142–144, 146, 156, 159, 162, 173, 174, 178, 180, 198, 211, 225, 237, 249, 251, 262, 268, 279, 280, 282, 290, 298, 300, 319–321, 332, 334, 344

Tower, The, 11, 120, 122, 130, 138–145, 157, 158, 232, 234, 253, 256, 265, 278, 287, 306, 315, 317, 343

Tree of Life, 9, 35, 37, 38, 42, 44, 50, 52–57, 63, 64, 67–74, 77, 78, 81, 82, 89, 96, 97, 101, 105, 109, 117–120, 122–125, 130, 133, 136, 138, 140, 141, 144, 149, 152, 156, 157, 161–163, 168, 169, 171, 173–181, 192–194, 196, 202, 203, 205, 211, 221, 232, 234, 237, 240, 241, 244, 245, 249–251, 253, 255, 257, 262, 267, 270, 272, 282, 284, 287, 300, 309, 310, 315, 318, 321, 327–329, 332, 333, 342, 343, 347, 348

Tzaddi, 91–93, 145, 146

Two, 5–7, 10, 13, 22, 28, 31, 32, 34–39, 43, 46, 48, 51, 52, 55, 57–64, 67, 70, 78, 79, 83–85, 88, 90, 92, 99, 104, 109, 114, 116, 119, 120, 125–127, 133, 135, 136, 141, 142, 148, 153, 155, 162–164, 170, 171, 173, 179, 183, 184, 194, 196, 197, 199, 205, 208, 214, 215, 217–219, 221, 222, 225, 228, 230, 232, 234, 235, 237, 240, 242–244, 250–253, 255–259, 270, 272, 273, 276–279, 281, 282, 288, 290–292, 295, 296, 298, 301, 304, 307–314, 316, 317, 325, 327, 332, 334, 336–338, 349

Upanishads, 2, 6, 7, 9, 10, 17, 21, 24, 32–33, 34, 35, 36, 58, 59, 61, 67, 72, 115, 149, 173, 175, 349

Universe, The, 159–162, 164, 343

Vav, 64, 95, 96, 99, 162, 167, 168, 173, 178, 179, 181, 198, 209, 215, 217, 220, 223, 225, 226, 235, 243, 290, 338, 344

Vijnanamaya kosha, 10

Virgo, 112, 113, 184, 187, 188, 202, 221, 222, 230–232, 323, 324, 326, 327, 329

Void, 20, 33, 58, 74, 102, 168, 192, 194, 200

Waite, Arthur Edward, 12, 15, 89

Wands, 34, 177–179, 181, 186–205, 211, 216, 217, 234, 235, 238, 240, 242–244, 246, 248, 253–262, 264, 265, 267–272, 276, 285, 288–290, 313

Water, 9, 22, 26, 37, 42, 48, 55, 62, 83, 87, 90, 105–107, 116, 123–128, 134, 135, 142, 143, 146, 148, 149, 163, 178, 181, 191, 195, 202–206, 209–212, 217, 218, 220, 224, 225, 232, 243, 270–272, 276–280, 282–287, 290, 292, 300, 319, 337, 344, 346

World, The, 4, 5, 7–9, 12, 14, 17, 21, 23, 26–29, 31, 35–39, 41, 43–45, 47, 48, 50, 57, 59, 61–64, 66–68, 71, 79–81, 84, 87, 89, 100, 101, 107, 109, 110, 114, 115, 121, 125, 129, 134–140, 146, 148, 151, 153, 155, 161, 163, 168, 170, 175–177, 179, 180, 182, 184, 189, 190, 192, 193, 195, 198–200, 202–204, 206, 210–226, 228–235, 237, 240, 246, 247, 251, 253, 255–257, 259, 260, 262, 264, 265, 267–270, 272, 274, 276, 277, 279–282, 284–287,

INDEX

289, 290, 292–294, 296, 298, 300, 302–306, 308–317, 319–321, 323, 325, 327–329, 332, 334, 335, 337, 338, 340, 342, 343

Yechidah, 10, 85, 217, 246

Yesod, 57, 63, 64, 66, 72, 93, 122, 133, 135, 143, 144, 146, 153, 161, 246, 249, 252, 267, 268, 284, 304, 325, 343, 344

Yetzirah, 9, 51, 54, 57, 61–67, 77, 81, 83, 108, 123, 129, 135, 140, 143, 145, 149, 163, 168, 170, 179, 184, 215, 219, 222, 246, 249, 257, 287, 289, 292, 294, 296–298, 300, 302, 304–306, 309, 311, 348

YHVH, 32, 38, 105, 162, 167, 168, 170, 176, 181, 188, 206, 208, 242–244, 246, 292, 294, 309, 328, 331, 336, 338

Yod, 60, 64, 71, 78, 105, 112, 114, 162, 163, 167, 168, 170, 173–176, 181, 193–195, 198, 200, 202, 205, 206, 215, 217, 223, 230–232, 243, 249, 254, 337

Yoga, 25, 28, 33, 36, 59, 82, 102, 108, 118, 135, 138, 144, 161, 171, 174, 203, 209, 241, 255, 271, 340

Youniverse, 21, 28, 30, 33, 47, 53, 76, 81, 110, 111–112, 113, 141, 155, 161–162, 246, 252

Zayin, 99–101

Zodiac, 48, 49, 60, 78, 91, 93, 122, 139, 143, 161, 164, 176, 182–185, 196, 205, 252, 253, 287, 348

Zohar, 51

TO WRITE TO THE AUTHOR

If you wish to contact the author or would like more information about this book, please write to the author in care of Llewellyn Worldwide Ltd. and we will forward your request. Both the author and publisher appreciate hearing from you and learning of your enjoyment of this book and how it has helped you. Llewellyn Worldwide Ltd. cannot guarantee that every letter written to the author can be answered, but all will be forwarded. Please write to:

Joe Monteleone
℅ Llewellyn Worldwide
2143 Wooddale Drive
Woodbury, MN 55125-2989
Please enclose a self-addressed stamped envelope for reply,
or $1.00 to cover costs. If outside the U.S.A., enclose
an international postal reply coupon.

Many of Llewellyn's authors have websites with additional information and resources. For more information, please visit our website at http://www.llewellyn.com.

NOTES